The Cossacks

Manchester University Press

The Cossacks

Shane O'Rourke

Manchester University Press

Manchester and New York

distributed exclusively in the USA by Palgrave

The right of Shane O'Rourke to be identified as the author of this work has been asserted by him in accordance with the Copyright, Designs and Patents Act 1988.

Published by Manchester University Press
Oxford Road, Manchester M13 9NR, UK
and Room 400, 175 Fifth Avenue, New York, NY 10010, USA
www.manchesteruniversitypress.co.uk

Distributed in the United States exclusively by
Palgrave Macmillan, 175 Fifth Avenue,
New York, NY 10010, USA

Distributed in Canada exclusively by
UBC Press, University of British Columbia, 2029 West Mall,
Vancouver, BC, Canada V6T 1Z2

British Library Cataloguing-in-Publication Data is available

Library of Congress Cataloging-in-Publication Data is available

ISBN 978 0 7190 7680 0 paperback

First reprinted 2013

The publisher has no responsibility for the persistence or accuracy of URLs for any external or third-party internet websites referred to in this book, and does not guarantee that any content on such websites is, or will remain, accurate or appropriate.

Printed by Lightning Source

For Amina, Finn and Molly

Contents

Acknowledgements

It is my pleasure now to thank all the people who have contributed in many ways to the writing of the book. I would first like to thank my colleagues in the History Department of the University of York. In particular Stuart Carroll, Bill Sheils, Claudia Haake and Guy Halsall have been good friends and sources of advice. The department itself has contributed research leave for this project and I grateful for that. The AHRB funded an extra term of research leave during the writing up process and the British Academy contributed towards trips to Moscow. Professor Edward Acton and David Moon supported my application for funding and I would like to thank them. I know how boring these forms are.

In Russia there are many many people who have helped in one way or another. Arch-Getty's organization, Praxis International, has unfailingly helped with the labyrynthine process of getting a visa every year. Staff at the libraries and archives in Moscow have been always been considerate and concerned to help. The Coffee Bean Cafe and its staff on Tverskaia street in Moscow have provided a pleasant and congenial atmosphere in which to review the day's work from the archive.

Russian friends have been immensely supportive all the times I have been in Moscow. Alexey and Anna Yurosovky provided me with a base in Moscow and many substantial meals while I was there. Alexey was generous enough to read the manuscript and comment on it for which I am deeply grateful. Madina Iuldasheva, Elena Chastova and Elena Bukreevaya also provided much help and support.

Finally I would like to thank my own family. My cousin Paul Holmes has taken a keen interest in this book. My mum and dad have helped in uncountable ways as always. Above all Amina, Finn and (very recently) Molly have been a source of endless love and delight and it is to them that this book is dedicated.

List of figures

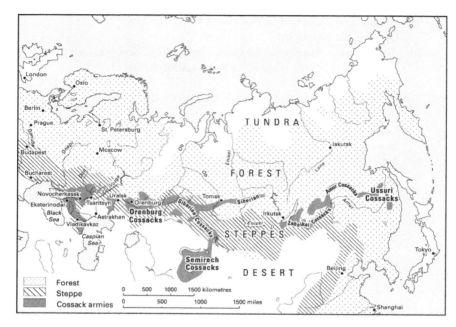

The Cossack armies of the Russian Empire

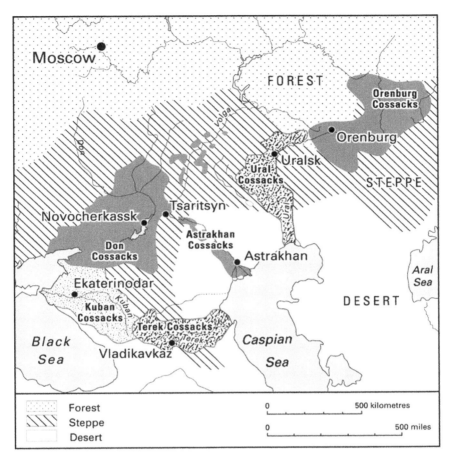

The Cossack armies of European Russia, 1914

Part I
Beginnings to 1600

Introduction

Who were the Cossacks? What were the Cossacks? Many people in the past have attempted to answer these questions. Some of the greatest writers, poets and painters have been drawn to the Cossacks, seeking to understand them and explain them to a wider audience. Pushkin, Gogol, Tolstoy, Sholokhov have all written unforgettable accounts of the Cossacks. Vasilii Surikov and Ilya Repin found inspiration in the Cossacks to produce some of the most famous canvases in Russian art. Yet the very multiplicity of images and fragmented interpretations have blurred definitive answers to the questions who and what were the Cossacks. And this is how it should be. Any historical subject worthy of interest always generates contested understandings and contrasting portraits.

Most people in the West have some conception of the Cossacks, conjuring up vague images of recklessly brave, wild horsemen, careless of their own lives and contemptuous of death. Perhaps these images would owe something to Yul Brynner playing Taras Bulba in the Hollywood version of Gogol's great novel or seeing Cossack dance troupes or horsemen giving spectacular displays in circuses or theatres. Some Europeans might recall folk traditions of less pleasant encounters with the Cossacks. The Seven Years War and the Napoleonic Wars brought the Cossacks into the heart of Europe where their prodigious feats of looting surpassed the best efforts of all other armies: no mean achievement given the high level of competition. Darker memories of the Cossacks as brutal mounted policemen in the late nineteenth century would also figure prominently in any collage of popular memory. Darkest of all would be Jewish memories of the terrible pogroms of the seventeenth and nineteenth centuries which are indelibly linked with the Cossacks.

Russian beliefs about the Cossacks are both more complex and more emphatic than those in the West. In Soviet times, the regime never forgave the Cossacks for their support of the Whites during the civil war and they became literally a non-people. The *First All-Russian Congress of Toiling Cossacks* pronounced in 1920 that 'the Cossacks are by no means a separate people or nation, but are an indivisible part of the Russian people'.[1] That remained the official attitude for the next seven decades. But the Soviet regime is no more and the Cossacks have been brought in from the cold by a new Russia, desperate to establish continuities with a pre-Soviet past. Cossacks are no longer a dubious element about which the less said the better, but have become the embodiment of a new Russian patriotism.

One thing, however, that most people in the West and in Russia would agree on is that the Cossacks are an indisputably Russian phenomenon. Semen Nomikosov, an official in the Cossack administration in Novocherkassk in the late nineteenth century, had no doubts on this score. The Cossacks were, he wrote, 'flesh of one flesh, bone of one bone with the Russian people'.[2] Most of his contemporaries would have heartily endorsed his description and even today few disagree with it. A century after Nomikosov the Union of Cossacks, the leading organization of the Cossack revival, declared 'We were always the guardians of the Russian frontiers and defenders of the motherland.'[3] There seems little reason to question a consensus that is at least two centuries old, but far from being 'flesh of one flesh, bone of one bone with the Russian people', the Cossacks, as we shall see, have a much more mixed pedigree.

Even the most cursory investigation of the Cossacks undermines much of the received wisdom about them. The very name, that most fundamental marker of any identity, that the Cossacks took for themselves pulsates with allusions to a world and to a culture radically different from the Russian one. 'Cossack' is simply a westernized version of the Russian *kazak*. *Kazak*, however, is not a Russian or even a Slavic word, but is a Russian rendition of the Turkic *qazaq*. Why would a quintessentially Russian phenomenon take its name from a world that was not just alien to Russia, but for many centuries was a mortal threat to Russian existence? This alone suggests that influences other than Russian formed part of the Cossack tradition.

Nor do Russian claims to sole ownership of the Cossacks pass uncontested. Ukrainian historians rightly argue that Cossacks are central to their country's history even more so than Russia's. Much of modern Ukraine's historical identity is built on the Cossacks: both the Zaporozhian Cossacks, who were one of the two original Cossack communities, and the Hetmanate Cossack state established in the seventeenth century.[4] Poland and Lithuania, although they have little inclination to celebrate the Cossacks, could equally well claim that their actions were critical to the formation of the Cossacks. The waters are further muddied by the newly independent nations of Central Asia. Free from the stultifying controls of Soviet historiography, historians there now quite properly point out that Cossacks were originally a part of the world of the Turkic nomads; a phenomenon rooted in the steppe lands of Central Asia.[5] Since plausible cases can be made for all of these, claims of national exclusivity appear somewhat dubious to say the least.

If we cannot say with certainty who the Cossacks were, can we at least be clear as to what they were? The answer that commands the widest agreement is that the Cossacks were an estate (*soslovie*) whose rights and duties were defined by the state.[6] This form of social organization was common all over early modern Europe and remained the foundation of the social order in Russia until 1917. Essentially every estate fulfilled a particular function. In the case of the Cossacks they fulfilled their obligations to the state through military service. All the estates were dependent on the central state for their existence and continuation. Naturally enough when the state abandoned the concept of an estate based society, or in the Russian case ceased to exist, the various estates themselves soon disappeared.

It can be argued that the Cossacks conformed closely to this model, fulfilling a particular function within the state and disappearing shortly after the imperial state itself collapsed in 1917. Yet the Cossacks do not easily fit into the estate mould. All the early Cossack communities or hosts (*voiska*) as they called themselves were founded in defiance of any state. For much of their history they proved anything but loyal servitors of the state. More fundamentally, they displayed characteristics that were reminiscent of a people as much as an estate. The Cossacks, particularly those of the Don and Kuban, developed passionate attachments to their particular regions often using the word 'motherland' (*rodina*) to describe it. Similarly they created a rich folklore around their Cossack status, commemorated Cossack history and life in songs, differentiated themselves from the wider society in their dress, diet, and through many of their customs. Most importantly, they believed they were different. Consider the answer that was given in the mid-eighteenth century to Alexander Rigel'man, one of the first modern investigators of the Cossacks, when he directly asked a Don Cossack who he thought he was: 'I am not Muscovite, but Russian, and even this only through custom and the Orthodox faith, not through birth.'[7] The answer, ambiguous and contradictory, does not fit neatly into any category of identity; in this at least, the Cossacks were no different from most other peoples, effortlessly juggling many different identities.

Perhaps looking beyond Russia, Ukraine and the steppe lands of Central Asia can throw some light on who or what the Cossacks were. Similar circumstances in other parts of the world and at other times produced groups who shared many traits with the Cossacks. Some combination of open frontiers, oppressive social systems and constant warfare produced communities with a heightened sense of their status as freemen, democratic systems of rule and very highly developed military skills. The collapse of authority in the Roman West in the fifth century left large territories controlled by *bagaudae* who were a mixture of fugitive slaves, former soldiers and assorted desperados not so very different from the first Cossacks.[8] In the Middle Ages, many states on both sides of the Christian/Islamic frontier acquiesced in the creation of autonomous militarized groups or sought to use any such groups which had spontaneously formed on the frontier.[9] The pirate brotherhoods of the Carribean in the eighteenth century had some striking resemblances to the early Cossack communities: the male cameraderie, the rough and ready democracy, and a life dedicated to robbery.[10] In Jamaica, runaway slaves, or Maroons as they were known, came together in the impenetrable mountains and forests of the island to live in free communities. The Maroons were perfectly at home in these inhospitable regions, easily able to outfight any forces sent to eradicate them.[11]

On the other hand, similar circumstances did not inevitably produce such groups. Colonial America in the eighteenth century with its large slave population, extended frontier and warlike indigenous peoples did not produce anything on the scale of the Cossacks or the Maroon communities in Jamaica largely because the slave-owning class and the authorities took great pains to prevent it happening; bounties were offered to native peoples to capture or kill runaway slaves and similar incentives were offered to attack any nascent runaway communities.[12] Frequently these groups emerged spontaneously, often in the absence of government or in direct opposition to it. Yet nearly always they existed in a symbiotic relationship with the state from which they had emerged. With the exception of the Maroons who still exist as distinct communities, most of them were eventually suppressed by centralized states once they were strong enough to do so or once they had outlived their usefulness to the state.

The Cossack hosts

One of the reasons why it is so hard to arrive at a satisfactory answer to who or what the Cossacks were was that there was never a single Cossack community, organization or territory. In 1914 there were eleven Cossack hosts strung out from the River Don in the West to the Rivers Amur and Ussuri in the Far East. Each of these hosts had there own distinct history and traditions. The Don, the Terek and the Ural Cossacks were the oldest surviving hosts and had all come into being independently of government action.[13] The remaining eight hosts had all been formed by deliberate acts of the government. This dichotomy of experience might explain why some Cossacks exhibited traits that did not sit easily with the estate model while others fitted it perfectly. The Don, Terek and Ural Cossacks all had powerful, deep rooted identies that went far beyond what the state prescribed for them. Other hosts which had been created directly by the government such as the Semirech'e, the Amur and Ussuri Cossacks demonstrated a very limited capacity to survive without the imperial state. It could be argued that a fundamental difference existed between Cossack hosts which had emerged without government permission or oversight and those that had been founded entirely through government action. The former were much more than estates while the latter remained locked within their estate confines.

Useful as this basic division is, it is not entirely satisfactory. Some of the hosts created by the government did begin to show startling parallels with the Don, Terek and Ural Cossacks in terms of their perception of themselves and their sense of difference from other people. The Orenburg Cossacks founded by the government in the 1740s sank deep roots into their territory, forming a cohesive Cossack identity which was closely attached to a regional one.[14] Much more significantly, the Kuban Cossacks, created in the 1860s out of the Caucasian (*Kavkazskaia*) Line Cossacks and the Black Sea (*Chernmorskoe*) Cossacks, very rapidly assimilated an overarching Kuban identity that proved to be remarkably resilient surviving the fall of the Tsarist regime in 1917 and even the subsequent civil war. A major Party Plenum in Moscow in 1925 noted with exasperation that the Cossacks, and particularly the Kuban Cossacks, 'have an extraordinarily great cohesion as groups preserving the survivals of their previous position'.[15]

By now it should be clear that Cossack as a concept does not easily lend itself to short or uncomplicated definitions. It is elusive because it is subjective and was never fixed or static. Cossacks like other people had many identities; at different times and in different circumstances some were more important than others. For some Cossack communities their identity as Cossacks remained peripheral to them and it could be abandoned relatively lightly without seriously harming their sense of self.

For other communities, however, it was central to their existence and they could not conceive of a life in which they had ceased to be Cossacks. Perhaps this offers one way of understanding Cossack identity and differentiating between types of Cossacks. For those communities where 'Cossack' was what you did, that is provide military service to the state, the Cossack part of their identity existed only as long as they provided that service. Thus in 1918 the Amur Cossacks agreed to dissolve themselves into the surrounding peasant communities.[16] On the other hand for those communities for whom being a Cossack was not what you did but who you were, the Cossack part of their identity survived regardless of whether they provided a service to a state or even when the state itself no longer existed.

No doubt many descendants of the Amur Cossacks would furiously dispute this categorization of their great grandfathers. Many individuals in these hosts must have seen themselves first and foremost as Cossacks, but, unless the community as a whole did, such individual choices remained just that – individual choices. Those communities which did choose Cossack as their primary identity had several things in common. Firstly, they had become Cossacks through an act of free choice or had been born into communities made up of such Cossacks. Secondly, they had a territorial aspect to their identity which went beyond simply a collective allotment of land. This territory was compact enough to imagined as a distinct area yet large enough to be conceived as more than simply the means of earning a living. Thirdly, the communities were sufficiently large to form a critical mass both in relationship to the territories they occupied and the surrounding non-Cossack population. Where these conditions coincided, Cossack identity had either always been more than an estate one or developed over time into something more.

At the very least powerful regional identities developed among the Ural, Orenburg and Terek Cossacks. But in two of the hosts this went further. The Don and the Kuban Cossacks showed the potential to move beyond a regional framework to a national one. On one side then were classic examples of an estate system while on the other were potentially distinct peoples. This I would argue was the central dividing line in Cossack experience.

Of course many people refuse to accept the idea that the Cossacks had ever been or could ever be anything more than an estate.[17] However, it does seem to me that if we are to understand anything of what the Cossacks were then we have to move outside the rigid conventional thinking about them and about what constitutes a state and what constitutes a nation. The experience of the post-Cold War world shows that our understandings of national identity based on big markers such as language, religion or occupation of territory are far too crude to explain the violent committment to national identity by groups who seem to outsiders to be indistinguishable from the surrounding peoples.[18]

We also need to be rather more flexible in what we understand by the term state. The absence of a large, formal bureaucratic structure in the early Cossack hosts makes it easy to argue that they never possessed a state or anything like it. Yet because Cossack organization did not correspond to notions of a state normal for sedentary societies does not mean that one did not exist. If the rudimentary organization of the first Cossack communities is set against the steppe and the nomadic world rather than the settled areas, then the boundary between communal organization and formal state structures dissolves and we are left with points on a continuum rather than qualitatively different things.

Nomads, contrary to widely held beliefs, were not hopeless state builders. They actually built states that were extremely effective for their own purposes: the mobilization of their societies for war, negotiating with surrounding powers and distributing loot. These tasks did not necessitate large bureaucracies or extensive record keeping. The Scythian dominion, the Hsiung-nu Empire based in the Mongolian steppe and the Khazar Khaganate all lasted for hundreds of years. Yet since they left no written records of themselves, they can be dismissed as nothing more than banditry on an epic scale. A distinguished American historian of China working on the paradox of entities that existed for hundreds of years while leaving only minimal written traces of themselves wrote:

> We might think of confederations as "nations" even though they lacked the enduring, consolidated territorial definition that some theorists consider necessary to the definition of the state. As such definitions gradually transcend Western cultural parochialism, the case for considering the political form achieved by the nomadic nation-builders to have been states becomes stronger.[19]

The Cossacks of course never approached the scale of any of these confederations yet the 'political forms' built by the Cossacks delivered their limited objectives in an effective manner. The first Cossack communities on the Don and Dnieper created political institutions with claims of authority over distinct territories and all those living within them.[20] They negotiated with surrounding states, sending diplomatic delegations and receiving them. They sought the sponsorship of powerful states under whose protection they could flourish, but in their minds at least this relationship was reciprocal, contractual and in existence only for as long as it was mutually beneficial. Such forms corresponded closely to the world of the steppe and had been part of the complicated relationship between steppe peoples and sedentary societies for two thousand years when the Cossacks appeared on the Pontic steppe in the fifteenth century.

In a similar way, the claims of the Don and Kuban Cossacks to be a nation are routinely dismissed as misguided, misconceived or, more bluntly, plain wrong. Russian speaking and Orthodox or Old Believer in faith, how could the Cossacks claim a separate identity from Russia? Yet nationality or ethnicity does not depend on the quantity of cultural difference between two groups. Max Weber wrote 'Any cultural trait, no matter how superficial, can serve as a starting point for the familiar tendency to monopolistic closure.'[21] This is not a new discovery; Herodotus was aware of it. Listing the different tribes of Scythia, he noted how one of the tribe's claim to a separate collective identity was based solely on the colour of their clothes: 'The Black Cloaks all wear black clothing, which is how they got their name. Their way of life is Scythian.'[22]

In the 1920s the Soviet government, as part of its promotion of minority cultures, decided that Ukrainian was to be the language of instruction in all schools in the Kuban. When parents were asked which language they wanted their children taught in – Russian or Ukrainian – a whole series of meetings replied 'our native Kuban language and not Ukrainian'.[23] Perhaps this is no more than straw in the wind, but it does suggest that lines between dialects and national language can be matters of degree as well as of kind. If that is true of speech then why cannot it be true of other 'hard' markers of identity? What matters ultimately is what people believe about themselves. The 'proofs' of their nationhood can all be constructed later. University departments of philology can demonstrate that their language, far from being a dialect, is and always has been a separate language in its own right. Archaeologists can provide material evidence 'proving' a particular people's right to a particular territory even if they have not occupied that territory for centuries. Nationalist historians can show a separate national history has existed in an unbroken line since at least the fall of the Roman Empire and so on. The point is not whether claims to nationhood can be measured against abstract criteria, but whether they are believed by the people concerned which is not the same thing at all. As one wise historian put it recently 'Peoples or nations, it is rightly said, are the products of their members belief that they exist.'[24]

The Cossacks are one of the groups that seem to fall outside all the conventional categories of labelling either in terms of the administrative structures that they created or in their collective identity. Yet if we are sensitive to the broad historical context in which they originated and developed and remain aware of how potent even relatively small differences can be in defining and sustaining a separate collective identity then much about the Cossacks that is confusing or obscure can become clear.

In recent years there has been a substantial amount of new research which has contributed a great deal to our understanding of the Cossacks. Firstly, the relationship between the steppe and the settled areas has been reconsidered in several important new works. David Christian has written a marvellous synoptic view of the complex interaction between the steppe and the sedentary world over the course of two millenia.[25] Mikhail Khodarkovsky's work on the steppe frontier has illuminated the encounter between the Muscovite and Imperial Russian states and the peoples of the steppe in which the Cossacks were both victims and agents of a colonial state.[26]

Concerning the Cossacks specifically, a new generation of graduate students and scholars in the West have added greatly to the breadth and depth of our knowledge about the Cossacks. Tom Barrett's work on the Terek Cossacks is the first monograph on them to appear in English.[27] Sergei Plokhy has written several important works on the Ukrainian Cossacks, including a magisterial account of them in the turbulent middle years of the seventeenth century.[28] Our understanding of the Cossacks during the civil war has been greatly enhanced by Peter Holquist's work although I do not share his understanding of the Cossacks.[29] My own work on the Don Cossacks has, I hope, made some contribution to the history of the Cossacks.[30]

In Russia and Ukraine there has been a long tradition of scholarly interest in the Cossacks. In the pre-revolutionary period work of the highest quality was produced. The great Ukrainian historian M. Hrushevsky produce a multi-tome epic on the history of Ukraine, devoting several volumes to the Zaporozhian and Ukrainian Cossacks. These are now becoming accessible in English for the first time and are listed in the bibliography. In Russia pre-revolutionary historians covered all aspects of Cossack history from a variety of points of view. Most of this work was based on meticulous archival research and I have made extensive use of it. Again there is a full listing in the bibliography.

In Soviet times history divorced from politics became impossible to write. Historians of the Cossacks were under particular difficulties given the Soviet regime's suspicions about the Cossacks, particularly the closer one came to the Soviet era. Nevertheless Soviet scholars produced a great deal of value particularly in respect of the history of the great Cossack rebellions of the seventeenth and eighteenth century where the Cossacks found themselves on the side of the angels or in the Soviet scheme of things on the side of the oppressed people. Many volumes of documents and commentary have been published on this turbulent era of Cossack history. Later Cossack history, however, had to be written within a much tighter ideological straightjacket. Above all, the history of the revolution and civil war had to be written according to strict Leninist formulas, giving a wholly distorted view of the history of the Cossacks during this critical period of their existence.

Since the end of the Soviet Union there has been a veritable outpouring of books on all aspects of Cossack history: general surveys, the history of particular hosts, the lives of individual Cossacks, documentary collections and so on. Particularly valuable have been the publication of documents from previously inaccessible Soviet archives which allow a much fuller reconstruction of the Cossacks under Soviet rule than had been possible earlier. All these collections are listed in the bibliography.

The present book is an attempt to put together a synoptic view of the Cossacks. I very much hope that it will be accessible to readers who know nothing of the Cossacks, but also will be of use to specialists. Much of the book is obviously based on the work of other historians: both recent and older. However, it is not just a work of synthesis. For the early period of Cossack history I have tried to use the accounts of foreign observers in conjunction with native sources. The foreign observers often had quite a lot to say about the origins of the Cossacks, their customs and their relationship to surrounding states. Many of them were writing close to the events they were describing and they offer an invaluable source on early Cossack history. Large parts of it, particularly from the nineteenth century onwards, are based on my own archival work. Much of this material especially that relating to the civil war and the early Soviet period up to collectivization has only become accessible since the demise of the Soviet Union. Some of this has been published in Russian, and a smaller amount has been translated into English. However, many of the documents that I use are appearing for the first time in any published source.

Inevitably any one volume of history covering 500 years and millions of people involves a large amount of compression, foreshortening and excision and alas this volume is no exception. I have had to leave out a great deal. In particular I regret not being able to write more about the Time of Troubles, the revolt of Kondrati Bulavin in the Don and Ivan Mazeppa's attempt to break Ukraine away from the Russian Empire in the early eighteenth century. Other people no doubt would have made different choices, but what I have chosen to write about will, I hope, still convey the broad sweep of Cossack history even if many of the details are missing.

The Cossacks emerged out of the steppe and were indelibly marked by it. For this reason I have chosen to begin the book with an account of the steppe world to show how the Cossacks and the states they dealt with were part of a pattern of relationships that was already 2,000 years old when the Cossacks first appeared. In tracing the origins and development of the first Cossack communities in the sixteenth century I hope to make clear just how much part of that world the Cossacks were. The next section will look at the relationship of the Cossacks to the surrounding states in the seventeenth and eighteenth centuries through the prism of three great conflicts: the revolts of Bohdan Khemelnytsky, Stepan Razin and Emel'ian Pugachev. The third section of the book will look at the Cossacks between the end of the Pugachev revolt in 1774 until the outbreak of the First World War. Although the book is basically chronological in structure I have deviated from this to provide a thematic chapter on Cossack women whose importance to the Cossack way of life is difficult to exaggerate. This is not the most elegant solution as I am well aware, but hopefully readers will see why I included such a chapter after they have read it. The fourth section will look at the Cossacks in the revolutionary period up to the end of the civil war. The final section will examine the tragic fate of the Cossacks under Soviet power. A brief epilogue will take the book up to the re-emergence of the Cossack movement in the present.

Notes

1 *Gosudarstvennyi Arkhiv Rossiiskoi Federatsii* (hearafter GARF) f.1235, op.85, d.2, ll.3–4.

2 S. Nomikosov (ed.) *Statisticheskoe Opisanie Oblasti Voiska Donskago* (Novocherkassk, 1884) p. 247.

3 T.V. Tabolina (ed.) *Vozrozhdenie Kazachestva 1989–1994* (Moscow, 1994) p. 294.

4 S. Plokhy, *The Cossacks and Religion in Early Modern Ukraine* (Oxford, 2001) p. 2.

5 M.Zh. Abdirov, *Istoriia Kazachestva Kazakhstana* (Almaty, 1994) p. 14.

6 R. McNeal, *Tsar and Cossack, 1855–1914* (London, 1987) p. 84.

7 A. Rigel'man, *Istoriia o Donskikh Kazakakh* (Moscow, 1846) p. 7.

8 P. Geary, *The Myth of Nations: The Medieval Origins of Europe* (Princeton, 2002) p. 106.

9 C.W. Bracewell, *The Uskoks of Senj: Piracy, Banditry and Holy War in the Sixteenth Century Adriatic* (New York, 1992) p. 36.

10 M. Rediker, *Between the Devil and the Deep Blue Sea: Merchant Seamen, Pirates and the Anglo-American Maritime World 1700–1750* (Cambridge, 1987) pp. 254–287.

11 A. Taylor, *American Colonies: The Settling of North America* (Harmondsworth, 2001) pp. 220–221.

12 Taylor, *American Colonies*, p. 235.

13 The Ural Cossacks were originally the Iaik Cossacks. They were renamed as punishement for their part in the Pugachev rebellion of 1773–74.

14 V.P. Bakanov, 'Orenburgskoe Kazachestvo' in N.I. Bondar' (ed.), *Ocherki Traditsionnoi Kul'tury Kazachestv Rossii* (Moscow-Krasnodar, 2002) p. 277.

15 *Rossiiskii Gosudarstvennyi Arkhiv Sotsial'no-Politicheskoi Istorii* (hereafter RGASPI) f.17, op.2, d.179, l.57.

16 M. Astapenko, *Istoriia Kazachestva Rossii* (3 vols, Rostov-na-Donu, 1998) vol. 3, p. 406.

17 See for example, P. Holquist 'From Estate to Ethnos: The Changing Nature of Cossack Identity in the Twentieth Century' in N. Schleifman (ed.) *Russia at a Crossroads: History, Memory and Political Practice* (London, 1998) pp. 89–123.

18 See for example, L.M. Danforth, *The Macedonian Conflict: Ethnic Nationalism in a Transnational World* (Princeton, 1996) pp. 11–13.

19 F.W. Mote, *Imperial China 900–1800* (Cambridge, Mass., 1999) p. 412.

20 F.A. Shcherbina, *Istoriia Kubanskago Kazach'iago Voiska* (2 vols, Ekaterinodar, 1910–13) pp. 439–440.

21 M. Weber, *Economy and Society: An Outline of Interpretive Sociology* (2 vols, Berkeley, 1978) vol. 1, p. 388.

22 Herodotus, *The Histories*, trans. R. Waterfield (Oxford, 1998) p. 270.

23 L.S. Gatagova (ed.), *TsK RKP(B)-VKP(B) i Natsional'nyi Vopros 1918–1933* (Moscow, 2005) p. 572.

24 D. Carpenter, *The Struggle for Mastery: Britain 1066–1284* (London, 2003) p. 2.

25 D. Christian, *A History of Russia, Central Asia and Mongolia. Vol I. Inner Asia from Prehistory to the Mongol Empire* (Oxford, 1998).

26 M. Khodarkovsky, *Russia's Steppe Frontier: The Making of a Colonial Empire 1500–1800* (Bloomington, 2002).

27 T. Barrett, *At the Edge of Empire: The Terek Cossacks and the North Caucasus Frontier, 1700–1860* (Boulder, 1999).

28 Plokhy, *The Cossacks and Religion*.

29 P. Holquist, *Making War, Forging Revolution: Russia's Continuum of Crisis 1914–1921* (Cambridge, Mass., 2002).

30 S. O'Rourke, *Warriors and Peasants: The Don Cossacks in Late Imperial Russia* (Basingstoke, 2000).

Prologue: the world of the steppe

Cossack life, legend and imagination was filled by the steppe-the endless plains of grass that stretched out to the horizon until the sky and the land flowed into each other. The Cossacks sang of the steppe, told tales about it and named it their motherland or *rodina*. The Cossacks hosts, spread out along the Pontic and Caspian steppes, had such visceral devotion to their small portion of it that it seemed to them there could be no Cossacks without the steppe or even steppe without the Cossacks. Yet the mysterious burial mounds or *kurgany* that littered the steppe from the Dnieper to the Volga spoke to the Cossacks of other peoples, long gone and long forgotten, who had once felt the same way about the land now occupied by the Cossacks. In truth the Cossacks were only one of many steppe peoples who occupied the Pontic and Caspian Steppes which themselves were only one part of the great steppe, linking China with Europe. The Cossacks were formed in a world that had its own particular cultural eco-system. Despite the diversity of the peoples of the steppe and the profoundly different cultural influences which shaped them, the steppe itself imposed its patterns on the life of all who lived there. This gave steppe peoples a certain familiarity with each other and a shared understanding of what life in the steppe meant. It also produced a broad pattern of similar relationships across the length of the steppe between steppe peoples and the civilizations on the periphery of the steppe.[1] The Cossacks were one piece of this much broader mosaic.

The steppe

The steppe is a vast grass flatlands stretching from Mongolia to Hungary. It forms one of the horizontal belts that dominate the Eurasian plain from Eastern Europe to the Pacific Ocean. In the far north lies the *tundra* or area of permafrost. Immediately beneath this is the forest zone which gradually thins as it moves south, shading into the steppe until finally the trees disappear and the true steppe begins. In the south, the steppe is bounded by the deserts and mountains of Central Asia and successively by the the Caspian Sea, the Caucasus mountains, and by the Black Sea. Although there are patches of steppe east of the Enesei River, the true steppe begins at the foothills of the Altai Mountains and rolls westwards along the 50th parallel passing Aktyubinsk and Uralsk in the Southern Urals. From Uralsk, it flows southwards towards the Caucasus before turning north-westwards through the Volga, Don and Dnieper Rivers. As it approaches Eastern Europe, the steppe narrows eventually petering out in the Hungarian plain. Its flatness and expanse have often drawn comparisons with the sea or even the ocean. Rivers and ravines are the only interruptions in this otherwise featureless landscape; trees occur naturally only along river banks as there is too little precipitation to support them elsewhere. Most of the steppe is covered by tough grasses either of the feather or needle type which are best suited to resist the rigours of the climate. In spring, however, much of the steppe of European Russia is a blaze of colour with tulips, peonies and sage transforming the mono-chrome landscape. Silvery feather grass predominates in early summer which ripples gently in the breeze, adding to the illusion of a sea rather than a landscape. In late summer tough needle grass predominates.

The climate of the steppe is continental; harsh, hot summers and piercingly cold winters are characteristic of the steppe. The moderating influences of the Black and Caspian Seas and the Sea of Azov are localized and do not extend far inland. Precipitation either in the form of rain or snow is low. As in the landscape, the climate is relatively uniform adding to the sense that steppe is a distinct ecological zone.[2]

Nomads

From early in the first millenium BC until the eighteenth century of the present era, nomadic peoples were the undisputed masters of the steppe.[3] Nomads lived by raising flocks and moving them from pasture to pasture. Pastoralism was a triumph of human adaptation to one of the harshest environments on the planet. Following herds through the biting cold of the steppe winters or the blazing heats of the summer months required people of exceptional toughness. Remaining in the saddle for weeks on end bred rare abilities of endurance and survival that were common to men and women. The weather, however was not the only or the worst enemy; other humans were the greatest threat. The steppe was a predatory environment in which the weak were deprived of property, family and life.

Warfare became a part of steppe life from the very beginnings of nomadic existence. The harshness of life on the steppe produced people ideally suited to war. Individual toughness, unprecedented mobility and ingrained habits of organization and cooperation in moving animals produced peoples whose military effectiveness far exceeded those of sedentary societies. Almost every able-bodied man was available for war. The transition from peace to war was much easier for nomadic societies since their peace-time way of life constantly honed their military capacities.[4] Nomadic skill in warfare was first recorded by Herodotus who provided the classic description of a nomadic confrontation with the army of a mighty sedentary state: in this instance the expedition led by the Great King Darius:

> . . . the Scythians decided against any straight fighting and open warfare, and in favour of retreat. The plan was as they rode back in retreat they would fill in any wells and springs as they passed, and destroy any vegetation they found growing in the ground. They also decided to divide their forces into two. One detachment, which was ruled by Scopasis, would be reinforced by the Sauromatae, and if Darius turned in their direction, they were to pull back along a route that would take them past Lake Maeetis and straight towards the Tanais River; however, if Darius withdrew, they were to pursue him and attack him.[5]

After a vain pursuit through the Pontic steppe and across the River Don (Tanais), the Persians, exhausted and running short of supplies, abandoned the pursuit. Now, however, they became the hunted, pursued across the steppe by the Scythians. Darius extricated himself only by abandoning a large part of his army in the steppe and fleeing headlong towards Thrace. This scenario repeated itself almost exactly in the Mongolian Steppe in 200 BC when the army of the Chinese Emperor Han Kao-tsu was cut off and annihilated by the Hsiung-nu.[6] Until the end of the eighteenth century, it was almost impossible for the armies of sedentary societies to operate effectively in the steppe. The expeditions launched by the regent Sofia against the Crimean Tatars in 1687 and 1689 came to grief in circumstances that Herodotus would have recognized.[7]

Warfare was endemic to the steppe, but the absence of war did not mean peace. Banditry in all its forms thrived in the steppe, differing from warfare only in its scale. William of Rubruck, a Fransican Friar, who made the incredibly journey across the steppe to Karakorum in Mongolia in the mid-thirteenth century, described the dread these bandits inspired as they moved through the upper Don:

On the road between him and his father we experienced great fear. For there Ruthenian, Hungarian and Alanian slaves, of whom there is a very large number among them, band themselves together in groups of twenty or thirty and run away by night and they have bows and arrows, and whomsoever they come across by night they kill. By day they stay in hiding, and when their horses are tired they come during the night up to a large group of horses on the pasture lands and change their horses; they also take away one or two with them so they can eat them when the need arises. And so our guide was very much afraid of meeting such men.[8]

Those that survived and prospered were exceptionally skilled in the use of all weapons: those that were not perished.

The steppe environment forced nomads to adapt their society at least as much as their economy. Women were much more prominent in nomad societies than in those on the periphery of the steppe. The difficulties of steppe life forced women to play a full role in the nomadic economy. The dangers of steppe life from natural hazards to warfare and abduction compelled women to be able to defend themselves if necessary.[9] Not coincidentally, the Pontic Steppe was regarded as the home of the legendary female warriors, the Amazons. Herodotus described their direct descendants, the women of the Sauromatae: 'And ever since then the Sauromation women have kept to their original way of life: they go hunting on horseback with or without their husbands, they go to war and wear the same clothes as the men do.'[10] Usually dismissed as nonsense, Herodotus' claims have been supported by extensive archaeological evidence from tombs which have contained women and their weapons and armour.[11] Another intrepid Franciscan, John of Plano Carpini, on his journey to Karakorum in 1245–47 gave an eye-witness description of Mongol women that bears an uncanny resemblance to Herodotus and descriptions of Cossack women much later:

Young girls and women ride and gallop on horseback with agility like the men. We even saw them carrying bows and arrows. Both the men and the women are able to endure long stretches of riding. They have very short stirrups; they look after their horses very well, indeed they take the greatest care of all their possessions. Their women make everything, leather garments, tunics, shoes, leggings and everything made of leather; they also drive the carts and repair them, they load the camels, and in all their tasks they are very swift and energetic. All the women wear breeches and some of them shoot like men.[12]

The high profile of women in the lives of their community gave them a respect and value that often seemed shocking to observers from the sedentary world. The Mongols in particular honoured their women and they became formidable players in the Mongol world.[13]

Nomadic political organization

Nomads lived in small groups based around kinship networks. These networks were linked into wider clan groups which were in turn organized into tribal units. Confederations larger than the tribe came together and stabilized only under certain conditions which occurred relatively rarely. When that happened, they created societies with a military potential dwarfing those of any of the settled states on the periphery. Once these conditions no longer applied, larger confederations began to disintegrate into their constituent parts back down to the kinship group until conditions once more proved favourable for larger organizations. The most spectacular example of this process was of course Temujin, later Chingis Khan, who at one point had no companions other than his mother and brothers.[14]

Two conditions were required for nomadic societies to transcend the normal limits of their social organization. One was a charismatic leader and the other was the ability to supply a constant source of goods to followers: luxuries for the elite and basic necessities for the lower orders. Without these conditions, no large coalitions could be created or sustained.[15] The emergence of a powerful new state on the periphery or the first contact between nomads and a powerful state acted as stimuli to the emergence of nomadic political organization. The Hsiung-nu Empire emerged just at the point when China was unified for the first time under the Han dynasty in the late third century BC.[16] Hun political organization, such as it was, appeared to develop when the opportunities offered by the Roman Empire became apparent.[17] Other nomadic states such as the Khazar one depended on controlling the steppe trade routes, or part of them, between China, the Middle East and the West. Nomadic political organizations under the right conditions have been as stable as any in the world.

Nomadic states needed certain goods and services from the settled periphery which they could not supply themselves. Nomadic elites craved luxury goods while ordinary nomads sought to trade for basic utensils and supplies from the markets of the border towns and fortresses The most prized possession was a princess from the ruling dynasty. A Chinese or Byzantine princess conferred enormous prestige on a nomadic leader, raising him far above his followers and rivals. One of the treaty conditions established by the Hsiung-nu after their great victory over the Chinese in

200 BC was the delivery of a Chinese princess to the Hsiung-nu ruler.[18] Attila went to war with the Roman Empire in 450 partly because the Romans had failed to deliver Augusta Honoria, the sister of the Emperor Valentinian III, as his bride.[19] The Byzantines and Khazars frequently exchanged royal brides: the Emperor Justinian II married the sister of the kagan, the Khazar ruler, at the end of the seventh century while Leo the Isaurian chose the daughter of the kagan to be the bride of his son Constantine in 732.[20]

Nomads possessed many strategies to obtain these goods. The most obvious method for nomads to obtain what they needed was to seize it by force. The military option, however, was risky, uncertain and unsystematic. An alternative was to trade the goods of the steppe for those of the settled areas. This was a constant feature of nomadic life, but it did not produce the surpluses necessary to sustain a state. By far the most effective method of obtaining goods from the surrounding societies was to have a formal agreement in which goods were received in return for promises not to plunder and to prevent other nomads from doing the same.[21] Once this level had been reached, the nomadic state possessed the resources to sustain itself over many decades and sometimes centuries.

Exacting a steady flow of tribute sufficient to sustain a large nomadic state was the culmination of nomadic strategies for exploiting the wealthy empires on the periphery. Of course these great empires deeply resented the nomadic extortion racket. The Byzantine Emperor Constantine Porphyrogenitus advised his son:

> Know therefore that all the tribes of the north, have as it were implanted in them by nature, a ravening greed of money, never satiated, and so they demand everything and hanker after everything and have desires that know no limit or circumspection, but are always eager for more, and desirous to acquire great profits in exchange for a small service.[22]

No doubt his Chinese counterpart would have heartily endorsed these sentiments. The great empires did not passively accept nomadic domination, but developed strategies to ensure that nomads served their purposes rather than the other way round. Both sides were locked into a competitive relationship in which each sought to gain the upper hand. This depended on many factors: military, economic, diplomatic, political and so on, which gave the advantage to one side and then the other. Only the spectacular population growth of the sedentary areas in the modern era tipped the balance irreversibly against the nomads. Before this, however, strategies had to be developed that could neutralize the threat posed by them.

Chinese, Byzantine, Persian and later the Russian Empires had to find some means of reconciling nomadic dominance with their own world views. All these empires in their own ways regarded themselves as the centre of the universe. The Great King Darius, for example, would have been willing to accept token acts of submission from the Scythians symbolizing their recognition of his claim to be lord of the earth.[23] For a great empire to pay tribute to people that they regarded as barbarians and savages was intolerable much more for the violence it did to their view of the world than for the economic losses. All of them developed rationales which disguised the real nature of the relationship and allowed them to maintain their sense of superiority over the nomads. A recent study of Chinese relations with the nomads wrote:

> Over time the issue of cultural relations probably troubled court scholars more than nomad military attacks for the nomads refusal to accept Chinese values struck at China's own definition of itself as the centre of the world order. This was true even during times when the Chinese were quite successful in employing their own ideological framework of foreign relations. Frontier peoples became quite skilful at manipulating this system, often accepting the Chinese forms while rejecting their content, thereby developing reputations as insolent or insincere barbarians.[24]

China, Byzantium and later Muscovy insisted that nomadic peoples approach them through a cultural framework in which they acknowledged their subjection to imperial power, even if this was far removed from the reality of the relationship. When the Hsiung-nu crushed a Chinese army in the steppe in 200 BC and established their empire, they were powerful enough to insist that the Chinese treat them as equals. This was profoundly humiliating for the Chinese and for 150 years they sought a formal expression of subordination from the Hsiung-nu, finally achieving it in 53 BC.[25] The Chinese were willing to pay the Hsiung-nu far more if only they would agree to express their relationship in terms acceptable to the Chinese. They also accorded the Shan-yu, the leader of the Hsiung-nu, precedence over every Chinese prince or aristocrat outside of the imperial family itself. As soon as the Hsiung-nu understood this, they readily agreed to do so. Once nomads agreed to express themselves in the cultural idiom demanded, the payment of tribute could be disguised as a gracious gift from the emperor. The awarding of titles became a favourite tactic for co-opting nomadic elites from China to the Roman west and from classical times to the nineteenth century.

A powerful nomadic state could ensure a constant supply of tribute from the peripheral states. Yet even here, this gave some leverage to the state paying tribute. It could seek to manipulate the payment in order to advance its own goals, create tensions at the highest levels of the state, factionalize it and ultimately bring about open conflict within it. Opening and then shutting border markets to nomadic peoples proved to be an effective way of causing strife within nomadic polities.[26] Alternatively, the power of Chinese or Byzantine culture, its magnificence, its luxury could be fatally seductive for a nomadic elite. Nomadic delegations would be deliberately subjected to a series of receptions and rituals designed to impress upon them the magnificence of the civilization they were dealing with and their own insignificance. The award of titles we have already seen was usually an irresistible bait for nomadic elites particularly in the long run.

It would take an extraordinarily ascetic ruler not to want to abandon the harshness of steppe life for the blandishments of the most civilized societies in the world. Motun, the founder of the Hsiung-nu Empire, and Chingis Khan remained in the steppe but their successors showed an ever greater willingness to exchange the harshness of the steppe for the luxury of the Chinese court. Once trodden there was no return from this primrose path. Elites became sinicized or Byzantinized, alienated from their own societies and secretly still despised as barbarians by the conquered peoples. The sources of their military strength were imperceptibly eroded until their dominance suddenly collapsed and they were brusquely ejected back into the steppe whence they had come. The Mongols, as is so much else, were the most complete expression of this cycle of conquest and collapse, but it was a recurrent pattern of relationships between nomadic and sedentary states through the whole steppe corridor.

The Pontic and Caspian steppe

The Cossacks became the masters of the Don and Dnieper Steppe in the sixteenth and seventeenth century. The Cossacks were the latest in a long line of peoples, stretching back at least to the time of Herodotus to control that particular part of the steppe. Cimmerians, Scythians, Samartians, Goths, Huns, Avars, Khazars, Pechenegs, Cumans, Mongols and Tatars had all ruled the steppe in their time. Sometimes their dominion lasted only a few years as in the case of the Huns; in others it lasted for centuries as in the case of the Scythians and Khazars. Each group left its mark on the steppe and its subsequent history. In understanding the transition of control in the steppe, it is of critical importance to grasp the continuing influence of defeated groups on the new masters. Confronted with defeat or an insurmountable threat nomads could respond in two ways: they could move on or submit to the new dominant power and become part of it.

A constant process of contact, conquest, assimilation and synthesis was at work in the steppe. The triumphant new grouping did not erase the previously dominant culture, but slowly absorbed parts of it and were themselves changed in the process. No nomadic confederation consisted of a single ethnic group and in this labels are often misleading. On the contrary, all nomadic confederations were made up of several groups who had become part of a victorious coalition. The dominant group became the aristocracy of the state and gave it their name, but the state itself was never ethnically based:

> Cimmerians, Scythians, Samartians, Goths, Huns, Avars, Bulgars, Khazars, Magyars, Pechenegs Cumans and Tatars emerge and vanish in turn on the historian's horizon. Modern scholarship has done much to modify this over-simplified pricture. It has taught us to read the political history of the steppe no longer as a kaleidoscope of successive populations, but primarily as a sequence of conquering minorities, each of which imposed its political authority and often its name on the earlier inhabitants, without wholly displacing or absorbing them. What changed in each case was the ruling race and the designation of its conquered subjects, not the basic ethnographic substratum.[27]

The Scythian dominion contained a variety of ethnic groups who cooperated in times of threat and then dispersed. The Mongols were only the apex of their empire; the vast majority of the Mongol army consisted of Turkic peoples who joined with them. Over and over again this pattern repeated itself, making any attempt to ascribe ethnicity to steppe peoples anachronistic and pointless. All steppe peoples had their roots in a wide variety of steppe cultures, drawing on aspects of all of them and bringing their own specific customs to the wide gene pool of steppe culture.

Kievan Rus

The first state of the eastern branch of the Slavs was based at Kiev which was situated on the western edge of the steppe. The steppe was a matter of the utmost geopolitical importance to the Kievan state from its foundation in the ninth century until its destruction in the thirteenth. Possibly Kiev began life as a tributary to the Khazars.[28] The Khazar dominion provided security from nomadic attacks for the vulnerable new state. Within a hundred years, however, the Kievans had been become powerful enough to challenge the Khazars for control of the lucrative trade routes that were the foundation of Khazar prosperity.[29] In 964 Prince Sviatoslav destroyed the Khazars in a campaign that extended the territory of the Kievan state, nominally at least, to the Volga and the North Caucasus. But in destroying the Khazars, Sviatoslav had removed a powerful buffer between Kiev and the steppe nomads.[30]

The territory of Kiev was now exposed to constant attack by powerful nomadic confederations: first the Pechenegs, then the Cumans and finally the Mongols. The Kievan state developed strategies that closely resembled the methods used by China and the Byzantine Empire, if on a smaller scale. Warfare, bribes, alliances and royal marriages were all used to foster links with nomadic societies of the steppe. These worked reasonably well until the Mongol invasions of the thirteenth century. The Kievans learned that one of the most effective defences against nomadic attack was another group of nomads. Familiar with the ways of the steppe and its methods of waging war, they provided invaluable service guarding the eastern borders. This would have been a tactic familiar to China and Byzantium. In the eleventh century, the Kievans began to recruit nomads into their service from various steppe tribes: the Torks, the Pechenegs, the Berendei and others. As far as we can tell, this group had little in common apart from service to Kiev. Over the course of a century, this diverse group took on a common identity defined by their service to Kiev and their uniform which included black hats, giving them their name: *Chernye Klobuki.*[31] There is an obvious analogy, even if no direct link, between the Kievan *Chernye Klobuki* and the later use of the Cossacks by Muscovy and the Polish-Lithuanian Commonwealth.

Conclusion

From the Great King Darius to Chingis Khan, from the walls of Constantinople to the Great Wall of China, the steppe reproduced certain patterns of interaction in time and space. The steppe gave rise to a particular way of life, pastoralism, which bred in its turn nomadic societies with a military potential that under the right conditions was sufficiently great to overwhelm the most powerful of sedentary empires. For those conditions to be met, nomadic society had to overcome its naturally fractious state and concentrate its energies which were otherwise dissipated in endless internal struggles. The existence of a powerful and wealthy civilization on the edge of the steppe provided the external stimulus necessary for the initial drive to unity among nomads. Maintaining that unity over the long run depended on the ability to extract sufficiently high quantity of material and cultural goods to satisfy the desires of the nomadic populations. Control of trade routes served a similar function in other places and times. Essentially, nomadic states could not survive without a steady external stream of goods and services.

Sedentary societies strove to establish their dominance over the nomads by relying on broadly similar strategies. They insisted on formal acknowledgement of the empire's superiority, they used the payment of tribute to factionalize the nomadic state and ultimately bring it to a position of real as opposed to nominal dependence. Cutting off the supply of goods or closing the border towns to the nomads was an effective means of exerting pressure. Judging the strength of one's hand was always a delicate and risky business for both sides and frequently mistakes were made, provoking a return to hostilities. By the time the Cossacks appeared in the fifteenth and sixteenth centuries, this pattern of interaction between the steppe and the sedentary peoples had already existed for the better part of two millennia. With little consciousness of earlier history, both the Cossacks and Slavic states on the edge of the steppe immediately began to move according to the ancient rhythms of the steppe.

Notes

1   D. Sinor, 'Introduction: The Concept of Inner Asia' in D. Sinor (ed.) *The Cambridge History of Early Inner Asia* (Cambridge, 1990) pp. 1–18.

2   R.N. Taaffe, 'The Geographic Setting' in Sinor, *Early Inner Asia*, pp. 33–37.

3   T. Barfield, *The Perilous Frontier: Nomadic Empires and China 221 BC to AD 1757* (Oxford, 1989) p. 1

4   E. Hildinger, *Warriors of the Steppe: A Military History of Central Asia 500 BC to AD 1700* (Cambridge, Mass., 2001) p. 7.

5   Herodotus, *The Histories*, trans. R. Waterfield (Oxford, 1998) p. 274.

6   Barfield, *The Perilous Frontier*, pp. 35–36.

7   L. Hughes, *Sophia: Regent of Russia 1657–1704* (New Haven, 1990) pp. 199–201.

8   C. Dawson (ed.) *Mission to Asia* (Toronto, 1998) p. 124.

9   T.J. Barfield, *The Nomadic Alternative* (New Jersey, 2001) pp. 146–147.

10 Herodotus, *The Histories*, p. 273.

11 A.I. Melyukova 'The Scythians and the Sarmations' in Sinor, *Early Inner Asia*, pp. 111–112.

12 C . Dawson (ed.), *Mission to Asia* (Toronto, 1980) p. 18.

13 D. Morgan, *The Mongols* (Oxford, 1986) p. 40.

14 P. Ratchnevsky, *Genghis Khan: His Life and Legacy* (Oxford, 1991) p. 22.

15 Barfield, *The Nomadic Alternative*, pp. 149–151.

16 Barfield, *The Perilous Frontier*, p. 35.

17 E.A. Thompson, *The Huns* (Oxford, 1999) pp. 67–68.
18 Ying-Shih Yu, 'The Hsiung-nu' in Sinor, *Early Inner Asia*, p. 122.
19 D. Sinor, 'The Hun Period' in Sinor, *Early Inner Asia*, p. 192.
20 P. Golden, *Khazar Studies: An Historico-Philological Inquiry into the Origins of the Khazars* (Budapest, 1980) pp. 60–65.
21 Barfield, *The Perilous Frontier*, pp. 8–16.
22 Gy. Moravcsik (ed.) *Constantine Porphyrogenitus De Administrando Imperio*, trans. R.J.H. Jenkings (Dumbarton Oaks, 1967) p. 67.
23 Herodotus, *The Histories*, pp. 276–277.
24 Barfield, *The Perilous Frontier*, p. 3
25 Ying-Shih Yu, 'The Hsiung-nu' in Sinor, *Early Inner Asia*, p. 140.
26 Ying-Shih Yu, 'The Hsiung-nu' in Sinor, *Early Inner Asia*, pp. 124–125.
27 D. Obolensky, *The Byzantine Commonwealth: Eastern Europe 500–1453* (London, 1971) p. 56.
28 S. Franklin and J. Shepard, *The Emergence of Rus 750–1200* (London, 1996) pp. 95–96.
29 Franklin and Shepard, *The Emergence of Rus*, pp. 144–145.
30 Christian, *History of Russia, Central Asia and Mongolia*, p. 357.
31 P. Golden, 'The Peoples of the South Russian Steppes' in Sinor, *Early Inner Asia*, p. 277.

1

The origins of the Cossacks

In the winter of 1444 a Tatar raiding party crossed into the principality of Riazan on the southern frontier of Muscovy. The border militia pursued the raiders, ran them to ground and destroyed them completely. Incursions like these were part of the routine of life on the frontier barely rating a mention in the chronicles. Only a passing reference to a hitherto unmentioned group in the list of forces making up the militia struck an unusual note. The chronicler recorded:

> Grand Duke Vasilii Vasilievich of Muscovy dispatched Prince Vasilii Obolenskii and Andrey Feodorovich Goltiaev, and his Court, and the Mordva on skies . . . And the Riazan Cossacks were also on skies. The troops were [armed] with cudgels and axes.[1]

Not the least bizarre aspect of this report was that the Cossacks made their first appearance in the Russian historical record not on horses but on skis! This laconic, enigmatic reference is the earliest extant mention of Cossacks in Russian sources. Understanding its significance and drawing out the meanings compressed within it only becomes possible when it is put in the context of the traditions of steppe society and the geo-political conditions of the southern frontier.

The *qazaqi* of Turco-Mongolian society

The word used by the Russian chronicler to describe these people was *kazaki*: a Russian rendition of the Turkic work *qazaq*[2]. This name in its Turkic context contained a cluster of meanings both flattering and unflattering: freebooter, vagabond, freeman, steppe brigand. The chronicler clearly expected his audience to understand his reference to Cossacks since he did not bother to include an explanation which suggests that they were already a familiar part of life on the frontier at that time. In this he was right

Figure 1 *The Zaporozhian Cossacks writing an insulting letter to the Turkish Sultan*, by I.E. Repin, 1980–91 (oil on canvas)

since *qazaqi* had existed from the time of the Mongol conquests and the disruption these had brought to the traditional steppe order.

The constant warfare of the steppe had created societies superbly conditioned for war, but warfare was only part of the life of a nomadic people. For a minority of men, however, fighting was the only life they knew and wanted. Bored by family ties and resentful of the very hierarchical nature of traditional steppe society, these ambitious, restless men found an outlet for their energies as *qazaqi*.[3] Such men, gathering with others of their kind, formed gangs under leaders chosen by themselves. They were willing to hire themselves out as professional soldiers or make their living by working for themselves as bandits.[4] There was even a verb, *qazaqliq,* to describe being or acting like a *qazaq*. The profession of *qazaq* was open to all who were able to follow it and ethnicity was no barrier to membership. *Qazaq* was not an ethnic label but a trade reminiscent of the original meaning of *viking*. Followers of the trade did not consider themselves a separate community nor did they develop territorial claims. They remained very much a part of the world of steppe nomads; no doubt desiring to merge back into it once they had found fame and fortune.

Qazaqi occupied an ambiguous place in steppe society as the various meanings embodied by it reveal. These highly skilled fighters were welcome in time of war, but in times of peace they were a dangerous and unpredictable element all too likely to revert to banditry. Nobody illustrates better both the opportunities open to a *qazaq* and the potential dangers to his employers than the great conqueror Tamerlane who began his career as a *qazaq*.[5] All across the Turco-Mongolian world *qazaqi* could be found, working on their own account or hiring themselves out as soldiers in the various wars of the steppe. In times of instability and uncertainty, such as the collapse of one steppe empire or the rise of another, the number of men seeking to make a living as *qazaki* increased sharply.

The southern frontier

When the hegemony of the Kipchak Khanate came to an end in the fifteenth century, the political map on the western edge of the steppe had changed beyond recognition. Three lesser but still very powerful khanates at Kazan, Astrakhan and the Crimea laid claim to the inheritance of the Kipchak Khanate. However, these khanates were not alone in their claims. Far in the north-east, a new power saw itself as the true heir to the Khan's throne. Moscow, which had been an insignificant principality before the Mongol conquests, had emerged as the dominant Russian principality when the Mongol Yoke was finally lifted in 1480. In the west, Lithuania had become the most powerful state under a series of able rulers. In 1569 Lithuania entered a dynastic union with Poland to create the Polish-Lithuanian Commonwealth, becoming one of the most dynamic states in Europe.

The disintegration of the Kipchak Khanate left a power vacuum over a vast area of steppe between the Volga and Dnieper Rivers. The open grasslands became a place of great terror for the settled populations to the north of them. Out of the steppe came nomadic raiders, looking for booty in any form but especially slaves for the booming markets of the Ottoman Empire. In the course of two centuries, hundreds of thousands of Slavs were carried off to slavery by the Tatars.[6] Sometimes these were small operations carried out by groups acting on their own initiative while on other occasions they were great state enterprises, involving thousands of nomads and tens of thousands of victims. Even formal peace treaties between the states brought little respite as many bands in the steppe refused to respect any peace and continued their lucrative trade. Guillame Le Vasseur, a French military engineer in the service of the Polish crown in the mid-seventeenth century, saw the trauma of slaving expeditions at first-hand:

> During the interval of this week-long stop, they bring together all their booty, consisting of slaves and livestock, and divided the entire quantity among themselves. The most inhuman of hearts would be touched to see the separation of a husband from his wife, of a mother from her daughter, there being no hope of their ever seeing each other again. They are to become the wretched slaves of Mohammedan pagans, who abuse them atrociously. The brutality [of these Tatars] causes them to commit an infinite number of filthy acts such as ravishing young girls, raping women in the presence of their fathers and husbands, and even circumcising children before their parents very eyes, so that they may be offered to Mohammed. Indeed the most sensitive of hearts would tremble to hear the shouts and chants, amid the weeping and moaning of these unfortunate Ruthenians, since these people mingle singing and shrieking with their tears. These wretches are then seperated, some being designated for Constantinople, others for the Crimea, still others for Anatolia. That, in a few words, is how the Tatars round up and carry away groups numbering more than 50,000 souls in less than two weeks . . .[7]

Fear of raids led to a rapid depopulation of the areas close to the steppe, but distance was no guarantee of safety. Even Moscow was subject to attack on several occasions. As late as 1571 Moscow experienced a terrible raid in which the whole city outside the Kremlin was burnt. The steppe became known as *Dikoe Polia* which is usually translated as the *Wild Field,* but *Savage Field* captures its meaning better.

Guarding the steppe frontier

The exposed southern frontier of Muscovy and Poland-Lithuania ran for hundreds of miles. With few natural obstacles to movement it was extremely difficult to defend.[8] Fortresses and defensive lines astride the main Tatar raiding paths offered some protection but demanded an exhausting mobilization of human and material resources by both states. There were never enough of either and determined raiding parties could always find a way through. The southern frontier existed in a constant state of tension and expectation of a new attack: danger was continuous and all around. For those living on the frontier it was a mundane fact of life. When asked by the authorities why he had not reported a recent incursion by the Tatars, the commander of Cherkassy on the Ukrainian steppe frontier replied sarcastically:

> It is nothing new for the Tatars to put in an appearance near a borderland castle several times a week; if one were to report such minor alarms each and every time there would not be enough messengers.[9]

Few voluntarily chose to live there, but for those who did they found a way of life dramatically different from the relatively safer life of the interior.

The population of the frontier was a heterogeneous mix: socially, ethnically and culturally.[10] The governments of Poland-Lithuania and Muscovy established garrisons in the frontier fortresses, but many of those who served in the military on the frontier did so of their own volition. Minor gentry down on their luck, adventurers, criminals, fugitives of one sort or another were all drawn to the frontier, throwing different social strata together in a uniquely promiscuous fashion.[11] There were even cases of a great magnates such as Dmitrii Vyshnevetskii in the mid-sixteenth century making a career for himself on the frontier. Many of these people were there illegally and local officials were supposed to arrest them and send them back to their places of origin. Few bothered to do so. Manpower was always short and the authorities were loath to return anyone who had made their way voluntarily to the frontier. Both governments frequently made noises about the return of illegal residents, but in reality colluded with the actions of the local officials.[12]

Ethnically, Slavs made up by far the largest group in the frontier towns but there were significant ethnic minorities including Tatars. Despite their inveterate enmity, Slav and Tatar encountered each other on the frontier in much more intimate ways. Tatars traded with the border towns, took up residence there and many entered into government service. Tatar language, customs and culture became part of life in the frontier towns. Living cheek by jowl in a highly pressurized setting, both groups developed a familiarity with the other culture, gaining an understanding that was unique to the frontier.

The frontier was distinctive in another way as well. The rigid social hierarchy that was such a prominent part of life in Poland-Lithuania and Muscovy softened the closer one came to the frontier. The peasant communities nearest to the frontier tended to be independent, self-reliant farmers well used to looking out for themselves and their families. Nobles as yet had few footholds among these proud peasants who cherished their free status.[13] On the Ukrainian side of the frontier these peasants eventually became incorporated into the Cossacks themselves, forming the settled Cossacks in contrast to those living at the *Sich*. Those living on the frontier itself displayed these qualities in an even more marked way. These men, drawn by the dangers and excitement of the frontier, did not lightly submit to any authority. The tough, competent commanders responsible for defending the frontier had to learn to work with the volatile population under their authority, accepting attitudes and behaviour that in the interior would have been savagely punished. As a whole, the southern frontier constituted a distinct society: more turbulent, less deferential and taking a certain collective pride in its dangerous existence.

The Cossacks

When the words of the chronicler for 1444 are put against the institution of *qazaqi* and the political context of the southern frontier, it becomes easier to make sense of them. There is little point in trying to work out the ethnicity of the group mentioned by the chronicler since *qazaqi* did not have ethnic connotations. These men could have been Tatars, Slavs or some mixture of the two. It is not possible to tell from the meagre information given to us by the chronicler, but his words are suggestive of important processes taking place in the steppe.

Qazaqi as we have seen were an accepted part of Turkic nomadic society. Operating in small bands they offered themselves to whoever could afford to hire them. It is highly likely groups such as these were active in the

southern steppe and had been since the collapse of the Kipchak Khanate.
Qazaqi knew the steppe intimately, were completely at home in Tatar
society and were superb warriors, having forsaken all other ties to follow
this career. They could go where no ordinary soldiers would dare to
venture, track and pursue raiding parties and give warning about imminent attacks.[14] Like soldiers of fortune everywhere, solidarity with their
ethnic group came a poor second to loyalty to their paymaster. Always on
the look out for prospective employers, the fortresses of the southern
frontier were an option worth considering for the *qazaqi*. To the hard-
pressed fortress commanders, the skills that these men offered for hire
were precious commodities. No doubt, the same qualities had attracted the
Kievan state to the *Chernye Klobuki*.[15] That they first appear to have been
hired in the principality of Riazan was no surprise. Riazan constituted the
southernmost part of the defence line in mid fifteenth century and was
the most exposed and vulnerable of all Russian principalities. Over the
next few decades, more and more border towns hired *qazaqi* as part of
their defensive efforts.

As some of the Tatar nomads entered service with the Russian principalities, some of the Slavic frontiersmen began to venture into the *Savage
Field*.[16] Alongside all its dangers, the open steppe had opportunities. The
steppe was a pristine wilderness; its rivers brimmed with fish and wild
beasts roamed in great numbers. A resourceful man and a few companions
could easily find enough to sustain themselves and build up a surplus
to trade back in the fortress towns. More tempting, but much more
dangerous were the Nogai Tatars who lived in the steppe. They had much
worth taking particularly their herds and their women. For those ready to
run the risks, the rewards were substantial. Among the restless spirits
attracted to the frontier, there must have been many who felt the pull of
the open steppe and the lure of the perilous, but free life it dangled before
them.[17]

Individually and in small groups these men entered the steppe to take
their chances there. Later on, fugitve peasants would enter the steppe in
great numbers, but the first Slavs to do so must have been the frontiersmen
of the southern borders.[18] Only these men possessed the requisite skills to
survive in the steppe. Peasants, moving directly on to the open steppe from
the settled areas, would have stood little chance against Nogai warriors. The
frontier acted as a transitional zone, providing essential experience of the
steppe and its ways.

The frontiersmen usually set out in early spring and remained until late
autumn when they returned to the border towns to sell off whatever they

had acquired in the steppe and to sit out the long winter.[19] This movement developed in parallel on both the Polish and Muscovite sections of the frontier and over the decades it became an established part of life, adding yet another hue to the rainbow population there.

By the beginning of the sixteenth century this movement into and out of the steppe had become a matter of concern to the Grand Prince of Moscow, Ivan III. In 1502 he wrote to Princess Agrippina, the ruler of Riazan principality, demanding that she put a stop to it:

> All your serving people, and others and the fortress Cossacks are to be in my service and if any of them do not obey and foolishly go to the Don for freebooting, you must execute them.[20]

The Grand Prince's instruction confirmed that more and more people were entering the steppe and that most were attracted by the prospect of robbing the Nogai Tatars resident there. The Polish and Lithuanian authorities were equally concerned about the unauthorized activities of the Cossacks, but by the second decade of the sixteenth century they had began to see ways in which the Cossacks might be of use to them. In 1524 Grand Duke Sigismund I mooted the idea of recruiting Cossacks into service after a company of Cossacks had held river crossings against the Tatars for a whole week:

> ... His Majesty the Sovereign orders this to be said to Your Graces: If with such a small number of men, such services were rendered to us, we see from this that if one or two thousand Cossacks were stationed there on the Dnipro, a greater and very significant service and defense of our dominions would result from that.[21]

For both states, the Cossacks were developing into something more than just the perennial problem of steppe bandits.

The flow of people into the steppe reflected the heterogeneous population of the southern frontier. Some fortress Cossacks were content to remain in the service of the Grand Princes or the Polish kings; over time this group became an hereditary part of their armed forces. Other fortress Cossacks, however, were just one among many who found freelancing in the steppe more lucrative than serving as hired guards for the government. But the opposite movements of Turkic *qazaqi* and Slavic frontiersmen were beginning to converge. Increasingly the two were following a common way of life and the barriers separating them were breaking down.[22] Doubtless they found they had far more in common with each other than with the populations from which they had sprung. As yet these people had no collective identity or group consciousness. They did not even have a name.

The Muscovite and Polish governments had various names for this free floating border population, most of them unflattering: bandits, thieves and vagrants. On the Polish side of the frontier they were often referred as *Cherkassy*, taking their name from the frontier fortress from which many set out. Steadily however, one name began to supersede all others among both the men who followed this way of life and those to whom they were a matter of concern. In 1517 the renowned Polish scholar and rector of Cracow University, Matvei Mekhovskii, published a highly influential work, *Treatise about Two Sarmatias*, in which he discussed, among other things, the *Savage Field* and its inhabitants:

> The Field of the Alans occupies a wide expanse. It is a wilderness in which there are no rulers-neither Alans nor others. Cossacks alone sometimes wander there 'searching' according to their custom for somebody to devour.
>
> Kazak is a tatar word, but Kozak is Russian and signifies a slave or subject-a vagrant on foot or on horse.
>
> They live by booty and are subordinate to no-one. They roam through the wide and empty steppe in detachments of three, six, ten, twenty or sixty persons and sometimes more.[23]

The various subgroups that flowed in and out of the steppe were acquiring a common name to identify them which was spreading far beyond the confines of their own theatre of operations. The mixed Tatar and Slavic heritage of the Cossacks was evident in Mekhovskii's understanding of the them. Mekhovskii's view of the Cossacks differed little from either the Polish or Muscovite governments, regarding them as ferocious outlaws who were a law unto themselves. Interestingly, however, he was also aware that the Cossacks were operating in gangs from the tiny to the substantial. The Cossacks were discovering the advantages of crime on an organized scale and were learning how to cooperate among themselves.

Another important change was taking place among those who practised the trade of Cossack in the first decades of the sixteenth century. Many of them abandoned their transitional existence between the steppe and the border towns and moved permanently into the steppe.[24] Attempts by the two governments to control the movement of Cossacks, the heavy taxes they levied on whatever the Cossacks had acquired in the steppe and the equally hefty bribes they were forced to pay frontier officials helped persuade many Cossacks that the open steppe was a less predatory enviroment than an avaricious state and its officialdom.[25] What had been a trade for these men was becoming a way of life.

Over the next couple of decades the numbers and organizational capacities of the Cossacks continued to grow. On the Polish part of the frontier, a series of spectacular raids on the Crimean Tatars by Cossacks under the leadership of Ostafei Dashkovich began in the early sixteenth century and continued until Daskkovich's death in 1535. In mid-century the Ukrainian magnate Dmitrii Vyshnevetskii enjoyed spectacular success as a Cossack chieftain gathering thousands of Cossacks around him. The Cossacks were moving from being an irritant to the Nogai Tatars to becoming a major threat. Nor did they restrict their activities to the Tatars. Polish and Muscovite interests were just as likely to attract the attention of the Cossacks. In 1538 Khan Iosef of the Nogai Tatars complained to Muscovy about the destruction wreaked on his people by the Cossacks. The Muscovites denied any responsibility for the Cossacks, claiming that they suffered from their activities no less than the Nogai:

> Many Cossacks are roaming in the field: kazantsy, azovtsy, Crimeans and other idle Cossacks. And Cossacks from our borderlands when mixed with these do like these people. So these robbers who are thieves for you are also thieves for us.[26]

The government may have been disingenuous in its denial, but it was equally possible that it was telling the truth and that the Cossacks were as much outside of its control as anybody else's. Again this account, like Mekhovskii's and nearly every other contemporary observer, stressed the multi-ethnic nature of the Cossacks. What gave them a common identity was not ethnicity, but the trade they plied, i.e. that of being a Cossack.[27] The joint enterprise of living in the steppe and robbing all who were not Cossacks mattered more than ethnic difference.

Mekhovskii and the Polish and Muscovite states understood that more and more Slavs were entering the steppe to follow the Cossack way of life. What had originally been a Turkic phenomenon was becoming increasingly Slavicised in its ethnic make up.[28] The Turkic *qazaqi* were turning into the Slavic Cossacks. But the process was more complex than the Slavs simply imposing their identity on a Turkic institution. While weight of numbers led to the predominance of Slavic languages and the Christian religion, the traditions of the Turco-Mongolian *qazaqi* were changing the Slavic frontiersmen into something else. In the early sixteenth century, a new social formation was coming into being on the steppe frontier.[29]

The move towards communities

The middle third of the sixteenth century was to be a watershed in the history of the Cossacks. In these thirty years the organizational capacity of the Cossacks took a qualitative leap forward. The autonomous gangs roaming the steppe coalesced into two organized, self-conscious communities on the Dnieper and Don Rivers with territorial pretensions, rudimentary institutions and a claim of allegiance over all who entered the steppe to live as a Cossack.[30] No less important they developed the capacities and structures to negotiate with the surrounding states. Why did these momentous developments come about?

Two conditions were required for the Cossacks to make the transition from isolated bandits to proto-state organisms. One was the political space for this to happen while the other was the stimulation of outside forces. The collapse of the Kipchak Khanate provided the space for the Cossacks to grow and develop. It is inconceivable that the Khanate would have tolerated an independent, organized community with territorial claims within its dominion. This gave the Cossacks the possibility to become organized, but it was not sufficient on its own. There had to be an incentive, making the effort of organization worthwhile. This was provided by the powerful Slavic states on the northern edge of the steppe.

The successes of the individual Cossack gangs operating without any outside support against the Crimean and Nogai Tatars had made a deep impression on the Poles and Muscovites.[31] Unlike their own forces which could not operate in the steppe, the Cossacks were completely at home there. After so many decades of frustrating incapacity in the face of Tatar raids, a force had finally appeared that was capable of taking on the Tatars on their home ground. The swelling chorus of complaint from the Nogai and Crimean Khans provided effective corroboration of the Cossacks' abilities. Yet these gangs were unruly and uncontrolled as apt to strike Muscovite and Polish interests as Crimean or Nogai. If they could be harnessed into the service of either state and disciplined, they would be an invaluable asset. But as long as they remained divided into dozens of different gangs, each pursuing their own interests, it would be impossible for them to construct any lasting relationship with them. Both Muscovy and Poland-Lithuania began to see advantages for themselves in the construction of a more consolidated political authority among the Cossacks. By appealing to all Cossacks to enter government service, both governments were addressing the Cossacks as if they were already a distinct phenomenon. For example Ivan appealed to the Cossacks to join him in his campaigns against Kazan and Astrakhan which many did.[32] Such appeals had the effect of helping to bring to fruition a collective identity that was still only embryonic. These external stimuli joined with internal evolution of the Cossacks.

As the numbers following the Cossack way of life grew in the early sixteenth century, a sense that they shared something more than simply a means of making a living developed among them. The self-identification of these people as 'Cossacks' and outsiders recognition and use of this name helped foster a belief that they shared a common identity. The success of Cossacks such as Ostafei Dashkovich and other chieftains spread the fame of the Cossacks far and wide, releasing a profound pride in all who shared that way of life and helping them conceive of themselves as something more than a band of cut throats.[33] The developing self-consciousness and increasing organizational capacity of the Cossacks fed off each other taking both to new levels. Gradually the Cossacks on the Dnieper and the Don began to develop a sense of identity that was rooted in their shared way of life and a distinct territory.[34]

It is of course impossible to say at precisely what point the internal and external stimuli to organization came together. Probably it happened on the Dnieper before the Don, but the two were so closely related in time and circumstance that it makes sense to see them emerging simultaneously. The process was facilitated on the Dnieper by a site ideally suited to the needs of a military brotherhood. Just beyond the rapids of the lower Dnieper were a series of islands which could be accessed only with the utmost difficulty. The intricate passage of the rapids demanded great skill and experience to negotiate. Hostile forces attempting to reach the islands would be acutely vulnerable to any attack while they were making the crossing. Prince Dmitrii Vyshnevetskii was the first Cossack leader to establish a base on one of the islands.[35] Out of this stockade eventually emerged the *Sich*, the focal point of the Cossacks on the Dnieper. The location of the Cossack headquarters became such a part of their identity that they became known as the Zaporozhian Cossacks, literally *the Cossacks beyond the rapids*. The Habsburg Ambassador, Erich Lassota Von Steblau, on a diplomatic mission to the Zaporozhians in 1594 was guided by the Cossacks through the rapids and left a vivid account of the crossing:

> The porogi are whirlpools or rocky places where the Dnieper continuously rolls over rock and boulders, some of which are under water and others, just even with it. Several boulders are higher than the water level and make travel past them very dangerous, especially when the water is low. The travellers must leave their boats, at these extremely dangerous spots. Then getting into

ЗАПОРОЖСКІЯ ГАЛЕРЫ И ЧАЙКИ ПО РОВИНСКОМУ И БОПЛАНУ.

Figure 2 *Drawing of Zaporozhian Galleys and Chaika*

the water, by means of ropes or poles they lift the boats over the sharp rocks and carefully let them down on the other side. Those who are holding the boat with the ropes must pay great attention to those who are in the water, listening to their commands when to pull or release the ropes so that the boat will not crash and be completely destroyed. There are twelve of these places . . .[36]

On the Don the lack of such a uniquely well-suited place probably retarded the process of consolidation, but not for very long. There were many easily defensible sites in the ravines and woodlands of the Don and its tributaries. By mid-century the Cossacks on the lower Don were operating out of several bases much to the discomfiture of the Nogai Tatars. Khan Iosef complained to Ivan the Terrible that 'His Cossacks in three or four places have built fortresses and collect dues from Azov and do not allow anybody to drink water from the Don.'[37] Ivan's reply was the almost the same as had been given a decade earlier:

> There are none of our Cossacks on the Don, only fugitives from our states . . . bandits live on the Don without our knowledge. We earlier sent people to eradicate them, but our people cannot get them.[38]

A significant difference from the earlier reply was the confirmation of the Khan's claim that there were now Cossacks living permanently on the Don. Interestingly as well, both Khan Iosef and Tsar Ivan used the name 'Cossack' to describe the people on the Don rather than the amorphous labels used a few decades earlier. Whether there was as yet one centre or a few is more difficult to say. But there was a momentum to larger levels of organization among the Don Cossacks no less than among the Zaporozhians.

Consolidation, however, brought costs as well as advantages. Three or four men living alone could probably supply all their own needs. Several hundred or even thousands living together needed a constant supply of food and other necessities if they were to stay together. The Cossacks could not produce for themselves the food, guns and other equipment necessary to support central organization. Even simply coming together for a prolonged period caused considerable logistical problems. Isaac Massa, a Dutch merchant, living in Moscow through the Time of Troubles described the difficulties the Cossacks faced even when they had to discuss something of vital interest to themselves. In this particular case it was whether to support the first False Dmitrii in 1604:

> And since 8,000 cossacks could not long wait in one place as they had to find provisions for themselves in the field, they fixed a time for the envoys [to return] and if the envoys had not returned then each could follow his own road. But until that time everyone had to remain . . .[39]

On the other hand Muscovy and Poland were willing to supply guns, ammunition and food if the Cossacks entered into their service.[40] The coincidence of interest between the Cossacks and the Slavic states developed rapidly from the mid-sixteenth century. It was by no means a smooth or unproblematic relationship; in fact it was to be the most explosive issue in the life of the Cossacks over the next two centuries. Nevertheless, it was a vital part of Cossack existence.

The expansion of the Cossack hosts

The coalescence of Cossack communities on the Don and Dnieper generated an extraordinary dynamism in the second half of the sixteenth century. The urge to explore the steppe, to follow the river systems, to find new places to occupy and new sources of booty drew more and more Cossacks from the two established hosts and from those who had never belonged to either. As the century wore on, Ivan the Terrible's ruinous policies set off the first of what would be many waves of peasant migration to the Cossacks from Muscovy. The harshness of serf existence within the Polish-Lithuanian Commonwealth provided a similarly effective recruiting sergeant for the Cossacks. Fortunately for these peasants there were already Cossack communities waiting to receive them. More members and the restlessness inherent in the Cossacks drove them to establish new communities on the Volga, the Iaik in the Caspian Steppe, the Terek in the North Caucasus and even on the Irtysh in Western Siberia. Although a great deal of energy has been expended attempting to pin down the precise ethnic make up of these new Cossack communities, it seems most likely that they consisted of the same heterogeneous groups that had formed the Don and Zaporozhian Cossacks.

Far more important than what these men might have been was what they became. The Cossack ethos and Cossack institutions were reproduced in locations hundreds and even thousands of miles from the Dnieper and the Don.[41] Stable communities were formed on the Iaik and Terek Rivers which rapidly developed their own territorial identity to go alongside that of a broader Cossack one. These communities, although distinct entities, were as yet not at all exclusive. Passage from one Cossack host to another was easy and many Cossacks were constantly on the move between them. This made cooperation between different hosts relatively straightforward. Zaporozhian, Don, Terek and Iaik Cossacks all participated in joint expeditions, sent appeals to each other for volunteers and acknowledged a common bond between them.[42] This never approached the point of creating one overarching authority or host for all the different Cossack communities, but it reinforced the sense of uniqueness that all Cossacks shared.

Not every Cossack expansion was successful. The Volga Cossacks who appeared not long after the Don Cossacks were never allowed to consolidate their control over the lower Volga.[43] The Volga had become a vital state interest to Muscovy in economic and, even more importantly, symbolic terms. The conquest of Kazan and Astrakhan symbolized Muscovy's claim to be the heirs of the Mongol khans. Having wrested dominion over the river from the Khanates of Kazan and Astrakhan, the government was in no mood to concede it to the Cossacks. In 1560 the first of many military expeditions was despatched down the Volga to expel the Cossacks from their bases on the river as the chronicles recorded:

> Cossacks pillaged along the Volga. The Godfearing Sovereign sent his commanders against them with many military men and he ordered them to catch them and hang them.[44]

This turned out to be an endless task as Cossacks from the Don, Terek and Iaik continually made use of the Volga either to attack trade passing along it or to enter the Caspian Sea to attack Persian cities or shipping. Seventy years after Ivan despatched the first expedition, the Governor of Nizhnii-Novgorod warned Ambassador Adam Olearius en route from Moscow to the Persian Empire to watch out for Cossacks:

> He asked if we were afraid of the Cossacks, who engaged in brigandage along the Volga and were not apt to leave us in peace. They were a cruel inhuman lot who love pillage more than their God, and fell upon people as they [the Cossacks] were beasts.[45]

Although the river figured constantly in Cossack plans and operations until the defeat of Pugachev in 1774, no free Cossack community took permanent root on the Volga. For different reasons, the Cossack attempt to establish themselves in Siberia also failed although it remained one of their most remarkable exploits.

The Cossack campaign in Siberia 1582–85

The tiny group of Cossacks who penetrated into Western Siberia in the 1580s, overthrowing the Khanate of Siberia and opening the way for the eventual Russian expansion to the Pacific Ocean and into the North American continent down as far as modern California, have drawn comparisons with Cortes and Pizarro in Mexico and Peru. The Cossacks were led by ataman Ermak Timofeevich who if ever there was an archetypal Cossack could claim to be it. He and his band of Cossacks had fought in many of Ivan the Terrible's wars including the disastrous twenty-five year Livonian War. When peace was finally concluded at the beginning of 1582, the Cossacks were immediately thrown off the payroll in a desperate attempt to salvage something of the government's finances. Released from the army, Ermak and his followers had to find another way to support themselves.[46] Ermak's company made its way to the Volga and, along with many other now superfluous Cossacks, pillaged everything that moved along the river. The so called *New Chronicle* described Ermak's subsequent flight from the Volga:

> Not far from the Don there is a river called the Volga and on it live Cossacks. These rob a great deal along the Volga and along other rivers. They looted vessels of the sovereign and robbed and killed ambassadors from the Kizylbashkii and Buchartsev and many others. Tsar Ivan, seeing their banditry and their wicked unruliness, sent his commanders against them and ordered them to capture and hang them. Many were caught and executed, but others, like wolves, fled in all directions. Six hundred people fled up the Volga away from them, following the appeal of Maksim

Figure 3 *Ermak's Conquest of Siberia in 1582*, by V.I. Surikov, 1895
(oil on canvas)

Stroganov. The most senior ataman was named Ermak but there were many other atamans among them.[47]

Salvation of a sort had come in the offer of employment from the Stroganov family of merchants. This family was one of the wealthiest in Muscovy in spite of its non-noble status. Among the Stroganovs' considerable interests were various enterprises in the Ural Mountains and in the lands east of the Urals. Although profitable, these enterprises were vulnerable to attacks from nomadic tribesmen. Stroganov offered the Cossacks employment protecting these enterprises. In keeping with Cossack tradition, a *krug* convened to discuss the Stroganov's proposal. With no other options, the Cossacks agreed to work for the Stroganovs.[48] When Ermak and his Cossacks arrived at the Stroganov's headquarters in Perm in the Urals, they discovered that the brothers had far more ambitious plans than their original proposal had suggested.

What they now proposed to the Cossacks was an audacious strike at the source of their problems: the Siberian Khanate. The Khanate had at one time been a vassal of Muscovy, but it had long since ceased to acknowledge its distant suzerain. Under its able leader, Kuchum, the Khanate had become a powerful nomadic confederation able to put at least 30,000 warriors of its own into the field.[49] Military forces from subject tribes augmented this total considerably. Most daunting of all, however, was the sheer distance of the Khan's capital, Kashlyk from Perm: at least 1,500 kilometres. Ermak agreed to the brothers proposals possibly because it appealed to his Cossack nature but there may have been more practical reasons as well. Ermak knew it would not be long before Ivan discovered that he had taken refuge with the Stroganovs and that he and his followers were extremely dependent upon the brothers' goodwill. How long that goodwill would last following any refusal to agree to the expedition must have been on Ermak's mind. Whatever the reason or combination of reasons, Ermak and 540 men set out on their epic journey at the beginning of September 1582.[50]

Leaving Perm, the Cossacks followed the Kama River through the Ural Mountains until it came close to the Irtysh: one of the great rivers of Siberia. At this point the Cossacks were forced to leave the Kama and drag their boats the 20 or 30 kilometres to a tributary of the Irtysh. Taking to the water again, they followed this tributary to the Irtysh itself. The Cossacks now had a direct route to Khan Kuchum's capital Kashlyk. They arrived at Kashlyk towards the end of October and immediately stormed the capital. The capture of the capital by a tiny Cossack band was another testimony to Cossack skill in military operations. However, the Khan himself escaped and was determined to recapture his khanate. The Cossacks found themselves engaged in a protracted war of attrition that increasingly took its toll on them. Ermak could ill afford to lose any men, but he was starting to lose them at such a rate that soon there would be no Cossacks left. In desperation he decided to appeal to Ivan for help.

Shortly after the Cossacks had left Perm, messengers had arrived from Ivan to the Stroganovs demanding the Cossacks be expelled. Ivan's fury was even greater when he discovered that they had set out to make war on Khan Kuchum.[51] Ermak and his companions had already inflicted serious harm on Russian interests and Ivan feared that the Cossack expedition would provoke a major war all along the Urals frontier. Large-scale revolts were already taking place among the recently conquered peoples of the Volga and, with the Livonian War in its final, disastrous stages, Muscovy's forces were already over stretched. When envoys led by Ermak's deputy, Ivan Kol'tso arrived in Moscow to appeal for help, Ivan ordered their arrest. Fortunately for Kol'tso and his companions, Ermak had anticipated Ivan's anger and had instructed Kol'tso to offer Ivan the crown of Siberia in recompense for the earlier damage the Cossacks had done. Ivan was mollified, graciously accepting the crown and pardoning the Cossacks. Three hundred streltsy were sent to aid Ermak.[52]

Over the next few years the government sent several more expeditions to consolidate control over Ermak's initial conquest. Very few other

Cossacks made their way to Siberia and soon the survivors of Ermak's expedition formed only a tiny minority among the amorphous government forces in Siberia. Ermak himself was killed in August 1585 when his Cossacks were caught in an ambush. Ermak escaped the ambush by leaping into the river. Weighed down by his armour, Ivan's present to him, Ermak drowned.[53] By the time of Ermak's death there were only ninety surviviors of the original 540 men who had set out with Ermak.[54] Without their leader and forming an ever smaller element among the tsar's servitors in Siberia, the Cossacks lacked the critical mass to create a Cossack host with its own identity. They were certainly not nearly large enough to make the consolidation and conquest of Siberia a Cossack enterprise. Instead, Ermak's Cossacks lost their distinct identity in the nebulous mass of servitors who were painstakingly continuing Ermak's work and the government influence over the Siberian Cossacks remained much stronger than over other hosts.[55]

The Cossacks and the Slavic states

The Don and Zaporozhian Cossacks had complex, shifting relationships with the two powerful states who acted as their sponsors. The Polish kings and Muscovite tsars claimed the Cossacks as their subjects and demanded unconditional obedience from them. The Polish monarchy, however, was well used to dealing with recalcitrant estates and corporations and knew how to negotiate with them. For the Polish Crown the Cossacks were just one of several groups with whom it was in constant negotiation. In 1572 King Sigismund Augustus II issued a charter to the Cossacks in which the crown acknowledged the Cossacks were now a corporate group like others within the Commonwealth.[56] Muscovite political culture on the other hand demanded, literally and figuratively, that all prostrate themselves before the throne. Although this disguised a more complicated relationship between the tsar and his great lords, it was an essential part of that culture.[57] For the Cossacks to claim they were in some sort of contractual relationship with the Tsar was intolerable. Yet beyond the mask of ideology, the Muscovite state dealt in political realities just as the Polish one did and the reality was that the Cossacks behaved as if they were free men. The compromise which made it possible for any relationship to exist was the willingness of Cossacks to express themselves in the idiom of Muscovite culture while completely ignoring its content when it did not suit.[58] In this respect, as in many others, Muscovite experience followed, unwittingly, Chinese and Byzantine precedents.

Within these confines, the respective monarchies did all they could to transform their claims of authority into reality. They used persuasion, coercion, rewards and punishments to tame the unruly nature of the Cossacks and turn them into obedient servitors. The Polish Crown made repeated efforts to compile a register of Cossacks so a more effective track could be kept on their movements. Payment for service was withheld, border towns were closed to the Cossacks and Cossacks were frequently executed by government forces. None of these measures had much effect in limiting Cossack freedom of action. They continued to behave as if they were completely free and had no overlord.

Yet the Cossacks were dependent on the two states if they wanted to survive as organized communities. Without employment in the armed forces of the monarchies and the supplies received from them, the Cossacks could not maintain a central organization. Lacking such an organization it was inevitable that the Cossacks would drift back into isolated groups of bandits, making a living by whatever means came to hand. The Cossacks did not look to create independent states in the modern sense, but they did want to be absolutely free to organize their lives, choose when, where and under what conditions they wished to serve and, above all, to ensure that their territory and communities remained completely autonomous.[59] Under these conditions they were willing to acknowledge the overall suzerainty of the Polish King or the Muscovite Tsar.

Jacques Margeret, a French soldier of fortune who entered the service of Tsar Boris Godunov and came to have a great deal of contact with the Cossacks, described Cossack/state relations in the following terms:

> Then there are the true Cossacks who maintain themselves along the rivers in the plains of Tartary, like the Volga, the Don, the Dnieper, and others. They often do more damage to the Tatars than the whole Russian army. They do not have large stipends from the emperor, but they do have liberty, it is said, to do the worst they can against the Tatars. They are permitted to withdraw sometimes to the frontier towns, there to sell their booty and to buy what they need. When the emperor wishes to make use of them, he sends them powder, lead, and some seven, eight, or ten thousand rubles.[60]

Another foreign contemporary, Issac Massa, concurred in this analysis:

> These Cossacks serve for money almost all the states which call them, but also without money for robbery alone. Notwithstanding this, they almost always served the Muscovites when the various Tatars have attacked them which has often happened. But from time to time, through God's will, the Cossacks have revolted against Muscovy and have started to rob all the

merchants trading with Persia, Armenia and Shemakhe and along the shores
of the Caspian Sea and even killing many of them . . .[61]

In this, the Cossacks were much like regional groups or corporations
elsewhere in early modern Europe who sought a complete break with a
dynastic overlord only in the most extreme circumstances. Usually they
were content to extract the best deal possible under the existing arrangements. The idiom in which this was expressed differed sharply in Poland-
Lithuania and Muscovy, but the process was essentially the same. The
Cossacks understanding of their relationship with the two monarchies was
needless to say very different from the two monarchs understanding of
it.[62] Nevertheless, it provided a capacious framework in which the two
could constantly renegotiate that relationship.

The culture of the Cossacks

Once relatively stable and self-conscious Cossack communities existed, all
who entered the steppe seeking to live as a Cossack had to become a part
of them. These communities, moreover, were fast developing their own
traditions and way of life which newcomers were expected to accept. A
Cossack was more than a Russian or Ukrainian peasant on a horse. By
joining the Cossacks he was adopting a new means of making a living,
but he was doing much more than this as well. He was subscribing to a new
way of viewing himself and the world around him. Essentially he was
exchanging one identity for a radically different one. What made up this
new identity?

First and foremost the Cossack were warriors like their *qazaqi*
forerunners. It is hard to exaggerate the ferocity of life on the steppe and
the endless struggle for survival with their formidable Tatar foes. To
survive, the Cossacks had not only to learn all the ways of the steppe and
steppe warfare, but they had to demonstrate exceptionally high levels of
skill in these arts. The Cossacks rapidly assimilated the experiences and
traits of steppe warfare and soon surpassed their Tatar teachers. Their
reputation as ferocious warriors was already well established by the reign
of Ivan the Terrible. Giles Fletcher the English sea captain who left one of
the first foreign accounts of Muscovy noted the awesome reputation the
Cossacks enjoyed:

At handie strokes (when they to ioyne battaile) they are accounted farre better
men than the Russe people, fearse by nature, but more hardie and blouddy
by continual practice of warre; as men no knowing no arts of peace, nor any
ciuill practice.[63]

Figure 4 *Don Cossacks Capturing the Fortress of Azov, 18th July 1637,*
by N.M. Kochergin, 1940 (pencil, pastel and w/c on paper)

The Cossacks soon revealed a prodigious capacity for all forms of
military knowledge. Unlike their Tatar enemies or for that matter the
gentry cavalry of Muscovy, the Cossacks were enthusiastic proponents
of the gunpowder revolution.[64] They were adept not only in the use of
small arms, but in highly complex and technical aspects of gunpowder
technology such as artillery and mining operations as we shall see. Equally,
Cossacks were completely at home on the rivers of the steppe and the open
sea. Moving down the river systems on their little boats or *chaiki*, the
Zaporozhian and Don Cossacks learned to navigate the Black and Caspian
Seas by the stars, developing the capacity and the daring to strike at the
mighty Ottoman Empire. No part of the Ottoman shore line was safe from
the Cossack raiders, even Constantinople. Ottoman galleys were a favourite
target and the Cossacks in their boats stalked a galley like a hunting pack
pursuing its prey. Pierre Chevalier described the ruthless efficiency of the
Zaporozhian Cossack pirates:

> When they meet with any Galley or Vessel (which they discover at a better
> and greater distance than they can be discovered) their boats being but two

foot and an half above water) they approach towards them till night, keeping about a League's distance, and then well observing the place where they saw the vessel, they begin to rowe about midnight with all their force, and encompassing it about, take it unawares, it being impossible for a Vessel beset with such a number of boats all at once to disengage or defend itself; they take out the Money, Guns, and all the Merchandise which they can conveniently carry away, and afterwards sink the ship, they being not dextrous enough to carry her off . . .[65]

The Don Cossacks similarly used the Volga to access the Caspian Sea and attack the wealthy cities and ships of the Persian Empire. The fast, manoeuvrable Cossack boats were difficult to catch and impossible once they left the open sea for the rivers.

Even the most difficult and draining of all military operations, siege warfare, provided another opportunity for the Cossacks to demonstrate their prowess either in defence or attack. Cossacks are not usually associated with the long, drawn-out tedium of siege warfare, but time and again they seized supposedly impregnable fortresses and held them against overwhelming odds. The capture and defence of the key fortress of Kromy during the Time of Troubles attracted the admiration of the foreign veterans in Muscovite service. Conrad Bussow's account of the Cossacks contrasted them favourably with the inept Muscovite forces besieging them:

> The Cossacks had dug slit trenches all around and within the fortifications. From both sets of trenches they threw up earth, and under the fortifications they made so many loopholes that they could, as the need arose, enter and sally forth in an instant. The Cossacks also built their dwellings in the earth like mice, so that nobody could disturb them with their shots.
>
> From the other earthwork they ran slit trenches toward the Muscovite redoubts and took cover in them. When the Muscovites came forward to skirmish, or sent men in for an assault, the Cossacks crept forward like mice out of their holes and defended themselves bravely and if the Muscovites began to get the better of them they quickly scrambled through the loopholes to regain the inner rampart, and their awaited the Muscovite pursuit. But the Muscovites were chilled to the bone and did not want to go in, and lay in siege for three months, wasting much powder and lead, and achieving nothing . . .[66]

Azov, Tsaritsyn, Astrakhan, Lvov, Bar, all mighty fortresses fell to the Cossacks during the seventeenth century even though all should have been able to withstand sieges by the best equipped and most advanced armies of the day.

The Cossacks possessed an extraordinary elan that enabled them to achieve far more than comparable numbers of regular troops. They were full of initiative, always seeking unexpected ways to throw the enemy off balance and demoralize him. The Cossacks understood the psychological aspects of warfare far better than their enemies.[67] Brazenly daring, they frequently unnerved much larger, more powerful opponents. To achieve their objectives Cossacks used anything that would tilt the balance of forces in their behaviour. During the great Cossack wars of the seventeenth and eighteenth centuries against Poland-Lithuania and Muscovy (later the Empire), the Cossacks demonstrated a rare capacity for precisely targeting discontented groups of the population and inciting them to join Cossack rebellions. Little wonder the Polish and Muscovite states desired their skills yet feared their unruly natures.

The Cossacks, however, were more than just ruthless condottierri offering themselves to the highest bidder. Unlike the Turkic *qazaqi* who had been rootless in a territorial sense, regarding the whole of the steppe as their base, the Cossack communities on the Don, Dnieper, Iaik and Terek rapidly developed proprietary claims over a substantial areas of territory.[68] The Don Cossacks, probably no later than the mid-sixteenth century, already had a concept of their territory which they called the *Land of the Host of the Don* (*Zemliia Voiska Donskogo*).[69] They sought by every means to protect their claims and have them recognized by the surrounding powers. The Zaporozhian Cossacks had their claims confirmed by the Polish crown while Ivan the Terrible was supposed to have issued a charter granting the Cossacks the Don and it tributaries in perpetuity. Although that charter was lost and may never have existed, the Don Cossacks believed it had existed and behaved as if it did.[70] The Iaik Cossacks claimed to have received a similar charter from Tsar Mikhail and repeatedly petitioned for its provisions to be confirmed.[71] Over the following decades and centuries these initially vague and fluid claims developed into a deep rooted, passionate bond with the land and rivers that the Cossacks identified as theirs. The universal attachment of the Cossacks to the land of their host would have profound political consequences over the next four hundred years.

Within these territorial bases, the Cossacks created political structures that were as much a part of their identity as their warrior way of life. In stark contrast to all the surrounding societies, the Cossacks were passionately committed to democracy in a most radical and crude form. At least once a year, more often if circumstances demanded it, the Don and Zaporozhian Cossacks would gather in their separate communities to decide matters

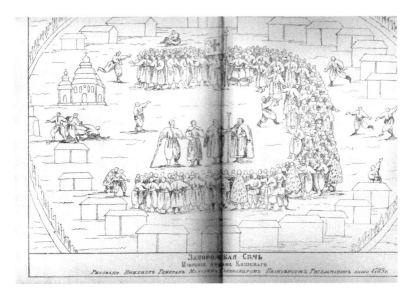

Figure 5 *Election of the ataman by the Zaporozhian Sich*,
drawing by A.I. Rigel'man

relating to their lives and elect leaders for the coming year.[72] These gatherings were named *krug* or *kolo*, literally circle or ring, which symbolized the Cossacks' commitment to unity and equality. The Cossacks stood around the in a circle and discussed, often over the course of several days, everything that impinged on the life of the host. All members of the community had the right to speak whatever was on their mind and give their opinion on the subject under discussion. Such discussions could often be stormy, but equally they could be sober occasions with the Cossacks weighing all the options before them. Ambassador Erich Lassota participated at the Zaporozhians' *Kolo* in the *Sich* when they debated the offer of service with the Holy Roman Emperor. The eight thousand Don Cossacks, referred to earlier, had come together to discuss whether to accept the claims of the young man who claimed to be Ivan the Terrible's murdered son, Dmitrii. This must have been almost the whole Don Cossack community at the time:

> The Cossacks, hearing about this, gathered an assembly to which more than eight thousand with their atamans came. They discussed this matter in a

mature manner and, finally, decided to send several envoys from themselves to Poland in order to find out about all and everything that had been relayed to them. And if they discovered that he was the real Dmitrii, then they would come forward to help gain his kingdom, but if he was not then they would move against him.[73]

The annual assemblies represented the summit of Cossack democracy. The assemblies bound the disparate Cossack groups together and provided a focus for the loyalty of the host as well a decision making body. The assemblies proved themselves effective decision makers. However stormy or bitter the deliberations, once the assembly had decided all Cossacks obeyed under pain of death.[74] The Cossacks developed powerful emotional attachments to their assembly and passionately resisted efforts to emasculate or abolish them as we shall see.

The annual assemblies had another function. They had to elect the men who were going to run the host for the next year. These men were vital to preserving the cohesion of the hosts when the assembly was dispersed which was most of the year. Negotiations had to be conducted with the surrounding governments, decisions regarding war and peace had to be made quickly, and, above all, the ataman and his assistants ensured that the Host acted and was seen to act as a unified body. The leader of the host was known as the ataman among the Don Cossacks and hetman among the Zaporozhian Cossacks and his assistant was an *esaul*. Both these titles were Turkic: yet more evidence of the *qazaq* roots of the Cossacks. It is probable that the leaders of the host were chosen by acclamation rather than any more sophisticated voting system. These elections could be relatively straightforward, but on occasion they were bitterly contested.[75] Again this had deep roots in steppe culture. The power of the ataman in wartime was absolute: as the Cossacks expressed it 'wherever the ataman throws a glance, there we throw our bodies'.[76] Yet away from campaign, the Cossacks with their cult of non-deference dealt bluntly with their atamans. Each year the assembly passed judgement on the outgoing atamans which could be an acutely uncomfortable experience for them.

The separate groups of Cossacks that made up the host chose their own atamans and *esauls* by exactly the same process, electing men they knew and would trust with their lives.[77] The hero of the siege of Kromy became ataman in just this way:

> The leader of these Cossacks was Korela, a mangy little man, covered with scars . . . and for his great courage Korela was elected ataman by this party of Cossacks while still in the steppe.[78]

Korela was chosen because he commanded the respect and admiration of his comrades. He was certainly not chosen for his looks or his birth or previous life. Later on, when Cossacks began to found permanent settlements and create societies more complex than military brotherhoods, they retained this form of decision making. In its essentials the basic democratic structure survived at the local level long after the democratic assemblies at the level of the *voisko* had been abolished. As we shall see they survived into the mid-1920s much to the annoyance of Soviet officials.

The radical democratic institutions of the Cossacks were accompanied by a commitment to egalitarianism in a particularly uncompromising form. Cossacks took great pride in the way that they divided everything equally, regardless whether a man was ataman of the host or a simple Cossack. When Tsar Feodor in 1592 sent payment to the Cossacks for their services, his ambassador was nonplussed at the reaction of the Cossacks. First, the Cossacks immediately complained that it was too small. Once this had been resolved, Ambassador Nashchokin, in keeping with the custom of his own society, and nearly every other one of the time, wanted to distribute it according to rank. The Cossacks famously replied, 'We have no great ones here, all are equal. We ourselves divide among the whole host according to need.'[79] While the Cossacks showed themselves absolutely shameless in always asking for more whenever they were being paid, among themselves they behaved as if material possessions were of little consequence. As well as disturbing the Muscovite ambassador's sense of propriety, the refusal to divide according to rank deprived the government of one of the means of creating a client base among the Cossacks. This had been one of the favoured tools through which sedentary societies had exercised control over steppe peoples

The Cossack sense of self went deeper than their political institutions and ideology. Becoming a Cossack involved a complete transformation of identity that extended to the way they looked and the way they conducted themselves with the outside world. Cossacks looked much more like Tatars than Slavs in their dress, their hairstyle and their weaponry. Tatar kaftans over the baggy trousers of nomadic horsemen, the single forelock of hair on an otherwise bald head were dramatic statements of a new identity. Many sources of the time were struck by how visibly alien the Cossacks were from the Slavic societies to the north of the steppe. As late as the last quarter of the eighteenth century Alexander Rigel'man observed during his time in the Don that all Cossacks still wore Tatar cloths.[80] It was not simply that these clothes were better suited to life in the steppe, the wearing of Tatar clothes and hairstyles represented a deliberate statement of identity.

Just as deliberate as the choice of clothes was the specific modes of behaviour adopted by Cossacks between themselves and to outsiders, particularly the great and powerful. Where other men cringed and abased themselves, a Cossack strutted. Where a peasant or a lowly townsman cast his eyes to the floor when he was addressed by a lord or an official, a Cossack stared him in the eye and spoke his mind bluntly. When the first False Dmitrii captured Moscow in 1605, he stationed Cossack guards within the Kremlin. Issac Massa described the behaviour of the Cossacks now in the very heart of the Muscovite Tsardom:

> . . . and fully armed Cossacks and other soldiers were stationed in the Kremlin with loaded guns. They feared nobody and they were so impertinent they even dared answer the great lords rudely.[81]

This was more than Dmitrii having chosen a particularly uncouth group of Cossacks as his bodyguards. It was a tangible expression of Cossack contempt for the grandees and all that they represented. Wherever and whenever they could, Cossacks publicly demonstrated their contempt for the hierarchal and deferential order symbolized by the boyars. Gathering in Moscow in 1613 for the election of a new tsar, Don and Zaporozhian Cossacks took the opportunity to display their loathing of the boyars. An eye-witness account 'The Tale of the Zemskii Sobor' recounted the behaviour of the Cossacks in the city:

> At that time forty thousand Don and Polish Cossacks entered Moscow, and the victors, while strolling idly through the city of Moscow in crowds of 20 or 30 persons, were all armed without any authorization. And none of them moved in crowds of less than 15 or ten persons. And those of boyar rank did not dare to say a word to contradict them, and when meeting [them] they stepped aside and only bowed their heads to them.[82]

In Astrakhan in 1669, Razin and his Cossacks treated the governor and his officials with a studied insolence that was a form of public theatre as well as a political act.[83] The only exceptions to this were the Tsar and the Polish King whom the Cossacks did treat with respect personally even as they completly ignored their wishes.

Ilya Repin's great painting, *The Zaporozhian Cossacks writing an insulting letter to the Turkish Sultan*, captured the spirit of the sixteenth century Cossacks perfectly. Although a nineteenth century recreation, Repin understood that becoming a Cossack meant adopting a radically new identity, leaving behind whatever one might have been before. This involved a fundamental transformation on every level. It was not just that the plough or the axe was exchanged for the sword as a means of making a living, but social and political relations, codes of dress, conduct and speech were also transformed. In many ways it was as if the Cossacks had deliberately fashioned their own identity by standing the world they had left behind on its head. The symbolic importance of Cossack culture cannot be overestimated for the oppressed masses of Poland-Lithuania and Muscovy. To see or even hear about a boyar or great lord treated with contempt by a Cossack demonstrated to those masses that an alternative and viable social order did indeed exist. This was to prove far more threatening to Poland-Lithuania, Muscovy and the Russian Empire than Cossack swords and muskets on their own could ever be.

The transformative power of Cossack identity has some striking similarities in its scope and completeness with the religious transformations taking place in other parts of the continent in the sixteenth century. For those who believed and became Cossack, the effect was so liberating, so all consuming that they in effect became different people. Even for the millions who remained behind in bondage, the power of the Cossack idea to stir the belief that an earthly liberation was possible was as potent as those appeals that promised a heavenly one.

Conclusion

The raw materials out of which the Cossacks were made had existed for a long time on the steppe: the incessant conflict between the steppe and the sedentary periphery, the internecine warfare among steppe peoples themselves, the existence of a professional class of soldiers and powerful states for whom the steppe was both a threat and an opportunity. Over the centuries these elements had combined to produce phenomena that were similar to the Cossacks, but not identical to them: steppe bandits, the *Chernye Klobuki* of Kievan Rus, the Turkic *qazaqi*. In the fifteenth and sixteenth centuries when the steppe kaleidoscope was shaken again, these elements coalesced to produce the Cossacks. The constituent roots of the Cossacks such as the *qazaqi* and the Slavic frontiersmen can be easily traced, but the Cossacks were greater than the sum of their parts. They transcended both the ethnic groups and the societies that had produced them. Cossacks belonged wholly neither to the Turkic *qazaqi*, the Slavic frontiersmen, the steppe or the settled areas. In the course of amalgamating all these elements something new was produced. The Cossack communities that emerged on the Pontic Steppe were different in the sense that becoming a Cossack was not a means to an end in the way it had been with the Turkic *qazaqi*, but an end itself. Self-conscious, possessing an ideology that transformed their understanding of their place in the world, and exhibiting powerful proprietary instincts over a specific and substantial territory, by the mid-sixteenth century at the latest, 'Cossack' was no longer what some men did, but had become who they were.

Notes

1 V.F. Mamonov, 'Teorii i fakty' in N.I. Bondar' (ed.) *Ocherki Traditsionnoi Kul'tury Kazachestv Rossi* (2 vols, Moscow, 2002), vol. 1, p. 171.

2 I am extremely grateful to Professor Peter Golden for his advice on the linguistic meanings of *qazaq*.

3 A.A. Gordeev, *Istoriia kazakov Zolataia Orda i Zarozhdenie Kazachestva* (Moscow, 1991) pp. 14–15.

4 B.V. Gorbunov, *Riazanskoe Kazachestvo v 15–18 v.v.: opyt istoriko-etnograficheskogo issledovaniia* (Riazan, 1994) pp. 5–6.

5 B.F. Manz, *The Rise and Rule of Tamerlane* (Cambridge, 1990) p. 45.

6 R. Hellie, *Slavery in Russia 1450–1725* (Chicago, 2002) pp. 21–24.

7 Guillaume Le Vasseur, Sieur de Beauplan, *A Description of Ukraine*, trans. and ed. A.B. Pernal and D.F. Essar (Cambridge, Mass., 1993), pp. 52–53.

8 C.S. Dunning, *A Short History of Russia's First Civil War: The Time of Troubles and the Founding of the Romanov Dynasty* (Pennsylvania, 2004) p. 50.

9 M. Hrushevsky, *History of Ukraine-Rus': The Cossack Age to 1625*, trans. B. Struminski, vol. 7 (Edmonton, 1999) p. 112.

10 Gorbunov, *Riazanskoe Kazachestvo*, p. 14. V.V. Glushchenko, *Kazachestvo Evrazii* (Moscow, 2000) p. 58.

11 Dunning, *Russia's First Civil War*, pp. 57–58.

12 C. Belkin Stevens, *Soldiers on the Steppe: Army Reform and Social Change in Early Modern Russia* (Dekalb, 1995) p. 26.

13 Dunning, *Russia's First Civil War*, pp. 91–94.

14 Gorbunov, *Riazanskoe Kazachestvo*, p. 21,

15 O.V. Matveev, 'Iavlenie Kazachestva v Istorii i kul'ture Rossii' in Bondar', *Ocherki Traditsionnoi Kul'tury*, p. 12.

16 R.G. Skrynnikov, *Sibirskaia Expeditsiia Ermaka* (Novosibirsk, 1982) p. 64. Hrushevsky, *The Cossack Age to 1625*, p. 64.

17 A. Ia Efimenko, *Istoriia Ukrainskago Naroda* (St Petersburg, 1906) pp. 160–161.

18 Hrushevsky, *The Cossack Age to 1625*, pp. 44–45.

19 Hrushevksy, *The Cossack Age to 1625*, p. 40.

20 V.K. Shenk (ed.), *Kazach'i Voiska* (Moscow, 1912) p. 5.

21 Hrushevsky, *The Cossack Age to 1625*, p. 80.

22 V.G. Druzhinin, *Raskol na Donu v Kontse XVII Veka* (St Petersburg, 1889) p. 36.

23 M. Mekhovskii, *Traktat o Dvukh Sarmatiiakh* (Moscow, 1936) p. 72.

24 Gorbunov, *Riazanskoe Kazachestvo*, p. 8.

25 Hrushevsky, *The Cossack Age to 1625*, p. 105.

26 Shenk, *Kazach'i Voiska*, p. 5.

27 Skrynnikov, *Sibirskaia Expeditsiia Ermaka*, p. 64.

28 S.V. Chernitsyn 'Donskoe Kazachestvo' in Bondar' *Ocherki Traditsionnoi Kul'tury*, vol. 1, p. 221.

29 Gorbunov, *Riazanskoe Kazachestvo*, pp. 12–13.

30 S.G. Svatikov, *Rossiia i Don 1549–1917: Issledovanie po Istorii Gosudarstvennago i Administrativnago Prava i Politicheskikh Dvizhenii na Donu* (Belgrade, 1924) pp. 15–16.

31 A.P. Pronshtein, *Zemlia Donskaia v XVIII Veke* (Rostov-na-Donu, 1961) p. 107.

32 A. Savel'ev, *Trekhsotletie Voiska Donskogo 1570–1870* (St Petersburg, 1870) p. 2.

33 Shcherbina, *Istoriia Kubanskago Kazach'iago Voiska*, vol. 1, p. 423.

34 Svatikov, *Rossiia i Don*, p. 16.

35 Hrushevsky, *The Cossack Age to 1625*, p. 107.

36 L.R. Wynar (ed.), *Habsburgs and Zaporozhian Cossacks: The Diary of Erich Lassota Von Steblau 1594* (Colorado, 1975) p. 81.

37 Shenk, *Kazach'i Voiska*, p. 5.

38 Shenk, *Kazach'i Voiska*, p. 5.

39 A. Liberman (ed.) *O Nachale Voin i Smut v Mosckovii* (Moscow, 1997) p. 67.

40 Svatikov, *Rossiia i Don*, p. 47.

41 I.L. Omel'chenko, *Terskoe Kazachestvo* (Vladikavkaz, 1991) pp. 51–52.

42 E.P. Savel'ev, *Istoriia Kazachestva* (Novocherkassk, 1916) p. 228.

43 Svatikov, *Rossiia i Don*, p. 17.

44 Shenk, *Kazach'i Voiska*, p. 16.

45 S.H. Baron (ed.) *The Travels of Olearius in Seventeenth Century Russia* (Stanford, 1967) p. 294.

46 Skrynnikov, *Sibirskaia Expeditsiia Ermaka*, p. 84.

47 A. Liberman (ed.) *Khroniki Smutnogo Vremeni* (Moscow, 1998) p. 265.

48 Skrynnikov, *Sibirskaia Ekspeditsiia Ermaka*, p. 97.

49 Skrynnikov, *Sibirskaia Ekspeditsiia Ermaka*, pp. 105–07.

50 Iu G. Nedbai, *Istoriia Kazachestva Zapadnoi Sibiri 1582–1808* (4 vols, Omsk, 1996) vol. 1, p. 97.

51 A. Rigel'man, *Istoriia o Donskikh Kazakakh* (Moscow, 1846) p. 32.

52 Tabolina, *Rossisskoe Kazachestvo*, p. 301.

53 Rigel'man, *Istoriia o Donskikh Kazakakh*, p. 34.

54 Tabolina (ed.), *Rossiisskoe Kazachestvo*, p. 301.

55 Nedbai, *Istoriia Kazachestva Zapadnoi Sibiri*, pp. 7–8.

56 Hrushevsky, *The Cossack Age to 1625*, pp. 109–110.

57 D. Ostrowski, *Muscovy and the Mongols: Cross-Cultural Influences on the Steppe Frontier, 1304–1589* (Oxford, 1998) pp. 88–90.

58 Svatikov, *Rossiia i Don*, p. 42.
59 A.L. Stanislavskii, *Grazhdanskaia Voina v Rossii XVII v.* (Moscow, 1990) p. 10.
60 J. Margeret, *The Russian Empire and Grand Duchy of Muscovy: A 17th Century French Account*, trans. and ed. by C.S.L. Dunning (Pittsburgh, 1983) p. 49.
61 Liberman, *O Nachale Voin*, p. 67.
62 Svatikov, *Rossiia i Don*, p. 42.
63 G. Fletcher, *Of the Russe Commonwealth* (London, 1591) p. 249.
64 Dunning, *Russia's First Civil War*, p. 54.
65 P. Chevalier, *A Discourse of the Original, Countrey, Manners, Government and Religion of the Cossacks* (London, 1672) p. 15.
66 C. Bussow, *The Disturbed State of the Russian Realm* trans. and ed. G.E. Orchard (Montreal, 1994) pp. 42–43.
67 Dunning, *Russia's First Civil War*, pp. 54–55.
68 Shcherbina, *Istoriia Kubanskago Kazach'iago Voiska*, vol. 1, p. 439.
69 Svatikov, *Rossiia i Don*, p. 14.
70 Svatikov, *Rossiia i Don*, p. 42.
71 S.K. Sagnaeva 'Ural'skoe Kazachestvo' in Bondar', *Ocherki Traditsionnoi Kul'tury*, vol. 1, p. 256.
72 Svatikov, *Rossiia i Don*, p. 35; Efimenko, *Istoriia Ukrainskago Naroda*, p. 184.
73 Liberman, *O Nachale Voin*, p. 67.
74 Svatikov, *Rossiia i Don*, p. 37.
75 Shcherbina, *Istoriia Kubanskago Kazach'iago Voiska*, p. 446.
76 M. Astapenko, *Donskie Kazaki 1550–1920* (Rostov-na-Donu, 1992) p. 14.
77 Gorbunov, *Riazanskoe Kazachestvo*, p. 10.
78 Liberman, *O Nachale Voin*, p. 78.
79 Savel'ev, *Trekhsotletie Voiska Donskago*, p. 4.
80 Rigel'man, *Istoriia O Donskikh Kazakh*, p. 96.
81 Liberman, *O Nachale Voin*, p. 95.
82 Liberman, *Khroniki Smutnogo Vremeni*, p. 457.
83 M. Perrie, *Pretenders and Popular Monarchism in Early Modern Russia* (Cambridge, 1995) p. 138.

Part II
The era of Cossack rebellion 1600–1774

The two hundred years between the reigns of Ivan the Terrible and Catherine the Great were momentous ones for the Cossacks. The unstable, shifting, bandit hordes of the steppe coalesced into permanent, deeply rooted, self-conscious warrior communities. On the Don, the Dnieper, the Terek, and the Iaik Rivers, Cossack communities became permanent fixtures on the geographical and political landscape. The age opened with the Cossacks at the peak of their power in relation to the surrounding states, but closed with the destruction of one of the two original Cossack communities and the brutal subordination of all the others to the Imperial Russian state. The Polish-Lithuanian Commonwealth was rocked by a series of progressively more devastating Cossack revolts that culminated in the Khmelnytsky rising in 1648 which fatally wounded the Commonwealth. On the Russian side, the attempt to subordinate the Cossacks to the state was ultimately more successful, but was punctuated by violence and brutality on an unprecedented scale. The first systematic attempt to bridle the Cossacks by Tsar Boris Gudonov backfired spectacularly and almost brought Muscovy to an end as an independent polity. Subsequent trials of strength ended progressively in the government's favour, spilling rivers of blood in the process. Yet even at the end, the Cossacks were still there as distinct communities. Chastened, subdued and restricted they certainly were, but they had survived.

The Cossack story in this period was full of wars, revolts and bloodshed but there was more to it than that. Their communities evolved from male brotherhoods dependent on new arrivals for renewal into fully self-reproducing communities with powerful family attachments and deep sense of belonging to the land of their host. The Cossack economy developed from one based on military service and plunder, supplemented by fishing and hunting, to stock raising and the first attempts at farming. Cossack hosts, now at the instigation of the state rather than spontaneously, pushed eastwards into Siberia and deeper into the North Caucasus. A few hardy souls went north-east and crossed the Bering Straits into Alaska. These developments will be explored more fully in the next section. This section will concentrate on the internal political evolution of the Cossacks Hosts and their relations with the surrounding states.

This was the critical relationship for the Cossack communities and decisively effected their evolution not only externally, but internally as well. Muscovy, and to a lesser extent Poland-Lithuania, became more skilful in their manipulation of the Cossack hosts, learning to create and exploit for its own advantage tensions and divisions within the hosts. Force was always an option and appeared to the preferred one of the post-Petrine state, but there were occasions when that might have undesirable consequences. Baits were offered in the form of the supplies, subsidies and outright bribes which were necessary for the hosts survival, but gave the Muscovite and Polish governments leverage over them much as Chinese and Byzantine governments had found in the past.

For the Muscovites, the Cossacks also proved a testing ground for methods of dealing with the non-Russian indigenous peoples of the steppe frontier. The imperial ideology of Muscovy, based on Byzantine and Mongol preconceptions to which the empire from Peter's time added a more contemporary gloss, insisted remorselessly on the tsar/emperors' sovereignty over all the peoples of the steppe, however, nominal that sovereignty might be in reality. Over the decades and centuries, the state worked to transform that nominal declaration of sovereignty into something much more substantial and real. The swearing of an oath of allegiance, the founding of government fortresses, the constraints on the right of movement and access to traditional sources of livelihood, the deliberate stimulation of factional conflict within a society ultimately broke its powers of resistance and allowed for it to be incorporated into the new imperial order. All these tactics were used against the Cossacks and many were actually developed first in relation to them. Later on the Cossacks would be one of the means by which the government subdued the nomadic peoples of the steppe.

This strategy helped stimulate processes of internal differentiation that were already underway within the Cossack hosts. The original egalitarianism of the Cossacks had always been an aspiration rather than an absolute reality. Differences existed within the hosts at all times, but in the beginning these remained dependent on an individual's own qualities rather than inherited wealth and status. This was an acceptable form of differentiation in a society which valued individual achievement highly.

But as the hosts grew in numbers and they became more stable environments, wealth and status began to flow from inherited sources as much as individual deeds. This is probably a natural development, but both Muscovy and Poland-Lithuania did all that they could to foster division and turn the Cossack elites into faithful clients.

Central to this process was the emasculation and the elimination of the *voiska* assemblies. As long as these existed, they provided a counter-balance to the power and wealth of the elites. The assemblies were the one time and place that weight of numbers could be effectively mobilized against the elites. The government identified the assemblies as a potent threat to its alliance with the Cossack elites and moved to eliminate them as soon as it was able. In 1722 the Don *krug* was abolished and replaced with a chancellory. The Zaporozhian *Sich* was broken by the Imperial army in 1775. On the Iaik the *krug* remained until the crushing of Pugachev's revolt. Once the assemblies had been abolished, ordinary Cossacks were deprived of any institutional means of checking the power of the elite and the policies they followed. So the Cossack story in this period becomes not only heroic resistance to external force, but an internal war in which the poor and rank and file defended the original ethos of the Cossack hosts against elites that aspired ultimately to incorporation into the Polish and Russian nobility.

Of course the lines of conflict were more complicated than that. In the Polish case, the ongoing contest between the Cossacks and the crown merged with religious conflict to fuel a much wider ranging revolt that for a time saw the existence of a truly independent Cossack state. Some members of both Cossack elites remained committed to the founding principles of the Cossacks, others vacillated torn between Cossack ideals and the prospect of riches and status dangled before them by king and tsar, as well as fear of the brutality which hovered very close to the enticements. Religious conflict cut across class lines in a way that nothing else did. In Poland the defence of Orthodoxy and Cossack self-interest united all sections of Cossack society against the crown. It made possible as well alliances with the secular and religious elites of Ukrainian society which were vital to the success of Khmelnytsky's rebellion. In Muscovy, the religious reforms of Patriarch Nikon in the mid 1660s was almost as potent in impact as the stuggle between Orthodoxy and Catholicism in the Ukraine. The old faith had its staunchest defenders in the Cossack territories particularly the Don, the Terek and the Iaik; its adherents were as much among the elite as the rank and file. Gradations of power and status within the elite also generated internal conflict, providing a leadership strata for the rank and file. Nevertheless, the picture painted by Soviet historians of communities riven by conflict between the elites and the rank and file seems to me to be substantially correct. The starkness of the conflict might be exaggerated, but its basic truth is well founded.

The story of these two centuries then is of two related but distinct struggles. One was directed outwards to maintain the freedom and autonomy of the host while the other was an internal one based on competing and irreconcilable visions of what the Cossacks were. If the struggle had simply been a triangular contest between the Cossacks and the state and within the Cossacks, in all probability the subordination of the Cossacks would have been achieved much earlier and with far less bloodshed. But the strife within the Cossack territories resonated across Poland-Lithuania and Muscovy. Cossack ideals of freedom and equality were the stuff of popular dreams. For humiliated and oppressed peasants, the Cossacks represented a living and viable alternative to the existing social order.

Cossack insurgency always had the potential to explode out of its regional, local character into a matter of kingdom wide significance, drawing into its ranks hundreds of thousands of desperate people by design and spontaneously. Rumour of Cossack rebellion was often enough for the enserfed masses to shake of their sullen obedience to a hated system, proclaim themselves Cossacks and wreak a bloody vengeance on their oppressors. The extreme violence of Cossack inspired revolts and the immediate shedding of blood distinguished them from most other revolts in Europe at the time. The memory of the abrupt transition from glowering docility to mob fury terrorized the imperial nobility down to the end of the old regime. This was no atavistic nightmare dimly held in the collective consciousness of the nobility, but a living menace which returned in 1905 and 1917 to complete what the Cossacks had attempted.

Less obviously, the appeal of the Cossacks extended to their ancient steppe enemies. Despite the constant warfare between the Cossacks and the steppe nomads, both sides understood each other very well. Cossacks were part of a steppe culture and were at home with other steppe peoples. Seeking allies among steppe peoples or even decamping en masse to the Ottoman or Persian Empires and exchanging the tsar for the sultan or the shah was a completely serious prospect for the Cossacks. The Zaporozhians did it; Razin, Bulavin and Pugachev all considered it. After the death of Kondratii Bulavin, ataman Nekrasov led 1,000 Cossacks and their families over the border into the Kuban where a distinct Cossack community survived in the Ottoman Empire well into the twentieth century. Nomadic peoples had culturally much in common with Cossacks while they shared virtually nothing with Russian peasants. Cossacks understood their needs, their anger and their hopes. With their roots in both societies, the Cossacks were uniquely placed to fuse the grievances of the frontier with those of the interior provinces. Little wonder the governments of Poland, Muscovy and the Empire regarded the Cossacks with such suspicion and sought so assiduously to put a halter on them.

The Cossacks during the Time of Troubles 1598–1613

The issues that dominated relations between the Cossacks and the two states to the north of them over the next 200 years crystallized in the period known as the Time of Troubles. Although there is insufficient space to provide anything more than a bare outline of this traumatic period of Russian history, it is important to highlight its significance for the Cossacks for it showed just how far the Cossacks had come in barely half a century. Literally and metaphorically, they moved from the periphery of Muscovite politics to the very centre. By 1613 the Cossacks had become the arbiters of Muscovy's fate and their support for the election of Mikhail Romanov as Tsar was central in bringing the troubles to an end.[1]

The crisis began with death of Tsar Feodor in 1598. Feodor had died childless and there were no other legitimate surviving members of the dynasty. Ivan's youngest son, Dmitrii, did survive, but, as child of Ivan's sixth wife, Dmitrii was illegitimate under Orthodox law. In the competition for power among the great aristocrats that followed Feodor's death, Boris Gudonov, the tsar's brother-in-law emerged victorious. However, Boris Gudonov's legitimacy was widely questioned and a series of political and natural disasters further undermined it. The death of Dmitrii in mysterious circumstances shortly after Boris' accession to the throne did nothing to bolster his legitimacy.[2] The Cossacks had particular reason to hate Gudonov.

Boris Gudonov (1598–1605) was the first Russian tsar to attempt systematically to transform the Cossacks into loyal servitors.[3] He sent expeditions against them, executed many Cossacks for disobeying him, closed the border towns to them and withheld payment for their services. Loathing Boris, the Cossacks waited for their opportunity. It arrived in 1604 when a mysterious stranger declared himself to be Dmitrii, having miraculously escaped Boris' assassins. The Cossacks of the Don and the Dnieper immediately rallied to Dmitrii's cause. For the next nine years, the Cossacks were deeply involved in the bitter struggles that convulsed the

Muscovite state. As the struggle progressed and intensified the Cossacks more and more became the single most important factor in deciding the fate of the country.[4] What did the conflict reveal about the Cossacks?

Apart from their obvious military abilities which were touched on in the last chapter, the Time of Troubles left no doubt that the Cossack communities could act as collective bodies, capable of reaching decisions and ensuring that all followed that decision. In a time when every other group in Muscovy was paralysed by division and rivalry, the Cossacks displayed impressive unity of purpose and clarity of vision. From their rallying to the banner of Tsar Dmitrii in 1604 to their support for the candidacy of Mikhail Romanov in 1613, the Cossacks fought for their own interests as always, but one of these interests was to have a legitimate tsar occupying the throne. The Cossacks and the throne were bound together in complicated ways, each believing they had the right to interfere in the affairs of the other. This relationship continued to develop over the next two centuries.

Cossack influence in Muscovite society was in direct proportion to the disintegration of that society: above all to division within the ruling elite. The boyars and the lesser gentry were hopelessly divided, pursuing different interests and backing different candidates for the throne. In the process they nearly lost everything. By the end of the Troubles they were confronted with the very real prospect that Muscovy would disappear and along with it everything that had given them wealth and status. It was a lesson that was to be burned into the collective consciousness of all sections of the elite: the great and the minor. Whatever the divisions that existed between the throne and nobility and within the nobility, they were of much less consequence than what they had in common. As far as the Cossacks were concerned, a united Muscovy was a much tougher proposition both in terms of resisting Cossack pressure and bringing pressure to bear on the Cossacks.

The obvious imbalance between a powerful central state and the relatively small Cossack communities on the frontier was offset by a factor which had become apparent for the first time during the Time of Troubles. The ideological appeal of the Cossack idea which had become manifest for the first time was stunning in its breadth and impact. Thousands of slaves, peasants, and townspeople had declared themselves Cossacks, formed themselves into gangs and terrorized the countryside. The rage of these self proclaimed Cossacks against the hated social order covered the spectrum of protest from highway robbery to a full scale assault on the social order. These neophyte Cossacks had little of the military skills or organization of the Cossacks of the Don or Dnieper and were useless against regular soldiers, but their ubiquity paralysed government efforts to mobilize its forces for long periods. More worryingly they signified a colossal fury among the lower orders towards the existing social order which the ending of the troubles in 1613 did nothing to abate. Cossack ideals and capabilities, a powerful expansionist state and an enraged subordinate population would prove to be a fiery brew over the next two centuries.

Notes

1 Stanislavskii, *Grazhdanskaia Voina*, p. 90.
2 For a sympathetic account of Boris Gudonov, see S. F. Platonov trans J. Alexander, *The Time of Troubles: A Historical Study of Internal Crisis and Social Struggle in Sixteenth and Seventeenth Century Muscovy* (Kansas, 1970) pp. 50–54.
3 Stanislavskii, *Grazhdanskaia Voina*, pp. 18–19.
4 Svatikov, *Rossiia i Don*, pp. 51–59.

2

Bohdan Khmelnytsky

Of all the great Cossack rebels, none was more unlikely than Bohdan Khmelnytsky yet none was more successful. Khmelnytsky's career had more parallels with that of his English contemporary Oliver Cromwell than of his fellow Cossack rebels. Unlike Razin and Pugachev, Khmelnytsky had no millenarian vision of exalting the lowly and casting down the mighty. Like Cromwell, he was thrust from provincial obscurity on to the national stage to lead a great popular rebellion and, again like Cromwell, he came to believe that he had been specifically chosen by God for this task. By nature conservative, cautious and a firm believer in social hierarchy, Khmelnytsky found himself a rebel by circumstances far more than by inclination. A loyal servitor of the Polish crown, Khmelnytsky was driven to revolt by the brutal murder of his young son by a local official. What began as a personal tragedy and a quest for justice merged with broader currents of unrest in Ukraine before spilling over its borders, drawing in the Crimean Khanate, Muscovy, the Ottoman Empire and Sweden. The grievance of one man combined with Cossack frustration, peasant fury, and religious and ethnic hatred to unleash a revolt of a magnitude and ferocity that was shocking to all, not least Khmelnytsky himself. The consequences of the revolt were no less momentous. By the time it had subsided in 1654 there had been a tectonic shift in the political landscape: an independent Cossack state exercised authority over a large part of Ukraine, the Polish-Lithuanian Commonwealth had suffered a grievous wound from it never really recovered, and Muscovy had gained a bridgehead in Ukraine which it would expand remorselessly over the following decades and centuries.

The Polish-Lithuanian Commonwealth
in the seventeenth century

The Polish-Lithuanian Commonwealth was in many ways a unique polity and a remarkable success story. It was a multi-ethnic, multi-confessional state presided over by an elected monarch. It had managed to avoid the worst excesses of the religious conflict unleashed by the Reformation that had brought so much turmoil to the rest of Europe. Catholic, Protestant, Orthodox and Jewish communities existed if not in harmony then at least with a degree of mutual toleration that was astonishing given the times[1] It possessed a vibrant and dynamic culture which greatly influenced intellectual life in Ukraine and indirectly Muscovy. Territorially, militarily and culturally, the Commonwealth was one of the great powers of Europe.

The Polish-Lithuanian Commonwealth was dominated at every level by the nobility who elected the king, controlled the finances, ran the administration and exercised far-reaching authority over the non-noble population, especially the peasantry.[2] The nobility was a broad class, ranging from fabulously wealth magnates such as the Vishnyvetsky clan, who were virtual rulers in their own right, to penniless men who had little apart from an acute consciousness of their noble status to distinguish themselves from the servile population. Without the support of the noble class, the king was powerless. His dependence was embodied in the famous 'veto' of the *Sejm* or noble assembly in which a single opposing vote was enough to block any measure. The only way the king could get the notoriously tight-fisted Sejm to release any money was to confirm and extend noble privilege. Money for defence of the borders or waging war was a perennial nightmare for the Polish kings even more than for most other early modern monarchs.

In such a context, the king had to be extremely solicitous of noble interests especially those of the great magnates. Noble wealth derived mainly from agriculture and the unlimited exploitation of a servile population. The development of a highly profitable export market for grain in the sixteenth century led to a rapid spread of serfdom throughout the Commonwealth.[3] Polish serfdom like its Muscovite counter-part was extremely oppressive in its economic costs to the peasantry and its violation of their personal dignity. The French Huguenot, Guillaume Le Vasseur, who was working as military engineer in Poland in the 1630s and 1640s, commented on the plight of the peasantry in his famous *Description of Ukraine*:

> The local peasants are in a very miserable state, being obliged to work, themselves and their horses, three days a week in the service of their lord, and having to pay him in proportion to the land they hold, many bushels of grain, and plenty of capons, hens, goslings, and chickens, specifically at Easter, Pentecost, and Christmas. What is more, they must cart wood for their lord, and fulfill a thousand other manorial obligations to which they ought not be

subject . . . In short, since they must give to their masters what the latter choose to ask, it is no wonder that these wretches never accumulate anything, being subjected, as they are to such harsh circumstances. However, that is still not all, for the lords have absolute power over not only their possessions, but also their lives, so great is the liberty of the Polish nobles. Thus, if it happens that these wretched peasants fall into the bondage of evil lords, they are in a more deplorable state than convicts sentenced to the galleys.[4]

Most peasants, however, rarely saw their noble masters particularly if the master was a magnate. Usually his authority was delegated to a steward who exercised the noble's autocratic powers with an eye to his own interests as much as those of his employer. Many stewards happened to be Jewish as this was one of the few lucrative professions opened to them which added an ethnic and religious dimension to the grievances that the peasants felt.[5] Peasant rage at the system was expressed in flight to the frontier and in frequent uprisings which could be set off by disturbances whose causes had little or nothing to do with peasants.

The religious toleration which had been such a pronounced feature of the Commonwealth throughout most of the sixteenth century began to break down at the end of the century and diminished rapidly in the seventeenth century. Succumbing to the passions of the Counter-Reformation, the Polish state and nobility began to pursue a more aggressive pro-Catholic policy.[6] The Union of Brest in 1596 was the most important manifestation of an intensified drive for uniformity in religious affairs. The Union established the Ukrainian Catholic or Uniate Church which followed Orthodox rites but recognized the authority of the pope. However, most of Orthodox believers rejected any union with Rome and were determined to maintain an independent Orthodox identity.

Once the Uniate Church had been established, pressure on the Orthodox Church and faithful increased significantly. Sections of the Orthodox aristocracy, the traditional protectors of the Church, began to convert to Catholicism, which increased significantly the vulnerability of the Orthodox Church. The Jewish scholar, Rabbi Nathan Hanover wrote of the worsening plight of the Orthodox Church from the reign of King Sigismund III in 1587:

Formerly most of the dukes and the ruling nobility adhered to the Greek Orthodox faith, thus the followers of both faiths were treated with equal regard. King Sigismund, however raised the status of the catholic dukes and princes above those of the Ukrainians, so that most of the latter abandoned their Greek-Orthodox faith and embraced Catholicism. And the masses that followed the Greek Orthodox Church became gradually impoverished. They were looked upon as lowly and inferior beings and became the slaves and the handmaids of the Polish people and of the Jews.[7]

Persecution of the Orthodox faith, however, carried grave risks for the Commonwealth. It mobilized the urban laity in defence of the Church, provided the stimulus to revitalize the intellectual life of the Church so that it could meet its Catholic rivals on equal terms and even as it deprived the Orthodox Church of its aristocratic guardians created the space for newer, much more turbulent defenders of the faith: the Cossacks.[8] It was the one issue that had the potential to transcend the entrenched sectional interests which were such a marked feature of protest in the Polish-Lithuanian Commonwealth. The Orthodox hierarchy, gentry who remained steadfast in the faith, urban burghers and lay brotherhoods, peasants and Cossacks found common cause in the defence of Orthodoxy. Religion was one of few means of legitimizing violent resistance to lawful authority, providing a protective mantle for the rebels in this world and in the next. Although the Orthodox Church and especially the hierarchy had a capacious view of the things they had to render unto Caesar, this did not extend to allowing Caesar to destroy the Church. For the less pious, religion offered a convenient cover for the advancement of rather more mundane interests. At the very least, the persecution of the Orthodox faith opened up the possibility of a much broader mobilization of Ukranian society than any other issue.

The Ukrainian Cossacks

The Ukrainian Cossacks had developed in a rather different manner to those on the Don, Terek and Iaik. The Zaporozhian Cossacks were virtually identical in their structure, ethos and behaviour to their counterparts further east with whom they cooperated on many occasions. As well as the Zaporozhians, however, the Ukrainian Cossacks contained a group without any parallel among other Cossack hosts. These were the 'settled' Cossacks in distinction from the 'wild ones' who existed in Zaporozh'e. As the Zaporozhians established a precarious mastery over parts of eastern Ukraine, peasant settlers followed. Pulled by the prospect of a better life on the frontier and pushed by the intensification of serfdom in western Ukraine, waves of peasant migrants crossed the Dnieper into the steppe from the end of the sixteenth century.[9] The cause of peasant flight was well known to contemporaries like Guillaume Le Vasseur: 'It is this slavery which goads many of them to take flight, the most courageous of them fleeing to Zaporozhe, which is an area on the Borysthenes [Dnepr] to which the Cossacks retreat.'[10] Settling first around the border castles, they gradually penetrated deeper into the steppe.

Small clusters of individuals and families established farms and eventually villages on the steppe expanses. These settlements were acutely vulnerable to the frequent slaving expeditions of Tatar raiders, but steppe predators were infinitely preferable to rapacious landlords. Fearing more than anything that eventually their former masters would catch up with them, these migrants claimed Cossack status for themselves because they believed that would ensure their freedom and that of their descendants in perpetuity.[11] The Zaporozhians acknowledged that status, seeing in the peasant settlers a source of potential recruits and possibility of a family life for themselves if they ever tired of the excitements of life in the *Sich*.

These migrants represented a transitional group between the full-blooded Zaporozhian and Don Cossacks and the peasantry of the interior – a sort of Cossack-lite. Even so, they lived on an active frontier in constant expectation of attack. These Cossacks had to be able to defend themselves individually and collectively, creating a population with a formidable military potential. They adopted the Cossack system of democratic assemblies and elected officers. Between themselves and the Zaporozhians there was an obvious community of interest.[12] Many of the settlers had spent some time at the *Sich* before turning to a more secure if still dangerous life of the settled Cossacks. On the Muscovite side of the southern frontier, a similar class of tough, independent peasants existed as we have seen. But these always existed either just behind the defensive lines or on them while the territory of the Don Cossacks remained many dangerous miles to the south. Although these peasants embodied many similar traits to the Cossack farmers in the Ukraine, they never formally claimed Cossack status nor did the Don Cossacks consider them as Cossacks. An independent, settled group of Cossacks in distinction to those following the traditional way of life never emerged on the Don.

The existence of the 'settled' Cossacks gave the Ukrainian Cossacks a broader base than those of the Don. By recognizing the settlers as Cossacks and creating institutional, administrative and military structures there came to exist in eastern Ukraine a large, militarized population with a deep antipathy to serfdom. Any attempt to reimpose serfdom on such people would be extremely difficult as well as dangerous.

The Polish kings like their Muscovite counter-parts had an ambiguous relationship with the Cossacks. They desperately needed the Cossacks to protect the frontiers, but found that the Cossacks created as many problems as they solved. Their unauthorized raids threatened to bring war with the Crimean Khanate or even worse the Ottoman Empire and their appeal to the enserfed peasantry of the interior was constant source of instability within the Commonwealth. As early as the 1520s the Poles had attempted to control the Cossacks by establishing a register of all those officially entitled to be Cossacks. Although the register remained very much a dead letter for most of the sixteenth century, it had become real enough by the end of the century. By 1589 there were approximately 3,000 registered Cossacks, but probably between 40,000 and 50,000 unregistered ones.[13]

The creation of a register deepened divisions within the Ukrainian Cossacks as no doubt the government intended. Between the Zaporozhians and the settled Cossacks there were tensions inherent in the different ways of life that they followed.[14] Put bluntly, the settled Cossacks had much more to lose than the Zaporozhians by needlessly provoking the Poles or the Tatars. Within the settled Cossacks, however, there were also growing divisions. Over the decades a strata of families had emerged whose wealth and influence separated them sharply from recent migrants to the Cossack areas. These wealthy men were the ones most likely to be on the register. As they accumulated wealth and status the original egalitarianism of the Cossacks lost much of its appeal. Slowly pushing its way into their belief system were some of the values and obsessions of the society their ancestors had fled from. The obsessive pursuit of status, privilege and dominance that was the hallmark of the Polish nobility began to find echos among the wealthier Cossacks.[15]

The register was part of a strategy to control the Cossacks, creating a faction loyal to and dependent on the crown. By holding out to the registered Cossacks the prospect of financial reward and constantly hinting at the prospect of noble status, the crown hoped to tie the interests of this influential group to itself rather than the Cossacks as whole. The Polish statesman Adam Kysil while recovering from illness in 1636 articulated this as part of a broader strategy for dealing with the Cossacks:

> In my feverish state I formulated a kind of discourse on the matter of dealing with the Zaporozhian Host. One must treat this foolish rabble in three ways. For the officers, gifts. For the conservative Cossacks and those who have homes and take care of them, favor. Remind them of the integrity of the fatherland, the freedoms that will be enjoyed not only by them, but also by their heirs. And as for the wild rebels, the have-nots who live only from booty, like the Horde – these must be curbed by annihilation and fear of the sword, for arguments, pietism faith, freedoms, wives, and children – in their heads it all flows down the Dnipro with them. Dividing them thus into three groups, I apply three methods in my dealings with these dubious brethren of mine.[16]

Kysil's strategy was one with a venerable tradition in the steppe. He understood that the Cossacks were not monolithic and that by astutely tailoring policy to take account of this the government could exacerbate these differences and make them irreconcilable. Implicit in his advice was a warning to do nothing that might lessen tensions within the Cossacks or even worse cause the Zaporozhians, the registered Cossacks and the unregistered to unite in defence of their common Cossack identity.

If the Polish kings had been able to pursue this strategy over the course of several decades, there is little doubt that eventually they would have succeeded in taming the Cossacks. This after all is what happened in the eighteenth century when Ukraine became incorporated into the Russian Empire. The Polish kings, however, were never able to do this. The always empty coffers of the treasury did not allow the elite to be paid regularly or expanded sufficiently to fulfil the role the government desired. Equally, longstanding members of the elite were frustrated by the refusal to grant noble status. In failing to meet these demands, the government left the elite disgruntled and not above siding with more radical Cossack elements at moments of particular frustration.[17]

The unregistered Cossacks received little sympathy from the crown, which, in the usual course of events, denied that it had ever granted them Cossack status. However, not infrequently its actions contradicted its words, particularly when their was an acute military threat from the Tatars or when the government needed more soldiers to fight in its interminable wars with Muscovy. King Stepan Bathory made extensive use of registered and unregistered Cossacks in his war against Muscovy between 1579–81. On such occasions the government appealed to the whole steppe population as Cossacks, calling on them to participate in the common defence of the Commonwealth.[18] Even though the crown usually reneged on any promises once a particular emergency had passed, there was sufficient ambiguity in its attitude over the decades to encourage the unregistered Cossacks to believe that they would eventually achieve formal recognition of their status.

Cossack/crown relations were not conducted in a vacuum. What happened between the crown and the Cossacks impinged directly on other social groups. The great magnates, like their boyar counter-parts in Muscovy, loathed the Cossacks. The Cossacks as we have seen constructed at least part of their identity on the habitual insolence they deployed in their relationships with aristocrats. This was bad enough coming from the Zaporozhians, but to experience it from men who themselves had been serfs on their estates or were the descendants of such serfs was intolerable.

The settled Cossacks were also economic rivals to the magnates. Settling on the frontier lands, these new Cossacks restricted the magnates' own opportunities for expansion.[19] Probably most dangerous of all was the mere existence of the Cossacks and threat that implied to whole noble order based on serfdom. One Polish nobleman in a circular letter to other nobles in 1617 outlined the threat posed by the Cossacks:

> Their willfulness disturbs you; you who live here especially feel this. In time this brush fire may prove dangerous and unpleasant to the Commonwealth in the more remote areas as well, because this peasantry, hostile by nature to the nobility may, if neglected even undertake something different and worse.[20]

The threats posed by the settled Cossacks far outweighed any advantages to the state as far as the magnates were concerned. At every opportunity, especially in the aftermath of any revolt they demanded thoroughgoing pacification of the Cossacks. To most magnates, there was little difference between the Zaporozhians, registered and unregistered Cossacks. All of them were a threat and had to be dealt with accordingly. The crown for its part had to manoeuvre between the demands of the magnates on whom it depended absolutely and the Cossacks on whom it depended for the security of the frontier. Which way it inclined depended very much on which group it needed most at any particular time.

The various tensions accumulating on the frontier ignited into rebellions with monotonous regularity from the last decade of the sixteenth century onwards. In the 1590s and the 1620s there were major rebellions of the Cossacks. The first rebellion in 1591 began with a dispute between a Cossack leader, Krystof Kosynski and the magnate Janusz Ostrozky over land. What began as a range war between two sets of armed bands, drew in many thousands of peasants who took the opportunity to settle scores with their own masters.[21] This was to become a persistent feature of all subsequent rebellions in the Commonwealth. After the Union of Brest in 1596, the defence of the Orthodox Church was routinely deployed by rebelling Cossacks and peasants, partly because they were genuinely outraged by the attacks on their Church and partly because it legitimized their revolts.

In 1637–38 the biggest Cossack rebellion yet rocked the Commonwealth. Beginning in the usual manner with a dispute between a group of Cossacks and magnates, it rapidly burst these limits, unleashing a peasant rebellion whose scale threatened the entire serf order. With great difficulty the Poles crushed the revolt. This time, however, they were determined not just to wreak a bloody vengeance on the Cossacks, but pacify them once and for all. Led by the newly appointed Polish hetman of the Ukraine, Stanislaw Potocki, a reign of terror was instituted in all the Cossack territories. Executing hundreds of rebels and placing their heads on pikes along the road, Potocki regretted only that he could not kill more:

> Although punishment is for a few, fear is for all. Therefore I ordain that only the principles be set out along the roads – ten will be an example for a hundred, and a hundred for a thousand . . . Now the time is ripe to mold anything one likes out of them as though from wax, so that this bane may no longer nest in the bosom of the Commonwealth.[22]

Terror was complemented by a radical abrogation of Cossack privileges. The numbers of registered Cossacks was drastically cut, the settled Cossacks lost their right to elect their leaders and instead had Polish officials imposed on them. Even the Zaporozhians were curtailed somewhat with the imposition of a large garrison of registered Cossacks on them. Rabbi Nathan Hanover noted approvingly:

> When the King realized that the Cossacks were still rebellious, he meted out further punishment to them. Of the twenty thousand which prior to this rebellion had enjoyed special privileges, only six thousand were to receive them now, while the remainder were to be subject to taxes, like the rest of the wretched Ukrainians. To prevent another outbreak he placed over them captains of the Polish army.[23]

Even after the initial frenzied reaction to the rebellion had calmed down, the change in atmosphere in Eastern Ukraine was palpable. The new Polish officials rode roughshod over Cossack sensibilities, subjecting them to a terrifying regime of arbitrariness, violence and intimidation.[24] In the aftermath of the rebellion, Polish policy was unequivocally directed towards the subjugation of all Cossacks, regardless of which section the Cossacks they belonged to and indeed whether they had taken part in the rebellion or not.

Bohdan Khmelnytsky

Bohdan Khemelnytsky was typical of those Cossacks who had achieved a modicum of prosperity and success on the frontier. His father was a member of the petty gentry who made a living on the frontier alongside the Cossacks. Although not formally members of the Cossacks, the petty gentry of the frontier had much in common with the Cossack elite. As well as the dangers of the frontier, they shared a commitment to private

Figure 6 *Portrait of Bohdan Khmelnytsky*, by the Russian School, seventeenth century (oil on panel)

property, social hierarchy and a craving for formal recognition of their status, regarding both the Zaporozhians and newly arrived peasant settlers as their social inferiors. The boundary separating the two groups was soft, allowing easy and frequent movement between them. At some point Khmelnytsky's father crossed over to the Cossack side and his family became Cossacks.

Bohdan Khmelnytsky was born into this milieu in the mid-1590s.[25] His father, Mykhailo, had been a successful local official, becoming prosperous, at least by the unassuming standards of the frontier, over the course of his life. Like many other members of the frontier elite, Mykhailo was ambitious for his son, sending him off to be educated by the Jesuits. Shortly after his return from school, Bohdan took part alongside his father in a campaign against the Tatars in 1620. Mykhailo was killed at the Battle of Tutora and Bohdan was captured. For the next two years Bohdan languished in a Turkish prison before his mother managed to ransom him. Difficult as that time had been, it was not without use for Khmelnytsky. It gave him a familiarity with the language and customs of the world of his neighbours which would stand him in good stead later on.

When he returned home Khmelnytsky continued in his father's footsteps as a prosperous farmer and a member of the Cossack elite. Over the next twenty years, Khmelnytsky consolidated his position, becoming a registered Cossack and holding various official posts in the Cossack administration; in 1637 he became secretary of the Host. Khmelnytsky was exactly the sort of prosperous Cossack identified by Adam Kysil who could be co-opted into Polish service with a minimum of effort. He had taken no part in the rebellion of 1637, probably regarding the peasant revolt that had accompanied it with as much distaste as his gentry counter-parts. In the difficult aftermath of the uprising, his good standing with the Polish administration indicated that he had made the right choice in remaining aloof from it.

Until his rebellion was well under way there had been nothing in Khmelnytsky's life to suggest that he saw himself as anything other than a loyal servitor of the king.[26] Khmelnytsky had achieved a modest prosperity, was a local official of some consequence, and gave every appearance of a middle-aged man settling down to enjoy the remaining decades of his life in comfortable obscurity. His refusal to take part in the rebellion of 1637 was eloquent testimony to his belief that his own future and that of his family lay in service to the Polish crown.

Yet Khmelnytsky could not isolate himself from the wider anti-Cossack atmosphere sweeping through Ukraine in the aftermath of the 1637 rebellion. While King Wladislaw far away in Warsaw might be sympathetic to his loyal Cossack servitors, the local Polish administration had an entirely different agenda. It was imbued with the vengeful spirit of the magnates, determined to reduce all Cossacks to the level of servile obedience, including those of previously impeccable loyalty. Khmelnytsky described the years after the rebellion as ones of great danger and insecurity for the entire Cossack host:

> Whenever the lords officers fancy taking something by force in a Cossack home, or a Cossack's wife, or a Cossack's daughter, then one must jump to their tune: concerning these grievances, the Lord of Cracow wrote several times to the officials and leaseholders, admonishing them, but this did not

do any good . . . We have become unfree not only with respect to our meager property, but also to our own persons; they seize homesteads, meadows, newly cultivated hayfields, plowed fields, ponds, mills, beekeeping tithes; they forcibly confiscate anything belonging to us Cossacks to which they take a fancy and swindle us, beat us, murder us, and throw us in jail, all without cause, and in this manner they have wounded us and crippled our comrades.[27]

In 1646 the anti-Cossack reaction reached the doors of Khmelnytsky's own manor in an unholy combination of lust, greed and violence. Daniel Czarplinski, the head of the local Polish administration, coveted the woman with whom Khmelnytsky had been living since the death of his wife. Arriving with a gang of armed retainers, Czarplinski carried off the woman and forcibly married her. Not content with coveting his neighbour's wife, Czarplinski also desired his goods. Claiming that Khmelnytsky had large tax arrears, Czarplinski forcibly seized a large quantity of Khmelnytsky's property. In response Khmelnytsky protested to higher authorities about the unlawful actions of Czarplinski. Czarplinski was enraged at what he considered the insolence of Khmelnytsky's response and was determined to teach him lesson he would not forget. Saddling up his retainers once more, Czarplinski abducted his young son and had him publically flogged in the market place. In terrible pain, the child lingered for a few days before dying. Czarplinski had not done with Khmelnytsky, however, He attacked his manor, burning it to the ground and making clear that he intended to arrest Khmelnytsky on a charge of treason.[28]

In the space of twelve months, Khmelntysky's comfortable existence had been shattered. Contemplating the ruins of everything he had striven for over the past few decades, Khmelnytsky understood that Czarplinski would not be satisfied with anything less than his death and that of his entire family. Towards the end of 1647, leaving his remaining children with friends, he abandoned his home and his previous life for the doubtful security of the *Sich*.[29]

Lust, theft, false witness and murder gave the feud between between Khmelnytsky and Czarplinski a biblical quality which retrospectively fitted easily into a providential process of selection. Czarplinski's actions had their origins in more earthly circumstances. His brutal assault on the Khmelnytsky family reflected his own innate viciousness, but it chimed perfectly with the prevailing Polish policy towards the Cossacks. Knowing he could count on the support of his superiors, Czarplinski acted without regard to law, justice or the personal loyalty of Khmelnytsky to the Polish

Crown. By treating Khmelnytsky in such a brutal fashion, Czarplinski was signalling to all Cossacks in the clearest possible way that no Cossack, however loyal and unblemished his previous service, had any rights before the Polish administration. This blunt application of terror against all Cossacks was as far away from the policy of Adam Kysil as it was possible to be.

The revolt

Many men would have been broken by what Khmelnytsky had experienced over the previous twelve months. The calamities that had afflicted Khmelnytsky, however, unleashed an eruption of moral fury that transformed the staid, middle-aged gentleman farmer into a charismatic leader, yearning for justice and vengeance on those who had wronged him. At the *Sich*, he found many exiles like himself: formerly prosperous men who had been ruined by the depredations of the Polish administration. There was no particular reason for the Zaporozhians to accord Khmelnytsky any particular honour; after all, he and they represented very different incarnations of what it was to be a Cossack. Yet something in his fury and desire for revenge must have struck a chord with the mood of the Zaporozhians whose own grievances since the crushing of the earlier rebellion had grown steadily. Khmelnytsky was elected Hetman by the Zaporozhians, traditionally the most turbulent element of the Cossacks. Within days the large garrison of registered Cossacks came over to him. With the defection of the garrison, any Polish influence or control over the Zaporozhians vanished. By the end of January 1648, Khemelnytsky was master of the *Sich*.[30]

Khmelnytsky's own moral fury had communicated itself to all the Cossacks at the *Sich*, uniting their grievances with his own. Yet he was not blinded by anger nor did he lose his capacity for rational judgement. He knew the power of the Polish state and limits of what the Cossacks of Zaporozh'e could achieve. If the rebellion was to have any chance of success it needed a much more broader base than the Zaporozhians could provide. Messengers were despatched to the settled areas appealing for support where they found a ready response. Khmelntysky's vision, however, stretched beyond the borders of Ukraine. Envoys were sent to the Crimean Khan seeking an alliance and offering to place the Cossacks under the Khan's protection in return. An unspoken inducement was the acceptance of the inevitable round up of slaves that always accompanied Tatar expeditions whether as allies or enemies:

> Desiring your protection for the future, in alliance with you we will serve
> body and soul for the benefit of Islam in future wars; we have severed all ties
> with the Liakhs [Poles]. We ask you take hostages from us and agree to an
> alliance with us.[31]

The Khan, confronted with famine at home, responded favourably and
promised to send his armies in support of the rebellion.[32]

Khmelnytsky's flight to Zaporozh'e did not unduly alarm the Poles. He
was not the first registered Cossack to have fled there and his flight
confirmed the charge of treason against him. The Poles evidently believed
that they had little to fear from the Zaporozhians and chose to send five
hundred Cossacks under Polish officers to arrest Khmelnytsky. This turned
out to be an important miscalculation. As soon as they arrived at the
Sich, the Cossacks mutinied, slaughtered their officers and came over to
Khmelnytsky. At the same time rumours of Khmelnytsky's attempts
to rouse the settled Cossacks and ally with the Crimean Tatars began to
reach Polish officials.

Even this news provoked little misgivings among the Poles. In fact the
Polish Hetman of the Ukraine, Potocki, saw it as an opportunity to teach
the Cossacks another bloody lesson on the costs of revolt. The magnates
of the Ukraine were similarly gripped by desire to settle with the Cossacks
once and for all. Only the ill and aged King Wladislaw urged caution
in dealing with the rebels. Potocki, however ignored the advice of the
King and made plain his intentions towards the Cossacks, issuing a
bloodcurdling warning to any rebels:

> To all who are loitering near Khmelnytsky! I warn and admonish you to
> disperse from that unruly band and to surrender him to me, being aware that
> if you do not carry out this instruction of mine I will order all your wealth
> that you possess in your settled area and your wives and children to be cut
> down . . . And in order that my promise may be fulfilled, I will not leave
> Ukraine until I am satisfied by the submission and surrender of that traitor.
> In addition, I promise that you will not be able to settle in Zaporozhia: not
> only will your lives not be safe from me, but also from the Tatars and from
> Muscovy – this unruliness will be punished everywhere.[33]

For Cossacks in the settled area who might have wished to ignore
Khmelnytsky's appeals, the warnings of Potocki were ominous indeed.
Polish retribution in the aftermath of the 1637 rebellion and in the
subsequent ten years had struck at the Cossacks indiscriminately. The tone
of Potocki's warning suggested that the coming retribution would be
significantly worse. The settled Cossacks, rich and poor, understood that

trying to stand aside from the burgeoning rebellion offered no guarantee of safety. Potocki's obvious intentions left the Cossacks with little choice about which side of they line they were on when the fighting started. Polish pressure was sealing fractures with the Cossack community, drawing together groups whose interests had frequently diverged in the past.

As winter gave way to spring in 1648, both sides were readying themselves for the decisive first encounters. Defeat for Khmelnytsky at this stage would probably prove fatal for the revolt and for himself. To succeed the revolt had to have the time and space to develop momentum. Victory would bring both while defeat would drive the rebels back into Zaporozh'e where it would only be a matter of time before the rebellion was crushed. The first battles of the campaign took place in May and resulted in crushing victories for the Cossacks. A Tatar army had linked up with the Cossacks and together they routed the advance-guard of the Polish army. Drawing encouragement from these first battles, the Cossacks and their Tatar allies met the main Polish force at Korsun on 26 May.[34]

Korsun was a unmitigated disaster for the Poles. Their armies were crushed and their leaders including Potocki were captured. The scale of the victory at Korsun was breathtaking and transformed the strategic situation in Ukraine beyond recognition. Compounding the disaster for the Poles was the death of King Wladislaw on the eve of the battle. The Polish state was now leaderless and would remain so until the election of a new King which would take several months at the earliest. Adrift in the midst of a great storm, the Polish-Lithuanian Commonwealth was no longer engaged in a punitive expedition against rebels, but was fighting for its very existence.

Khmelnytsky was probably as staggered by his achievement as anyone else. A stalemate at Korsun or a more limited victory might have suited his aims better than the annihilation that the battle had been in reality. His aims at this point were still modest, seeking redress for the injustices he had suffered and the restoration of Cossack freedoms as they had been before 1637.[35] As is clear from a letter he sent to the now deceased Polish King, Khmelnytsky continued to see himself as a loyal subject of the crown. After outlining a long list of grievances suffered by the Cossacks, Khmelnytsky outlined his demands which in the circumstances were modest:

> When he [Potocki] advanced on our lives with large forces against the will and command of Your Royal Majesty, we were obliged to avail ourselves of the assistance of the Crimean Khan, who indeed helped us this time, remembering that on several occasions we rescued them from their enemies in similar circumstances. Well, by God's will, some green wood got it along

with the dry. Who is the cause of this, let God determine! For our part, just as previously we were loyal subjects of your majesty, so now, too, we are steadfastly prepared, for any service to the Commonwealth against any enemy, to give our lives for the honor of Your Royal Majesty. . . . Therefore we humbly request that your Royal Majesty show fatherly mercy to us, your lowliest underlings, and pardon us that involuntary sin and deign to leave us with our ancient rights and liberties, so that Your Royal Majesty in your own holy person and we, the most humble servants of Your Royal Majesty, no longer endure that slavery, etc. Signed: Bohdan Khmelnytsky, Chief at this time of Your Royal Majesty's Zaporozhian Host.[36]

The consequences of the Battle of Korsun rippled out beyond what either Khmelnytsky or the Poles intended or wanted. Khmelnytsky's victory wove the disparate strands of unrest in Ukraine into a seamless revolt. Immediately following Korsun, Polish authority in the urban and rural areas of Ukraine started to haemorrhage. Rabbi Nathan Hanover witnessed the dramatic collapse of Polish self-belief across Ukraine as news of the disaster of Korsun spread closely followed by news of the death of the King:

> The same day on which the Polish army and its two generals were captured, also brought the evil tidings that King Wladislaw died, and the whole Kingdom of Poland became as sheep which have no shepherd. When the dukes and the nobles heard that their king had died, and that all the Polish nobles, the mighty warriors, and also the two generals were captured, they became disheartened. The hearts of the Jews melted like wax before the fire, for fear of the enemy. All the nobles, who governed the provinces beyond the Dnieper, and west of the Dnieper up to the City of Polannoe, fled for their lives.[37]

The Ukrainian peasantry, so acutely attuned to the smallest shift in the register of noble power, could not miss the thunderclap of Korsun. Decades of anger and frustration found their release in an elemental explosion of popular anger that turned into one of the bloodiest rampages in European history. Social injustice fuelled by ethnic hatred and legit-imized by religion, regardless of the attitude of the hierarchy, ignited into a series of massacres of Jews and Poles that would see no parallel until the Nazi occupation of Ukraine in the Second World War. Peasants slaughtered Jews and Poles wherever they could find them. Most had fled to the cities as soon as they had received news of Korsun, but these offered no safe haven. Soon cities began to fall to the peasant rebels, joined by Cossacks and the urban poor who shared many of their grievances. The fall of every city was marked by hideous orgy of killing in which neighbours and 'friends' betrayed Jews to the rebels or killed them themselves. By the time the rebellion had subsided as many as 56,000 Jews had been massacred.[38] Nor was it enough simply to kill; the rebels sought to inflict the maximum suffering and humiliation on their victims. Rabbi Nathan Hanover described in terrible detail massacre after massacre over the course of the rebellion:

> Many communities beyond the Dnieper, and close to the battlefield . . . perished for the sanctification of His Name. These persons died cruel and bitter deaths. Some were skinned alive and their flesh was thrown to the dogs; some had their hands and limbs chopped off, and their bodies thrown on the highway only to be trampled by wagons and crushed by horses; some had wounds inflicted upon them, and thrown on the street to die a slow death, they writhed in blood until they breathed their last; others were buried alive. The enemy slaughtered infants in the laps of their mothers. They were sliced into pieces like fish. They slashed the bellies of pregnant women, removed their infants and tossed them in their faces. Some women had their bellies torn open and live cats placed in them. The bellies were then sewed up with the live cats placed in them.[39]

So desperate was the plight of the Jews that many sought out to give themselves up to the Tatars who as well as fighting alongside Khmelnytsky were engaged in the usual slaving expeditions. The Tatar slave gangs offered immediate security and eventual release through ransom.

Khmelnytsky through the summer of 1648 still hoped for a limited, negotiated settlement with the Poles, returning the Cossacks to the situation that had existed before the 1637 Rebellion. But the ethnic massacres and the social revolution taking place in the countryside made any hopes of return to the status quo ante illusionary. The stakes had become too great for such a limited settlement. The Poles spent the summer gathering a new army. Almost reluctantly, Khmelnytsky abandoned his waiting stance and took to the field against them. The Polish army proved to have little stomach for the fight. The two armies faced each other at Pyliavtsi on 2 September 1648, but before any fighting began rumours swept the Polish camp that a large Tatar army had just linked up with the Cossacks. The rumours were not true, but the panic stricken army fled before any fighting had began.[40] The defeat at Pyliavtsi was even more significant than at Korsun. It did not mark the end of the war, but it did mark the end of any Polish control over Ukraine which was now under de facto Cossack administration in so far as anyone exercised authority there.

In nine months Khmelnytsky had gone from a hunted, penniless fugitive to master of Ukraine. His position now far exceeded that of gentleman farmer from which he fallen in 1647. He had become a national figure, uniting all the diverse elements of the revolt in his person even if a great deal of what was being carried out in his name appalled him. The destruction of noble authority and property in the countryside was particularly galling to a such a firm believer in social hierarchy and order. Whatever his inclinations though, Khmelnytsky recognized that he was powerless to halt the popular rebellion which had to be left to run its course. Polish negotiators reported that 'Even if Khmelnytsky himself wanted peace, the peasant masses and the Ruthenian priests do not want to allow it-but for him to finish the war against the Poles, so that the Ruthenian faith may spread, and so that they may not have any lords over them.'[41] Khmelnytsky's de facto position as the ruler of Ukraine was becoming ever more incongruous with his desire to restore the constitutional position to what it had been in 1637 in which he and the Cossacks were loyal servitors of the Polish King. Yet for him to reject that required a revolution in his world view at least as profound as the political and social transformation taking place all around him.

There was only one institution that could plausibly bridge the crevice separating Khmelnytsky's achievement from his ambition, turning him from the de facto ruler of Ukraine into the de jure one and that was the Orthodox Church.[42] Khmelnytsky's anointment by the Church was the culmination of two connected processes that had been operating since the Union of Brest in 1596 if not earlier. Persecution of the Orthodox Church by the Catholic Church was one strand while the emergence of the Cossacks as the defenders of Orthodoxy was the other. Although at times the Church and the Cossacks made uncomfortable bedfellows, the community of interest between them grew steadily in the first half of the seventeenth century. This process reached its apotheosis at Kiev on Christmas Day 1648.

As Khmelnytsky and his victorious army approached Kiev, the cradle of Christianity among the East Slavs and the former capital of Rus, the whole city, people and clergy, emptied to greet his triumphal entry. En route to Moscow at the time was the Patriarch of Jerusalem, one of the most senior figures in Orthodox Christianity, who anointed Khmelnytsky as a second Constantine, the protector of Orthodoxy and the deliverer of his people.[43] The role of the Church in building up Khmelnytsky's conception of himself as God's chosen instrument cannot be overestimated. Nor was it done simply in a transient mood of euphoria. Six years later when Patriarch Macarius of Antioch visited Khmelnytsky, Macarius blessed him saying 'Truly God is with thee Khmelnytsky. He raised thee up to deliver his people as Moses delivered Israel, so thine host destroyed the filthy Poles with thy depopulating sword.'[44]

Moses, Israel, Constantine – such extravagant titles and imagery from the leaders of the Orthodox world gave Khmelnytsky the confidence to break his ties with the Poles. Why should a Moses or a second Constantine consider himself beholden to a mere Polish prince? Even Khmelnytsky's first name Bohdan (*God given*) now seemed providential. In a deeply religious age, it was not difficult for Khmelnytsky to conceive of himself as God's chosen instrument. He would not be the first or last to do so, but rarely has any rebel against a Christian monarch had such unambiguous support from the established Church. From his entry into Kiev onwards, Khmelnytsky's tone changed completely. He no longer presented himself or the Cossacks as the King's loyal servitors, seeking only justice for the outrages visited upon them. Gone was the supplicant tone and in its place was Moses addressing Pharaoh:

> I shall fight to free the whole Ruthenian nation from Liakh [Polish] bondage! At first I fought for my own damage and injustice-now I shall fight for our Orthodox faith. All the common people will help me in this-all the way to Lublin and Cracow, who do not abandon it [the Orthodox faith] and I shall not abandon them, for they are our right hand: so that you, after doing away with the peasants, do not strike at the Cossacks as well.[45]

Even as his image was boosted into celestial realms, Khmelnytsky's policies remained firmly grounded in the more mundane and still perilous world. Practically, Khmelnytsky understood that while divine approval was indispensable, on its own it was insufficient: an earthly protector was also necessary if Ukraine was not become of a victim of the avaricious powers, hovering around it. Muscovy was the obvious choice given the affinities of language history, and religion, but it was one Khmelnytsky hoped to avoid if at all possible. He knew enough of Muscovy to know that the protectorship of the Tsar was not something to be entered into lightly. His preferred choice was the Ottoman Empire which was sufficiently powerful enough to make potential aggressors think twice yet was distant enough to discourage excessive interference.[46] The long experience of all the Cossacks with the Islamic world gave them a familiarity and ease with it that made such choices eminently practical and sensible. Popular antipathy to the hated Tatars, however, eventually brought this to nothing and Khmelnystky was forced to turn to Moscow. In 1654 the Treaty of Periaslavl was signed between Ukraine and Moscow in which the Hetmanate as it became know acknowledged the suzerainty of the tsar while the latter promised to respect the autonomy of the Hetmanate. Khmelnitsky's misgivings about the Muscovite alliance were confirmed as early as the signing ceremony when the Muscovite delegation refused to swear in the name of the tsar to respect the treaty, claiming it was infringed on the dignity of the tsar as an autocrat to swear a binding oath with those to whom he offered his protection. Although the incident was papered over, it was an ominous sign of things to come.[47]

Conclusion

Bohdan Khmelnytsky is today the central symbol of Ukrainian nationhood. Although other Cossacks have become celebrated as folk heroes, none have become the centrepiece of a national mythology. His progression from genteel obscurity to father of the nation was remarkable by any standards. For a Cossack, on the periphery of society geographically and socially, it was all the more so. Khmelnytsky's genius was to be able to transcend the limitations of his circumstances, drawing in to his struggle all elements of Ukrainian society. Other Cossack rebels failed because their appeal was limited to their own kind and to the dispossessed, but to the institutional and social powerbrokers they had not the slightest appeal. Part of Khmelnytsky's success in broadening his appeal was due to the context in which he operated. Indiscriminate oppression by the Poles united the Cossacks as they had never been before. Significantly, hardly any section of the Cossack elite sided with the Poles unlike the revolts of Razin and Pugachev later on when the Cossack elites made very clear their hostility to the rebels. The appeal of the Cossacks to the peasantry was obvious and needs no further explanation. But it is the appeal beyond this that is the key to Khmelnytsky's success. Above all, it was the fusing of sectional interests with the religious question which provided the glue to keep such a disparate alliance together. A war for defence of the faith was much more acceptable to notables in town and countryside than a war for the restoration of Cossack rights and even more so one for peasant rights. The acceptance of Khmelnytsky by the Church gave him a credibility internationally as well as nationally which he used to achieve a precarious independence for Ukraine.

Circumstances alone, however, do not explain everything. They after all had existed for decades and many men had stories similar to Khmelnytsky's. Khmelnytsky from the moment he fled to Zaporozh'e brought energy and purpose to widespread anger among the Zaporozhians. From the very beginning of the revolt he showed himself a shrewd strategist, seeking allies not just at home but abroad as well. This breadth of vision surpassed that of any other Cossack rebel. Tactically he was astute as well. His own conservatism and ill-concealed dislike of peasant revolution eased the transition to his side of the Orthodox gentry whose willingness to fight in defence of Orthodoxy might have been much less if the fight was being led by a millenarian intent on overturning the social order. Transcending the differences within his movement, he was able to unite all its elements around his own person. He succeeded in driving out the Poles and establishing an independent state. It would be up to his successors to find a way of binding such a diverse collection of interests into coherent national community.

Notes

1 D. MacCulloch, *Reformation: Europe's House Divided 1490–1700* (London, 2003) pp. 340–344.
2 N. Davies, *Heart of Europe: A Short History of Poland* (Oxford, 1984) pp. 296–306.
3 Efimenko, *Istoriia Ukrainskago Naroda*, pp. 164–166.
4 Le Vasseur, *A Description of Ukraine*, pp. 14–15.
5 Efimenko, *Istoriia Ukrainskago Naroda*, p. 214.
6 MacCulloch, *Reformation*, p. 362.
7 N. Hanover, *Abyss of Despair*, trans. A.J. Mesch (New Brunswick 1983) p. 27.
8 Plokhy, *The Cossacks and Religion*, pp. 340–344.
9 Hrushevsky, *The Cossack Age to 1625*, pp. 197–205.
10 Le Vasseur, *A Description of Ukraine*, p. 15.
11 Hrushevsky, *The Cossack Age to 1625*, p. 209.
12 Hrushevsky, *The Cossack Age to 1625*, p. 210.
13 O. Subtelny, *Ukraine A History* (Toronto, 1988) p. 111.
14 Hrushevsky, *The Cossack Age to 1625*, p. 242.
15 M. Hrushevsky, *History of Ukraine-Rus': The Cossack Age 1626–1650*, vol. 8, trans. M.D. Olynyk (Edmonton, 2002) p. 112.
16 Hrushevsky, *The Cossack Age, 1626–1650*, p. 183
17 Plokhy, *The Cossacks and Religion*, pp. 40–48.
18 Hrushevsky, *The Cossack Age to 1625*, p. 127.
19 Efimenko, *Istoriia Ukrainskago Naroda*, p. 183.
20 Hrushevsky, *The Cossack Age to 1625*, p. 211.
21 Hrushevsky, *The Cossack Age to 1625*, p. 140.
22 Hrushevsky, *The Cossack Age 1626–1650*, p. 218.
23 Hanover, *Abyss of Despair*, p. 33.
24 Hrushevsky, *The Cossack Age 1626–1650*, p. 253.
25 The biographical details of Khemlnytsky are taken from Hrushevsky, *The Cossack Age 1626–50*, pp. 376–382.

26 Efimenko, *Istoriia Ukrainskago Naroda*, pp. 215–216.
27 Hrushevsky, *The Cossack Age, 1626 to 1650,* p. 318.
28 Hrushevsky, *The Cossack Age, 1626–1650*, pp. 382–387.
29 Efimenko, *Istoriia Ukrainskago Naroda*, p. 218.
30 Hrushevsky, *The Cossack Age 1626–1650*, p. 389–390.
31 Hrushevsky, *The Cossack Age 1626–1650*, p. 397.
32 Efimenko, *Istoriia Ukrainskago Naroda*, p. 218.
33 Hrushevsky, *The Cossack Age, 1626–1650*, pp. 400–401.
34 Efimenko, *Istoriia Ukrainskago Naroda*, pp. 219–220.
35 Efimenko, *Istoriia Ukrainskago Naroda*, p. 222.
36 Hrushevsky, *The Cossack Age, 1626–1650*, p. 425.
37 Hanover, *Abyss of Despair*, pp. 41–42.
38 N. Davies, *God's Playground: A History of Poland Volume 1. The Origins to 1795* (Oxford, 1981) p. 467.
39 Hanover, *Abyss of Despair*, p. 43.
40 Efimenko, *Istoriia Ukrainskago Naroda*, p. 222.
41 Khmelnytsky, *The Cossack Age 1626–1650*, p. 522.
42 Plokhy, *The Cossacks and Religion*, pp. 227–229.
43 Hrushevsky, *The Cossack Age 1626–1650*, p. 518.
44 *The Travels of Macarius: Extracts from the Diary of the Travels of Macarius Patriarch of Antioch, written by his son Paul Archdeacon of Aleppo in the years of their journeying, 1652–1660* (London, 1836) pp. 15–16.
45 Hrushevsky, *The Cossack Age, 1626–1650*, p. 535.
46 Subtelny, *Ukraine*, pp. 133–134.
47 Subtelny, *Ukraine*, p. 134.

3

Stepan Razin

When Mikhail Romanov died in 1645 he passed on to his son Alexei Mikhailovich an immeasurably more stable inheritance than he himself had received in 1613. The shattered state and society that had elected Mikhail Tsar had largely recovered during his long reign. The early years had been difficult with banditry rife, the treasury empty and powerful foreign enemies still circling like vultures, hoping that the revival of Muscovy might prove temporary.[1] There was good reason to believe that Muscovy would sink once more into chaos. Mikhail was only a boy with little experience of the world when he became Tsar. The Assembly of the Land (*Zemskii Sobor*) that had elected him had been riven with divisions and had come to Mikhail only as a compromise candidate. In short, Mikhail's prospects did not seem much brighter than those of his immediate predecessors Vasilii Shuiskii or Boris Gudonov.

Yet the very scale of destructiveness of the Time of Troubles aided Mikhail. All those who had some stake in the society, however small, recognized that the passions and hatreds unleashed by the troubles threatened them all with ruin. Aristocrats, gentry, merchants, petty traders, clergy, even the Don and Zaporozhian Cossacks saw some value in stability.[2] For those without any stake in the society, bandits, enserfed peasants and slaves a newly revived Muscovy did not have much attraction. Many remained in the large gangs that continued to operate on Muscovite territory for years after the formal ending of the troubles. But the momentum towards stability and the restoration of order proved unstoppable. Mikhail benefited from the large amount of goodwill towards him in the country. He avoided the wild imperialistic visions of Ivan the Terrible and some of his successors. Mikhail's father, Patriarch Filaret who returned from Polish captivity in 1619, became in effect the real ruler until his death in 1633 by which time Mikhail was more than ready to govern on his own. Apart from the recurrent conflicts with the Poles and Tatars,

Mikhail did not undertake anything on the scale of the Livonian War nor did he engage in mad social experiments. Instead slowly but steadily he put his own house in order.

The base of the new order was an confirmation of the alliance of throne and gentry which had been so disastrously interrupted by the Time of Troubles. The victims of this alliance of course were the peasantry, the urban poor and the serfs who found their position even more debased than it had been previously. Peasants were fixed to their lords without right of departure, the state imposed higher taxes and the gentry squeezed what little was left out of their peasant bondsmen[3]. As the state stabilized, the government made extensive grants of land and peasants to the gentry especially in the Volga valley and on the southern frontier. Not only did this spread serfdom, it started to displace the indigenous non-Russian peoples of the lower Volga.[4] Rising peasant anguish only reinforced the mutual dependence of crown and gentry. Peasant unhappiness seemed to be a reasonable enough price to pay for this stability. A draconian legal code and ferocious punishments for the most petty of offences ensured that any discontent remained containable. The large floating population of the towns especially those of the southern frontiers remained volatile. But without leadership or organization they presented little threat to either Mikhail or later his son Alexei.

A social order built on a combination of unremitting exploitation and ferocious punishment could never be truly stable. Even by the standards prevailing in the early modern world, Muscovy was a harsh society. Jan Struys a Dutch seaman in the employ of Muscovy and no friend of social upheaval recognized that the peasantry '. . . indeed are very tyrannically dealt with throughout all the Emperours Dominions . . .'[5]. Disturbances were always a possibility both in the urban and rural areas. In 1648 a riot exploded in Moscow which threatened the life of Alexei himself. It was followed by riots in many provincial towns.[6] The execution of Charles I by his English subjects in the following year profoundly shocked Alexei and added to his sense of insecurity. Once order had been restored, the elite responded not by alleviating the conditions of the poor but with an even harsher legal code, the *Ulozhenie* in 1649. A few years later a new wave unrest of struck the capital in response to the government's debasement of the currency in 1661. The 'Copper Riots' as they were known frightened the government sufficiently to execute a few treasury officials by pouring molten lead down their throats, but popular anger remained unappeased. As long as it remained diffuse or scattered, however, it had little chance of threatening the social order.

The Don *voisko* after the Time of Troubles

The Don *voisko* emerged from the Time of Troubles with its prestige and power considerably enhanced. It had resisted the crude attempts of Boris Gudonov to coerce it, had thrown its weight behind the first False Dmitrii and had been the decisive influence in the election of Mikhail Romanov.[7] This was an impressive list of achievements by any standard. Yet the achievements did not stop there. The power of the Cossack idea had resonated throughout the whole of Russian society. Thousands of peasants and slaves without any formal link or connection to any Cossack host had spontaneously declared themselves Cossacks, formed *krugs*, elected atamans and began to settle accounts with their social superiors. The rage of the dispossessed and their close association with the Cossacks was etched into the memory of the Muscovite ruling elite. At all costs the two had to be kept apart in future.

The Don and Zaporozhian Cossacks had displayed an impressive degree of collective identity and cohesion. The fragmentation of Russian society had not found any echo among the Cossacks of the Don or the Dnieper. Both hosts acted as cohesive units and both were able to cooperate with each other. Between the Cossack elite and rank and file there was a shared sense of values and identity. Cossack loyalty was first and foremost to their host and all other loyalties were secondary. Friendship existed between the separate hosts and Cossacks knew that they could count on sanctuary and support from each other.[8]

Inevitably the power of the Cossack hosts relative to Muscovy would decline at it crawled out of the mire in which it had almost been swallowed up.[9] Yet as long as the Cossack hosts remained united around their values of democracy and egalitarianism, they were in strong position to resist all pressures from the surrounding states. Mikhail knew that he owed his throne to Cossack support in 1613 and, although he personally disliked them, was cautious in his dealings with them.[10] Occasionally he attempted to persuade the Cossacks to take the oath of loyalty to him, but the Cossacks firmly rejected this. The one attempt he made to put serious pressure on the Don Cossacks in 1630 ended in disaster. Mikhail's envoy, Ivan Karamyshev, so outraged the Cossacks with his message that he was seized, sewn into a sack and thrown into the Don.[11] Mikhail did not send any more envoys to the Cossacks to their satisfaction and no doubt to the relief of possible envoys.

For all of Mikhail's reign, the Cossacks carried out their own foreign policy, refusing to subordinate it to the interests of Muscovy.[12] The most spectacular example of this was the capture of Azov from the Ottoman Empire in 1637. This had been undertaken without Mikhail's knowledge let alone his blessing. For four years the Cossacks held the fortress against the might of the Ottoman Empire. In 1642 when it became clear that Mikhail would not come to their aid as requested, the Cossacks evacuated Azov. The failure to come to the Cossacks' aid rankled with them long after the abandonment of Azov and they became even more truculent in their dealings with the Muscovite state, angrily rejecting an order from Mikhail's successor, Alexei, to attack the Tatars.[13]

The Cossacks must have seemed as stubborn and dangerous at the end of Mikhail's reign as they had at the beginning. Yet changes were taking place in the host which were to Muscovy's advantage. The homogeneity of Cossack society had began to disintegrate along with its absolute commitment to democracy. An elite whose position had originally rested on charisma and the acclaim of the Host found more permanent substitutes for such evanescent criteria. Long term residence, family background and wealth emerged as the basis for membership of the elite.[14] This cannot be dated precisely since it was a process not an event, but by mid-seventeenth century it was well under way.

The emergence of an elite is an inevitable part of any human society. On the Don, however, the speed at which the elite crystallized and the peculiar ideology of the Cossacks ensured that the process would be particularly bitter and divisive. Sometime around mid-century the divisions within Cossack society hardened and became ever more difficult to cross.[15] There were many reasons for this. The two most important were the elite's increasing success in consolidating its hold over the Cossacks and the parallel process of an unceasing flow of fugitives to the Don through the reigns of Mikhail and Alexei. After the *Ulozhenie* of 1649 which closed the last remaining legal loopholes permitting peasant movement, the flow became a flood.[16] This influx of newcomers most of whom had little more than the shirts on their backs could not be absorbed in the traditional way by the Cossacks. In the past newcomers had generally to serve a long apprenticeship to show that they were worthy of becoming a Cossack. The *krug* would then admit them to the status of full Cossack with political rights and a right to the share of the tsarist salary. In this way newcomers had been absorbed into the Host. But such methods could cope neither with the scale of the influx nor the depth of anger that these arrivals felt.

The new arrivals (*novoprishlye*) had few opportunities to make their living. The traditional means of winning acceptance in the society through demonstrations of martial prowess were narrowing. Raiding the Ottoman

Empire, Persia and the Crimean Khanate was becoming steadily more difficult as more sophisticated defensive tactics were developed.[17] Similarly Muscovy exerted unceasing pressure on the Cossacks not to undertake raids without its permission. The only opportunity for the new arrivals to put food in their stomachs was to work as labourers or barge-haulers for the Cossack elite. Few of them were reconciled to this situation, their anger fuelled by the disparity between their expectations of life on the Don and the reality of it.[18] Yet like the enserfed masses of Muscovy itself, these remained little more than a nuisance. The elite in Cherkassk controlled the levers of power. They also played on the community of interest between themselves and those who were rank and file Cossacks but full members of the Host. Any increase in the number of Cossacks would result in the salary being spread even more thinly.[19] Thus both within Russia and the Don, tensions were rising but lacked any apparent outlet.

The strange case of Vasilii Us

In 1666 a bizarre episode took place which gave a severe fright to the government.[20] In the midst of years of hunger and want, a Cossack ataman Vasilii Us and 300 of his followers left the Don ostensibly to offer themselves for service to the tsar. They managed to evade government watch posts and pickets and their northward march was not detected until they reached Voronezh. The governor of the town refused to allow them to go any further, but did permit them to send a small delegation on to Moscow. The rest of the Cossacks, the governor insisted, must return to the Don. However, Us refused and his decision was confirmed by his Cossacks in a *krug*. As suddenly as the Cossacks had appeared they vanished, leaving a worried governor behind. Although the authorities had trouble finding the Cossacks, thousands of peasants and slaves did not. Within a short time, fugitive peasants and slaves had swelled Us' band to over 8,000. Many of these fugitives took the opportunity to settle scores with their masters, on their property if not their persons. Gentry of the surrounding districts inundated Moscow with complaints about Us.

The delegation that had gone on to Moscow had received a categorical refusal of their request for service and were told in no uncertain terms to return to the Don. They met up with Us on his northward march. Again as with the peasants and unlike the government, they had little trouble finding Us. Confronted with a categorical rejection of their demand, the Cossacks summoned a *krug* to discuss their position. They were in the heartland of Muscovite territory, hundreds of miles from the Don and far from any possible help. Still Us was undaunted and decided to send a new delegation to Moscow this time led by himself.

By now the government was seriously alarmed and commissioned a senior commander, Prince Bariantinskii, to lead a reliable regiment to force the Cossacks to return to the Don. Bariantinskii made it clear that as a condition of safe passage to the Don the Cossacks were to hand over all the fugitives who had found refuge with him. Those who had committed violence against their landlords were to be hanged while all the rest were to be flogged with the knout through the villages of the local districts. Us returned empty handed from the government and under heavy escort. The Cossacks were to be taken to Bariantinskii and placed under arrest until they had agreed to his conditions. However, just before they arrived at Bariantinskii's camp, Us and his delegation gave their escort the slip and returned to the Cossack camp. There they decided that they had no choice but to return to the Don. Nevertheless they were determined not to hand over any fugitives. They struck camp and vanished as they had done at Voronezh. Bariatinskii was furious and pursued them all the way to the Don. But even burdened with a much larger gang than he had set out with, Us evaded the government pursuit and crossed safely into the Don where the government for all its bluster still did not dare to follow.

Why had such a trivial incident so alarmed the government that it had brought it to the brink of invading the Don? Us had defied the government and inflicted some damage on gentry property, but had been little more than an irritant. The government response, however, was not a mindless over-reaction. It was a measure of the seriousness of what Us had done and even more what he might have gone on to do. The failure of the government's early warning systems to pick up the Cossacks until they were deep into the Muscovite heartland was bad enough let alone their ability to constantly give government forces the slip. Much worse was the mere fact of their presence on the surrounding countryside. The fragility of the social order was exposed immediately there was some mechanism to focus discontent. Peasants and slaves in their thousands came to join Us and his tiny band. The Cossacks, as in the Time of Troubles, remained the single most potent catalyst for revolt. Nor could the government ignore the unpleasant truth that Us had been operating in the Muscovite heartlands not the turbulent borderlands where such things might be expected. The coincidence that the government had dreaded most, Cossack grievance and peasant unrest, had briefly come together in the summer of 1666. Us had given the government much food for thought.

Life and early career of Stepan Razin

Stepan Timofeovich Razin was born in Zimoveiskaia Stanitsa sometime in the 1630s. His father Timofei had been a fugitive peasant from Voronezh province and had arrived in the Don sometime in the 1620s.[21] Timofei must have been a remarkable man. Within a few years he had established his reputation sufficiently for the ataman of the host to agree to stand as the godparent for his midde son, Stepan. His rise to a position of respect in that society was witness to his innate abilities and to the still open nature of the Cossack community on the Don. Stepan's mother was a Turk, possibly a captive, and he was known as a '*tuma*' that is someone of mixed parentage. She died while he was still quite young and Stepan was brought up by a stepmother. Stepan, his older brother Ivan and his younger brother Frol inherited their father's abilities. Born into a widely respected family, talented and ambitious, Stepan had all the prerequisites for leadership. His early career suggested that he would indeed be a future ataman. A gifted linguist, an able military leader and already possessing wide experience of the surrounding world, Stepan fitted naturally in the world of the emerging Cossack elite. Had he wanted, there is little doubt that he could have made his home there.[22]

Why he chose a different course will always be something of a mystery. Contemporary foreign descriptions of his revolt point to the execution of his elder brother by Prince Dolgorukhii:

> The first occasion of this revolt (as he himself confessed) was to revenge his brother's death, who was killed by an Eminent Personage whose name was Iurie Alexowitz Dolgoroeky in the year 1665. The brother of Radzin was at that time in the service of the Great Duke in the Polish Wars under the command of the before mentioned boyar Iurie Alexowitz Dolgoroeky who commanded in chief. and when their camp broke up to go into their garrisons the young Radzin desired to be discharged with his Men, having done the Emperour very good service in that last Expedition and that there was no more occassion for their Aid: but the general refused to let them go . . . The Cosaks were hereat greatly discontented, being volunteers, and had deserved yet greater Civilities than their Request, or than ever they had received from the Russians: they therefore marched off silently, led by their Collonel, brother to this said Stenko Razin, which was so badly resented by the General, that he took the Collonel, and hanged him. This was the sum and the ground of his revolting, which prompted him to imploy his Weapons against the Russians . . .[23]

Russian sources contain no mention of this incident but if it is true it was obviously a potent source of Stepan's hatred of the Muscovite order. Other suggestions of Razin's animus against the regime came from his trips inside Muscovy as a pilgrim. Like many Don Cossacks, Razin had a particular fondness for the Solovetskii Monastery in the far north. He had intended to go as a pilgrim with his father, but the latter had died before he could make it. Stepan later on fulfilled this pilgrimage, passing through Moscow on his way north in 1652.[24] Razin was again in Moscow in 1658 as part of an official delegation from the Don. He visited Moscow a third time on his way to Solovetskii in 1661.[25] Tensions in the city were ominously high as a result of the government's attempt to replace silver coinage with copper. The resulting inflation pushed the price of bread beyond the means of the urban poor. A year later the tensions exploded into what became known as the 'Copper Riots.'

What he made of the gross inequalities and harsh oppression is difficult to say. Although young, Razin was already an experienced warrior and was familiar with bloodshed and accepted it as a way of life. Yet maybe something of the Cossack freedom in his nature was revolted by the abasement of life in Muscovy itself. No doubt the depth of alienation, the anger and pent up violence of the urban poor made a deep impression on him and was not forgotten. Whatever the reason or precise combination of reasons that led Razin to put himself forward as the champion of the dispossessed first of the Don and then of all Muscovy, he was the leader that had been missing until now.

The Persian campaign 1667–69

Razin's growing alienation from the elite within his own society and that of Muscovy did not express itself directly in open revolt. He let it be known that he was planning a great pirating expedition such as had not been seen for many years on the Don. An appeal from a proven leader and the most charismatic Cossack alive was bound to evoke a powerful response, particularly among the poor and dispossessed in the upper Don. The government too got wind of what was happening and despatched urgent messages to Cherkassk, demanding that Razin be stopped.

The elite in Cherkassk were in a difficult position. Like the government, they were suspicious of Razin and his turbulent followers. Yet enough of the piratical Cossack spirit remained in them to recognize that Razin's campaign offered a good opportunity of riches. Some of the Cherkassk elite secretly helped finance and equip Razin and his flotilla in return for a share of the booty.[26] Publically, the elite condemned the planned raid and forbade it. Privately they informed the government that they were

powerless to stop it. The elite would not openly defy the government, but
neither were they yet ready to concede their independence totally. If Razin's
raid failed and he and his followers did not return, then they were rid of a
serious nuisance. If he succeeded then they stood to receive a substantial
share in the booty.

Razin and his followers set out in early spring. To get to the open sea
would be a major achievement in itself. Access could only be via the Volga,
but the lower Volga was dotted with government fortresses including two
of the most powerful in the realm, Tsaritsyn and Astrakhan. Lesser but
still formidable forts lay between these two. The government had already
warned the governors of these forts not to let the Cossacks pass under any
circumstances: testimony to its lack of confidence in the Cossack elite's
ability or willingness to prevent Razin's departure. The Cossacks left the
Don at the point where it comes closest to the Volga. They carried their
boats overland and entered the river. Razin was acutely vulnerable at this
point. He and his followers could not hope to pass the fortresses if they met
with determined resistance. The Cossacks had no heavy ordinance nor the
time and provisions to batter their way past them. But Razin had no
intention of besieging these river bastions. Instead, relying on Cossack
cunning and the sympathy of the rank and file soldiers, he managed to
bypass or capture all the forts; Chernyi Iar, Krasnyi Iar and Tsaritsyn fell
without any seige. Even the great fortress of Astrakhan proved powerless
to block the entry of the Cossacks into the Caspian Sea. Despite its
immense strength and large garrison, the Governor I.S. Prozorovskii did
not wish to put his forces to the test and made only feeble efforts to stop
Razin's passage.[27]

Now the Cossacks were in their element. The sea was beneath them and
the wealthy coastal cities of the Persian Empire lay before them. For the
next two years Razin and his band terrorized and plundered these cities.
They inflicted spectacular defeats on the Persians on land and at sea and
collected enormous quantities of booty. Alongside their successes, the
Cossacks came close to disaster on several occasions. After sacking Baku,
Razin and his followers in true Cossack style went on a drinking binge that
lasted a week, as Jan Struys related:

> Here they found a great quantity of wine, which they divided among
> themselves and caroused for so long, till they were all besotted and drunk,
> being about six thousand men in all. In the meanwhile the Persians had drawn
> down several companies and all on a sudden fell on this Rout, and made such
> a slaughter that the twelfth part or little more were left alive, and Stenko

himself 5 times in danger of being taken. The Remainder betook themselves to the Stroegs.[28]

Razin knew that time and luck were running out and that it was necessary to return home.[29] Whatever success the Cossacks had in individual battles and gathering booty, a powerful state such as the Persian Empire could always gather new forces and attack again. The Cossacks, however, had no possibility of reinforcements. Fighting, illness, hunger and thirst had taken a heavy toll on Razin's band. On their own, however successful in the short run, the Cossacks could not hope to prevail against a state whose reserves of manpower and other resources far exceeded those available to the Cossacks. It was a lesson that was not lost on Razin.

Even more so than on his departure, Razin's return to the Volga placed him in an extremely vulnerable position. His men although laden with booty were in very poor shape. Food, water, powder and shot were almost exhausted and many of his men were ill with stomach problems. Energetic action by the Governor of Astrakhan, Prozorovskii, could have dealt with Razin once and for all. He was already an outlaw, his forces were weak and he once again found himself beneath the walls of one of the most powerful fortresses in Russia.[30]

Despite his weaknesses, Razin counted on a display of bravado that was the Cossacks' hallmark. Recognizing that appealing for mercy might give the governor the confidence to attack him, Razin instead brazenly demanded not just entry to Astrakhan, but a triumphal procession through it. At the same time, Razin banked on the greed and rapaciousness of the ruling class. Substantial bribes were offered to Prozorovskii to let the Cossacks pass through.[31] Razin had judged his man correctly. Fear and greed made an irresistible combination and the governor opened the gates of his city to Razin on condition that they surrender all Persian captives and heavy weapons. Once inside the city, the initiative passed to Razin. His Cossacks knew well how to make the most of their entry. Dressed in the finery of the Persian Empire, the Cossacks caused a sensation:

> They marched forward for Astrachan, where they were very kindly received and congratulated by those of the townsmen, everyone of them appearing in the most splendid manner he could, for they had rifled many Gentlemen's Houses where they found always Apparel, Jewels and other Plunder for habit and ornament.[32]

The populace flocked to greet him and his men and Razin responded by scattering silver coins to the crowd.

The Cossacks were immensely popular. Among the lower classes, they represented the living embodiment of freedom. Here was Razin, a Cossack, dictating terms to a Prince, turning the world upside down. Even among the wealthy merchants, the Cossacks were popular since they had vast quantities of booty to offload at knockdown prices. Jan Struys the Dutch seaman in Astrakhan at the time of Razin's return found the Cossacks selling their plunder off at about a third of its real value. He himself picked up a thick gold chain from a Cossack in this plunderer's bazzare.[33] The governor received his reward as well. Even Razin, however, had underestimated the greed of the boyar class. In a particularly shameless display of avarice, the governor demanded Razin's shuba or fur coat. With bad grace Razin handed it over.[34] But it rankled with him and he remembered it a year later when his forces retook the city.

For six weeks Razin remained in Astrakhan, resting his men and building a rapturous following for himself among the urban poor. Jan Struys despite his personal hostility to Razin and the Cossacks, grudgingly recorded his admiration for the man:

> Stenko Radzi the Ringleader of that Rout, could not be distinguished from the rest, but by the honour which was done him, being saluted by the name of *Batske*, Father, and certainly he was the father of many impious Sons. I have seen him several times upon the *stroegs* and in the City; he is a brave man as to his person, and well proportioned in his limbs, tall and straight of body, pock-pitted but only so as did rather become rather than disfigure him, of good conduct, but withall severe and cruel, as has been already been instanced.[35]

From this time in Astrakhan and from the accounts of foreigners in the service of the Tsar we can get some of our few glances of the man himself. All of these were hostile to Razin, but they recognized his qualities as a leader of men. Like a Cossack of old, Razin's distinction lay in the honour his men paid to him rather than in visible displays of wealth or power. By and large he showed himself restrained and lacking in personal cruelty. But he was a Cossack and a man of violence. On occasion he could be cruel and vindictive to both friends and enemies. Usually this coincided with drinking bouts. It was during one of these bouts that Razin threw a Persian princess who he had captured into the Volga. Razin was extremely fond of her and was said to have bitterly regretted his actions when he had sobered up[36]. His close followers learnt to give him a wide berth on these occasions, avoiding his wrath and dispensing with any subsequent regret on his part.

Razin and his followers remained in Astrakhan for several weeks before deciding to return to the Don. Although they were far from fulfilling all the conditions of their pardon, the governor of Astrakhan was only too willing to see the back of them. By their presence alone, Razin and his followers were raising tensions in the already bitterly divided city.[37] The urban poor saw before them an alternative social order acted out on a daily basis. Just as they had done during the Time of Troubles, the Cossacks took every opportunity to display their derision for the minutely graded social hierarchy. Razin did not disguise his contempt for the governor and the ruling elite of the city who were powerless to avenge the insults heaped upon them. For great nobles hyper-sensitive to their status and in an hierarchal society defined by deference, the studied insolence of Razin and his followers was deeply wounding, echoing Cossack behaviour during the Time of Troubles. To move against him was impossible. The urban poor were not alone in their admiration of Razin. The large strelsty garrison sympathized with him. His open-handed generosity in the city and the wealth his men brought back from their campaign made a deep impression on the garrison, particularly since its own pay was so niggardly and was several months in arrears. When Razin and his followers decamped from the city in September 1669, to the governor and the elite Razin's non-compliance with the terms of his pardon must have seemed a small price to pay.

The revolt of Stepan Razin 1670–71

Razin's return home to the Don was more akin to a triumphal procession than the return of a successful Cossack raiding party. He did nothing to minimize the furore surrounding his return or dampen the hopes and expectations among the poor on the Don that he had aroused. Razin's confidence and self-belief, neither of which he was short of, now appeared to take a qualitative leap forward. The Muscovite government issued a pardon in return for a promise not to undertake any more unauthorized expeditions, but this must only have added to Razin's growing self-assurance.[38] His success, the impunity with which he had defied the government, and the messianic idealization of him by the poor broadened his ambition. Although as yet there was no evidence of a desire to begin a great war of liberation within Muscovy, Razin was already pondering his next campaign. Usually a successful Cossack army disbanded and scattered as soon as it reached the Don. Razin, however, kept his men together and set up camp on a large island near Kagal'nitsskii Gorodok, about two days upriver from Cherkassk.

Ataman Iakovlev did not celebrate the return of his prodigal godson with a fatted calf.[39] The elite's earlier ambivalence towards Razin was now coming home to roost. Razin reneged on his promises to share his loot with his sponsors, but this was the least of their worries. His prestige and power were now so great that the opportunity to use force against him had passed. More worrying still was the support Razin was attracting among the rank and file Cossacks who up until now had remained aloof from what they had regarded as a movement of the impoverished newcomers.[40] From outside the *voisko*, pressure was mounting on the elite. The government's fears of Razin had not been quelled by his recent promises to avoid any further adventures. Through the autumn and winter of 1669, rumours circulated about Razin's intentions although little could be done until the weather broke the following spring.

As soon as travel was possible again, the government despatched an embassy to Cherkassk demanding that the Cossacks deal with Razin once and for all. Iakovlev's position was much weaker than the government realized, but Iakovlev had no desire to confess his weakness to a government envoy. He and the elite received the ambassador with great honour, bombarding him with assurances over their ability to neutralize the threat posed by Razin. Their deception succeeded. The ambassador was convinced by their promises and was on the point of leaving for Moscow when the whole charade suddenly collapsed.

Razin had spent the winter contemplating his next move. News of the arrival of the ambassador in Cherkassk signalled to Razin that the time for waiting was over. Gathering his followers, Razin set off for Cherkassk. Riding hard, they reached the capital just as the ambassador was taking his leave. Bursting into the *maidan*, the great public square of Cherkassk, Razin demand the *krug* be reconvened. Too late, the ambassador realized he had been lied to by Iakovlev. He was seized by the Cossacks and put on trial for his life. At the *krug*, Razin accused the ambassador of being a boyar spy. Up to this point the ataman and the elite had been able to play on the division between the rank and file Cossacks and the 'naked ones' who were the bulk of Razin's followers to ensure their control over the *krug*. Now as a sign of the growing power of Razin, the rank and file Cossacks who made up the *krug* swung behind Razin. The hapless ambassador and his assistant were immediately executed.[41]

The execution of the ambassador marked the point of no return as Razin was well aware. The government might forgive raids on foreign lands and even the killing of the odd governor or two, but the execution of an official envoy was a different matter. There could be no compromise now. Either Razin would triumph or he would pay with life for his actions. Iakovlev roundly cursed Razin, but Razin bluntly told him that 'you are the master of your army and I am the master of mine.'[42] But in the moment of his triumph Razin underestimated his opponent. He did not understand how implacably his godfather was opposed to him. By leaving the ataman and the elite in place, he left dangerous enemies in his rear who for the present had to bide their time.

After killing the ambassador, Razin and his followers held a *krug* to decide what to do next. The options before the *krug* were to repeat the previous year's raid into Persia, to try their luck against the Ottoman coastline or to move north into Muscovy itself. Razin spoke passionately in favour of the last option, summoning the people to a war to liberate the tsar from the evil boyars who had imprisoned him. The *krug* enthusiastically endorsed Razin's proposal for a war against the boyars.[43] Razin now faced a series of tactical choices on the best way to proceed. He could follow the Don northwards which offered the most direct route to Moscow. But this was the old Tatar raiding path and the government had constructed several defensive lines to block this approach. The Volga was another possibility. It was a more roundabout route, but it was less heavily defended. Razin could cross to the Volga and move directly northwards, using the elements of speed and surprise to catch the government before it had time to react. This, however, would leave a string of powerful government fortresses in his rear, cutting off any line of retreat and possibly providing a base for government forces to pursue him up the Volga. Razin opted to secure the lower Volga before turning north. This decision carried its own costs. It would delay the turn northwards for several vital weeks, giving the government time to mobilize its forces.

Once the decision had been taken, Razin acted with characteristic decisiveness. Splitting his forces in two, he advanced on Tsaritsyn by land and river. Razin himself led the land contingent while Vasilli Us led the river force. The Cossacks left the Don at the same point as Razin had done the year before, dragging their boats to the Volga. However, instead of entering the Volga at the point closest to the Don which they knew would now be watched, they moved further downstream, embarking through dense reeds. The authorities in Tsaritsyn were completely unaware of the movements of the Cossacks. The first they knew about them came when Us and his men suddenly appeared beneath the walls of the fortress. There was barely time to slam the gates and sound the alarm bells before the Cossacks were upon them. But the alarm bells only succeeded in bringing out the citizens who opened the gates for the Cossacks. Most of the *streltsy* garrison immediately joined the rebels, forcing the governor to retreat with a some loyal soldiers into the citadel. After a three-day siege, the

Cossacks stormed the Kremlin killing all the soldiers and seizing the governor. The governor was killed in the traditional Cossack manner by sewing him into a sack and tossing him into the Volga. Us then introduced Cossack administration into the city. The wealth of the rich was seized and divided among the poor.[44]

Razin meanwhile was preparing to deal with a relief column of 1,000 soldiers, advancing from Astrakhan. The Cossacks were in their element. They tracked the movements of the ponderous government forces and suddenly fell upon them. Half the government forces joined the rebels while the other half fled towards Tsaritsyn. They only realized that the city was in rebel hands when a cannonade greeted them from the walls. Realizing their position was hopeless they surrendered. The rebels, however, were in no mood to take prisoners. They slaughtered the soldiers and their commander. Another relief column mutinied and came over en masse to Razin.[45]

Razin now faced the daunting prospect of taking Astrakhan. Unlike at Tsaritsyn, there could be no question of taking it by surprise. In fact there should have been no question of taking it by any means. It was one of the strongest fortresses in Russia, strong enough to withstand a siege by any European army. The city was defended by a deep ditch, stones walls interspersed with towers and a heavily fortified inner citadel. The garrison was 5,000 strong and had over 500 artillery pieces mounted on the walls. Razin did not possess the means or the time to reduce such a powerful fortress.[46] But this had never been his intention. From his previous year in Astrakhan he knew the deep divisions within the city among the populace and the garrison. Razin was gambling on their willingness to open the gates to him when he appeared in front of them.

The governor and the city elite had not been idle once Razin's rebellion broke into the open. They did all they could to shore up the city's defences and prepare for a long siege.[47] When Razin arrived he sent two envoys demanding the surrender of the city. The governor's response was to mutilate the envoys and then hang them from the city walls in full view of the rebels. Both sides had signalled that this was to be a war in which no quarter was given or taken.[48]

On the night of 22 June a revolt broke out in the city. The Cossacks immediately began to storm the walls. The *streltsy* defenders encouraged them to come on and within a short space of time all of the outer walls and suburbs were in the hands of the rebels. The governor, metropolitan and the rest of the upper classes withdrew to the city kremlin with a few remaining loyal soldiers, mostly western mercenaries in the service of the tsar. Even these were beginning to have second thoughts. They knew that they could expect no mercy from the rebels. At meeting of the foreign soldiers, Captain Butler, an Irishman, spoke what was on everyone's minds:

> Gentlemen, I doubt not but that you are all sensible of the present danger which hangs over our Head, and that there is not much hope left to hazard our persons any longer here, the summ of what I have to say is briefly to advise and request of you all to pack up what you have in the shallop and that we forthwith betake ourselves to the Persian Coast.[49]

The situation was hopeless and their only chance was to flee. Many took his advice and left the city by whatever route they could. The governor and the remnants of his forces defended the kremlin bravely, but the final outcome was only a matter of time. Storming over the walls, the Cossacks broke into the kremlin and captured the citadel. The governor and the Metropolitan continued to resist from the cathedral, but this too shortly fell to the Cossacks. The city was now a Cossack one.

The next morning Razin summoned a *krug* of the citizens to pass judgement on the prisoners. The governor was among those taken. Given the hatreds within the city and his execution of the Cossack envoys he knew that his fate was sealed. But the rebels and the townspeople were determined to exact a horrific vengeance. Razin himself took a leading role in the bloodletting that followed. The governor was thrown down from one of the towers possibly by Razin himself. But then in a gratuitous act of cruelty he executed one of the governor's teenage sons and had the other suspended over the city walls. In all sixty six people were killed by the order of the *krug*.[50] Numerous other settling of scores took place across the city as the coiled hatred of the lower orders was unleashed.

Enemies of Razin depicted the occupation of Astrakhan as a bacchanalian orgy of violence and destruction.[51] Yet after the initial bout of bloodletting, Razin moved quickly to restore order. The only model of government that was acceptable to the Cossacks was their own and they introduced it to the city. The citizens were organized into 100s and 10s for the purposes of administration. This followed Cossack practice although it derived ultimately from the Mongols. For the city as a whole a *krug* was established while local districts had their own mini-*krugs* to manage neighbourhood affairs. This system of government although utterly alien to the Muscovite system corresponded closely with the wishes of the ordinary people not only in Astrakhan but all over Russia. As in the Time of Troubles, groups of peasants far from Razin's forces declared themselves

Cossacks and created their own *krugs*. Vasilii Us was appointed governor of the city.[52]

It is hard to judge the effectiveness of the Cossack administration. The city was in uproar, tensions between the ruling elite and the lower classes had passed their breaking point. It was no easy matter to control the city. Razin himself was not always to be relied upon as a force for stability particularly during his drinking bouts. The Captain Butler mentioned earlier was captured after his escape from Astrakhan and brought before Razin: 'the General sat at the Gates of the Bishop's Palace crosslegg'd after the Turkish manner drinking Brandy and was so drunk that his eyes rolled in his head'.[53] Razin in his cups was volatile and dangerous which could only have a destabilizing force on the city. Nevertheless, Butler survived his audience with Razin and lived to write a gripping account of his time in Astrakhan and his ultimate escape. It says something for the Cossack administration, that the city remained in rebel hands for months after the defeat of the rebellion and the execution of Razin.

Razin remained in Astrakhan for a month after its capture. This was a long delay and the government did not waste its time. An expedition was gathered for use against Razin and reinforcements were sent to the fortresses along the middle and upper Volga. The Cossacks held another *krug* and the decision to advance up the Volga valley was confirmed. At the same time Razin despatched his brother with a separate army to the upper Don in the expectation that he would lead an army north from the Don and at the very least tie down considerable government forces.[54] Rumours of his approach set the countryside aflame just as the revolt of Khmelnytsky had done in Ukraine.[55] Peasants turned on their hated masters when they were available or their stewards as a substitute. As in Astrakhan, the people needed only the smallest encouragement to vent their rage. Thousands flocked to join Razin's men, swelling his forces. Government authority in the Volga countryside went up in flames along with the property of its servitors.

Razin's choice of the Volga was well made. The area was still a frontier zone, but was one just being brought into the grasp of the landlord state. Serfdom was a recent introduction, but was introduced in its harshest and most exploitative form. There had not been enough time to grind peasant spirits into acceptance of the new order which was an affront to them economically and socially but more importantly morally as well. Moral outrage fuelled the savagery of the peasant war as it would again during the revolt of Pugachev a century later. Razin knew from his own experience the depths of social hatred within Muscovy and it was an essential part of his tactics to make as much use of this as possible. Charters were despatched by Razin throughout the countryside calling on the people to rise up and avenge themselves against their oppressors. They were couched in the direct simple language of the people, speaking directly to their grievances.

Razin's appeal extended beyond the peasantry. The Volga was also home to nomadic and semi-nomadic peoples such as Bashkirs, Tatars and Kalmyks whose way of life was disintegrating under pressure from Muscovy and its rapacious ruling class. Traditional grazing grounds were handed over to nobles, undermining not just the nomads' economy, but their way of life. Razin directed appeals to these as well. They brought a definite military capacity as well as their own anger.[56]

Control of the countryside, however, was not the key to victory as Razin well knew. If the rebellion were to succeed, the rebels had to secure the towns. If they failed in this, sooner or later the government would use them as bases to pacify the countryside. As in Astrakhan, Razin counted on the local people opening the gates of the cities to him. Saratov and Samara fell into his hands without a shot being fired. He was met at the gates with bread and salt, the traditional Russian symbols of welcome. The revolt was spreading out from its Volga heartland into the central regions of the country and eastwards towards the Urals and Siberia.[57] This was no mere revolt of a turbulent periphery against a stable centre. Us's tiny band five years earlier has roused thousands of peasants in the very heartland of Muscovy. Now as a major peasant war raged along the Volga, the peasantry of the central regions stirred in expectation of Razin's arrival. One of the most successful of these bands was led by a former nun who was known as ataman Alena. An English eyewitness described Alena shortly after her capture:

> Amongst the Prisoners, there was brought to Kneas Jurge Dolgoroek, a nun in Man's habit, put over her Monastical dress. This Nun had commanded Seven thousand Men and had done bravely in this War, till she was taken prisoner. There appeared not any alteration in her, not any fear of death, when the Sentence of being burnt alive was pronounced against her . . . A little before she died, she wished that many more had behaved themselves, and fought as courageously as she had done; that then certainly Kneas Jurge would have found his best safety in his heels.[58]

For both sides the critical moment of the rebellion was approaching. If Razin's advance continued up the Volga, the river would take him to Moscow via Kazan and Nizhne-Novgorod. Both cities were already experiencing unrest. In early September Razin's army arrived at Simbirsk.

Unlike other cities on the Volga, Simbirsk possessed an able and energetic governor who had done much in the time available to him to raise the morale of his troops. The outer city fell quickly to Razin's forces, but the kremlin held out. For a month the battle raged for Simbirsk. Three times the rebels attempted to storm the kremlin, but each time they were beaten back.[59] Then came news that a relief column was approaching the city. Razin knew that his forces would soon be trapped between the relief column and the Simbirsk kremlin. Despite the rigours of a month long siege and the beginnings of the autumn rains, Razin showed great decisiveness. He intercepted the relief column and a great battle raged. Razin himself was in the thick of the fighting and was wounded three times. There was no decisive outcome to the battle as both sides withdrew to recover. The tide however was turning against the rebels who had been badly battered in the encounter. In desperation Razin ordered one last attempt to storm the kremlin. He was too ill to lead the assault himself and had to entrust the matter to his subordinates. The assault was a disaster and it was repulsed with catastrophic losses for the rebels. Defeat turned into rout and slaughter. Those who could fled to the boats and back down river. Razin was carried by his comrades and just managed to avoid capture. The government forces then went on a horrific killing spree, far worse than Razin had been in Astrakhan. Hundreds were killed in the most horrible fashion and their bodies floated down river on scaffolds as signs of impending retribution.[60]

The defeat Razin had suffered was grievous but not fatal. The government armies were not yet ready to pursue him down the Volga. The peasant war in the countryside continued to rage in spite of the defeat at Simbirsk and the countryside had to be pacified before a serious pursuit of Razin could begin. Razin and his followers arrived safely back to the Don and he returned to his old island lair. There is no indication that Razin had given up the fight or was going to seek his own salvation in fight. He was an experienced Cossack warlord and knew that defeats or victories were rarely as overwhelming as they might have seemed at first sight. The kernel of his band was intact, the revolt in the countryside continued to spread even without his army as a central focus. His intentions as far as we can judge were to recover from his wounds during the winter when the Don would be inaccessible to government forces and then try again the following spring.[61]

At this point, however, his old enemy Iakovlev decided to strike. Like Razin, Iakovlev was an able Cossack ataman. Ruthless, brave and cunning, he knew that his own position in the aftermath of the revolt might be extremely awkward. He had after all been ataman when a government ambassador had been executed in his presence. The government might be less than impressed with his protestations of innocence. Gathering a large force of Cossacks from the lower Don, he suddenly struck at Razin's base on the island before Razin returned. The ataman of the base was killed and Razin's brother and wife were captured. Razin now recognized his mistake in failing to kill Iakovlev the previous spring. He gathered his forces to fight Iakovlev. But his followers were exhausted and many ordinary Cossacks who had supported him in the *krug* the previous spring saw which way the wind was blowing. A second battle took place at Kagalnitskii Gorodok and this time the defeat of Razin was final. He was taken alive and his base burnt. Iakovlev then proceeded immediately to the borders of the Don to hand Razin over to the government.[62]

Iakovlev's actions reflected both his own animus against Razin and his desire to placate the government but they violated the oldest principle of Cossack life: '*s Dona net vydacha*' (from the Don there is no extradition) Razin payed dearly for his failure to kill Iakovlev when he had the chance the previous spring. Perhaps he believed that whatever their differences both were still Cossacks committed to the Cossack way of life. But Iakovlev along with the rest of the Cossack elite were ready to abandon Cossack traditions in favour of accommodation with Muscovy. For them power, status and wealth were to be had as loyal servitors of Muscovy rather than through the old freebooting way of life represented by Razin.

All that remained now was for the government to extract the maximum possible value out of Razin's execution. Everything was stage managed to ensure the humiliation of Razin in the eyes of the people who had looked to him as a deliverer from their woes. An English sailor who happened to be in Moscow at the time of Razin's capture described his entry into the city:

> Stenko coming within a mile of Mosco, the Waggon met him that been made to bring him into the City according to his deserts. In the hind-part of it was erected the Gallows; himself was stripped of his Silken habit, which he had worn hitherto, and an old ragged Sute put upon him; and so he was placed in the Waggon under the Gallows with an Iron Chain about his Neck, fastened to the top of the same. Both his hands were locked fast to the Side-beams of the Gallows, and his Legs divaricated. His Brother Frolko was with an Iron-Chain fastened to the Waggon, and went afoot on the side of it.[63]

Razin and his brother were subjected to horrific tortures before their execution. In June 1671 Razin was quartered on Red Square in front of a large crowd. He died bravely, without making a sound. For the government, his execution did not have the desired effect. Far from humiliating Razin or destroying his myth among the people, it cemented his place as the greatest folk hero in Russian history.

Razin's revolt was one of the most ferocious in early modern Europe. Its scale, brutality and bloodletting was matched only by the Peasant War in the Holy Roman Empire in the sixteenth century. The revolt was a complex in origin and diverse in its development. It embraced Cossacks, peasants, townsmen, nomads, lower clergy. The only social group resolutely against it were the gentry. A critical difference from the Time of Troubles was the unity and solidarity of all the Russian elite. They recognized that the revolt was unmistakably directed at them and their way of life. Their support and the unwavering determination of the government to crush the revolt made Razin's task much more difficult than the First False Dmitrii's or Bolotnikov's. Critical to Khmelnytsky's success had been his ability to extend his base of support from the Cossacks and lower orders to the Ukrainian gentry and the Church. Unlike Razin, Khmelnytsky had no wish to overturn the existing social order, allowing him to forge alliances that ensured the success of his revolt. Razin's uncompromising assault on the entire social order ensured his isolation, making the success of the revolt immeasurably more difficult.

It is easy to dismiss the revolt as the last gasp of a periphery against the centre or despairing peasants hopelessly resisting their oppression. Yet as with Pugachev a century later, this seriously underestimates the degree of discontent within the country. The causes of discontent were not confined to a specific territory such as the frontier. Discontent was endemic to Muscovy. The riots of 1648 and 1662 in Moscow showed the depth of dissatisfaction in the very heart of the country. Us's march through the heartland of Muscovy in 1666 was sufficient pretext for thousands of peasants and slaves to turn on their masters and seek revenge and freedom with the Cossacks. If Razin had fought his way through to the centre of the country there is every reason to believe that peasants and townspeople there, no different from the periphery, would have risen in support of him. Large parts of the countryside were lost to government control even though they were far from the Volga or Razin's envoys. The revolt did fail, but the failure was far from inevitable.

The Cossacks were an essential part of the revolt for two reasons. Most pertinently they provided military ability which peasants on their own simply did not have. Secondly they had profound symbolic value for all of Muscovy's oppressed masses. The Cossack idea of freedom and self-government were deeply rooted in Russian folk culture. The spontaneous self-transformation of peasants into Cossacks was evidence of the alternative moral social order that existed among the ordinary people whether in the towns or countryside and the fragility of the one imposed by the government. This combination of practical ability and ideological belief made the Cossacks such a powerful and threatening force within Muscovite Russia.

The Land of the Don itself was far from the ideal held in folk memory. Divisions were bitter and deepening. The Cossack elite was ever more ready to enter the embrace of Muscovy, abandoning the traditions of the Don and the Cossacks, seduced by promises of wealth and status held out to them by Muscovy. This was an effective tactic for dividing and neutralizing the Cossack host. Byzantine and Chinese officials would have recognized and approved of it. Even so, it was not without risks. The ideals of the Cossack state were deeply ingrained particularly among the poor of the Don and revolt was always a possibility among that turbulent and violent people. Us had come close to precipitating a revolt, but it was the titanic figure of Stepan Razin who embodied in himself the unique combination of qualities necessary to bring all the discontents of the Don and Muscovy together. Razin failed, but the margin of failure was narrow.

Notes

1 Stanislavskii, *Grazdanskaia Voina*, pp. 103–115.
2 Dunning, *Russia's First Civil War*, p. 300.
3 E.V. Chistiakova and V.M. Solov'ev, *Stepan Razin i ego Soratniki* (Moscow, 1988) pp. 6–7.
4 V.M. Solov'ev, *Anatomiia Russkogo Bunta: Stepan Razin: Mify i Real'nost* (Moscow, 1994) pp. 21–22.
5 J. Struys, *The Voyages and Travels of John Struys Through Italy, Greece, Tartary, Media, Persia, East India, Japan, and other countries in Europe Africa and Asia* (London, 1684) p. 192.
6 Solov'ev, *Anatomiia Russkogo Bunta*, pp. 22–23.
7 Svatikov, *Rossiia i Don*, p. 59.
8 Svatikov, *Rossiia i Don*, p. 68–69.
9 Rigel'man, *Istoriia o Donskikh Kazakakh*, p. 73.
10 Svatikov, *Rossiia i Don*, p. 59.
11 Svatikov, *Rossiia i Don*, p. 74.
12 Svatikov, *Rossiia i Don*, pp. 67–69.
13 Savel'ev, *Trekhsotletie Voiska Donskogo*, p. 17.
14 Druzhinin, *Raskol na Donu*, p. 15–16.
15 Pronshtein, *Zemlia Donskaia*, p. 108.
16 Svatikov, *Rossiia i Don*, p. 98.

17 Rigel'man, *Istoriia Donskikh Kazakakh*, pp. 91–92.
18 Druzhinin, *Raskol na Donu*, pp. 11–12.
19 Svatikov, *Rossiia i Don*, pp. 98–100.
20 This section on Us is based on Chistiakova and Solov'ev, *Stepan Razin*, pp. 112–124.
21 Chistiakova and Solov'ev, *Stepan Razin*, pp. 9–10; Solov'ev, *Anatomiia Russkogo Bunta*, pp. 41–42.
22 Solov'ev, *Anatomiia Russkogo Bunta*, pp. 42–43.
23 Struys, *Voyage and Travels*, p. 184.
24 Chistiakova and Solov'ev, *Stepan Razin*, p. 12.
25 Solov'ev, *Anatomiia Russkogo Bunta*, p. 42.
26 Solov'ev, *Anatomiia Russkogo Bunta*, p. 45.
27 Solov'ev, *Anatomiia Russkogo Bunta*, p. 53.
28 Struys, *Voyages and Travels*, p. 188.
29 Solov'ev, *Anatomiia Russkogo Bunta*, p. 64.
30 Solov'ev, *Anatomiia Russkogo Bunta*, p. 64.
31 Solov'ev, *Anatomiia Russkogo Bunta*, p. 67.
32 Struys, *Voyages and Travels*, p. 186.
33 Struys, *Voyages and Travels*, p. 186.
34 Solov'ev, *Anatomiia Russkogo Bunta*, pp. 77–78.
35 Struys, *Voyages and Travels*, p. 186
36 Struys, *Voyages and Travels*, p. 187.
37 Solov'ev, *Anatomiia Russkogo Bunta*, p. 68.
38 Rigel'man, *Istoriia o Donskikh Kazakakh*, p. 97.
39 Savel'ev, *Trekhsotletie Voiska Donskogo*, p. 38.
40 Svatikov, *Rossiia i Don*, p. 107.
41 Savel'ev, *Trekhsotletie Voiska Donskogo*, p. 39.
42 Solov'ev, *Anatomia Russkogo Bunta*, pp. 78.
43 Chistiakova and Solov'ev, *Stepan Razin*, p. 34.
44 Chistiakova and Solov'ev, *Stepan Razin*, pp. 36–37.
45 Solov'ev, *Anatomiia Russkogo Bunta*, p. 83.
46 Solov'ev, *Anatomiia Russkogo Bunta*, p. 86.
47 Rigel'man, *Istoriia o Donskikh Kazakakh*, p. 102.
48 Chistiakova and Solov'ev, *Stepan Razin*, p. 43.
49 Struys, *Voyages and Travels*, p. 197.
50 Solov'ev, *Anatomiia Russkogo Bunta*, pp. 90–91.
51 Rigel'man, *Istoriia o Donskikh Kazakakh*, p. 103.
52 Chistiakova and Solov'ev, *Stepan Razin*, p. 125.
53 'Narrative Sent by Capt. D. Butler dated at Isaphan, March 6th 1671' in J. Struys, *Voyages and Travels*, p. 371.
54 Chistiakova and Solov'ev, *Stepan Razin*, pp. 49–50.
55 Rigel'man, *Istoriia o Donskikh Kazakakh*, p. 106.
56 Chistiakova and Solov'ev, *Stepan Razin*, p. 51.

57 Solov'ev, *Anatomiia Russkogo Bunta*, pp. 102–105.

58 *A Relation Concerning the Particulars of the REBELLION Lately raised in MUSCOVY By STENKO RAZIN* (London, 1672) p. 13.

59 Chistiakova and Solov'ev, *Stepan Razin*, pp. 58–60.

60 Chistiakova and Solov'ev, *Stepan Razin*, pp. 61–62.

61 Chistiakova and Solov'ev, *Stepan Razin*, pp. 60–61.

62 Solov'ev, *Anatomiia Russkogo Bunta*, pp. 208–209.

63 *A Relation Concerning the Particulars of the REBELLION*, pp. 16–18.

4

Emel'ian Pugachev

Peter the Great died in 1725, but all his successors embraced Peter's vision of Russia. True, none of them followed it with the exuberance, passion and cruelty of Peter himself yet neither did they deviate from it. Peter's signal achievement, marked by his stunning victory over the Swedes at Poltava, had been the entry of Russia into the club of European Great Powers. The preservation of great power status was an obsession of his successors and, indeed, of all Russian rulers since Peter's time. This desire institutionalized itself within the elite and, unlike some other of Peter's reforms which fell by the wayside when he was no longer there to drive them forward, was not dependent on the whim of the individual tsar. By the beginning of Catherine the Great's reign in 1763 Russia's position as a permanent member of the great power club was unquestionable. The achievements were impressive; Poland had been reduced to satellite status; Sweden was becoming a minor regional power; and the Ottoman Empire was being rolled back on all fronts. Even more significantly, the Russian army could now more than hold its own with undisputed first class powers. In any European war, Russian support was the difference between victory and defeat so much so that for the first time the other European powers began to discern dimly a threat to themselves from the vigorous power in the East.

The Russian Empire was Janus like in its gaze. One face, looking westwards, from St Petersburg represented a mighty empire, a glittering Empress and a dazzling court. The other looked eastwards into the depths of Russia and there aspect was wholly different; a peasantry crushed by social and economic oppression; native peoples caught in the clutches of a merciless colonial power and religious dissenters living in an eschatological world of the anti-Christ and his opponents. Great swathes of the empire were seething but the grievances of different groups were locked into isolation with their anger endlessly dissipating and renewing itself impotently against the empire.

The Cossacks in the eighteenth century

The process of incorporating the Cossack *voiska* into the Russian Empire continued in the eighteenth century. The autonomy and freedoms of the Hetmanate State established by the Treaty of Pereiaslav in 1654 were steadily whittled away by the Imperial Government. The Cossack elite eagerly cooperated in this process, abandoning Cossack freedoms for noble status within the empire. By Catherine's reign the autonomous status of the Hetmanate had ceased to exist in fact and by the end of her reign had been completely absorbed within the empire.[1] On the Don, the process of assimilation was progressing, but at a slower rate. The *krug* had already been abolished and the elite appeared firmly in control. The only real threat to the power of the elite now came from divisions within it.[2] However, from the 1730s one family monopolized the position of ataman. Daniil Efremov became ataman in 1738 and remained in place until 1753; he was replaced by his son, Stepan, who held the post until his violent deposition in 1772.

The Efremovs were rulers of the Don in all but name.[3] Stepan, however, had ambitions beyond this. Perhaps wishing to emulate Bohdan

Figure 7 *Russian Cossacks in the 18th century*, by the French School, nineteenth century (engraving)

Khmelnytsky, he appeared to want to establish an independent state with his family as the hereditary rulers. The government was increasingly suspicious of Efremov, but suddenly realized it had no mechanism for calling him to account. In the midst of the war with the Ottoman Empire, it was confronted with possibility of having to invade the Don *voisko*. Fortunately for the government, other members of the elite realized that Efremov represented a threat to them as well. Abandoning any attempt to remove Efremov by institutional means, they kidnapped him and fled to a government fortress.[4] With Efremov's capture, the plot fizzled out. However, it had been an extremely close call for the government. Just how close became apparent the following year when Pugachev led the Iaik Cossacks in the biggest revolt in Russian history before the 1905 Revolution.

The Iaik Cossacks

The Iaik Cossacks, like the Don Cossacks whose descendants they were, took their name from the river on which they made their home. Their chief settlement was Iaitskii Gorodok or Iaitsk on the Iaik River which flowed down from the Ural Mountains through the Caspian Steppe and on into the sea. The first Cossacks on the Iaik came from the Don who used the Iaik as a convenient place to make their winter quarters when raiding the Caspian shoreline of the Persian Empire.[5] By the early seventeenth century the settlements on the Iaik had become permanent and the Iaik Cossacks began their existence as an autonomous Cossack army or *voisko*. Apart from its convenience for raiding Ottoman or Persian territory, the Iaik had other advantages as well. The vast expanse between Moscow and Iaitsk was attractive to men who found even the limited reach of the government into the Don too restricting for their tastes. The new settlement was also a chance to recreate the heroic brotherhood of the original Don community without the corruption of wealth and the social divisions that were evident on the Don. Established before the Nikonian Reforms, the Iaik Cossacks remained steadfastly committed to the old faith. The 'born again' fervour of the founders of the Cossack host on the Iaik stamped itself into consciousness of subsequent generations and the Iaik Cossacks remained the most truculent, difficult and awkward of all the Cossack hosts.[6]

As with other Cossack hosts, the Iaik Cossacks needed the sponsorship of one of the sedentary states to provide them with supplies they could not produce themselves. The Muscovite state was willing to do this, but at a price. The usual services of the Cossacks in interdicting nomadic raids along the frontier was in the interests of both parties. More ominously the tsar's government insisted, as was its wont in dealing with the frontier and frontier peoples, that the Iaik Cossacks acknowledge the tsar's suzerainty. So when the Iaik Cossacks petitioned Tsar Mikhail to be brought under the 'high hand of the Tsar', he graciously consented, granting the Cossacks possession of the Iaik River from 'the heights to the mouth'.[7] For Mikhail the frontier services of the Cossacks were useful, but more important was the long term strategy of establishing claims on the territory which however tenuous in the present could be transformed into something much more real in the future.[8] The Cossacks were soon to discover that although the hand of the tsar might be high, it was also extremely long and its grip tight.

Less than sixty years were to pass before the Cossacks became all too aware of the Faustian bargain that they had made. Fittingly enough, it was Peter the Great, the anti-Christ to many of his contemporaries, who set about transforming the nominal suzerainty of the Muscovite tsars into the effective domination of a European emperor. For Peter the Iaik Cossacks were a useful, but unreliable tool. Too headstrong, too independent for his purposes, Peter determined to curb and discipline them as he had done with other groups of the population. Under Peter, the state made its presence known to the Iaik Cossacks in unmistakable terms. Increased service obligations, constructing and manning fortresses on a new defensive line stretching from the Urals to the Caspian Sea, were imposed on the Cossacks without any regard for their previous traditions or sensibilities. More grievously, Peter mobilized Iaik Cossacks to fight in wars far from their homes.[9] Protests were met with the brutality that was the hallmark of the Petrine state: a tradition which continued under Peter's successors. Even so, however much the government felt it had subdued the Cossacks, it never felt easy about leaving the defence of the frontier in the hands of such a notoriously unreliable group. In parallel with the strategy of subduing the Cossacks, the government began to establish non-Cossack troops in the fortresses along the Iaik frontier. Much more significantly in 1734 the construction of Orenburg began: a major new administrative and military centre to east of the Cossacks. This new city fortress was to become the real bastion of government power on the frontier, relegating Iaitsk and the Cossacks to a secondary role. Pressed between the new defensive line and Orenburg, physically and symbolically the Iaik Cossacks were unmistakeably being incorporated into the empire.

Resentful as the Cossacks were over the intrusion of the imperial state into their lives, this grievance shrank in comparison to the outrage felt by the majority of the Cossacks over the betrayal of the founding principles of the host and its material interests by the Iaik elite. As part of its frontier strategy, the government sought the allegiance of indigenous elites to help in the subordination of an independent frontier people. Crude material incentives coupled with unstinting and brutal support to any challenge to its authority coopted almost all of the Cossack elite. From early in the eighteenth century the Iaik polarized between the elites and the rank and file Cossacks: the former were known as the *poslushnoi* or obedient while the latter were known as the *neposlushnoi* or disobedient. While the starkness of the conflict between the factions is evident, it was not absolute. The Cossack elite who dominated the host was riven with its own jealousies and competitiveness, which always provided the possibility of some individuals for their own reasons breaking ranks to side with the ordinary Cossacks. Beneath the *voisko* elite existed a sub-elite much closer to the rank and file in their outlook, but with authority and standing sufficient to challenge the status quo if the circumstances were right. Blocked by the *voisko* elite who jealously restricted access to the inner circle, this sub-elite provided most of the leaders in the Iaik Cossacks' endless struggle with the authorities.[10] And cutting across all factional lines as ever was Old Belief, opening up new possibilities of alliance and organization. In the fifty odd years separating Peter's time from the Pugachev rebellion, the Iaik Cossacks remained in an extremely volatile mood. Despite the basic cohesion of the elite, neither it's position nor, by extension, that of the government's was secure. The speed and violence with which the elite consolidated their political and economic dominance of the Iaik Host provoked a feral anger among the Iaik Cossacks that lasted for decades before finding its apotheosis in the Pugachev rebellion.

In 1718 Peter sent an expedition to the Iaik to round up anyone who had arrived after 1695. Amidst scenes of great brutality, about 600 people were arrested.[11] Not satisfied with these results, Peter ordered a new search in 1720. The Cossacks responded by deposing their ataman and electing a new one in his place. Rather than challenging the authorities openly, the Cossacks sent a delegation to Peter to explain their grievances. Far from softening Peter's stance towards them, the delegation provoked Peter's fury. The Iaik Host was stripped of its still nominally autonomous status in its relations with the central government and was subordinated directly to the War College rather than the College of Foreign Affairs. The ataman now had to answer to the Governor of Orenburg rather than the *krug* and the symbol of the Cossacks' independence, the ataman's bunchuk or mace, was snatched away from them.[12] To make sure the Cossacks understood the new order of things another expedition was sent to the Iaik which resulted in the public execution of three Cossacks. A particularly outspoken critic of the government, an escaped convict, was quartered.[13] This set the tone of government/Cossack relations for the next fifty years in which the Cossacks petitioned over their grievances and the government responded with arrests, floggings and exiles. Decade after decade, this cycle repeated itself, forging a visceral hatred among ordinary Cossacks for their elite and the central government.

In 1771 the Iaik Cossacks refused orders to pursue fleeing Kalymks which led to the formation of yet another punitive expedition. Led by General Traubenberg, this expedition arrived on the Iaik in 1772. Confronted with a procession of Cossacks petitioning for the removal of the ataman and his assistants, Traubenberg panicked and ordered his artillery to open fire on the procession, killing over 100 Cossacks. Enraged the Cossacks attacked Traubenberg's detachment and overwhelmed them. Traubenberg himself sought to flee but was cut down by the incensed Cossacks.[14]

For the next six months the Iaik was in a state of open rebellion with the government. The weather and the distance delayed the despatching of a punitive expedition, giving the Cossacks time to plan their next move. Yet in truth the Cossacks had little idea what to do next.[15] For fifty years they had resisted the government and their own elite at great personal cost to themselves and their community. Now their imagination failed them. What could they do? They were isolated, without a recognized leader and no strategy for taking the rebellion forward. The *krugs* that the Cossacks held to discuss the situation only exposed the divisions within the community. Some argued for flight to the Kuban, others suggested that they should try to draw in the native peoples and the peasantry, but the majority still believed that some sort of accommodation was possible with the government. In the end the Cossacks simply awaited the arrival of government troops which finally crushed the rebellion after two days of bitter fighting in June 1772. The usual round of savage punishments followed immediately. Most, but not all of the ringleaders were arrested and marked for exemplary punishment.[16] Amidst these great events, unnoticed and without fanfare, Emel'ian Pugachev arrived on the Iaik in November 1772.

The early life of Emel'ian Pugachev

The man who would draw together all the disparate grievances of the empire, giving them purpose and direction, was the unlikely figure of a

lowly Don Cossack, Emel'ian Pugachev. We know far more about
Pugachev than we do about the other leaders of the rebellions partly
because the late eighteenth century state gathered more information, but
most importantly because Pugachev gave an account of his actions
and life story to his interrogators immediately after his capture.[17] This
testimony given in Iaitsk, Simbirsk and Moscow is unique. Of course it
was not given in ideal circumstances. Pugachev knew that his life was over
and the only uncertainty was the level of pain that he would be subjected
to before and during his execution. While some of what he said was
deliberately untrue, particularly during his second interrogation under
that vainglorious lout, Count Panin, the majority of his testimony was
frank and revealing.[18]

Pugachev's testimony gives many clues to his character and motiva-
tion. He was intelligent although uneducated, courageous, quick witted,
resourceful, attention-seeking and with a real ability to charm people even
in the most difficult circumstances. Pugachev usually presented himself as
responding to the actions of others rather than initiating them.[19] Thus his
brother-in-law's flight which precipitated his own flight was sprung on
him. Equally the idea of passing himself off as Peter III came about through
a chance remark of another companion. Yet other actions of Pugachev
showed him to be decisive, resilient and full of initiative. During his
numerous scrapes with authority, he was always able to persuade someone
to help him despite the risks. He had a flair for dramatic gesture and speech,
knowing exactly how to fulfill popular expectations of how the 'true' tsar
should behave. He could be ruthless, but was surprisingly soft hearted and
could easily be moved to pity unlike his co-conspirators from the Iaik who
were implacable in their hatred of their enemies be they men, women or
children.

Pugachev was only 32 years old when he was finally captured not far
from Tsaritsyn on the Volga in 1774. His early life provided few clues to
his subsequent career. What is most remarkable is the sheer ordinariness
of it[20]. He was born in Zimoveiskaia Stanitsa in the Don which, coincidentally, was also the birth place of Razin. There, however, the similarities
between the two men ended. Razin's father had been one of the leading
men in the host by reputation if not by position and Razin was a man born
to lead. Pugachev's circumstances were much more humble. He was
born into a family that had been Cossacks for several generations, but
had remained very much part of the Cossack rank and file. His father
was a native of Zimoveiskaia Stanitsa while his mother came from a
neighbouring one. He had a brother and two sisters. Pugachev was baptised

in the stanitsa church and made a point of telling his captors that he was Orthodox and not sectarian although his later behaviour seemed to belie this:

> But I am not a sectarian as are other Don and Iaik Cossacks, but am of the Orthodox Greek confession of the Catholic faith, and I pray to God with that cross as do all Orthodox Christians, and I make the sign of the cross with first three fingers (and not the last).[21]

As was usual for a Cossack family, Pugachev lived and worked alongside his father until he was called up for service in the Seven Years War after his nineteenth birthday. A week before he left for service he married a girl from the close-by Esaulovskaia stanitsa, Sofia Nediuzheva.

From the meagre information that he gives in his testimony, Pugachev's family life was stable and, despite the general harshness of life, was not without affection. His later concern for his mother, sisters and wife showed a surprisingly gentle side to his character, quite at odds with the prevailing image of family life among the lower orders of the empire. He does not appear to have suffered any great trauma during his childhood describing it fondly: 'Until seventeen years old I lived at my father's and just like other young Cossacks in idleness.'[22]

Pugachev left the tranquil Don and was thrust into the inferno of the Seven Years War. Even for a Cossack this was an abrupt transition into adulthood. Pugachev experienced the brutality of war at first hand, taking part in many battles and sieges. The killing, the dying and the cheapness of human life in general no doubt left its mark on Pugachev. The war, however, brought opportunities as well. Pugachev adapted quicky to life on campaign so much so that he attracted the attention of his commanding officer, Colonel Denisov. Denisov appointed Pugachev as his orderly which was a mark of distinction and offered further possibilities for advancement. Yet it was as Denisov's orderly that Pugachev received a lesson about the contempt and disdain in which he and all like him were held by their superiors. A night raid by a Prussian cavalry patrol on Pugachev's camp was beaten off with no great difficulty. However, one of Denisov's horses was lost in the confusion. Pugachev recalled 'Because I was responsible for Denisov's horses and being in a hurry because of the Prussians, I don't know how, but I somehow lost one horse for which Denisov punished me mercilessly with a whip.'[23] Neither Pugachev's age nor his personal acquaintance with Denisov mitigated the latter's rage at the loss of his horse. Pugachev would bear the physical scars of that flogging for the rest of his life. How the deep the psychological ones were can only be guessed at.

Pugachev came through the war unscathed, but he did bring himself once more to the attention of his new commanding officer. He boasted that the sword he carried had been given to him by the tsar and that the tsar was in fact his godfather.[24] Such claims could easily have landed Pugachev in the torture chambers of the Secret Expedition of the Senate if his commanding officer had chosen to take it further. Instead he laughed and did nothing. Evidently, Pugachev had a liking for the limelight, regardless of the consequences.

1762/63 was to be an extraordinary year in Russian history. The Empress Elizabeth died just as Russian armies were poised to crush the Kingdom of Prussia. Pugachev along with the rest of the army swore allegiance to the new emperor, Peter III. An ardent admirer of Frederick the Great, Peter not only ended the war against Frederick but signed an alliance with him.[25] Pugachev's former enemies were now his allies. Six months later, Peter was deposed by his wife who from then on ruled in her own name as Catherine II. Once more, Pugachev and the army swore allegiance to a new sovereign. This bewildering series of events was specifically mentioned in his testimony and, although he denied that it had anything to do with his later decision to call himself Peter III, at the very least it must have been deeply unsettling:

> . . . news came from Petersburg that Her Majesty the Sovereign Empress Elizabeth Petrovna had died, and the Sovereign Emperor Peter III had ascended the All-Russian throne. And immediately after this, peace was made with the Prussian king and the division of which I was a part was ordered to help the Prussian king against his enemies. . . .
>
> On returning to Russia, crossing the river Oder, news arrived from Petersburg, that Her Majesty Sovereign Ekaterina Alekseevna had ascended the throne and I took here the oath of allegiance to her. At that time I was about twenty, but the thought of calling myself Sovereign had still not entered my head.[26]

Pugachev returned home and for the next few years lived quietly with his wife. A son and two daughters were born and the only interruption came with a brief expedition rounding up fugitive Old Believers in Poland. The relative tranquillity of the time since the end of the Seven Years War ended abruptly with the declaration of war on the Ottoman Empire in 1768. Pugachev was mobilized and took part in the siege of Bender among other actions. There, like thousands of others, he contracted plague which left permanent scars on his chest and legs. Sent home on leave he had still not recovered by the end of it. He asked to be discharged from service, but this was refused. The authorities did, however, grant him permission to visit his sister and brother-in-law in Taganrog.[27] This was the turning point in Pugachev's life.

Pugachev spent three weeks at his sister's, chatting easily with his brother-in-law about the difficulties of life in general, and in particular the perennial fear that the government were going to turn the Cossacks into regular troops. The only moment of disquiet came when Pugachev's brother-in-law suggested if such a thing ever happened then he with many others would flee across the border to the Kuban. Pugachev said nothing to this.[28] When Pugachev left for home, he took with him his sister who wanted to see their mother. Some way into the steppe, Pugachev and his sister were overtaken by a small group of Cossacks. It was his brother-in-law and others determined to flee. They wanted Pugachev to help them get to the Terek. Most reluctantly he agreed. He said bitterly to his brother-in-law 'I am innocent of this, but I will be forced to answer for it.'[29] It turned out just as Pugachev had said. The brother-in-law was captured and immediately implicated Pugachev. Pugachev was now in serious trouble, having committed a capital offence by helping someone flee. Little remained for him now but to flee before he was arrested.

Pugachev made his way to the Terek, hoping to lose himself in one of the Cossack settlements there and, when the hue and cry died down, bring his family to join him. He might have got away with it, but his inability to keep his head down was his undoing. He put himself forward to carry a petition to St Petersburg, but was recognized and arrested.[30] Escaping, he found help in an Old Believer community by claiming that he was on the run for the faith. He was advised to cross the border into Poland and to return to the Russian frontier, presenting himself as a fugitive who wished to come home. The Old Believers advised him to make for the Iaik which was a good place for Old Believers. The pieces of the jigsaw were now beginning fall into place.

All returnees had to spend six weeks in quarantine. As was his nature, Pugachev easily struck up friendly relations with two other inmates, Alexei Semenov and Petr Kozhevnikov. One evening after supper Pugachev related how Semenov suddenly burst out 'This fellow is exactly like Peter III,' to which Pugachev replied '"You're lying, you fool."'[31] Later under interrogation Kozhevnikov denied ever having said this. Whatever the truth, Pugachev's intentions, which had not been fixed up this point, now hardened. With the two others he discussed the possibility of going to the Iaik, proclaiming himself Peter III and persuading the Cossacks to follow him to the Kuban and service with the Ottoman Empire.

Pugachev arrived on the Iaik in November 1772. Through his Old Believer connections he was put in touch with many of the Cossacks who had taken part in the recent Iaik rebellion, but had escaped arrest. The most delicate part of Pugachev's enterprise had now arrived. Very possibly his claims to be the deceased emperor would be ridiculed and he himself arrested. However, the Cossacks with whom he discussed the idea were embittered men, seeking vengeance for their recent suffering. They also understood that the Iaik Cossacks on their own could do nothing against the imperial state. Pugachev offered them the possibility of drawing in much larger sections of the population. They were willing to accept him as the true tsar although they knew full well who he really was.[32] What mattered now was his ability to carry off the charade.

The pock marks on Pugachev's chest left by the plague fitted perfectly popular beliefs about the 'royal signs' carried by the true tsar. His wanderings among the people, suitably embellished to include Jerusalem, Egypt and Constantinople, likewise were an essential part of the myth.[33] To this was added his miraculous escape from the hands of his murderous wife and the substitution of another victim in his place. It was up to Pugachev to live up to his new role. As rumours began to sweep the Iaik that Peter III was living among them, small groups of Cossacks made their way to Pugachev to see for themselves. At one such meeting, one asked, in terms both familiar and respectful, what was on everyone's minds: 'Well now your majesty show us the royal signs so that we can believe in you and do not be angry that I have asked you about this. Then I took my knife and slitting my shirt from the collar to the navel I showed them my wounds.'[34] Pugachev's Christ-like revelation to his would be followers revealed an unexpected talent for the dramatic and striking gesture, befitting a sovereign unveiling himself before his subjects. Those outside the immediate conspiracy, wanting to be convinced, accepted Pugachev as Peter III. It was decided that Pugachev would reveal himself openly to the Iaik Cossacks in January 1773 at the ending of the winter fishing and the start the revolt.

Disaster then struck. Pugachev was betrayed and arrested. He was interrogated under torture by the local commandant. Pugachev was accused of attempting to lead the Iaik Cossacks in flight and falsely taking the name of the deceased emperor, Peter III. The scars left on his body by his flogging in the army would have immediately aroused the suspicion of the authorities that they were dealing with a hardened criminal, regardless of what he was actually charged with.[35] Pugachev was flogged, but he refused to admit any charges. In the end, the commandant decided the matter was too serious for him to resolve and sent Pugachev off to Kazan to be interrogated there. Pugachev's prospects at this point were bleak. The best he could hope for was a flogging with the knout, the most fearsome of the whips used by the Russian authorities, and spending the rest of his life in Siberia; execution was a real prospect.

Once again, however, Pugachev demonstrated his reserves of courage, intelligence and charm. Somehow, he managed to make one of the senior administrative officials take pity on him. His shackles were removed and he was given permission to go on work details around the city, albeit under guard. This was the break Pugachev needed. Using his Old Believer contacts, a daring escape was planned. Pugachev received permission to visit a priest under guard. While at the priest's house a carriage drew up. One of Pugachev's two guards had been bribed to cooperate; the other was more difficult, but Pugachev solved the problem by paying for him to drink himself into unconsciousness. Immediately the soldier had passed out, he was heaved into the wagon and Pugachev was off. The incident also reveals something of Pugachev's sense of humour. He related 'as soon as they had travelled about 8 *versty* from the town, the drunk soldier asked him, Emel'ka, why are we taking so long? And he, Emel'ka, laughing said to the soldier 'you see we took the scenic road.' (literally *the crooked road*)[36]

Pugachev arrived back on the Iaik in the summer of 1773. Once more he was received enthusiastically by the Cossacks. More and more acknowledged him as tsar, but his presence was now drawing the attention of the authorities. By the beginning of autumn the pursuit was gaining on him. Pugachev had only narrowly avoided capture on a couple of occasions and both he and his fellow conspirators knew that their luck could not hold indefinitely. Therefore on 17 September 1773 with a handful of followers Pugachev issued his first manifesto to the Iaik Cossacks:

> Imperial Ukaz to the Iaik Cossack Host from the Autocratic Emperor, the Great Sovereign Peter Fedarovich of all the Russias etc, etc, etc.
>
> In the name of my Ukaz drawn up for the Iaik Host: Just as your fathers and grandfathers served earlier tsars until the last drop of their blood so you shall serve the fatherland and me the Great Sovereign Amperor. Peter Fedarovich. If you will stand firm for the fatherland, then your Cossack glory will never leaver you or your children from now until the end of time. You, Cossacks, Kalmyks and Tatars will be rewarded by me, the great sovereign. And whoever will be obedient to my imperial majesty sovereign Peter Fedarovich, I the Sovereign Peter Fedarovich will forgive all their sins and reward them with the rivers from the height to the mouth, with land and with money, and livestock, powder and bread.
>
> I the Great Sovereign Amperor Peter Fedaravich reward you.
>
> 1773 September 17.[37]

The course of the revolt

Pugachev's revolt lasted from September 1773 until September 1774 when he was betrayed and captured in the Caspian Steppe. His revolt fell into three distinct phases. The first was the campaign centred around the siege of Orenburg which lasted until the spring of 1774. The second phase encompassed Pugachev's flight into the Urals and culminated with his unexpected capture of Kazan in July 1774. The final phase of the revolt was Pugachev's march southwards through the densely populated Volga valley. Each of these phases had its own distinct characteristics yet each of them were part of the same movement united through the person of Pugachev and the general sense of grievance against Catherine's government.

Pugachev's prospects at the start of the revolt looked bleak. The local authorities were already on to him and his followers numbered less than 100.[38] With little more than his own self belief, they set out to challenge the might of one of the greatest powers in Europe. Pugachev decided that they could not take the government centre of Orenburg. Even the Cossack capital Iaitsk proved too strong for the rebels. Instead Pugachev moved against a series of forts along the Iaik River. These minor forts should have been able to defend themselves against the poorly armed rebels. But like Razin before him, Pugachev was not planning to take them by storm. He hoped to appeal to those Cossacks within the forts to join him. The non Cossack soldiers were of poor quality and unlikely to put up much resistance, particularly if the Cossacks had already defected. Fort after fort fell to Pugachev with the only resistance usually coming from the commander and some officers.

The depth of the hatred that the Iaik Cossacks had for their enemies and their desire for vengeance was evident from the first days of the revolt. Among the first prisoners taken by the rebels were Cossacks belonging to the faction supporting the elite. Pugachev was inclined to spare them, but the Iaik Cossacks were having none of it:

> In the morning when the Cossacks had got up, they came to me and said 'Well what does Your Majesty order us to do with the Cossacks taken into captivity?' I answered them 'We should persuade them to swear the oath.' Then the Cossacks said to me, 'We don't trust them.
>
> Your majesty, we know who to pardon and who to hang. There are some great villains among them.' And when I saw that what they wanted was to hang them, then I ordered them to build the gallows and then the eleven people who were suspicious in the opinion of the Cossacks were hanged and the rest pardoned.[39]

Even at this early stage the rebels gave no quarter to their enemies, brutally executing officers and their families. Most tragic of all was fate of seventeen year old Tat'iana Kharlova and her eleven year old brother. Having seen her husband, the commander of the Nizhne-Ozernoi, fortress, and her parents murdered by the Cossacks, she and her brother were dragged before Pugachev. The Iaik Cossacks wanted to kill them, but Pugachev impulsively took pity on them and forbad the Cossacks to touch them. He even put them in his own wagon for protection. Unfortunately, even Pugachev had not gauged the raw hatred of the Iaik Cossacks for all whom they identified as their enemies. During one of his absences, the Cossacks murdered both children much to Pugachev's real grief.[40]

Pugachev's early successes provided the movement with the critical space and time to develop a momentum. Garrison after garrison came over to him and Cossacks from all over the Iaik acknowledged him as the true tsar. Pugachev recognized that the Cossacks on their own could never succeed and from the beginning sought to attract other groups to his banner. Even before the rebellion began, he searched unceasingly for literate people who could issue manifestos to different groups. Pugachev's manifestos carefully reflected the grievances of the groups to whom they were issued. One of Pugachev's earliest followers was the Bashkir Kinsely Arslani who translated the Pugachev's manifestos into Tatar.[41] The factory serfs of the Urals were another group who responded enthusiastically to Pugachev's call. Few peasants as yet joined the revolt which at this stage was still confined to the frontier. But rumours of Pugachev and the events on the Iaik were spreading rapidly eastwards into the Urals and Siberia and westwards into the central provinces. Areas adjacent to the revolt began to destabilize while even in Moscow hushed talk of the appearance of the true tsar was being picked up by government informers.[42] Within a couple of weeks of starting his revolt, Pugachev had already transcended the narrow grievances of the Iaik Cossacks and was on his way to becoming an empire wide phenomenon. By October, his forces numbered several thousand and having survived the opening period of the revolt when his vulnerability was greatest, Pugachev faced decisions other than mere survival.

The rebels had to decide what to do next. They could take advantage of the speed and success of the movement and head immediately into the interior of the country seeking to rouse the peasantry against the government. Or they could try to secure their rear and take Orenburg which would give them a secure base from which to operate. Pugachev's inclination seemed to be a dash for Moscow before the government could react while his fellow conspirators and the Bashkirs favoured Orenburg which for them was symbol of government power and their oppression.[43] Pugachev deferred to the wishes of his followers not for the last time. In early October his forces arrived outside the gates of the regional capital. For the next five months the rebels besieged Orenburg and several times it was on the verge of falling to them.

The five month siege of Orenburg was the most stable and organized phase of the revolt. Far from being the mindless rabble or swine referred to by the government, Pugachev and his companions gave serious thought to organizing and directing the revolt. A Military College was set up at Pugachev's headquarters at Berde a few miles from Orenburg. Different departments were created and people appointed to run them.[44] Of course it was far from perfect, but in organizing the siege and spreading the revolt into hitherto quiet areas it was remarkabley successful. Pugachev appeared to be creating an embryonic state to replace the imperial one. It was not clear what type of state he had in mind, but it is probable that he envisaged a Cossack tsardom with himself as the true tsar. The surrounding nomadic chieftains began to send emissaries, people and presents to Pugachev's court, adding to Pugachev's confidence and authority. He set up a court parodying the imperial one and even named some of his cronies after Catherine's leading courtiers. Pugachev also dispensed a grim justice to any nobles or enemies brought before him.

The reaction of the authorities to events unfolding on the Iaik was strangely sluggish. Initially, the Governor of Orenburg, Reinsdorf, hoped to deal with the problem himself and only inform St Petersburg when it was all over. Only when he realized the scale of the revolt did he inform the government. Catherine received news of Pugachev on 14 October but her initial reaction was to view it as a local affair of minor importance.[45] She had other worries. The Turkish War was dragging on, becoming more unpopular as its costs, human and financial, rose. Frontline troops could not easily be spared to deal with a rising on a distant frontier. A punitive expedition was put together commanded by Baron Kars who was confidently expected to put down the revolt. However, many of the troops were of poor quality as was the commander himself. Kars had severe doubts about the reliability of the troops under his command, but set out nonetheless.[46]

Kars, however, was advancing through enemy territory, his every move watched by the local population. Pugachev's intelligence networks picked up and tracked Kars' movements as he approached the rebels. On 7 November Kars' units were ambushed by 1,500 Cossacks. Two days later he was attacked again. Kars was stunned not just by the rebels ferocity, but their organization and technical competence particularly with artillery. His forces suffered a crushing defeat. Only the shortage of powder among the Cossacks enabled Kars to save his forces from complete annihilation and extricate himself. But by this point his nerves failed him and he took to his heels abandoning the remnants of his forces.[47]

The complacent reaction of Catherine and her entourage to the rebellion up to this point was shattered by the defeat of Kars. For a major army unit to suffer such an ignominious defeat at the hands of rebels was deeply humiliating, but far worse were the psychological reverberations of the defeat. The unease of the nobility, not just in the frontier regions but in the interior as well, now gave way to outright panic. Rumours of Pugachev were everywhere. By this victory, Pugachev had transformed his rebellion from a shapeless rumour into a real threat. The nobility looked on with horror while the lower orders in the towns and the countryside were gripped by a sense of expectancy.

By sending a second rate military unit to crush the revolt, Catherine had achieved the worst possible outcome. The rebels were triumphant, the peasantry stirring across the empire, and the nobility were panicking. Catherine's vulnerability at this point was acute. Her son, Paul, had come of age in September and some felt that he should now rule in her place.[48] If there was a challenge to her from within the elite at this point, the whole imperial system built up since Peter could unravel producing a second Time of Troubles. Catherine, however, behaved like an empress born to rule. She was calm, decisive and publicly confident. General Bibikov, one of the empire's most able commanders was appointed to lead a new expedition. He, unlike Kars, would have first-class, regular troops. As Bibikov marched off, Catherine knew that her fate was now in his hands.

Bibikov arrived in Kazan on 25 December 1773 and was dismayed by what he found. The sense of despondency among the nobility and authorities was palpable. Many of the leading figures had already fled and those that were left were demoralized and incapable of organizing the city's defence. Bibikov immediately set about rallying their spirits. Catherine had chosen well. Bibikov projected confidence, authority and certainty in final victory. His speeches and vigorous actions shook the nobility out of their stupor into active participation in the defence of the city. In a letter to his wife, however, he confessed his deep misgivings about the outcome of his mission: 'I found such a filthy state of affairs here that I could not describe it even if I wanted to.'[49] Nevertheless once he had received reinforcements he immediately advanced on Orenburg. On 22 March 1774 the decisive battle of the first phase of the rebellion took place outside the fortress of Tatishchev. Pugachev's forces were comprehensively defeated. Although Pugachev escaped, the crisis appeared to have peaked.

The lifting of the siege of Orenburg and the rout of Pugachev's army convinced the government that the worst was over and that the capture of Pugachev was only a matter of time. Of the three army detachments pursuing Pugachev, however, only that of Colonel Mikhelson did so with any urgency. By late summer Mikhelson was forced to call a halt to refit and rest his troops. Pugachev meanwhile had vanished into the Ural mountains.[50] The government was not particularly alarmed at this, believing that even if Pugachev remained at large he would only be a minor irritant. Again the government had misjudged their man. Pugachev's self belief and resiliance combined with vast reservoir of anger that existed within the empire enabled the movement to flair up again. Moving out of the Ural mountains along the Kama River, Pugachev and his new army suddenly descended upon Kazan, one of the most important cities within the empire. Kazan was completely unprepared and the outer city fell to Pugachev. The city governor and the commission set up to investigate the revolt made an undignified bolt to the city kremlin where they awaited the arrival of Mikhelson's forces. The fall of Kazan shocked Catherine and her advisors and sent new waves of panic through the nobility. Mikhelson's rout of Pugachev's forces three days later did little to quell the sense of shock, particularly as Pugachev once again eluded capture.

From Kazan, Pugachev moved down the Volga, seeking to rouse the peasantry. His manifestos to the enserfed peasantry set the countryside aflame. The revolt now entered its final and most bloody stage as peasants along the Volga and surrounding countryside gave vent to their long suppressed fury.[51] The embers of peasant revolt flew across the land, setting off risings as far away as Voronezh and the central provinces. Pugachev's intentions at this point were not clear. He might have been trying to reach the Ottoman border or he might have been seeking to arouse the Don Cossacks. The latter, although sympathetic, showed little willingness to commit themselves to someone whose cause was already lost; they knew Mikhelson was close behind Pugachev.[52] Mikhelson finally overtook him at Chernyi Iar and inflicted another defeat on him. Once more Pugachev slipped away. This time, however, he was betrayed by his followers in return for their own pardon. In September 1774 his closest followers handed him over to the authorities in Iaitsk.[53]

Pugachev had few illusions about his fate. He was interrogated in Iaitsk, then Simbirsk and finally Moscow. In December 1774 he was tried and sentenced to death. On 10 January 1775 he was executed in Moscow

with some of his followers. Government repression in the Volga countryside was ferocious. Potempkin held the power of life and death over the
countryside for nearly seven months and made full use of that power.
Thousands of peasants were executed in revenge for noble losses. The
frenzy of government bloodletting far exceeded that of the rebels just as it
had done under Razin a century earlier.

Conclusion

In Emel'ian Pugachev many of the discontents of Imperial Russia came
together and found their outlet. The depths of anger and alienation among
large sections of the population whether the Cossacks, native peoples,
peasantry or townspeople had been building for generations yet until
Pugachev they had dissipated themselves in small scale, minor outbursts
that were bloody but brief affairs. Only with the appearance of Pugachev
did the disparate strands of anger and despair coalesce to form a movement
that in scale and violence was the largest outburst of popular discontent
in the eighteenth century before the French Revolution.

The long term dispute among the Iaik Cossacks with the government
was the link between general discontent and a specific point of origin
for the revolt. The increasing restrictions on their autonomy in which the
Iaik elite were active accomplices provoked open and unceasing conflict.
With extraordinary stubborness, the ordinary Cossacks fought for their
traditional way of life in spite of escalating brutality which culminated in
the repression of 1772. The government believed that by this it had cowed
the host and that it would experience no more trouble from it. But not
only had it failed to break the will of the general mass of the Iaik Cossacks,
it had left several leaders of the opposition at large. These were men whose
sense of injustice and hatred for their own elite and government was
undimmed although they now recognized that alone they could not prevail
against the government. In the late autumn of 1772 they found what they
had been looking for in Emel'ian Pugachev.

Pugachev was the last link in the chain connecting anger with action. He,
as the true tsar, united groups whose interests diverged and clashed.
Without him, it is extremely unlikely that the movement would have taken
on such a scale. By raising the banner of the true tsar groups such as the
Bashkirs who would never have participated in a local Cossack quarrel saw
the opportunity to take revenge for what they had suffered. Peasants
likewise found in Pugachev the legitimacy for their bloody struggle against
the nobility and the imperial state. Pugachev played his role with great

aplomb and gave a convincing display. Certainly those closest to him knew the truth and probably a much wider circle had their doubts. Yet this was not important. Most of his followers were ready and wanted to believe Pugachev was who he claimed to be. The peasants of the Volga valley rose on the rumour of his coming; they did not wait for incontrovertible proof of his identity. Early success validated Pugachev's claims. So desparate was the anger of the people even the nearly unbroken series of defeats suffered after Orenburg did not dampen their ardour for Pugachev. Only his capture and execution enabled the government to fully re-establish control.

In western historiography the rising is usually portrayed as a frontier jacquerie that was at most an irritating distraction at a difficult time for the imperial government. The absence of overt rebellion in the central provinces is cited as proof that the heartland of the empire rejected Pugachev and all that he stood for. I think that this view is mistaken and minimizes the potential threat from Pugachev. The legitimacy of the ruling sovereign was a perennial weakness in the eighteenth century and Catherine's legitimacy was the most suspect of all: a target for pretenders and palace coups alike. The early 1770s was a time of particular crisis for Catherine. The war with Turkey had been dragging on for five years producing little but plague, losses in human life and increased taxation. When Pugachev began his revolt, it was probably the bleakest point of the war. Although it ended in brilliant success in the summer of 1774, there was little optimism about its outcome in 1773. The ordinary townspeople and peasantry in the central provinces were hardly more integrated into the regime than those on the frontier. After all, Moscow no less had been rocked two years earlier by the vicious Plague Riots. The quiescence of the central provinces seems to me to have far more to do with the levels of force that the government could deploy there rather than any increased legitimacy that it enjoyed. In 1905 and 1917 the peasantry of the central provinces demonstrated their capacity for revolution once the power of the state had collapsed. Crisis of legitimacy, an unpopular war and generalized discontent produced a much more threatening coalescence of circumstances than Pugachev's meagre military forces on their own might suggest. Even though Pugachev was defeated, the causes which had given rise to his rebellion continued. In his own way Pugachev said as much to Count Panin during his interrogation in Simbirsk. Count Panin scornfully asked his now powerless prisoner how he, a criminal, dared to name himself Sovereign. Pugachev playing on the similarity between the word for criminal (*vor*) and raven (*voron*) answered 'I am not the raven, only his offspring. The raven himself is still flying.'[54]

Notes

1 Efimenko, *Istoriia Ukrainskago Naroda*, pp. 314–317.
2 Pronshtein, *Zemlia Donskaia*, p. 235.
3 Svatikov, *Rossiia i Don*, p. 151.
4 Svatikov, *Rossiia i Don*, pp. 211–214.
5 A.S. Pushkin, *Istoriia Pugachevskago Bunta* (St Petersburg, 1834) p. 2.
6 I.G. Rozner, *Iaik Pered Burei* (Moscow, 1966) pp. 5–7.
7 Shenk, *Kazach'i Voiska*, p. 215.
8 See for example Khodarkovsky, *Russia's Steppe Frontier*, pp. 51–56.
9 Pushkin, *Istoriia Pugachevskago Bunta*, p. 7.
10 Rozner, *Iaik Pered Burei*, pp. 100.
11 Rozner, *Iaik Pered Burei*, p. 15.
12 M.D. Mashin, *Orenburgskoe Kazach'e Voisko* (Cheliabinsk, 2000) pp. 87–88.
13 Rozner, *Iaik Pered Burei*, p. 21.
14 Rozner, *Iaik Pered Burei*, p. 119.
15 Rozner, *Iaik Pered Burei*, p. 122.
16 Rozner, *Iaik Pered Burei*, pp. 162–165.
17 R.V. Ovchinnikov, *Emel'ian Pugachev na Sledstvii* (Moscow, 1997).
18 R.V. Ovchinnikov, *Sledstvie i Sud nad E.I. Pugachevym i ero Spodvizhnikami: Istoricheskoe Issledovanie* (Moscow, 1995) pp. 61–62.
19 V.V. Mavrodin, *Krest'ianskaia Voina v Rossii v1773–1775 godakh* (3 vols, Leningrad, 1966) vol. 2, p. 78.
20 These biographical details are all from Pugachev's own testimony. Ovchinnikov, *Emel'ian Pugachev*, pp. 56–57.
21 Ovchinnikov, *Emel'ian Pugachev*, p. 56.
22 Ovchinnikov, *Emel'ian Pugachev*, p. 56.
23 Ovchinnikov, *Emel'ian Pugachev*, p. 57.
24 J.T. Alexander, *Emperor of the Cossacks* (Kansas, 1973) p. 45.
25 I. de Madariaga, *Russia in the Age of Catherine the Great* (London, 1981) pp. 23–24.
26 Ovchinnikov, *Emel'ian Pugachev*, p. 57.
27 Ovchinnikov, *Emel'ian Pugachev*, p. 59.
28 Ovchinnikov, *Emel'ian Pugachev*, p. 59.
29 Ovchinnikov, *Emel'ian Pugachev*, p. 60.
30 Mavrodin, *Krest'ianskaia Voina*, vol. 2, p. 77.
31 Ovchinnikov, *Emel'ian Pugachev*, p. 141.
32 Mavrodin, *Krest'ianskaia Voina*, vol. 2, pp. 93–95.
33 Ovchinnikov, *Emel'ian Pugachev*, p. 74.
34 Ovchinnikov, *Emel'ian Pugachev*, p. 74.
35 E. Anisimov, *Dyba i Knut: Politicheskii Sysk i Russkoe Obshchestvo v XVIII Veke* (Moscow, 1999) p. 320.
36 Ovchinnikov, *Emel'ian Pugachev*, p. 156.

37 R.V. Ochinnikov (ed.) *Dokumenty Stavki E.I. Pugacheva, Povstancheskikh Vlastei i Uchrezhdenii* (Moscow, 1975) p. 23.
38 Mavrodin, *Krest'ianskaia Voina,* vol. 2, p. 103.
39 Ovchinnikov, *Emel'ian Pugachev,* p. 80.
40 Ovchinnikov, *Emel'ian Pugachev,* p. 86.
41 Mavrodin, *Krest'ianskaia Voina,* vol. 2, pp. 143–144.
42 Anisimov, *Dyba i Knut,* p. 89.
43 Mavrodin, *Krest'ianskaia Voina,* vol. 2, p. 121.
44 Alexander, *Emperor of the Cossacks,* pp. 83–84.
45 Mavrodin, *Krest'ianskaia Voina,* vol. 2, p. 168.
46 Mavrodin, *Krest'ianskaia Voina,* vol. 2, p. 171–172.
47 Mavrodin, *Krest'ianskaia Voina,* vol. 2, p. 178.
48 R.E. McGrew, *Paul I of Russia 1754–1801* (Oxford, 1992) p. 42.
49 Pushkin, *Istoriia Pugachevskago Bunta,* p. 71.
50 Alexander, *Emperor of the Cossacks,* pp. 148–149.
51 Pushkin, *Istoriia Pugachevskago Bunta,* p. 140.
52 Svatikov, *Rossiia i Don,* p. 220.
53 Ovchinnikov, *Sledstvie i Sud nad Pugachevym,* p. 32.
54 Pushkin, *Istoriia Pugachevskago Bunta,* p. 162.

Part III
The Cossacks in the long nineteenth century 1774–1914

The long reign of Catherine the Great took the autocracy to the pinnacle of its power. Internally and externally the empire went from strength to strength. The defeat of Pugachev confirmed the existing serf-based order which continued to expand and become ever more exploitative. Military successes in the west and continued expansion in the east similiarly legitimised the empire's social order and raised the prestige of the autocracy. Catherine's grandson, Alexander I, led Russia to triumph in the Napoleonic Wars, the greatest conflict yet seen in Europe. Victory provided incontrovertible proof of the potency of the system created by Peter and perfected by Catherine.

Yet even as it basked in its reputation in the post-Napoleonic era, the strengths of the Russian autocracy were imperceptibly turning to weaknesses. The intellectual ferment generated by the French Revolution lost nothing by the defeat of French armies. On the contrary, the disassoication of the ideas of nationalism and liberalism from French imperialism only strengthened their appeal. No less important to Russian power was the economic challenge of the industrial revolution which fundamentally shifted the balance of power away from serf-based societies like Russia. Only defeat in the Crimean War in mid-century galavanized the Russian elite into action led by the new Tsar Alexander II.

Alexander II introduced a series of reforms which created the basis for a modern society, most notably the Emancipation of the Serfs in 1861. His son Alexander III began a program of rapid industrialization which achieved astonishing results. By 1914 Russia was the fourth industrial power in the world. Such root and branch transformation, however, had its costs. Politically the empire was stagnant. The last two tsars obstinately refused to share power with their rapidly developing society. Political instability gave way to revolution in 1905 which the regime barely survived.

Although the revolution was defeated, it had altered the political landscape irrevocably. An elected parliament, the Duma, was established and, in spite of its weaknesses and the hostility of Nicholas II, remained in existence until 1917. The prestige of the monarchy was diminished beyond redemption by the events of the revolution. Most importantly of all the underlying causes of the 1905 revolution remainied unresolved while the resources of the monarchy to meet future challenges had diminished considerably.

In just over a century the Russian autocracy passed from its apogee to its nadir. Catherine the Great brought the autocracy to unprecendented heights and her grandson took Russia to the top of the great power league by 1815. But far from marking the beginning of a Russian Century or a *Pax Rossiia*, it marked the exhaustion of the potential of such eighteenth century regimes. Very rapidly the empire was surpassed by the industrializing societies of western and central Europe. When the autocracy attempted to catch up it created a situation where the political system was increasingly out of kilter with the economy and society. The limitations of the last two autocrats, particularly Nicholas II, exacerbated the divergence, but ultimately problem was systemic not personal. The autocracy itself, not the ruler, had become the source of the empire's weakness. The defeat of the 1905 Revolution could not disguise the fact that the autocracy as a poltical system had reached a dead end.

The Cossacks were just one part of this larger story in the nineteenth century. They experienced their own abasement before the autocracy at the start of this period, but survived to see the autocracy brought to its knees at the end of it. The Cossacks became more integrated within the empire not just in legal and administrative terms, but in the ways in which changes within the empire impacted ever more rapidly on their own lives and communities. Yet even as they were tied more closely to the internal rythms of the empire's existence, they retained a sense of their own distinctiveness and identity. The Cossacks showed, as they had in the past and would again in the future, the capacity to adapt to changing circumstances and political realities without ever losing the belief that they formed unique communities with their own history and traditions. How they adapted these to the demands of a wider context, which was changing with bewildering speed, forms the peculiarly Cossack part of the empire's history in the nineteenth century.

5

Government, administration and economy

Cossack reputation among the imperial elite, never very high, plummeted to its nadir in the aftermath of the Pugachev revolt. The Cossack vision of an alternative social and political order had been decisively and bloodily defeated after nearly two centuries of struggle. Never again would the Cossacks place themselves at the forefront of the popular struggle to overthrow tsarism. Prostrate before imperial power in 1775, the Cossacks faced a very uncertain future. If the Cossacks were to survive in the post-Pugachev era, they had to find some way of accommodating themselves to the imperial state.

The government had many reasons to consider the Cossack hosts more trouble than they were worth. The Iaik Cossacks had unleashed the most destructive rebellion in Russian history while the Don Cossacks had been severely compromised by the Stepan Efremov affair and the unmistakable signs of sympathy displayed to Pugachev who was after all one of their own. The chequered history of the Zaporozhian Cossacks in relation to the Muscovy and the empire hardly inspired confidence in them as loyal and obedient servitors. Yet the government never seriously considered abolishing the Cossacks. Suitably chastened, it regarded the Cossacks as an ideal force for subduing the ever expanding frontier in the south-east and east. Several more Cossacks hosts were created to carry out the long, grinding process of subduing the frontier territories. First, however, the government was determined to bring the Cossacks to heel.

The immediate reaction of the government was to strike out at the guilty parties. The Iaik Cossacks were collectively punished by having their name expunged from the historical record. They became the Ural Cossacks and their capital, Iaitsk, became Uralsk. On a more practical level, they were stripped of all their artillery: a backhanded compliment to the rebels effective use of it. The vindictiveness of the government extended to Pugachev's wife and family even though they were entirely innocent of any role in the rebellion. The family house in Zimoveiskaia Stanitsa was destroyed and his wife and children were shut up in the grim Keksgol'm fortress. Pugachev's last surviving daughter, Agrafena, died in Keksgol'm in 1833. It was not only the Bolsheviks who visited vengeance on innocent children.[1]

In the same year that Pugachev was executed the government turned its attention to the Zaporozhian Cossacks. Government forces surrounded the *Sich*, bombarded it and then dispersed the Zaporozhian Host for good. The remnants of the Host fled to the Ottoman Empire.[2] Within a few years, however, the government decided that the dispersal of the Zaporozhians had been premature. People were needed to protect the newly conquered areas on the Black Sea littoral and who better than the Cossacks? In 1783 Potemkin issued an appeal to all the Zaporozhians to return to the empire.[3] Significantly, however, the government symbolically sought to draw a line between the old Zaporozhians and the new host by naming it the *Chernomorskoe* or Black Sea Host.

After the initial wave of repression had subsided, more thoughtful members of the government recognized that it was not just malevolent individuals that were at the root of the rebellion but that systemic failure had played its part. Catherine's favourite, Count Potemkin, took it upon himself to carry out a root and branch reform of the Cossack system. Potemkin identified the lack of control over the ataman as the key problem. Up to that point the government had relied totally on the personal loyalty of the ataman. It had no institutional mechanism for controlling him if he decided to oppose government policy. The situation in the Don had only been saved, as we have seen, by the kidnapping of ataman Efremov by other members of the elite and their subsequent flight to a government fortress.

Bodily seizing an incumbent ataman and bundling him off in the middle of the night was an effective, but rather extreme, method of removing a disobedient official. Potemkin was determined that no ataman would ever exercise such power again. Rather than allowing the ataman to gather into his hands all the administration of the *voisko*, Potemkin's reforms divided the *voisko* administration into civil and military wings with their functions split between six people. The ataman would become the coordinator of policy rather than its maker. The six separate senior officials assisted the ataman, but also provided a check on any untoward ambitions.[4]

Potemkin's reforms, initially restricted to the Don but extended piece-meal to the other hosts in the course of the next few years, did not alter the crude bargain between government and local elites in which the latter gave loyalty in return for status and economic rewards, nor were they designed to. The reforms tied the interests of the elites more closely to the government, integrating them further into the imperial ruling class. The Cossack officer of 'elder' became a hereditary title almost but not quite on a par with noble status. As the government intended, Cossack elites devoted their energies to obtaining this coveted status which the government doled out parsimoniously to the different hosts. In 1798 the Don Cossack elite were granted noble status, a year later the Ural Cossacks were given the same rights. Other hosts had to prove they were worthy of the title.

The Cossack elites were expected to identify their interests with those of the imperial state. Whenever these clashed with the interests of ordinary Cossacks, the elites always sided with the government. Sometimes the issues were minor; sometimes they affected the lives of thousands of people. In 1792 the government decided to transfer 3,000 Don Cossack families to the Kuban to create the Caucasian (*Kavkazskaia*) Line Cossacks. The Cossacks selected for removal refused to go and began a campaign of passive resistance. The government, with the elite in Cherkassk's cooperation, brutally crushed the resistance through floggings, brandings and nose slittings; over 5,000 Cossacks were flogged during the pacification campaign. In the end, however, only a thousand families were transferred.[5]

The Cossack elites' ambitions now flowed exclusively into achieving wealth and status within the empire. The imperial government always rewarded its elites generously and the Cossacks were no exception. The government allowed them to seize unlimited quantities of land that was the property of the whole host for their own use. This had already been going on for some time in the Don, Ural and Terek hosts, but after the Pugachev rebellion the process accelerated considerably. Changes in the Cossack economy giving land a new value intensified the seizure of communal land. Even when new hosts were created, such as the Black Sea Cossacks, the elites of these host immediately set about seizing the economic assets of the *voisko* for themselves.[6] The government tolerated this although it refrained from giving legal recognition to the seizures partly out of inertia and partly to keep the Cossack elites dependent on the government for their property. The elites' seizure of property and the formalization of their status created deep divisions within the Cossack communities. The land they appropriated was the property of all Cossacks while their status was elevated at the expense of ordinary Cossacks. The legacy of bitterness would be a source of permanent tension among the Cossacks.

The reform process which had begun promisingly under Potemkin faltered when he died. No-one else had the same interest in implementing systematic reform in the Cossack territories and, as so often in Imperial Russia without a dominant personality to drive reform through, a combination of bureaucratic inertia and other priorities eased the pressure on the Cossack *voiska*. The accession of Paul I to the throne further slackened government pressure on the Cossacks. Paul even reversed many of Potemkin's reforms largely out of spite towards his mother. By the time Alexander I became tsar the administration of the Cossack territories was in a parlous state largely devoid of central supervision and once again run almost completely by the local elites. Any major change, however, could not be contemplated while the Napoleonic Wars lasted.

The Napoleonic Wars

Napoleon's bid for European hegemony reached its climax with the invasion of Russia in June 1812. The campaign of 1812 was to be one of the defining events of the nineteenth century for the Cossacks as well as for the empire as a whole. The patriotic fervour unleashed by the invasion brought the Cossacks closer to the imperial regime than any time previously. The legacy of bitterness among the Cossacks to their own elites and the imperial state was softened, at least in part, by the common struggle against the foreign invader. Cossacks, of course, had already participated in campaigns against Napoleon. These, however, had been in Europe not on their home soil and had involved Cossacks called up for service in the usual way. But it was the invasion of the empire that transformed the war from one waged by the professional army into patriotic war waged by the people as a whole. Because of its numbers and closeness to the invasion route, the Don *voisko* was the Cossack host most heavily involved in the war against Napoleon. Other Cossack hosts made important contributions, but it was only on the Don that the whole Cossack population was mobilized.

Immediately after the invasion, the government issued orders for the creation of a militia in the sixteen provinces of European Russia. The Don *voisko* was specifically exempted from this due to the large numbers of Cossacks already on service. However, ataman Denisov decided to ignore the government instructions and proceed with the mobilization of all male Cossacks between 17 and 55 years old.[7] Ordinary Cossacks responded enthusiastically to the call and by September twenty-two regiments had been formed. There was no government money available to pay for this

Figure 8 *Part of the Allies Entering Paris, 1814. The Russian Contingent, Cossacks and Plunder*, by the English School, nineteenth century (lithograph)

out of turn mobilization. All the men who answered the appeal had to equip themselves out of their own resources. Their families, likewise, had to manage as best they could.

The twenty-two militia regiments were joined by four other Cossack regiments on internal service in the Don. They left the Don between 11 and 18 September to link up with the main army under General Kutuzov. Covering an extraordinary sixty kilometres a day, the twenty-six Cossack regiments had all arrived at Kutuzov's headquarters by early October. The Cossack militia distinguished itself over the course of the next few months, particularly in the harrying of the Grand Armee's terrible retreat from Moscow. Fighting with the regular cavalry, operating just behind enemy lines like latter day special forces and linking up with partisan units deep in the French rear, the Cossacks once more displayed their extraordinary versatility in all aspects of warfare. The militia was honourably discharged once the French had been driven out of the empire, but the Cossacks serving on a regular basis continued to pursue the French with the Russian army through eastern, central and finally western Europe.[8]

The legacy of the Cossack participation in the war against Napoleon was profound. By the end of the war, the Cossacks enjoyed a European wide reputation and they were feted everywhere. The Cossacks, who accompanied the Emperor Alexander on his visit to England in 1814, were particularly popular with the London crowds. But it was in Russia that the legacy of the war was to be most profound. It not only completely rehabilitated the Cossacks in the eyes of the imperial elite, but also created the basis of new, mythic relationship between the dynasty and the Cossacks Tsar Alexander showered the Cossacks with banners, medals and charters for their heroic deeds. Cossack and tsar had never been closer and this relationship continued to develop under Alexander's successors.[9] The Cossacks, naturally enough, basked in the warm glow of imperial approbation and readily signed up to the myth of a special relationship. Both sides would find this myth extremely useful in the later stages of the nineteenth century.

Administrative reform

In 1819 the government at last felt able to turn its attention once more to the Cossack system. The unswerving loyalty of all the Cossack elites during the Napoleonic Wars testified to the effectiveness of the Potemkin reforms in tying the elite psychologically and materially to the imperial regime. There were no Ivan Mazeppa's or Stepan Efremovs thrown up by the Napoleonic Wars. The government was, however, increasingly concerned that the licence it had tacitly given the elite to seize communal resources had been so effectively exploited that it threatened to undermine the ability of the Cossack hosts to support themselves if it continued unchecked. In 1819 the government established the *Committee Concerning the Organiza-tion of the Don Voisko* to examine all aspects of local administration as a prelude to a comprehensive reform of all the Cossack hosts. Sixteen long years later, the work of the Committee finally bore fruit in the *Law Concerning the Administration of the Don Voisko.*[10]

This legislation was the most far-reaching reform of the Cossack administration ever attempted and, although devised for the Don, it became the template for the administration of all the Cossack hosts. The Law of 1835 was part of the continuing strategy the empire had devised for integrating frontier areas and peoples into the empire's heartland. The position of the ataman lost what remaining charisma it had retained and became much closer to a governor of any other province in European Russia. The administration of the *voisko* became less idiosyncratic and more like provincial administration elsewhere. Two subsequent pieces of legislation in 1870 and 1891 deepened and extended the process of integration to the point where it seemed that the only distinction between the Cossack administration and other provinces of European Russia was the retention of archaic Cossack names for some officials and administrative units.[11]

However, Imperial Russia was a polity of contradictions. The bureaucratic urge to regulate, homogenize and classify was countered by impulses from other parts of the system. Policy did not glide smoothly in one direction so much as moving in fits and starts with considerable detours on the way. Not all government attempts at closer integration were successful. The introduction of zemstvo into the Don in the 1870s, bringing it into line with other provinces of European Russia, mobilized the largest overt opposition among the Cossacks in the nineteenth century to government policy. After five years, the government backed down and abolished the zemstvo in the Don and dropped what was obviously intended as a pilot scheme for other territories. Critical to the resolution of this crisis was the personal intervention of the new Tsar, Alexander III, who supported the Cossacks and ordered the abolition of the zemstvo.[12]

Alexander III's action was a tangible example of a trend that had its roots in the romanticization of the relationship between the Cossacks and the dynasty after the Napoleonic Wars which had continued through the nineteenth century. In 1827 Nicholas I had invented the position of ataman of all the Cossack Hosts (something which had never existed) for his son and heir, Alexander.[13] This office was always held subsequently by the tsarevich. The links between the dynasty and the Cossacks were embroidered over the next few decades into a mythology of a unique and ancient bond between the two. So deeply did this myth take root that by the time of the last two tsars it had become a mystical expression of the tsar's charismatic authority that is his ability to act without regard to precedent, law or tradition.[14] There were ceremonial visits to the Cossacks territories which allowed ritualized expression of the link between throne and Cossacks. The bureaucracy with its obsession with rationality, order and routine expressed a very different conception of power.

Aware that their own charismatic authority was ever more restricted by the bureaucratic regime, the last two tsars reacted angrily to anything they regarded as encroachments on their authority. Alexander III saw the zemstvos as unwarrented and unwanted intrusion of an alien bureaucratic element into Cossack life which he needed little persuading to abolish. Nicholas shared his father's sense of a special relationship. His son's bodyguard and helper was a Cossack. At the point when the Cossacks were vulnerable to further state interference, they found an unexpected source of support in the tsars' determination to assert their charismatic powers. This government could pass major legislation such as the Law of 1891, but the protectiveness the last two tsars felt towards the Cossacks was a clear signal that this was an extremely sensitive area.

Local administration of the Cossacks

The three major pieces of legislation relating to the Cossacks successfully integrated the officials and institutions of the Cossack *voisko* into the provincial administration of European Russia. Much more important to the lives of ordinary Cossacks, however, than the institutions of the *voisko* were the systems of local self-government that existed in every Cossack host. These had existed since the first Cossacks had grouped together in the *Savage Field* and had developed untouched and unnoticed by the government over the next three centuries. The Laws of 1835, 1870 and 1891 were widely seen as increasingly ambitious attempts by the government to wrest control of the local administration out of Cossack hands into its own. Each of the three pieces of legislation worked towards widening the sphere of government authority and constricting the space for local autonomy. The passive acquiescence of the population to the existing order was no longer deemed an acceptable goal of policy. Cossacks, like other groups, now had to be disciplined into actively supporting government objectives. The ambitions of government planners to mould the population to suit its needs grew markedly as the century progressed. The committee preparing the Law of 1870 initially had little sympathy with the Cossacks and was considering drastically reducing or even abolishing the Cossacks.[15] Even though it backed away from this most radical piece of social engineering, it showed how ambitious government planners had become.

It has become something of a cliche among historians of the Cossacks to record the destruction of Cossack autonomy over the course of the nineteenth century.[16] The three pieces of legislation were widely seen as removing the last vestiges of Cossack autonomy and completing the process of turning them into an estate whose rights and obligations were defined by the government in the same way that it defined those of any other estate in the empire. However, most of those lamenting the supposed effects of the laws rarely bothered to see how they operated in practice.

The Law Concerning the Social Administration of the Cossack Stanitsas of 1891 turned out to be the last major piece of legislation regarding the Cossack *voiska* passed by the tsarist government and represented the deepest penetration of the government into the lives of the Cossacks. All the substantive elements of Cossack democracy, the link between the stanitsa and its satellite settlements, the *khutora*, the competence and functioning of the local assembly, the *sbor*, the role and conduct of the ataman and his election were confirmed more or less as they had existed over the previous 100 years.[17] In the 1820s a history of Verkhne-Kumoiarskaia Stanitsa in the upper Don had described a remarkably similar list of duties for the stanitsa ataman.[18] In fact the only substantive change as far as the ataman was concerned between the 1820s and 1890s appeared to be that the ataman was no longer responsible for the defence of the community against steppe nomads as he had been in the early part of the nineteenth century. In the Kuban, Terek and other frontier hosts the ataman still had this duty. It is hard to avoid the conclusion that the government legislation was more concerned with the smooth functioning of the Cossack administration rather than its wholesale replacement. If the government had really wanted to break Cossack autonomy, it is inconceivable that it would have conceded to the ataman and the *sbor* virtually everything that touched on Cossack life as it was lived in the stanitsas. Whatever the government in distant St Petersburg wanted and intended, however, was no guarantee of what it actually got when the reforms were implemented.

Judging from the level of abuse that the Cossacks directed against their local administration and particularly against the ataman one could be forgiven for thinking that the system was in a state of terminal crisis. Cossacks complained about the corruption of their atamans, the length of time it took to get any decision made or, once made, implemented, the conduct of meetings in the *sbor*, the dominance of wealthy cliques and so on. Many of these complaints had the excessive or illicit consumption of vodka as a common factor.

The *sbor* by Cossack custom and government legislation was the lynchpin of Cossack democracy. As we have seen it possessed competence over every public sphere of Cossack life outside of military service. All adult males were entitled to attend the meetings which usually took place on Sundays or holidays in the stanitsa *izba* that is the main public building of the stanitsa. A contemporary in the Don described how these meetings should be conducted:

> Everyone has the opportunity of casting their vote for the common good, of comparing different opinions on a particular issue and then arriving at a conclusion meeting the needs. Neither graft nor friendship nor kinship must have any influence on the rightful course of business.[19]

Of course the reality of these meetings was nothing like this. Meetings either resembled the quiet of the graveyard because hardly anyone turned up or were so packed that a cacophony of noise, whistling, and jeering drowned out any discussion. An exasperated observer recounted his experiences of a stanitsa *sbor*:

> I have attended many stanitsa *sbory* but I have not yet seen one functioning properly. Always a half or at the very least a third of the members are either tipsy or hungover. For example going on to the porch of the stanitsa building, very frequently the first person you will meet will be a drunk Cossack staggering out. Go into the first room and you will meet ten similar people. And who are these people? They are our esteemed Commune meeting to discuss communal business.[20]

To many it seemed a marvel that such an institution could manage anything let alone the complex affairs of thousands of people. Yet the *sbor* did manage the affairs of the community remarkably well. When the time came to carry out the repartition of the communities' land this physically intricate and socially extremely delicate operation was carried out through the *sbor*.[21] When issues that were felt to threaten the vital interests of the community were under discussion, the sbor mobilized the community in defence of those interests. The anti-zemstvo campaign in the 1870s, the revolt of the Cossack stanitsas during the 1905 Revolution and the organization of Cossack life during the civil war were all made possible by the stanitsa *sbor*. It provided the institutional mechanism to convert numbers into effective action.

Of no less importance was the function of the *sbor* as a ritual manifestation of the collective identity of the community. The *sbor* involved all members of the stanitsa: rich, poor and middling alike. By providing a forum for the whole community to gather, it subliminally reinforced the notion that the Cossacks were indeed a community even if they were bitterly divided on an issue or a whole series of issues. Government influence on the *sbor* was marginal which left the sbor as what it had always been: an institution of the Cossacks and wholly dependent on their attitudes towards it.

The ataman

The office of ataman had existed from the point when Cossacks first began to cooperate with each other in the steppe as we have seen. Each community had its own ataman who was elected by the members of that community. This principle of an elected ataman was critical to the Cossack sense of identity and system of authority. The Zaporozhians, while united as members of one community in the *Sich*, were divided up into thirty-eight separate *kureni* or barracks, consisting of up to 500 men. Each *kuren'* had its own elected ataman as well as the general assembly to run the common affairs of the host.[22] In the Don, each separate stanitsa was led by an ataman chosen by the community. The Don and Zaporozhian Cossacks established the principle of elected atamans in the all the hosts set up by them. This principle had become so firmly established that the government while very definite in preventing the elections of *voisko* atamans was happy to allow it at local level. Only in one case did the government not allow a Cossack community to elect its own atamans; the Don Cossacks who became the Caucasian Line Cossacks were denied this right because of their mutiny in 1792.[23] The only outside intervention in the process was the confirmation of the elected ataman by the *voisko* authorities; this remained the position until 1917.

In the nineteenth century the principle of elected atamans was unchanged, but the scale and cost of electing an ataman rose dramatically.[24] The first atamans had emerged either by consensus or by nominations for the post competing before the stanitsa assemblies. The three yearly elections had become a major operation by mid-century. Candidates for the post campaigned relentlessly, haranguing the Cossacks and, most importantly, liberally distributing vodka and food to all and sundry. One dyspeptic observer wrote 'When faced with such important questions as the election of the stanitsa ataman, the *stanichniki* don't give it a lot of thought and decide the matter in a fairly original manner, i.e. whoever provided the most buckets of vodka will be ataman.'[25] A good description of a typical election campaign was provided by a journalist covering the campaign for his newspaper. He was invited into a tavern by a Cossack friend to witness Cossack democracy in action.

Inside there are two tables with drinks and snacks. Sitting around are several of the stanitsa bigshots whom I know. There is a frightful din going on. Everyone is yelling, everyone is talking at once. Each tries to speak before his neighbour, interrupting him but no-one is listening. When I enter several people cry out in unison.

'Semeon Semoneovich! Sit down, sit down. What do you want dear friend? Friendship! You can find it here.'

'Do you know whose health we are drinking?' whispers one of the party to me. 'Ivan Tolstopuzov has thrown this party,' my informant says with his eyes on the bottle, 'in order to convince the assembly to support him. He wants to be ataman.'

'I wouldn't advise it' I replied.

'But what do you think? Are we right to elect him?'

'Well if you're drinking his health then I can only think that you intend to thrust this rogue on our Commune again.'

'Yet that's true. We didn't ask him. He nominated himself and stood himself. (Already up to 10 people have gathered here and all are staggering from strong drink.) Today we will continue here but tomorrow we go to the gypsy's and the day after to Petrovna's.'[26]

Many outside observers were disgusted at what they saw as the shameless auction of votes to the highest bidder and demanded that the system of elections be reformed or, even better, abolished. However, Cossacks themselves never expressed dissatisfaction with the system of elections although they were frequently disillusioned with the person elected. For the community the elections were more than just a drunken binge at someone else's expense. Beyond electing the leader of the administration for the next three years (an important element in its own right) the elections served the community on many levels. They represented an opportunity for the community to manifest its collective identity. As the elections involved the whole community, rich and poor alike, they served to emphasize that whatever divisions existed they were all still members of one community. Similarly, the elections were another means to bind any satellite settlements (see below) to the stanitsa, reaffirming their membership of the community. Finally, the election of the leader which continued until the Soviet victory in the civil war was of incalculable importance in legitimizing the local administration as a something that originated with the community rather than the government.

The expansion of Cossack democracy

Bolshevik officials during the civil war were baffled by the ability of Cossacks to mobilize thousands of people into military units virtually overnight. In large measure this was due to the unique system of local administration that existed in the Cossack *voiska*. The uniqueness of the Cossack system did not lie in its autonomy as nearly all peasant communities possessed substantial degrees of autonomy, but in the number of the communities and the size of the population embraced by each stanitsa, the basic administrative unit.

Stanitsas, as we have seen, were the original components out of which each *voisko* was built. Beginning in the late eighteenth and continuing throughout the nineteenth centuries, stanitsas began to set up dozens of satellite settlements known as *khutora* to cope with the rising population.

Members of stanitsas who wanted or needed more land would move out into the steppe to found new settlements.[27] Emotional and familial attachments to the stanitsa and the still dangerous circumstances of the frontier, at least in the beginning, ensured that *khutora* not only retained links of affection to their original stanitsa, but remained integral parts of the stanitsa. Those who lived in a *khutor* were members of a stanitsa in the same way as the people who actually lived in the stanitsa settlement itself. Some stanitsas had dozens of *khutora* which created administrative units embracing thousands of people. All the *khutora* were an integral part of stanitsa institutions and all participated in the election of officials. In the Don and Kuban the number of *khutora* ran into thousands by the end of the nineteenth century. In the Don there were over 4,000 *khutora* while in the Kuban in the 1860s there were 63 stanitsas with 3,000 *khutora*.[28] The other Cossack *voiska* repeated this pattern though not on such a scale. Almost by accident an extensive system of local democracy had developed which had arisen out of the Cossack tradition of self-government and the internal colonization of the Cossack territories. This deeply entrenched and extensive system of self-government was the key to the Cossacks' ability to mobilize such large numbers in defence of their interests.

Earning a living

One of the distinctive features the Cossacks inherited from the nomadic peoples of the steppe was a set of beliefs in relation to the natural resources of their *voisko*. These beliefs created an overarching framework which governed the ways in which the Cossack economy developed. Other factors also had an influence. On a more practical level, the demands of military service limited the choice of economic activity open to the Cossacks and inhibited the development of those economic activities that the Cossacks did pursue. Beyond the purely mundane activity of providing a living for the themselves, the peculiar way Cossacks did this became another manifestation of their identity.

Most importantly, the Cossacks adopted nomadic values of territorial possession and ownership of natural resources within that territory. Every sub-division of a tribe or *ulus* to use its Mongol name had a specific territory to graze and water their herds. This territory belonged to the *ulus* as a whole and could not be appropriated by any individual no matter how powerful. Within the community of course there was a pecking order of who got access when, but this did not challenge the collective ownership of natural resources. Each Cossack stanitsa had a very roughly delineated territory over which it had exclusive control and which belonged to the stanitsa collectively.[29] The Cossacks even imported the nomadic label '*iurt*' to describe their territory which they continued to use until the abolition of all Cossack nomenclature after the civil war. The concept of collective ownership formed at the time that Cossacks became self-conscious communities proved to be remarkably obdurate when it was tested in the nineteenth century.

The Muscovite and Imperial governments repeatedly confirmed the corporate ownership of lands by the Cossacks. When new hosts were being formed by government fiat in the eighteenth and nineteenth centuries, the government always granted land to communities collectively.[30] In 1792 Catherine the Great issued a charter establishing the Black Sea Cossacks and granting them as a community exclusive ownership of the land:

> To the Black Sea *voisko* is given in perpetual ownership the island of Fangoriia with the lands lying between the Kuban and the Sea of Azov as a mark of particular concern and favour, for heroic deeds on land and water and fearless loyalty in the course of the favourable outcome of the war with the Ottoman Porte.[31]

In the nineteenth century Semirech'e, Amur and Ussuri Cossacks all received substantial land grants when they were formed. The 7,000 Ussuri Cossacks received over 600,000 desiatina to support them, obviously allowing them to meet the 30 desiatiny norm with ease.[32]

The collective ownership of land did not eliminate conflicts between Cossack communities or between different sections of the community. Nor was the government always scrupulous in respecting what it had granted. The Semirech'e Cossacks, for example, had a third of their land grant taken from them a few years after their foundation. None of this, however, undermined the belief that the community was the ultimate owner of land not any individual.

The developing Cossack economy of the seventeenth and especially the eighteenth centuries followed the patterns established by nomads. Stock raising became a central part of the economy until late into the nineteenth century.[33] Nomads had raised large herds for centuries on the steppe and the Cossacks easily slipped into this pattern. Herds could be left to graze for much of the year with minimal supervision which was always an important consideration for a society with large numbers of men absent on military service. The herds were vulnerable to rustling which was one of the great pastimes of the steppe, but, since the Cossacks were as good at it as anyone else the losses and gains probably balanced each other. The

Don and Kuban Cossacks provided vast numbers of horses for the national market in the nineteenth century.

Fishing was for some hosts the mainstay of the economy and was an important activity for all of them. Like land, waters were communally owned and controlled. In the Ural *voisko* where it was particularly important fishing had been subjected to rigorous controls since at least the end of the seventeenth century.[34] Only full members of the community had the right to fish, the time of fishing was limited to the periods of the spring migration and a licence system was in operation to prevent overfishing. The Don introduced a similar system of control in the late nineteenth century.

Arable farming remained poorly developed among the Cossack hosts for most of their existence.[35] Initially Cossacks had despised agriculture because of its strong association with landlords and serfs and had threatened death to any Cossack practising it on the territory of the *voisko*.[36] In addition there were more practical reasons for its late development. Frontiers were dangerous places and men and women working in the fields were vulnerable to nomadic raiding parties. When the Cossacks of Verkhne-Kumoiarskaia stanitsa began ploughing fields for the first time in the late eighteenth century, it involved the whole stanitsa moving to the fields together with weapons as well as armed guards.[37] These conditions prevailed in the Don until the end of the eighteenth century and in the Kuban and Terek hosts until at least the 1860s while the new Cossack hosts continued to experience them right up to the end of the old regime. Even when an individual *voisko* ceased to be a frontier, commentators were struck at the small percentage of land that the Cossacks sowed compared to their peasant neighbours.

Because cereal agriculture was such a minor part of the Cossack economy for so long, there were few controls operating on the use of agricultural land. In the Don, land was allocated according to the principle of '*gde udobno, skol'ko udobno*' literally wherever and as much as convenient.[38] In the Kuban the only restriction on taking land was the rather vague injunction not to damage the interests of anyone else. In effect this allowed ambitious and powerful people to seize as much land as they wanted.[39] Similar systems operated in all the Cossack *voiska* and in the Ural, Amur and Ussuri hosts they were never abandoned. This system was open to all sorts of abuse, allowing individuals to seize far more land than they needed for their own use. Often, simply marking out the edge of area with a single furrow was enough to establish exclusive usage. Families also got into the habit of passing down land to the next generation even though technically it remained communal property.

While land remained in excess of demand this system of allocation and its abuses aroused few complaints. As the switch to arable farming gathered pace in the second half of the nineteenth century in response to the growth of population and the rising costs of military service, conflict over land allocation became intense. In the Don and Kuban, a movement for the reassertion of communal control over land developed into a very long and bitter campaign which left a long legacy of bitterness towards the elites.[40] Those who stood to lose by any reallocation resisted the change bitterly by whatever means were at their disposal – their wealth, their connections, patron client networks as well as more underhand means. A survey of the Don in 1874 found a widespread belief among the Cossacks that 'the land is not divided because of the wealthy'. In another stanitsa a few years earlier even the formal decision to reallocate land was no guarantee that it would be carried out:

> Originally the citizens agreed to divide the land on 27 October 1865 but when they set down to work out the division, they met extraordinary difficulties and obstacles. Several of the wealthy citizens who were against the division said 'our lives are at stake if the iurt is divided' and they tried by every means to hinder the division. They intended to ply the land surveyor with drink and steal the plans from him in order to delay the work and its completion by the appointed time. Because of this they only succeeded in completing the repartition in 1869.[41]

Ultimately, however, the principle that the land belonged to the community and that it should decide how its resources should be allocated prevailed in all the areas where it was tested. In the Kuban no less than the Don, the principle of communal ownership of land was so fundamental that in the end it could not be denied. That principle was felt almost viscerally by ordinary Cossacks as a leading nineteenth century historian of the Kuban Cossacks understood:

> The simple, rank and file cossack never knew the juridical points of the written legal code, but he understood well what this cossack land was that he used and his understanding of this subject was based on the right of collective ownership and use of land.[42]

The creation of new *voiska*

The middle years of the nineteenth century were years of uncertainty for the long established hosts. Paradoxically, these same years witnessed the unprecedented formation of new Cossack hosts in the still active frontiers of the empire. In 1851 the Transbaikal Host was created to be followed in 1858 by the Amur Host. In 1860 the separate Cossacks hosts forming the defensive lines in the North Caucasus were amalgamated into two basic hosts: the Terek and the Kuban. The Semirech'e Host was founded in 1867 and the Ussuri in 1889.

What lay behind this unprecedented expansion? The conquest of the Khanates of Bukhara and Khiva in the 1860s and the advance to the Chinese border in the 1870s brought vast new territories into the empire. These were occupied largely by nomadic peoples who resented and resisted Russian control. Securing these territories militarily and economically was going to be extremely expensive particularly for a government whose finances were always precarious and never more so after the Crimean War. Cossacks offered a cheap and effective solution to the problem securing the frontiers and supporting themselves at the same time. Creating new hosts had the additional advantage of allowing the government to strip out the many undesirable customs and practices of the existing hosts in theory at any rate.

Creating new hosts was not entirely novel. In the eighteenth century several new hosts had been established by the government. The Orenburg Host was created in 1736 while at the end of the century the Blacks Sea Host had been created from the remnants of the Zaporozhians and several thousand forcibly removed Don Cossacks became the Caucasian Line. All of these hosts, however, had at their kernel already existing Cossacks. They brought with them the habits, customs and expectations of their previous lives which the government had to take into account. The new hosts, however, were created out of a much more hetrogeneous mix. The Transbaikal Cossacks was formed out of Buriat Mongols, Chinese settlers, and 25, 000 peasants who overnight found themselves transformed into Cossacks.[43] The Semirech'e Cossacks had at their core two regiments from the Siberian Cossacks and 400 Chinese immigrants while a significant percentage of the Amur Cossacks was made up of penal battalions.[44] Often these new Cossacks were no more than bureaucratic reclassifications. The people involved had no knowledge of Cossacks or what the government now expected from them. When they did find out, not surprisingly they were deeply unhappy. Peasant migrants could also find themselves suddenly transformed into Cossacks. In 1846, 6,000 state peasants in Siberia were transformed into Cossacks with another 4,000 added two years later.[45]

Although the origins of all Cossack hosts was heterogeneous, those who had become Cossacks in the Don, Terek and Ural hosts had done so out of choice or had been born into long established communities. The new hosts, however, were formed out of people who had had little choice in the matter and were frequently extremely disgruntled with their new status. Establishing a strong corporate identity among these Cossacks proved to be extremely difficult. The frequent addition and subtraction of different groups did little to add to cohesion. The addition of a 2,000 strong echelon from penal battalions to the Amur Cossacks turned out to be an unmitigated disaster. The government had hoped that the influence of Cossack life would reform these reprobates. Unfortunately the moral influence was all in the other direction which the government belatedly recognized by removing the remnants of the penal battalions in 1879.[46]

The hetrogeneous nature of these Cossacks was not the sole inhibitor of a corporate identity. These new hosts often had few links between their individual settlements or an acknowledged centre to focus their identity. The Siberian Cossacks had at different times Omsk, Tomsk and Tobol'sk as their administrative centres. But these had never been Cossack towns and the Cossacks were simply one more branch of the provincial administration. Nor was their a distinct Cossack ataman to provide a personal focus of identity. Usually the governor doubled as the ataman which made the job of ataman a purely bureaucratic function and not one that resonated with charisma or a sense of history. Distances between settlements and tiny numbers of Cossacks compared to the territory as a whole further inhibited any sense of belonging to a collective organism wider than the immediate community.

These hosts founded by government initiative and regulated according to rules drawn up in central bureaucracies rather than local custom were much closer to *soslovie* than the Cossack hosts further west. This did not mean that their identity was immutable nor that a collective identity could not evolve, but time and stability were necessary for this. The routines of government administration, the continual identification of the host by its new name and the marking out of an official territory could subtly reinforce a new collective consciousness among the group as the Kuban Cossacks illustrated.

The Kuban Cossacks were made up of two separate hosts drawn largely from the Zaporozhian and Don Cossacks with other additions made along the way.[47] The Black Sea Cossacks (Zaporozhians) and the Caucasian Line Cossacks (Don) brought with them to the Kuban, strong pre-existing identities as Cossacks. From the 1790s to the 1860s these hosts were engaged in a bitter struggle with the peoples of the Caucasus. That seventy year struggle helped bond both Cossack hosts to their new homeland and to each other. The territory of the *voisko* was substantial but relatively compact. Furthermore, the Kuban Cossacks were the overwhelming majority of the population at the time of its formation in 1860. The Kuban Cossacks were neither lost in a territory so vast as to make them insignificant nor were they submerged in a much larger non-Cossack population. Unlike other newly created hosts, the Kuban Cossacks had a chief settlement, Ekaterinodar, that was originally an exclusively Cossack settlement. This provided a focus and a centre, giving a sense of coherence and unity for all the Cossack settlements in the Kuban. Over the half century between the foundation of the Kuban host and the First World War these earlier identities were overlaid with a strong collective Kuban identity.[48] A sure sign of that identity taking route was its celebration in song and folk tales of the Cossacks such as 'You Kuban, you – our Motherland'. By the end of the nineteenth century Cossacks in the Kuban answered retained an awareness of the different groups from which they had sprung, but routinely asserted that 'We are *Kubantsi*' (Kuban Cossacks).[49]

It suited the government's purposes to create groups whose only point of reference were those laid down for them by the government. The government had always wanted the military abilities of the Cossacks without the wilful nature that accompanied them. When it created new hosts, beginning with the Orenburg one in 1735, it deliberately excluded those features of Cossack life which it regarded as the source of all the problems. The Orenburg Cossacks had no general assembly nor did they have an ataman. Instead the Cossacks were subordinated to the governor of Orenburg who controlled the lines of communication between the different sections of the hosts. By inhibiting a collective identity the government hoped to avoid the sort of problems it had experienced with the Iaik and Don Cossacks. When the Zaporozhian Cossacks were refounded as the Black Sea Host, there was no place for the Assembly which had been the hub of the community's identity.[50] In this case and that of the Caucasian Line Cossacks the government did allow atamans for the whole host. The intensity of the conflict in the Caucasus and the absence of any other type of settlement, apart from the Cossacks, gave the government little choice but to accept atamans.

While careful to block central institutions or figures, the government did not regard elected assemblies which controlled the stanitsas as a threat. All the new Cossack settlements were administered by the community. Again given the weakness of the government in the frontier areas, it had little choice but to accept this old Cossack tradition. Individual stanitsas did not worry the government; only their ability to combine raised them to a real threat. The downside of this of course was that the esprit de corps which was key to the Cossack military prowess was considerably less among the new hosts. But to the government this reduction in military effectiveness seemed a worthwhile price to pay.

By the end of the nineteenth century the Cossack hosts had become ever more fragmented. The sense of kinship that the Don, Zaporozhian, Terek and Ural Cossacks felt for each other did not extend to the new hosts in the Far East. These hosts were estates in the real sense of the word. A Cossack identity had been imposed on them unlike the hosts that did not owe their existence solely to government action. These had much more robust Cossack identities and were much more intractable in their dealings with the government. However, as we have seen these lines were not clear cut as some hosts created by the government rapidly developed strong collective identities.

Conclusion

The Cossacks had recovered steadily from the suspicion and low esteem in which they had been held after the Pugachev revolt. Their service in the empire's wars against the Ottoman Empire and, above all, the Napoleonic Wars had lifted them out of their post-Pugachev pariah status to the most celebrated warriors in the empire. The tsars had even come to believe that a special link existed between the Cossacks and the throne which stood the Cossacks in good stead when they were faced with the reforming, rationalizing zeal of the bureaucracy in the second half of the nineteenth century.

Although the government did take a much closer interest in how ordinary Cossacks administered themselves, it never seriously attempted to transform the original Cossack hosts into estates. Rather it sought to regularize the procedures through which the Cossacks governed them-selves and give them a legal basis. This preserved the principle of demo-cratic administration among the Cossacks, which actually grew as the setting up of *khutora* continued unabated through the nineteenth century. Far from declining through the nineteenth century, the growth of popula-tion and the expansion of settlements had created a new potential for organization and mobilization in the Don and Kuban. The routine confirmation of the ties between the stanitsa and *khutor* through the meeting of the *sbor*, the election of the ataman, and the inclusion of the *khutor* in the stanitsa division land, gave institutional grounding to the deep ties of sentiment that existed for the stanitsa. Each *khutor* instinctively looked towards its own stanitsa for guidance and leadership. Because this leadership was elected by the Cossacks and because it was controlled by the *sbor*, Cossacks regarded the local administration based in the stanitsa as their administration not something foisted on them by outside agencies and therefore not dependent on that agency for survival. The significance of this would only become apparent during the civil war. None of this of course stopped the Cossacks complaining endlessly about the administration.

The expansion of the Cossacks in the nineteenth century had fragmented their identity and weakened any sense of unity embracing the entire caste. The links between the old Cossack hosts diminished and the free movement between them declined over the course of the nineteenth century. Nevertheless, the Don, Kuban, Terek and Ural Cossacks still recognized that they shared certain features in common which distinguished them from other peoples in the empire. However, between the old hosts centred in the North Caucasus and the Urals and the new ones in the east there was little in common apart from the name. Settlers from the old hosts often formed part of the new, but they were never the predominate part which might have helped established real links between the hosts in the west and east.

As the stability of the nineteenth century gave way to the turmoil of the twentieth, the Cossacks would face tests of far greater magnitude than anything they had faced before. Yet far from being transformed into estates wholly dependent on the state for their survival, the Cossack hosts in the North Caucasus and the Urals remained ones whose existence was rooted in their own traditions and history and their continuing autonomy which was both institutional and psychological. The remaining Cossack hosts, however, had far fewer autonomous resources to sustain them outside of the state.

Notes

1 Ovchinnikov, *Emel'ian Pugachev*, p. 246.
2 Shcherbina, *Istoriia Kubanskago Kazach'iago Voiska*, vol. 1, pp. 468–469.
3 Schcherbina, *Istoriia Kubanskago Kazach'iago Voiska*, vol. 1, p. 472.
4 Savel'ev, *Trekhsotletie Voiska Donskogo*, p. 94.
5 Svatikov, *Rossiia i Don*, pp. 234–238.
6 Shcherbina, *Istoriia Kubanskago Kazach'iago Voiska*, vol. 2, p. 623.
7 V.M. Bezotosnyi (ed.) *Otechestvennaia Voina 1812 goda* (Moscow, 2004) p. 252.
8 Bezotosnyi (ed.) *Otechestvennaia Voina 1812 goda*, pp. 251–253.

9 R.W. Wortman, *Scenarios of Power: Myth and Ceremony in Russian Monarchy* (2 vols, Princeton, 1995) vol. 1, p. 352.

10 Svatikov, *Rossiia i Don*, pp. 313–314.

11 For an extended discussion of the local administration of the Cossacks, see O'Rourke, *Warriors and Peasants*, pp. 102–133.

12 Svatikov, *Rossiia i Don*, pp. 379–381.

13 McNeal, *Tsar and Cossack*, p. 1.

14 McNeal, *Tsar and Cossack*, pp. 4–5.

15 Svatikov, *Rossiia i Don*, p. 348.

16 See for example, Svatikov, *Rossiia i Don*, pp. 3–4; McNeal, *Tsar and Cossack*, p. 84.

17 O'Rourke, *Warriors and Peasants*, p. 118.

18 E. Kotel'nikov, *Istoricheskoe Svedenie Voiska Donskogo o Verkhne-Kumoiarskaia Stanitse* (Novocherkassk, 1886) p. 20.

19 *Donskiia Oblastnyia Vedomosti*, 6 June 1879.

20 *Donskoi Vestnik*, 15 October 1869.

21 O'Rourke, *Warriors and Peasants*, pp. 112–114.

22 E.D. Felitsyn, *Kubanskoe Kazach'e Voisko 1696–1888* (Voronezh, 1888), p. 18.

23 Felitsyn, *Kubanskoe Kazach'e Voisko 1696–1888*, p. 159.

24 O'Rourke, *Warriors and Peasants*, p. 121.

25 *Donskaia Rech'*, 10 December 1891.

26 *Donskaia Rech'*, 19 November 1891.

27 Pronshtein, *Zemlia Donskaia*, pp. 58–59.

28 *Rossiiskii Gosudarstvennyi Voenno-Istoricheskii Arkhiv* (RGVIA) f.846, op.16, d.1872, l.21.

29 M. Kharuzin, *Svedenie o Kazatskikh Obshchinakh na Donu: Materialy dlia Obychnago Prava* (Moscow, 1885) p. 3.

30 Felitsyn, *Kubanskoe Kazache Voisko*, p. 61.

31 Shenk, *Kazach'i Voiska*, p. 112.

32 V.V. Glushchenko, *Kazachestvo Evrazii* (Moscow, 2002) pp. 135–138.

33 See for example, Felitsyn, *Kubanskoe Kazach'e Voisko*, p. 93.

34 Rozner, *Iaik Pered Burei*, pp. 55–56.

35 O'Rourke, *Warriors and Peasants*, pp. 64–69.

36 K.V. Markov, *Krest'iane na Donu* (Novocherkassk, 1915) p. 3.

37 Kotel'nikov, *Istoricheskoe Svedenie*, p. 26.

38 Kharuzin, *Svedenie o Kazatskikh Obshchinakh na Donu*, p. 10.

39 Tabolina, *Rossisskoe Kazachestvo*, p. 250.

40 Tabolina, *Rossisskoe Kazachestvo*, p. 252.

41 *Donskiia Oblastnyia Vedomosti*, 1 November 1875.

42 Felitsyn, *Kubanskoe Kazach'e Voisko*, p. 80.

43 Tabolina, *Rossisskoe Kazachestvo*, p. 362.

44 Glushchenko, *Kazachestvo Evrazii*, p. 138.

45 Astapenko, *Istorriia Kazachestva Rossii*, vol. 3, p. 368.

46 Astapenko, *Istoriia Kazachestva Rossii*, vol. 3, p. 403.
47 Shcherbina, *Istoriia Kubanskago Kazach'iago Voiska*, vol. 2, pp. 823–824.
48 N.I. Bondar' 'Kubanskoe Kazachestvo' in Bondar' '*Ocherki Traditsionnoi Kultury*', p. 243.
49 Tabolina, *Rossissikoe Kazachestvo*, p. 247.
50 Shcherbina, *Istoriia Kubanskago Kazach'iago Voiska*, vol. 1, p. 476.

6

Cossack women

Few societies have celebrated traditional masculine values as much as the Cossacks. The Cossack way of life was a paean to the physical and moral attributes of masculinity. Bodily strength, toughness and endurance alongside bravery, steadfastness and loyalty to ones brother Cossacks were the qualities that made a Cossack. Male dominance of Cossack culture, understandable enough in the military sphere, spilled over into the public life of the community; no women could be ataman, *esaul*, judge or even speak in the *sbor* as a right. Ostensibly at least women were relegated to the margins, confined by an inordinate male narcissism that could conceive of nothing finer than being a man and a Cossack man at that.

Paradoxically, it was a way of life wholly dependent on women for its survival. The Cossack woman or *kazatchka* was a towering figure in Cossack life to whom these most masculine of men deferred as a matter of course across a range of matters far exceeding the narrow spheres generally conceded to female control. If a Russian today is asked to describe a *kazatchka*, the list of adjectives used: *delovaia* (businesslike), *strogaia* (strict), *distsiplinirovannaia* (disciplined), *trudoliubivaia* (industrious) and so on invariably depict a woman who enjoyed the esteem of her community, including respect from the male half. The *Kazatchka* was the antithesis of the traditional peasant women, the *Baba*. *Baba* itself was demeaning, encapsulating the deeply misogynist view of women in rural Russia. While *Kazatchka* and *Baba* were stereotypes they do say something about the different values placed on women by Cossack and peasant communities.

Woman and the frontier

When the first self-conscious Cossack communities arose on the Don and the Dnieper steppe, there was no place for women among them. The original Turkic *qazaqi* had been warrior bands one of whose defining features was a rejection of the demands of home and family. The hazards of life on the steppe frontier attracted only the most restless and dissatisfied of men who retained few ties to the socieies they abandoned for the Cossacks. Scarcely any women from the settled Slavic areas then and not many more later made their way voluntarily to the Cossacks on the steppe. What probably began as a matter of practicality, rapidly became enshrined in Cossack custom. As early as the mid-sixteenth century women were forbidden to live among the Don and Zaporozhian Cossacks.[1] Later on in the century when the Terek and Iaik hosts came into being there were no women among them either. The absence of women was a matter of concern for the Muscovite and later imperial governments from the beginning. Ivan the Terrible supposedly ordered the Don Cossacks to marry, presumably to provide a source of replenishment other than his own subjects. The scarcity of women long remained a problem for all the Cossack hosts which the government periodically attempted to rectify without much success. In the eighteenth century the government offered to commute the death sentences of women convicted of murdering their husbands if they agreed to marry Cossacks on the Siberian or Terek frontiers which was hardly the most auspicious basis on which to build a relationship.[2]

Although the unceasing flow of fugitives constantly replenished Cossack ranks in the short term, in the long term depending on such an unstable and precarious source of supply threatened to make the Cossack communities of the steppe frontier as ephemeral as the pirate brotherhoods of the Carribean. Only with the arrival of women did Cossacks have the potential to evolve into something more than rather effective bandits.[3] Women were to be the means through which an indigenous Cossack population would be created and take root, knowing no life apart from that of a Cossack. Once this happened an unstable and potentially reversible identity hardened into a much more permanent and irreversible sense that Cossack was who you were not what you did.[4]

The exclusion of women from Cossack communities proved to be impossible to enforce absolutely. Joining a male brotherhood and revelling in the bonds of male companionship was all very well, but the desire and need for women remained strong. In a violent world and among men for whom violence was a way of life, the satisfaction of these desires took predictably violent forms. Adam Olearius, on his journey down the Volga in 1630, passed very close to the Don *voisko*. As they approached the government outpost of Tsaritsyn on the lower Volga he recorded in his diary:

Just below Tsaritsyn, on the right side, lies Sarpinski Island, 12 versts long. Here the streltsi pasture their cows and other cattle. Not long before our arrival, the Cossacks had observed that the wives and daughters of the streltsi daily crossed over to the island to milk the cows, often without guards; they lay in wait, seized and had their way with them, and then sent them unharmed back to the streltsi homes.[5]

More important to the future of the Cossack communities than these frenzied but brief encounters was the assimilation of one of the oldest traditions of steppe warfare by the Cossacks: the capture and abduction of women from their enemies.[6] Women were the most prized booty of the steppe whose intrinsic value was immeasurably heightened by the devastating humiliation their abduction inflicted on one's opponents. Although there are no specific or even vague dates for the permanent presence of women among the Cossacks, it is probable that women were present from the moment Cossacks began to raid the encampments of their nomadic neighbours sometime in the early sixteenth century. In other words, despite their formal exclusion, there were probably always women among the Cossacks even if only as part of the booty piled up after a successful raid. Within a few decades, the Don and Zaporozhian Cossacks bowed to the inevitable and accepted women among them. On the Don they became a part of the community, but the Zaporozhians found a solution that enabled them to preserve their male exclusivity while conceding to a Cossack the right to live with a woman. Women were banned only from the *Sich* itself, but Cossacks wishing to take wives and raise families or peasant fugitives arriving with families to live as Cossacks could do so outside of the *Sich*, giving rise to the settled Cossacks of Ukraine.

Seizing women from the nomadic peoples of the steppe and, in the case of Cossacks on the Terek, from the peoples of the North Caucasus decisively moulded an emerging Cossack culture. The Cossacks took women from the Nogai, Crimean Tatars, Kalmyks, Kirghiz, Chechen, Ingush, Ossetians and Kabardinians among others.[7] Steppe culture and fashion had already imprinted itself on the external aspect of the Cossacks in their dress, their weapons, parts of their speech, even their hairstyles. Already visibly alien to the Slavic cultures from which so many came, once Cossacks joined with women from the steppe, the influence of the common Turkic culture of the steppe took root at the very core of Cossack identity. Through these women, the Turkic and Slavic cultures merged creating the hybrid culture which gave the Cossacks their unique identity.

The influx of women from the indigenous societies of the steppe and the North Caucasus left a permanent mark even on the physiognomy of the Don Cossack host that was still visible in the nineteenth century. Bronevski in his history of the Don Cossacks published in 1828 noted the prevalence of dark eyes, dark skins and black hair particularly among the Cossacks of the lower Don. Two decades later a survey of the Don Cossacks commissioned by the General Staff again noted this legacy of the nomadic peoples.[8] Tolstoy during his stay among the Cossacks in mid-nineteenth century marvelled at the extraordinary beauty of the Cossack women of the Greben Host which was an off-shoot of the Terek Cossacks:

> The combination of the purest Circassian type of face with the broad and powerful build of the Northern women makes the beauty of the Greben women particularly striking. Cossack women wear the Circassian dress: a Tartar smock, the beshmet, and soft leather slippers; but they tie kerchiefs round their heads in the Russian fashion.[9]

There was even an echo of this genealogy in Sholokhov's great novel of the Cossacks in war and revolution not only in the fact of Turkic ethnicity in the ancestry of the hero Gregor Melekhov but in the way that ethnicity had been acquired as a result of the Russo-Turkic War of 1878:

> The Cossack Prokoffey Melekhov returned to the village during the last war with Turkey. He brought back a wife – a little woman wrapped from head to foot in a shawl. She kept her face covered, and rarely revealed her yearning eyes. The silken shawl was redolent of strange aromatic perfumes; . . .
>   Thenceforth Turkish blood began to mingle with that of the cossacks. That was how the hook nosed, savagely handsome cossack family of the Melekhovs nicknamed 'Turks', came into the village.[10]

These women brought and passed on to their children the cultural heritage of their societies which mingled with that of the Slavic ones. Although Turkic influence declined over time, it decisively shaped Cossack culture at its most malleable period, constituting an irreducible difference between the Cossacks and the societies around them.

However brutal their abduction and however alien the Cossack camp might seem to indigenous women taken in a raid, there was enough about the Cossacks that was familiar for them to seem an intrinsic part of the steppe world. Steppe women lived all their lives with the possibility of abduction and permanent removal to another society. Adapting to their new circumstances, however painful, was part of steppe tradition. Once children arrived most of these women had little choice but to reconcile themselves to their new homes. Whatever the idiosyncrasies of a particular society, all steppe societies had enough in common to facilitate this process. To their new Cossack homes, these women carried the values and assumptions of steppe society regarding women which were very different to those of a peasant society.

Nomadic women, as we have seen, at need protected their homes and fought alongside their men in defence of them. Cossack women stepped effortlessly into this familiar role. When the Cossacks captured Azov in 1637 and held it for four years against the mighty Ottoman Empire, Cossack women were prominent in the defence of the city. Rigel'man, writing a century and a half after the siege and basing his account on folk memories, wrote:

> During all these assaults, the women not only were unafraid to bring food, powder and other equipment, but also during the attacks hurled flaming barrels of pitch, hot oil, boiling water and other similar weapons. The women were no more afraid of bullets than they were of assaults. The Turks were no more able to defend themselves against the women than against their husbands.[11]

This was untypical only in that involved a full-scale siege by the most sophisticated military machine of the era. The circumstances in which Cossack women would routinely find themselves were on a smaller scale, but no less deadly for that.

Cossack stanitsas were frontier settlements exposed to all the dangers of the steppe frontier. Prolonged periods of male absence, sudden alarms as raiding parties were sighted placed women permanently at risk. The distinctions that settled society drew between war and peace or front and rear had no meaning on the frontier. Just as superfluous were traditional gender roles. Once the alarm had been sounded women and any able-bodied older men would bring the livestock into the stockade or hide them in the dense reeds of the river bank and await the attack of their enemies.[12] Sometimes raiding parties slipped through the various cordons undetected, descending on women working in the fields. But Cossack women were prepared for this as well:

> Cossack women in the absence of their husbands and fathers put on male clothing and repulsed attacks of enemies and also formed cavalry units etc. Even as recently as sixty years ago, going into the fields to work with scythes, pitchforks and rakes, the women also took weapons. In case of need at least one detachment of women transformed themselves into men and defended themselves courageously.[13]

These words described the lower Don at the beginning of the nineteenth century. Although the Don had officially ceased to be a frontier decades before this, it remained a dangerous place. The Cossacks along the Kuban and Terek rivers lived on an active frontier until the official ending of the war in the 1860s. In reality, raiding, seizing livestock and abducting women remained a feature of life into the 1920s. A Soviet official among the Terek Cossacks found himself living through what any Cossack settlement on the frontier might have experienced over the previous two hundred years:

> The life of the Russian population of all the stanitsas apart from Kabardia has become unbearable and is approaching the point of universal ruin and expulsion from the borders of the Mountain Republics. The complete economic ruin of the territory is caused by the daily raids and violence against the Russian population by the Chechen, Ingush and also the Ossetians. Going out for work in the fields even only 2–3 kilometres beyond the stanitsa is accompanied by the risk of being deprived of horses, spouse, tools and personal effects, of being stripped to the skin robbed and frequently being killed or driven off into captivity or slavery.[14]

Life on the frontier bred resolute, self-reliant, confident women just as it had among the nomadic women who were the first to live among the Cossacks. All Cossack hosts originated on the frontier and most remained frontiers until the end of the old regime. Nineteenth century creations such as the Amur, Semirech'e and Ussuri hosts placed women in the same positions they had been in on the Don, Dnieper, Terek and Ural.[15] Young Cossack men were nearly always on duty on the numerous picket lines and cordons of the frontier, returning home only briefly and irregularly. As the frontier and military service sucked men out of Cossack communities, it vacated wide spheres of activity and responsibility for women normally shut off to them.[16] The perils of the frontier, the needs of individual, household and communal security and economic survival fell squarely on the shoulders of Cossack women. In these circumstances it was hardly surprising that those shoulders turned out to be exceptionally broad.

Household and domestic economy

The hub of Cossack family life was the *kuren'* or hut and like other aspects of their domestic life was imprinted with the distinctive experience of the frontier and the prominence of women. *Kuren'* was not a Russian word, but derived from the Mongol word *kuriyen* meaning a defensive encampment of wagons drawn into a circle. It came to the Cossacks via

Figure 9 *Portrait of Cossack Girl L. Motorina* by V.I. Surikov

their steppe neighbours and is yet another example of how culturally porous steppe societies were in general and how open the Cossacks were to steppe culture in particular. With the adoption of a more sedentary lifestyle the *kuren'* took on new forms, becoming a permanent structure and able to adapt to the life cycle of the Cossacks. It was capacious enough to embrace the extended family and sufficiently flexible to survive as a nuclear unit. At different times it was both. At the heart of its life were women as grandmothers, mothers, wives and daughters. Men came and went according to the demands of military service, but women were an abiding presence.

Cossack women were faced with the responsibilities of running a household, bringing up children, working in the fields and, not infrequently, following a trade. A Cossack woman could be no more sure that there would be enough to eat in the coming year than a peasant woman. Yet for all the similarity of experience, the contributions of Cossack women to their way of life were filtered through a very different set of cultural assumptions; these were generated by the peculiar historical tradition of the Cossacks and the continued fact of life on a frontier. Peasant culture ruthlessly divided authority and labour within the peasant household so while women contributed an enormous amount of the latter they possessed very little of the former.[17] Authority to make decisions in all areas of life relating to the running of the farm, and in most other areas for that matter, was vested very firmly in the male head of household. Among the Cossacks any such separation of managerial powers from labour contribution was wholly notional. For much of the time there could be no such divisions since there was no-one to divide it between. The Cossack woman was in effect both manager and labourer.

All nineteenth century observers of Cossack life, regardless of the particular *voisko* commented on the extraordinary energy and drive of Cossack women. The official gazette of the Don *voisko* wrote:

> During the whole period the man finds himself on service, all male work and duties around the farm are carried out by the young wife who remains behind and is now mistress. The majority of Cossack women of the Transdon stanitsas work the land themselves. They sow the grain, they cut the hay with their own hands and manage the fisheries. Many of the women practice trades such as the making of fishing nets and agricultural tools, e.g. ploughs, harrows, carts and the other small tools necessary in an agricultural economy.[18]

This observation made in the late nineteenth century bore a striking resemblance to John of Plano Carpini's description of Mongol women in the thirteenth century. An observer on the Terek made the same point:

> A wife is the main wealth of a Cossack, from whence he receives his uniform, weapons and horse ... A wife in the economy and house is an Archimedes lever for him and he feels and sees her power everywhere. And woe to the Cossack who doesn't have such a wife! Then both in the house and in the field it is bad for him.[19]

Women of the Amur and Ussuri Cossacks found themselves in a similar position to those of the Don, Kuban and Terek in this respect.[20]

What distinguished a Cossack woman from peasant women was not so much the volume of labour contributed to the farm, but that the Cossack woman was the manager of the whole enterprise. She made the decisions about when to plant, when to harvest, when was the right time to sell and so on. She had to exercise her judgement, knowing that if she got it wrong her family and household faced ruin. When a Cossack returned from military service, it was impossible to push her aside and ignore her experience. Instead he found himself in a partnership with his wife and not necessarily the dominant partner at that:

> In order to judge correctly the division of labour in the Cossack family and the degree of intensity, it is necessary to watch and observe at length Cossack men and women at their work. The Cossack woman bakes the bread, cooks the dinner, milks the cattle and feeds the chickens and the swine. When she goes into the fields the work is carried out in a flash by her tireless hands. But the Cossack man if he comes to plough, ploughs less than a neighbouring peasant. If he goes to mow, he rests at every sheaf.[21]

The consequences of women's dominance of the Cossack domestic economy rippled through all areas of their lives. Women headed households when their husbands were absent and even when they were dead. Many peasant cultures were deeply troubled by women as heads of household and transferred authority to her adult sons or male relatives. Only if there were no adult males to take on this role did they reluctantly accept a woman as head of a household. For Cossacks, however, it was the norm. Even when there were adult, married sons living in the household it was the mother that became the the head.[22] Far better to have the farm run by an experienced, able woman than a less experienced, untested man.

When a woman became head of a household control over the common family property passed fully to her including the power to bequeath it to whom she wanted. Cossack custom was very unusual in placing such a high concentration of power in a woman's hands which she could use to reward, punish and control her adult children:

> 29 October 1880. I, the Cossack woman M.Z. with two sons S. and P.Z. and since my husband's death a widow, being of sound mind and firm memory have drawn up the following will. . . . This property which I have inherited and is mine by law is mine to manage as I see fit. Therefore I bequeath it forever to my son P.Z and his children. My other son S. and his family must not under any circumstances take legal action over my property since I have deprived him of his share on account of his disrespect for me.[23]

As in any peasant society, a share of the common family property made the difference between a tolerable life and years of impoverishment.

The sheer visibility and universality of women's dominance of the domestic economy shaped male perceptions of women far beyond narrow issues of economic competence. A exhaustive almanac of Cossack life produced by the Don Statistical Committee in the 1880s found that men, however grudgingly, were deferring to their's wives practical experience and organizational abilities. This was expressed by many seemingly insignificant tokens of respect such as addressing his wife by her name and patronymic. On a deeper level, Cossack men recognized the essential humanity of women which was far from universal among the peasantry.[24] Many Cossack proverbs extolled this companionate relationship between husband and wife: 'a wife is not a servant for her husband but a friend' or 'a female mind is the best of councillors'.[25] Proverbs of course express ideals rather than absolute reality, but it says much about attitudes to women that this was an ideal of that society.

When towards the end of the nineteenth century industrialization drew off millions of peasant men to the cities and peasant women were left in similar positions to Cossack women, their status too slowly began to rise.[26] But this had been a way of life for Cossack women from the very beginning and was an innate part of the tissue of Cossack experience, structuring the expectations and assumptions of generations of women and men. No matter which Cossack host one turned to, the descriptions and prestige of Cossack women were the same. We can end with a contemporary description of Cossack women in the Kuban in the nineteenth century which although sentimental reiterates the value of women for that society:

> . . . and the whole burden of civil life was placed on women. The *Kazatchka* of this time showed herself a kind of ideal person whose spirit did not fall under the heavy blows of the cruel Cossack fate. With unceasing fear in her heart for the life of her husband, children, and brothers serving on the line, she, this *kazatchka*, organized her domestic economy, ran the farm, comforted the elderly, guided adolescents, brought up the children and in general worried about creating a comfortable refuge which would be a joyful and bright picture in the mind of the Cossack while in the midst of military storms and demands.[27]

Family and household

Family life among the Cossacks did not get off to a very auspicious beginning as we have seen. The reluctance to have women among them, the general insecurity of life and the intense male bonding left little room for families. Most Don and Zaporozhian Cossacks when not on campaign lived out their lives in communal huts, again known as *kureni,* containing up to 200 or even 500 men. Even by the standards of the time, these dwellings must have been ghastly and were certainly not designed to encourage family life. Nevertheless as Cossack settlements took on more permanent forms in the seventeenth century the rudiments of family life did emerge.

The nomadic women seized in war or by raiding parties were the only source of partners for the first generations of Cossacks. Once Cossacks began to take more or less permanent partners as opposed to simply forcing themselves on women and then abandoning them, the exclusive male brotherhoods unravelled. From the eighteenth century onwards, the old communal huts gave way to individual dwellings which were more conducive to family life.[28] This was a long drawn out process with many men preferring the pleasures of communal living. When the remnants of the Zaporozhian Cossacks were reconstituted as the Black Sea Cossacks in the Kuban, single Cossacks again lived in a series of communal huts in the main settlement of Ekaterinodar just as they had done on the *Sich*. For the married men of Verkhne-Kumoiarskaia Stanitsa the attraction of the communal hut remained strong well into the eighteenth century especially when getting drunk. Angry women dragging their men out of the communal hut became a feature of stanitsa life.[29] The Cossack proverb 'the drunk Cossack is not afraid of his wife, but sleeps in the hayloft anyway' suggests that the stanitsa was not unique in this respect.[30]

The coarseness of life on the frontier did not lend itself to prolonged courtship or elaborate marriage ceremonies. What sources we have indicate that a Cossack simply lived with a woman without any formal recognition from the community or the Church. More elaborate ceremonies appeared to have developed first among the settled Ukrainian Cossacks where circumstances were rather more conducive to family life than among the Don and Zaporozhian communities. Beauplan in his description of Cossack life in Ukraine described Cossack ritual which although similar to peasant marriage customs was strikingly different in the prominence of the young woman in the process:

> In that country, contrary to the practice current in every [other] land, it is girls who are seen courting the young men who please them.
> ... Here is how these girls proceed. An amorous young lady goes to the father of the young man (whom she loves), at a time when she believes that the father, the mother, and her beloved will be together at home. Upon entering the house, she says, '*Pomahai Bih*,' meaning, 'May God bless you,' which is the usual form of greeting when one enters one of their homes. When she has sat down, she pays compliments to the one who has wounded her heart, and addresses him in these terms: 'Ivan,' 'Fedir,' 'Dmytro,' 'Voitek,'

'Mykyta,' etc . . . 'I recognize in your face something of an easy-going nature. You will know how to love your wife and govern her well, and your virtues make me hope that you will be a good hospodar. Your fine qualities lead me to beg you very humbly to accept me as your wife.' Having spoken thus, she addresses the father and mother in like terms, humbly requesting their consent to the marriage. However, if she receives a refusal or some excuse [or other], [perhaps], that he is too young and not yet ready for marriage, she answers them [saying] that she will not leave until she becomes his wife, as long as they are both alive.[31]

According to Beauplan, parents and fiancé eventually caved into to these strong-willed girls which makes one wonder who actually governed whom in these relationships. If Beauplan's account is accurate, and there is no reason to doubt it, the prominence of women in the marriage process began very early among the Cossacks and continued to the end.

Communal acknowledgement of relationships among the Don Cossacks began sometime in the seventeenth century for those Cossacks who felt a need for it, but it was not until the eighteenth century that marriage became common.[32] The first marriage ceremonies were secular affairs, involving only a brief declaration before the community. The man and woman approached the community gathered on the *maidan* and publically declared their intention to live as husband and wife. Offering up a short prayer, the couple bowed four times to each other and he said 'You, say you will be a wife to me' to which she replied 'You, say you will be a husband to me.' This somewhat minimalist ceremony ended with a flourish as the man cast his kaftan around the shoulders of the woman, signifying the completion of the marriage ritual.[33]

There was no sense that marriage implied any longer term commitment than the earlier arrangement of simply living together. Divorce was unproblematic and simply reversed the marriage ceremony. Husband and wife once again stood before the community only this time she was wearing his kaftan. He announced 'Honourable stanitsa, she is no longer a wife to me and I am not a husband for her' and as he finished speaking he removed his kaftan from her shoulders. Divorce continued to be common in Cossack societies well into the eighteenth century. The Church was noticeable only by its absence as few stanitsas had priests or churches before the eighteenth century and even when they did many Cossacks preferred their own ceremonies to those offered by the Church. When Razin captured Astrakhan in 1670 he introduced Cossack marriage ceremonies in front of oak trees and, despite the availability of sympathetic priests, promptly married off the daughters of the nobility to some of his followers according to Cossack rites.[34]

The development of more stable relationships of which marriage was an expression spread to the other Cossacks hosts as the wildness of the male, bachelor communities was gradually tamed by the growing presence of the Church among the Cossacks, the switch to agriculture as a means of making a living, and more onerous military obligations to the state. Stable families suited the Church, the government and offered the Cossacks the best means of paying for their military service. The ritual surrounding marriage steadily increased in complexity to mark its swelling significance in Cossack society. Ending a marriage at the drop of a kaftan had considerably more consequences towards the end of the eighteenth century than it had at the beginning. However, it is important to remember that these changes worked themselves out over a long period of time. In Verkhne-Kumoiarskaia Stanitsa a priest was permanently present from the 1720s, but the old civil marriage ceremonies survived until mid-century at least.[35] The old attitudes never completely died out, surfacing in attitudes to fidelity, divorce and remarriage.

By the nineteenth century marriage had become the paramount rite of passage in Cossack life. Complex inter-family negotiations, intricate rituals, the exchange of gifts and dowries, the payment of bride-price, known as the *kladka* and extensive celebrations replaced the earlier declaration made in front of the community. The rituals surrounding Cossack weddings were similar to peasant ones with the exception of the dominant role of Cossack women in the whole process.

The choice of a marriage partner was both a weighty and delicate matter for any family. Two families were entering into an alliance based on reciprocal obligations and expectations. Reputation, wealth, status, health were paramount considerations while the wishes of the two people being married came much farther down the list although this too became more important later on in the nineteenth century. Families, particularly parents, but also grandparents, uncles, aunts and godparents, had all to be consulted informally and formally at a family council. Unlike peasant families, however, the major players in the negotiations were the mothers of the prospective couple. When the anthropologist Mikhail Kharuzin worked in the Don in the 1870s he was told by Cossacks that in this matter 'the mother is the big person'.[36] In Tolstoy's account of the Greben Cossacks, women's control of the process was still more emphatic. The most delicate part of the negotiations that is the initial sounding out of whether a proposal would be welcomed or not was handled exclusively by the two mothers. Only when the two women had resolved everything to their satisfaction would the men be involved. Publically the man would be asked for his consent; privately he did what he was told:

> The teacher's wife knows what Luka's mother is after, and though she approves of Luka she hangs back: first because she is the teacher's wife and well to-do, whereas Luka is the son of a mere Cossack and a dead one at that; secondly because she does not feel ready to part with her daughter; but chiefly because propriety demands it.
>
> 'Yes when Marianka grows up 'twill be time enough to think of getting her wed,' she says with sober discretion.
>
> 'I'll go send the matchmakers round, that's what I'll do. Just let me get the vineyards done and then we'll come and wait on you,' says Luka's mother. 'We'll come and talk things over with your good man.'
>
> 'What's he got to do with it? I am the one you'll have to speak to,' says the teacher's wife haughtily. 'But all in good time.' [37]

Once a decision had been agreed in principle, a lengthy and frequently acrimonious dispute ensued over the precise contents of the dowry and the level of the bride-price. Usually bride-price is a payment made to the family of the bride to compensate for the loss of her labour. Under Cossack custom the bride-price went not to the bride's family but to the bride herself and in effect became a second dowry but this time paid for by the groom's family. The compiler of Cossack customs in the Don noted that 'the *kladka* always remains the property of the woman and even though she is a member of the husband's family, she can dispose of it as she sees fit'.[38] Cossack women, like peasant women, were extremely protective about their dowries, usually keeping it in a trunk that was permanently locked. Her new family had no access to it without her permission and only great need would force any decent family to ask the wife for the temporary use of its contents and always with the promise of replacing everything at the first opportunity. The sacrosanct nature of the dowry was one of the few rights that peasant women also could enforce against their families

Cossack women brought substantial dowries with them. Apart from the physical objects in the trunk, families gave their daughters livestock, tools, property; in short, they gave daughters a full share of the family property.[39] The main difference from her brothers was the timing of the inheritance: she received hers at her marriage while they received theirs when the parents died. The generosity of dowries affirmed the high abstract value placed on women, but on a more intimate level bore witness to the enduring ties between women and their natal families after her marriage. There is no evidence to suggest that Cossack girls were regarded as transient members of the family by her parents nor that they saw it as their chief task to marry her off at the minimum cost to themselves. On the contrary, the norm was for a daughter to remain extremely close to her own family even while she lived with her husband's family. Once she and her husband set up on their own, the absolute priority of her husband's family over her own receded.

The cost of a Cossack wedding was on a par with the costs of military service. The two great worries of any father were having enough money to put his son through service and to pay for his wedding.[40] All the costs of the wedding were borne by the bridegroom's family apart from the dowry which as we have seen they had no access to. The costs of a wedding were a sore blow to family finances particularly as many marriages took place only days or weeks before the son's departure for service: the two most expensive moments of Cossack life literally falling within days of each other. Some outside observers bemoaned the extravagance of Cossack weddings and rather unrealistically called for government action to limit the costs of them:

> Cossack weddings are extremely ruinous for the family of the man. Expenditure on the wedding feast and other necessities gets completely out of hand. . . . If the government does not turn its attention to this foolish custom and take measure to abolish it then sooner or later the majority of Cossacks will be reduced to poverty if a wedding is accompanied by a bad harvest or a cattle plague.[41]

But parsimony at a wedding would have been inconceivable for a Cossack family. No amount of money would have been worth the stigma and shame that would have inevitably followed the family around for years afterwards.

The first few years of a married couple's life were usually spent in the household of her husband's parents as part of an extended family. The extended household was not without benefits for a young woman. It offered economic security, a larger number of working hands and so less work, and a general sense of companionship. Nevertheless the extended household held many trials for a new wife; she was a stranger in the family, she had to adapt to their ways, she was under the authority of her mother-in-law, and she became the general dogsbody for the family. At its worst she could find herself the victim of unwanted sexual advances from other men in the family, particularly her husband's father. The anxiety that anyone would have felt moving into a new family was intensified for a new bride as her husband often departed for service within days of marriage. That was the last she would see of him for the next three years. This was no less true among the new hosts of the Far East as it was among the older hosts.[42] However kind her new family were, the emotional isolation and psychological readjustments required made those three years among the most difficult of any woman's life.

Not surprisingly, most women pressurized their husbands to set up their own households as soon as possible. Whatever the disadvantages of a nuclear household in terms of economic security and extra work, they were more than compensated for by the chance to be mistress within her own house. Not that Cossack men needed much persuading either. Most of them by the time they came back from military service chaffed at the thought of subordinating themselves once more to their fathers:

> As is well known, among us a large number of young Cossacks leave the family home on their return from service during which they strive by every means to gather the wherewithal to be their own masters. And so intoxicated with sweet hopes, the Cossack returns from service. But after a few days he is rudely awakened when he discovers that his dreams cannot become reality because his father has rented his share of land for the whole period of division.[43]

It did not always work out the way the son and his wife wanted. The timing of the division of a household was matter of persuasion, cajoling and compromise, but the desire to be one's own master and mistress could rarely be thwarted for long. The automatic right to a share of communal land undermined the will of even the most patriarchal fathers. In the example quoted above, one suspects that ways of circumventing the renting out of land were found and while they waited, the authority of the father would never be what it had been before. Most fathers eventually accepted the break up of their household.[44] They could not look to the community to keep the household together as a peasant father could, since the Cossacks regarded household division as private matter. In the end most allowed their sons to go their own way and the family cycle would begin again. Such was the underlying rhythm of Cossack life from generation to generation.

Relations between women and men

Cossack men and women encountered each other through idioms and modes of behaviour that differed significantly from modern Western society. Cossack tradition and life had their share of antagonism between the sexes which could be seen in its folklore, stories and observations of outside observers. Much that appears crude or boorish to us, particularly metaphors drawn from the farmyard which was natural enough in a peasant society, operated on a register different from ours. Cossack men feared domination by their women and yet understood their dependence on women. A Cossack might worry about who wore the trousers, but knew the truth of the proverb that 'the Cossack sits proudly in the saddle, but his wife holds the reigns in her hands'. Understanding that register on the basis of incomplete and scattered information is extremely difficult. Yet the majority of the evidence points unmistakeably to a culture that valued women for far more than their labour contributions. It was this above all that distinguished Cossack women from their peasant counterparts.

Tolstoy wrote of the Greben women that 'In their relationships with men the women, and especially the unmarried girls, are completely free.'[45] Many other writers were struck by the level of informality with which men and women habitually interacted. The easy social exchanges, the robust and frequently ribald banter between men and women, the presence of women in all aspects of economic life and the constant dealings of women with men outside their families and households allowed for much less inhibited encounters between men and women. The strict supervision that

Figure 10 *Azov Cossacks Boarding a Turkish Corsair full of Cherkessk Women on the Coast of the Black Sea,* by Adolphe Bayot (engraving)

was maintained over women and girls of the peasantry in the central Russian provinces had no place on the frontiers. With so many men absent for so long and with so many women heads of households in the absence of their husbands, the mechanisms for controlling women were much more limited. This extended even as far as sexual relationships outside marriage. Unlike the peasantry who regarded deviations from sexual norms as a public matter and severely punished them, the Cossacks in almost all cases preferred to see it as private matter which was up to the individuals to sort out.[46] As an individual a Cossack man, or woman for that matter, might react with extreme violence to infidelity, but the community as a whole seemed wearily resigned to it.

The rhythms of Cossack life left most adult women without their husbands for many months or even years at a time. The first time a husband rode off to the army was usually within days of marriage. As well as the first absence, it was also the longest. Three years he was away without leave, serving somewhere within the empire. Later, every year until he was thirty, summer camps took men away for at least a month while war could take men away at any time indefinitely. Probably some women welcomed these absences, but for most the departure of men brought extra work, more responsibility and ceaseless worry. The emotional costs of military service to a Cossack family were less written about than the military ones, but they were at least as high. Grandparents, parents and wives accompanying the young Cossacks leaving for service to the edge of the stanitsa were acutely aware that for some it could well be the final parting. The Cossack writer Feodor Kriukov caught the terrible poignancy of separation in one of his stories of Cossack life. A student in St Petersburg returning home to his stanitsa brought letters and presents from the Cossacks serving in the capital:

> He was forced to spend two whole days distributing these letters and parcels, drinking vodka, talking with the old men, comforting the old women who poured out tears over their own sons in spite of all his assurances that they all were living and healthy and safe, thanks be to God. But it was incomparably more difficult to satisfy the questions of the Cossack wives – the *odnosumki* [see below] – who came separately from the old men and women and who interrogated him in such unimaginable detail about their husbands that the dismayed student could either say nothing at all or else in despair lied mercilessly.[47]

The return of men from the army, especially those who had completed their first turn of service, was a momentous day in the life of the stanitsa and a real theatrical spectacle. News of the imminent arrival of the Cossacks would reach the stanitsa a day or so ahead. As the hour approached, the church bells would ring out and the whole stanitsa in holiday dress and carrying bread and salt, the traditional tokens of welcome, would walk out to the edge of the settlement to meet the returning men. *Donskaiia Oblastnyia Vedomosti* described one such return:

> Women with bouquets in their arms, clergy with banners and icons, grey-haired old Cossacks, deputies from the stanitsa with bread and salt, all went to meet the regiment which two years previously had been sent off by the same inhabitants.[48]

Parents, relatives and friends would all wait impatiently for their men to return, but the central drama was reserved for the meeting between wives and husbands. Dozens of mounted men in dress uniform would sweep into the stanitsa and as their wives bowed down before them, the passing Cossack, leaning down from his horse, swung his wife up on to his saddle as only a Cossack could. Flush with the accumulated pay of three years, the Cossack showered his wife with presents. A church service giving thanks for their safe return was followed by an extensive round of celebrations, often lasting several days before life slowly returned to normal.

Not all homecomings had such happy ends. Many ended in bitter grief and sometimes violence as men gave vent to what they knew or what they suspected about their wives' behaviour in their absence. For often emotionally isolated and always relatively free, many Cossack women took lovers. In Tolstoy's village among the Greben Cossacks there were several adulterous relationships going on fairly openly while in Sholokhov's great novel of the Don Cossacks the plot hinges on one of the most passionate relationships in Russian literature: the adulterous one between Gregor and Aksinia. It might be objected that these were novelist's devices for heightening drama and said nothing about the generality of Cossack life; except that they are supported by academic, anthropological and contemporary press accounts of Cossack custom. Kharuzin with considerable restraint wrote 'Betrayal of marital fidelity in Cossack custom is, generally speaking, by no means rare.'[49] Tom Barrett's findings support Tolstoy's description of the relaxed attitude to fidelity among the Cossacks:

> There was also, according to many observers, a loose sexual ethic among the Terek Cossacks. The evidence is rather sketchy, as it would be, but according to an officer who lived among the *Grebentsy*, married Cossack women and men kept 'lovers' in the open. They were called 'side' (*pobochnyi*) wives or husbands.[50]

Relationships that were visible to outsiders were hardly going to be secret from the members of the community. Like all face-to-face communities, Cossack stanitsas and *khutora* were hotbeds of gossip, rumour and inuendo which soon made any affair common knowledge. These rumour networks extended to absent husbands on service where news of home and family would regularly arrive by post. Malicious or interfering relatives and neighbours took it upon themselves to pass on any salacious gossip either directly to the husband or to one of his comrades, knowing full well that it would soon reach him. By the time a man's unit returned after a prolonged absence, little his wife had done would be a secret to him.

The sense of expectation that hung over the return of the soldiers was obviously heightened for those spouses who had scores to settle with each other. Kharuzin wrote that women who had been unfaithful received very different treatment on the great entry of Cossacks into the stanitsa. Instead of swinging her up on to his horse, the man would ride brusquely past without glancing at her, humiliating her in front of the whole stanitsa. Worse was to follow. '. . . if he had found out about her unfaithfulness he rode past, giving the appearance of not noticing her. After this public disgrace a beating would follow which would be carried out in the *kuren'*.'[51]

At this most tense of moments, however, the husband found himself under intense pressure to soften his rage. If his wife kneeling before him as he rode by implored his forgiveness, the husband nearly always relented and pulled his wife up on to his horse as all the other men were doing, publically signalling the reconciliation of husband and wife. Other men or relatives would also intervene on behalf of the wife. A comrade might remind him of his own sexual liaisons while away on service or some of the older men would point out that only God was without sin: 'who hasn't sinned against God; the green vine is not sweet nor a young mind strong, you can't punish someone severely for this.'[52] From all sides the couple were urged to leave the past behind them and get on with life. The official gazette of the Don *voisko* understood the contradictory pressures for vengeance and reconciliation that were at play here:

> As the time for the husband to return from service draws near, it happens that he waits impatiently for the day when he can see his better half. But when he arrives home not only does he not pay his wife back for the infidelity, he also does not raise his hand to strike her, but turns from ferocity and anger to love and kindness.
>
> Several of these unfaithful wives and mistresses end their affair when their husband returns and again become good wives and mistresses. But others

became accustomed to freedom during their husband's absence and neglect all their duties in the home and in the field.[53]

Men had affairs as well of course. While some women acquiesced in their husband's affairs many others reacted angrily even violently:

> If the husband is unfaithful the wife will destroy his lover in the end. She breaks her windows, smashes her porch, encourages young boys to cut the tails of her cows and to smear tar over her home and on a dark night will beat her severely so she should not take someone else's husband.[54]

But even this was a private matter that the community was distinctly reluctant to involve itself. The relative tolerance of the Cossacks for adultery was not born out of any enlightened attitudes to sexual freedom, but came from an unstated recognition that it was a humdrum part of their lives which there was no way of eliminating without tearing the community apart. Unable to suppress it, they had to find some way of coping with it. By choosing to look upon it as a misdemeanour rather than a heinous moral and religious transgression, it left open the way for reconciliation and the restoration of stability.

Cossack women were neither passive victims nor sexual predators. They were women of the frontier whose lives were a mixture of great responsibility and comparative freedom. Just as in other areas of life they exercised choice and made decisions, so they did in this most intimate area of human relations. What was unusual was not the fact of illicit sexual relations or how individuals reacted to them, but that women enjoyed a similar degree of freedom to men in choosing whether or not to avail themselves of the opportunity.

Female sociability

Although members of the immediate family and wider kinship networks had the primary claims on women's attention and time, the horizons of Cossack women, as in other spheres of life, extended beyond the narrow framework of household and family. Many traditional societies provide neither space nor time for women to form relationships beyond these boundaries. Cossack women, however, had the possibility to create powerful networks of solidarity and support based once again on the peculiarities of life on the frontier.

Cossack boys setting off from the stanitsa to start their military service had traditionally formed lifelong friendships with each other. As sign of trust they had placed all their valuables in one bag. This custom became an institution among the Cossacks which was known as *odnosumptsvo* (literally one bag). Lesser but still powerful networks of friendship were formed with men who served in the same regiment who referred to each other as *polchaniki*. What is less well known is that Cossack women also created these networks of support and obligation with the wives of men leaving for service together and with wives of men who were serving in the same regiment:

> It is well known that when Cossacks leave for service, they are sent off at the same time to a particular regiment and by an ancient custom refer to each other as '*odnosumki*'. Similarly their wives when seeing off their husbands by the same custom also address each other as '*odnosumki*'. From this time they are closely acquainted and for many this acquaintance began as a young woman, little by little is transformed into a close friendship for life.
>
> When travelling from the *khutor* to the stanitsa a Cossack woman counts it her greatest pleasure to catch sight of her *odnosumki*, usually as they come out of church after service. Here on the porch they question each other eagerly. Has anyone received a letter from the men on service? Who and when exactly? Are the men in good health? It goes without saying that the mothers of the men on service participate happily in this question and answer session.
> . . .
> In such a way on almost every holiday and Sunday or leaving Church or sometimes after dinner either in the house or at the local store, the *odnosumki* of one regiment gather along with their mothers and the simply curious where frequently apart from the chat about the news from service, they read out their letters.[55]

In the market place where arguments between groups of women were common, women who were *odnosumki* or *polchaniki* invariably supported each other as Kharuzin recorded: 'You're no relative to me, but she is my *polchanka* – it's necessary to respect her.'[56]

Female *odnosumki* and *polchaniki* took their attachments to each other just as seriously as men did. The quarrel recorded by Kharuzin clearly implied that both types of relationship were forms of fictive kinship. These relationships offered emotional support and sustenance that were all the more valuable since they came free of the complications and problems that came with family relationships to say nothing of those with lovers. In Kriukov's story the intense bonding between the women is evident from the desire to question the student separately from the wider family but with each other. As well as providing obvious benefits to women themselves, the autonomy embodied in such relationships was both a consequence and another marker of the status of women in Cossack life.

No men participated in these sessions or watched over them. They were areas of exclusive female sociability which reinforced a mutual sense of dignity and solidarity.

Conclusion

The unique Turkic/Slavic culture and the exigencies of life on the frontier produced the distinctive identity of the Cossacks. An intrinsic component of that identity were the Amazonian women who made up half the Cossack community. Women carried the economic costs of the Cossack system throughout their adult lives. For much of that time they had male support, but often it was alone. They became the key decision makers in the Cossack economy which the society accepted and acknowledged. Without women the Cossack way of life would have collapsed immediately: that it survived for so long was in no small way due to the Herculean efforts of Cossack women.

The economic contribution of women alone does not explain their standing. Peasant culture recognized that no peasant farm could survive without a woman, but in the same way that it calculated a viable farm needed a horse or bullock. The wider culture conceded only the most minimal spheres of authority to women based on their economic contributions. What Cossack women did, however, was refracted through a set of values and assumptions that valued them as people not just for their draught power. These in their turn derived from the nomadic heritage of the Cossacks and the realities of life on the frontier. The frontier forced women to take responsibility for economic decisions, the defence of the community and the preservation of the Cossack way of life. Equally it forced men to accept that wide swathes of their life outside military service were controlled by women who possessed clear notions of what was their territory and defended it from male intrusion. Often a public veneer of male dominance masked a process that was essentially female in organization and control. Inheriting from their nomadic ancestors certain assumptions about women, the experience of the frontier sustained and extended those assumptions, embedding them deeply in Cossack culture. Cossack women used their unique position to demarcate autonomous spheres of female activity to which their men acquiesced. These areas were considerably broader than in peasant Russia. Women paid a high price for their status not just in ceaseless labour but in the emotional costs that the system imposed on them as well. Women were not equal with men, but the degree of inequality was substantially less than in the wider peasant

society. Authoritative, powerful, and assertive, the *Kazatchka* defined
Cossack identity as much as the horseback warrior pursuing glory across
the endless steppe. Indeed on occasion it was the warrior who found
himself mastered:

> The Cossack Vasilli Alexandrenko summonsed Marfa Alexandrenko for non-
> payment of 75 roubles for work carried out over half a year. During the
> investigation it emerged that Vasilli and Marfa were husband and wife. Marfa,
> after six months of married life, decided that she no longer wanted to live with
> her husband and drove him out of their house. The court decided in the
> plaintiff's favour. Vasilli was to receive 60 roubles from Marfa Alexandrenko
> for six months work based on the average annual wage of a hired hand.[57]

Notes

1 Shcherbina, *Istoriia Kubanskago Kazach'iago Voiska*, vol. 1, p. 437.
2 Adirov, *Istoriia Kazachestva Kazakhstana*, p. 113; Barrett, *At the Edge of Empire*, p. 132.
3 Shcherbina, *Istoriia Kubanskago Kazach'iago Voiska*, vol. 1. p. 461.
4 Shcherbina, *Istoriia Kubanskago Kazach'iago Voiska*, vol. 1, p. 461.
5 Baron (ed.) *The Travels of Olearius in Seventeenth Century Russia*, p. 319.
6 Shcherbina, *Istoriia Kubanskago Kazach'iago Voiska*, vol. 1, p. 462.
7 See for example, Shcherbina, *Istoriia Kubanskago Kazach'iago Voiska*, vol. 1, p. 462.
8 V. Bronevski, *Istoriia Donskogo Voiska* (3 vols, St. Petersburg, 1834) vol. 3, p. 123; RGVIA, f.846, op.16, d.18721, l.112.
9 L.N. Tolstoy, *The Cossacks*, trans. R. Edmonds (Harmondsworth, 1960) pp. 180–181.
10 M. Sholokhov, *And Quiet Flows the Don*, trans. S. Garry (Harmondsworth, 1967) p. 13.
11 Rigel'man, *Istoriia o Donskikh Kazakakh*, pp. 82–83.
12 Bronevski, *Istoriia Donskogo Voiska*, vol. 3, p. 95.
13 *Donskaia Rech'*, 3 July 1888.
14 RGASPI, f.64, op.1, d.247, l.109.
15 G.G. Ermak, *Semeinyi i Khoziaistvennyi Byt Kazakov Iuga Dal'nego Bostoka Rossii: Vtoraia Polovina XIX–Nachalo XX Veka* (Vladivostok, 2004) p. 91.
16 Shcherbina, *Istoriia Kubanskago Kazach'e Voiska*, vol. 2, p. 830.
17 C.D. Worobec, *Peasant Russia: Family and Community in the Post-Emancipation Period* (Princeton, 1991) p. 204.
18 *Donskiia Oblastnyia Vedomosti*, 18 July 1876.
19 Barrett, *At the Edge of Empire*, p. 135.
20 Ermak, *Semeinyi i Khoziaistvennyi Byt Kazakov*, p. 91.
21 *Donskiia Oblastnyia Vedomosti*, 1 October 1881.

22 Kharuzin, *Svedenie o Kazatskikh Obshchinakh*, p. 205; Nomikosov, *Statisticheskoe Opisanie*, p. 321; *Donskoi Vestnik*, 11 August 1869.
23 Kharuzin, *Svedenie o Kazatskikh Obshchinakh*, p. 241.
24 Nomikosov, *Statisticheskoe Opisanie*, p. 322.
25 Makhnenko, *Donskoi Fol'klor*, pp. 211, 221.
26 B.A. Engel, *Between the Fields and the City: Women, Work, and Family in Russia, 1861–1914* (Cambridge, 1994) pp. 55–59; Worobec, *Peasant Russia*, pp. 203–204.
27 Felitsyn, *Kubanskoe Kazach'e Voisko*, p. 228.
28 Bronevski, *Istoriia Donskago Voiska*, vol. 3, p. 146.
29 Kotel'nikov, *Istoricheskoe Svedenie*, p. 15.
30 Makhnenko, *Donsksoi Fol'klor*, p. 223.
31 Beauplan, *Description of Ukraine*, pp. 70–71.
32 Kotel'nikov, *Istoricheskoe Svedenie*, p. 7; Bronevksi, *Istoriia Donskogo Voiska*, vol. 3, p. 123.
33 Bronevski, *Istoriia Donskogo Voiska*, vol. 3, p. 123.
34 Chistiakova, *Stepan Razin i ego Soratniki*, p. 47.
35 Kotelnikov, *Istoricheskoe Svedenie*, p. 15.
36 Kharuzin, *Svedenie o Kazatskikh Obshchinakh*, p. 116.
37 Tolstoy, *The Cossacks*, p. 185.
38 *Donskoi Vestnik*, 18 March 1868.
39 O'Rourke, *Warriors and Peasants*, pp. 158–159.
40 Kharuzin, *Svedenie o Kazatskikh Obshchinakh*, p. 116.
41 *Donskoi Vestnik*, 25 March 1868.
42 Ermak, *Semeinyi i Khoziaistvennyi Byt Kazakov*, p. 90.
43 *Donskiia Oblastnyia Vedomosti*, 17 July 1876.
44 Kharuzin, *Svedenie o Kazatskikh Obshchinakh*, p. 235.
45 Tolstoy, *The Cossacks*, p. 181.
46 O'Rourke, *Warriors and Peasants*, pp. 164–165.
47 F.D. Kriukov, 'Kazatchka' in *Rasskazy Publitsistka* (Moscow, 1990) p. 28.
48 *Donskaiia Oblastnyia Vedomosti*, 11 October 1878.
49 Kharuzin, *Svedenie o Kazatskikh Obshchinakh*, p. 180.
50 Barrett, *At the Edge of Empire*, p. 134.
51 Kharuzin, *Svedenie o Kazatskikh Obshchinakh*, p. 182.
52 Kharuzin, *Svedenie o Kazatskikh Obshchinakh*, p. 183.
53 *Donskiia Oblastnyia Vedomosti*, 9 July 1876.
54 *Donskiia Oblastnyia Vedomosti*, 9 July 1876.
55 *Donskiia Oblastnyia Vedomosti*, 14 May 1880.
56 Kharuzin, *Svedenie o Kazatskikh Obshchinakh*, p. 85.
57 E.I. Iakushkin, *Iuridicheskie Poslovitsy i Pogovorki Russkogo Naroda* (Moscow, 1885) p. 216.

7

Economic crisis and revolution

In its annual report on all the Cossack hosts for 1873 the War Ministry summarized government policy on the Cossacks as 'the unification of the Cossacks in their civilian life with the rest of the population and the formation from the Cossacks of such military forces as can compare with the regular army in case of a European War'.[1] There was nothing particularly new about this policy. In fact it merely reformulated in more modern idiom the fundamental objective of all government policy towards the Cossacks since the time of Ivan the Terrible: the harnessing of Cossack military prowess to the needs of the state while simultaneously reducing them to the same degree of subordination as the rest of the population.

As we have seen, by the end of the nineteenth century many contemporaries believed that the Cossack *voiska* west of the Ural Mountains had indeed been subdued and transformed into the obedient servitors so long desired by the government. Stripped of their former freedoms and subject to endless regulations emanating from St Petersburg, the Cossacks had become an estate in much the same way as the clerical, merchant and noble estates had long been. Ivan the Terrible's desire to make the Cossacks loyal and obedient servitors appeared to have become reality by the reign of the last two tsars, Alexander III and Nicholas II.

The triumphs of the state, however, were more ephemeral than anyone expected. From the late 1870s a debilitating economic crisis and growing opposition to the forms of service carried out by the Cossacks subverted the whole process of integration. What began in the 1870s with entreaties for subsidies to help with the costs of military service ended during the 1905 Revolution in mutiny and demands for the restoration of Cossack autonomy under the aegis of the State Duma. Even the re-establishment of tsarist power from 1907 onwards could not return the empire as a whole to the status quo ante. Nor could it erase the experience of the revolution or the possibilities opened up by it from the collective memory of the Cossacks.

Cossack military service

The terms of Cossack service were largely uncodified until the nineteenth century. The first attempt at codification in 1802 simply gave existing practice the force of written law; a Cossack was liable for service anywhere, at any time between the ages of twenty and fifty.[2] In 1835 the government took the first tentative steps to regulating the uniform and equipment of the Cossacks. Evidently little had been achieved in this regard two years later when Nicholas I took the review of Cossack regiments in Novocherkassk. As a rustic parade unfolded in front of him Nicholas remarked in disgust: 'I expected to see 22 Cossack regiments, but saw only muzhiks.'[3] After this the government took a much livelier interest in the equipment and appearance of the Cossacks. Despite this Cossack service remained recognizably what it had been down to the last quarter of the nineteenth century. A new law on military service in 1875 marked a radical departure from what had gone before.

The new law was part of the root and branch reorganization of the empire that had been ongoing since the Crimean War. To the reformers in the War Ministry the Cossack system seemed typical of the ramshackle nature of the Russian army that had failed so calamitously in the Crimean War. Many within the ministry even believed that the Cossacks had

Figure 11 *One for the Road*, by S. Gavriliachenko, 1999

outlived their usefulness and should be abolished. Even though it drew back from this most radical option, the ministry was determined that the Cossacks would be integrated much more closely with the regular army and that differences in service terms between the Cossacks hosts were to be eliminated as far as possible.[4]

The law reorganized and standardized Cossack service, establishing three basic categories: preparatory, active and reserve. Preparatory service lasted for three years and was intended to produce a fully trained cavalry trooper who could be integrated immediately into active service units. Active service was divided into three 'turns' of four year durations. On entering the first turn of active service, a Cossack had to provide himself with a horse, a uniform, a sabre and a lance. This period of service was always spent away from the Cossack's native *voisko* if it was one that was no longer a frontier and could be anywhere in the empire or outside it in the event of war. The second and third turns were spent at home on what was termed 'privileged service'. A Cossack on the second turn of service had to maintain a war horse and uniform which was inspected twice a year. On the third turn he only had to have access to a horse in the event of mobilization. All Cossacks on privileged service had to attend a training camp every summer for about a month.[5] The government intended to mobilize these units in the event of an emergency, but the Cossacks understood this more narrowly as mobilization in the event of war. This difference in understanding was to have important consequences. After completing three turns of active service, a Cossack spent five years in the reserves and then passed into the militia. Neither of the last two categories had much practical significance.

In the years after the introduction of the new law the first evidence of a crisis in the Cossack system began to appear. A system that was supposed to be self-financing soon required substantial amounts of outside aid. In 1878 Don Cossacks on privileged service were mobilized for war against the Ottoman Empire plunging the whole system into crisis. Many families were deprived of their only adult male labourer and less than half of the Cossacks mobilized from the third turn had access to a horse as required by law.[6] Only emergency aid of 225,000 roubles from the state and desperate selling off of livestock, the working capital of their farms, tided the Cossacks over.[7] The ministry might have been tempted to put the crisis down to teething troubles, but subsequent mobilizations, even partial ones, produced the same problems. In 1895 the government mobilized Cossacks on privileged service from the Don, Kuban and Orenburg hosts to take part in military exercises in Smolensk, but again substantial subsidies had to be paid to the families of mobilized men.[8] During the Russo-Japanese War 100 roubles was paid out to every Cossack mobilized from privileged service.[9]

There was evidence, however, of an even more fundamental malaise within the system. Local commentators repeatedly noted the growing impoverishment of the Cossacks and the difficulties they were having fulfilling their service obligations. Poor harvests, often several in a row, became a routine feature of life in all the Cossack hosts. By the start of the 1880s all the Cossack *voiska* in European Russia were suffering a string of poor harvests. In its account for 1881 the War Ministry wrote:

> The beginning of the present year was altogether difficult for all the Cossack hosts of European Russia and in particular for the Ural and parts of the Orenburg and Astrakhan hosts as a consequence of the complete harvest failure in 1879 and of the unusually dry winter of 1879/80.[10]

The ministry was beginning to understand that there was something seriously wrong, but it saw the problem in the way Cossacks farmed the land not in the demands that military service was placing on them. Writing specifically about the Don, but with clear reference to the entire steppe zone the ministry reported:

> Although in the present case the reason for the harvest failure was fortuitous, nevertheless it cannot be denied that in the Don *Oblast'* to a very large degree, there exists a constant cause of such failure, i.e. the lowering of the productivity of the soil from year to year . . . With the increase in population and the development of the southern ports, land of every type has gone under the plough, but the period of fallow has become altogether shorter. Along with this has gone the excessive destruction of the woods and consequently the shallowing of rivers, the drying up of their source and in general a decrease in the quantity of moisture both in the soil and in the atmosphere. These phenomena which are characteristic of all our southern steppe zone threaten if circumstances do not change to turn it into a wilderness good only for nomads.[11]

The early 1890s brought harvest failure on an empire-wide scale and a terrible famine in 1891. Although the Cossacks themselves escaped famine it was only thanks to government intervention. The cash handouts were described as 'extraordinary measures' by the War Ministry, but four years later 3,500,000 roubles was still being paid out in subsidies.[12] The government dealt with each crisis on an ad hoc basis, doing enough to keep the system going until the next one struck. Only towards the end of the century did the government suspect that they might be connected by an underlying cause. In 1898 a commission was set up under Lieutenant-General Maslakovets to investigate the causes of Cossack impoverishment.[13] Although the focus of the commission was the Don where the crisis was most acute, the government was well aware that where the Don went, the other Cossack *voiska* invariably followed.

The inquiry headed by Maslakovets was the most exhaustive investigation of the impact of military service on the Cossack economy carried out by the old regime. He investigated the costs of military service, the organization and practices of Cossack agriculture and the income this generated for each family in order to evaluate the capacity of the Cossacks to pay for their military service. Maslakovets was remarkably honest in his analysis, avoiding the easy option of pointing out separate failings and instead identified the problem as the Cossack system itself:

> Such an obvious disparity between the burden of military obligation with the means of the Don Cossack population to fulfill them will absolutely and unavoidably lead the Don *voisko* in the more or less immediate future to a barely survivable economic crisis. There can only be one outcome to this: the transformation of the Don Cossacks into the category of the general tax paying rural population and their subjection as far as military service is concerned to the general state requirements and rules.[14]

In plain language Maslakovets was saying that military service was the cause of Cossack impoverishment and that collapse was imminent; the only solution to the problem was to transform the Cossacks into peasants, bringing to an end the centuries old existence of the Cossacks. But Maslakovets realized that this was politically unacceptable to the government and that the Cossacks would rightly see it as an attack on their very existence:

> But such a depressing outcome of the present state of affairs after three glorious centuries of military service of the Don host would not be desirable in any respect either for the cost to the state nor for its lack of correspondence with the world view and basic way of life of the Don Cossacks.[15]

The government characteristically shelved Maslakovets' report. It knew a crisis was imminent and unavoidable without drastic action, but chose to do nothing and hope for the best. The Cossack system had become gridlocked, but this was symptomatic on a local scale of a more general paralysis within the empire as a whole. By the start of the twentieth century solutions to all the empire's problems, including the Cossacks, appeared to have been closed off.

The failure of the Cossack economy

How had such a situation come about in less than twenty five years? Military service had always been a strain, but the Cossacks had managed to cope from year to year. The key to Cossack success had been an ample supply of land and relatively low costs of military service. Neither of these conditions applied in the last quarter of the nineteenth century. In 1835 the government had fixed 30 *desiatiny* of land, just under 90 acres, as necessary to put one Cossack through military service.[16] The Cossack *voiska* in the Urals and east of the Urals had little problem meeting this norm. Among the Amur Cossacks the average allotment at this time was 48.2 desiatiny while the Ussuri Cossacks luxuriated in an average allotment of 64.6 *desiatiny*.[17] But in the Don and Kuban it was a very different story. Population rise had put intense pressure on land supply, causing a fundamental reorganization of the way land was used. This, however, was only a palliative. By 1895 the average share of land on the Don had fallen to 18.5 *desiatiny* and by 1900 it was down to 13.[18] In the Kuban it was even worse with average allotments falling to 11.3 by 1905.[19] Even if everything else had remained unchanged these figures alone would go far to explain Cossack impoverishment. But other things had not remained unchanged. Most importantly the law of 1875 had set in motion costs that spiralled upwards uncontrollably. Preparatory service which had existed only on paper before 1875 now cost each family over 200 roubles in cash and lost labour. That it was a complete fiasco only rubbed salt into the wounds. Maslakovets concluded that a Cossack was as untrained at the end of the three years as the day he started. The cost of a uniform and equipment rose from 40 roubles to around 120. Previously there had been a thriving second-hand market in uniform and kit, but the requirement that Cossacks on privileged service had to keep all their equipment brought this market to an abrupt end. New standards of uniform ended domestic production of them, forcing Cossacks to turn to professional suppliers who were guilty of all sorts of sharp practices. The bureaucratic love of tinkering with the uniform and continually adding items to the list of what was necessary added to the cost, as well as burdening the Cossack with much unnecessary equipment. Maslakovets fumed that 'a Cossack going on service resembles not so much a light cavalry trooper but a mounted pedlar'. Finally, the price of a horse rose from an average of 35 roubles before 1875 to between 75 and 125 roubles by the end of the century. Thus even before setting out on service a Cossack family had to find over 500 roubles. Before 1875 it had been less than a hundred.[20]

The army bore the costs of the Cossack while on active service, but his family had to cope with the loss of his labour. Maslakovets believed that this was about 10 per cent of the male adult labour force. Privileged service brought new costs particularly the maintenance of a war horse and annual summer camps. The latter removed another 20 % of the male labour force at the most critical point of the agricultural cycle. In all, the total cost of twelve years of military service was around 1000 roubles.[21] The average Cossack family had little hope of meeting the cost of sending one soldier on service; sending two was an impossibility. Caught between the pincers of shrinking resources and rising costs, Maslakovets' gloomy conclusions about the future of the Cossacks were fully borne out by the evidence he had assembled.

The Don and the Kuban faced the most acute economic crisis but the Cossacks of the other *voiska* were not far behind. In all the hosts east of the Ural mountains the land supply dwarfed the population able to work it. Cossacks in the Ussuri, Amur or Semirech'e or Transbaikal hosts could take as much land as they wanted. Yet without the labour to work it, the land was valueless. Even if labour was available there was no market for any surplus. The absence of large urban centres and poor communications confined any production to the levels of domestic consumption. The minuscule levels of land under the plough in these *voiska* told their own story. In the Transbaikal and Ussuri hosts just over 1% of the land available to the Cossacks was given over to grain production; in the Ural, Astrakhan and Siberian hosts it varied between 2–4%; the Orenburg and Semirech'e managed 6%.[22] Commercial livestock raising offered a better use of scarce labour resources, but in the absence of a market was pointless. The only option for most Cossacks was to rent out their land to peasant migrants for whatever they could get for it. This was a desperately inefficient use of land both for the Cossacks who received a pittance for it and for the peasants who had no incentive to improve the land and every incentive to exploit it ruthlessly. The governor of the Semirech'e *voisko* in 1895 bitterly criticized such land usage, attributing it to Cossack idleness rather than the structural problems of their lives:

> As far as the Russian rural population is concerned, Cossacks and peasants, the former receive bigger allotments, but they work little of it themselves. Rather they rent it out and exist on the income received in rent. Such easy income secures for them a comfortable and idle life. Cossacks hardly ever take up a craft. The peasantry on the other hand are altogether industrious.[23]

The Cossack economy was thus caught in a bind. All Cossacks faced rising costs of military service which they could not meet. In the Don, Kuban and Terek more was having to be produced from less and less. In Asiatic Russia on the other hand land was plentiful but the absence of labour and markets gave the Cossacks little possibility of developing the opportunities available to them. By the turn of the century, the Cossack economy had been squeezed dry in an attempt to meet the costs of military service. The numbers of Cossacks forced to turn to the stanitsa or *voisko* for help in paying the costs of service or asking to move straight into the 'privileged service' category rose sharply. By the end of the century 26% of Don Cossacks eligible for active service were being excused on the grounds of poverty. Even more worrying was that 10% of this total was made up of men rejected for service because they were physically unfit.[24] Those families that did scrape together enough to send their sons on service found the strain immense. The simple truth was that at the end of the nineteenth century and the beginning of the twentieth military costs were rising so rapidly that it was impossible for a peasant farm to cover them. No amount of government propaganda celebrating the special relationship of the Cossacks with the dynasty or their privileged position could counteract the daily reality of anger, frustration and poverty caused by military service.

Active service

Service to throne and motherland legitimized the sacrifices that the Cossacks imposed on their families. The Cossacks conceived of themselves as a warrior caste, heroically defending the country against its foreign enemies. The reality, however, in the last quarter of the nineteenth century was very different. Rather than being deployed against the Ottoman Empire or one of the European great powers, Cossacks found the enemies that they were expected to fight were not on foreign fields but in the cities and villages of Russia itself. With increasing frequency, the state used the Cossacks as a paramilitary police force suppressing urban and rural unrest. Within a few decades Cossacks had fashioned a new and enduring image for themselves as the vicious hirelings of the tsarist regime. It was not an image they were entirely comfortable with. They sang no songs about internal police service, had no proverbs encapsulating collective wisdom about it and in fact rarely made any mention of it at all. Yet for each cohort called up every year, service in St Petersburg, Moscow, Warsaw or some other great city was far more likely to define their military experience than participation in a major war.

The phenomenal tempo of industrialization in tsarist Russia from the 1880s replicated all the horrors of early industrialization elsewhere in Europe, but in a particularly concentrated form. Such conditions created an extremely volatile workforce which could erupt into a lethal, alcohol fuelled riot, or *bunt* as it was known in Russia, without warning. Later on political demonstrations also became common on the streets of large cities. To the government, however, both types of protest were equally unwelcome and were regarded as a threat to the social order which had to be firmly repressed. It lacked, however, a reliable and appropriate instrument for dealing with unrest. The tiny urban police force could not cope with peaceful processions, let alone major riots. On the other hand the use of the regular army and application of lethal force on a large scale particularly in Moscow or St Petersburg severely damaged the reputation of the regime at home and abroad. The War Ministry itself was very reluctant to see the army employed in this role except in the direst emergency and it resolutely resisted any attempt for the routine use of the army in suppressing internal unrest.[25]

Rather fortuitously, the government hit upon filling the space between the police and the regular army with the Cossacks. Cossacks had been used on an ad hoc basis against rioting peasants, rebellious native peoples and factory workers in the Urals since the eighteenth century.[26] But it was only in the last quarter of the century that they were used systematically in this role. Mounted horseman turned out to be an extremely effective way of dealing with urban unrest. Speed, power and a rapidly established ferocious reputation could sweep even the largest demonstrations from the streets in a matter of minutes. Relying mainly on their fearsome whip, the *nagaika*, the Cossacks inflicted painful lessons on demonstrators without leaving dozens of them dead on the streets of the capital. With tight group cohesion, few contacts in the city and isolated in barracks, the Cossacks excelled themselves in their new role.

The War Ministry reluctantly acquiesced to the use of Cossacks, probably seeing it as preferable to exposing the rest of the army to this kind of work. Very rapidly governors of provinces across the empire clamoured to have Cossacks stationed in their jurisdiction to enforce order. Most governors had very low opinions of the police under their command: the governor of Lifland province commented for example 'that drunkeness is the distinguishing characteristic of the Russian police guards'.[27] The opportunity to have a reliable, disciplined and effective body of men at their disposal was too good an opportunity to pass up. Governors from Moscow, Odessa, Minsk, Tula, Ekaterinoslav among others bombarded the War Ministry with requests for Cossacks. Even the Don ataman requested permission to keep some of the mobilized Cossacks within the Don *voisko* to help contain unrest in the turbulent city of Rostov-na-Donu.[28]

Urban unrest in late tsarist Russia was not transient, but was an entrenched part of city life. The commander of Moscow Military district commented on this in his report to the War Ministry in 1897:

> Disorders in the factory areas of Moscow military district which repeat themselves every year compel the sending of military units in order to stop them. The most suitable type of units for this are unquestionably the Cossacks.[29]

If anything the violence appeared to be growing and spreading into the countryside as the new century began. The sheer destructiveness of agrarian riots in Poltava and Kharkov provinces in 1902 was a harbinger of a qualitative change in the nature of peasant protest.[30] There were never enough Cossacks to go around nor could there be. The solution to the problems of the empire lay in political reform not in ever larger numbers of riot police. By the end of the nineteenth century the War Ministry was becoming increasingly exasperated at the endless requests for more Cossacks from the Ministry of the Interior and testily pointed out that there were no more Cossacks to be mobilized. Unfortunately, Tsar Nicholas himself scrawled across one such report 'I doubt this', forcing the ministry to scrape the barrel even deeper.[31]

The Cossacks engaged in these vicious operations appeared to have few qualms about them. No units expressed unhappiness or showed much sympathy to their victims. On the contrary, as we have seen, they established a reputation for the utmost reliability. Among workers, students, peasants and members of revolutionary organizations, the Cossacks achieved iconic status as the embodiment of tsarist brutality. How did the Cossacks reconcile this role with their heroic image of themselves?

Relatively few Cossacks were carrying out police work at any one time. Usually it was only men of the first turn of service who were in their early twenties. Recently married but without children and still part of their father's household, the young men on service were freer of responsibility than at any other time of their lives. Being sent to one of the great cities of the empire was probably rather exciting to say nothing of being a good deal safer than service on one of the frontier cordons. Although this is only speculation, one suspects that fighting mostly with other young men of

Figure 12 *Cossack confronts villagers in Kazan,* by R. Caton Woodville

the same age possessed a certain exhilaration, particularly as the Cossacks literally had the whip hand. The authorities were well satisfied with the way the Cossacks carried out their duties. No one seems to have considered whether the same Cossacks a few years later but with young children and as heads of independent households would still have the same enthusiasm for such service. When war erupted between the Russian and Japanese empires over competing claims in China to be followed by revolution in 1905, this issue was no longer a matter for speculation, but was to be tested in reality.

The mobilization of the Cossack territories

Throughout 1905 the regime teetered on the edge of destruction, power-less to halt the urban and rural unrest. Mutiny in the army deprived the government of the means to put down the revolution even if it had possessed the will. Stripped of all other supports the government turned desperately to the one group whose loyalty it believed was unshakeable. In spring 1905 the government began the most extensive mobilization of the Cossack territories since the Napoleonic wars. Well aware of the devastating impact that even partial mobilizations had on the Cossack economy, the government had little choice but to throw caution to the wind and call up as many Cossacks as possible.

The Cossack territories had already been partially mobilized for the war against Japan, but only a few second turn regiments had been called up.[32] No-one questioned the right or the need for the government to mobilize Cossacks in time of war even if the Cossacks themselves were well aware of the hardship it would cause to families left behind. Very soon thousands of Cossack families from the Don, Kuban, Terek, Ural and Orenburg hosts would find themselves facing financial ruin and harvest failure worse than the famine years of the 1890s.

The mobilization of the Cossack territories faithfully followed the rising crest of the revolutionary tide. A month after Bloody Sunday sixteen second turn regiments were mobilized from the Don, Kuban, Terek and Orenburg hosts. In June as the revolution spread into the countryside, the government called up six more regiments from the Don, four from the Kuban and one each from the Terek and Orenburg hosts. In the aftermath of the October General Strike in St Petersburg as the survival of the regime hung by a thread, the order was issued for the mobilization of any remaining second turn and substantial numbers of third turn units. Twenty-four regiments were called up from the Don and Kuban and another twelve from the Orenburg host.[33]

By October the supply of men in the Cossack territories was running out. Yet still the demands for Cossacks poured in on all sides. Another six regiments of the third turn were mobilized from the Don in December 1905.[34] Governors, watching helplessly as their provinces slipped into anarchy, had little sympathy to spare for the problems of the Cossacks and inundated the War Ministry with demands for more Cossacks. The ministry was in an impossible position unable to meet all or even most of the requests. The governor of Nizhne-Novogorod province in March 1905 for instance complained that he had been promised six sotnias of Cossacks, but had suddenly been told that this was being cut to two. To make the pill even more bitter, the War Ministry had no idea when these were going to arrive.[35] Desparately scrabbling round to put a few more units together the War Ministry put pressure on the atamans of the *voiska* to find a few more Cossacks. By now however, the *voisko* administrations were seriously concerned at the impact of mobilization on the Cossack economy and the possibility of unrest in the Cossack territories themselves. They began to complain to the War Ministry of the dangers of further mobilization:

> In the present time the *Voisko Nakaznyi* ataman is petitioning for the revocation of the mobilization appeal of the remaining three regiments of the third turn as their mobilization coincides with the spring field work and could undermine the Cossack economy and arouse dissatisfaction among the Cossack population.[36]

Police service

Mobilization was having a devastating effect on thousands of Cossack households. In itself this was deeply damaging for the morale of the Cossacks on service, but far worse was the campaign in which the Cossacks now found themselves at the forefront. In cities, factory settlements and mines Cossacks were set against strikers and demonstrators, flailing about them with their nagaikas, trampling workers with their horses or slashing them with their sabres. In the countryside the Cossacks found themselves acting as private security guards for the property of the nobility. They were split up into small units of a dozen or less and expected to carry out a savage war of reprisals against rebellious peasants. Cossacks had little in common with the nobility whose property they were defending, but the peasants they were beating differed only in that their plight was even worse than that of the Cossacks. Hungry peasants demanding food and an end to their poverty were uncomfortable reminders to the men of the second and third turns of their own families suffering back home.

The campaign in the countryside was endless as no sooner had one disturbance been quelled than others broke out. A report which could have come from anywhere in the empire during the revolution, but actually came from Kursk province, identified the Sisyphean task in front of the Cossacks:

> General Adjutant Dubasov, telegraphing about the seriousness of the peasant movement in Kursk Province pointed out that this movement in the present time had taken on a character which makes the struggle difficult. All the riots are carried out in the absence of the army, cease with its appearance and upon withdrawal of the military units flares up again with new force.[37]

Exhausted, resentful, and living on frayed nerves, Cossacks relieved their frustrations on the unfortunate people in front of them. Like many soldiers in similar situations before and after them, the Cossacks relied on copious amounts of alcohol to dull their senses. Burning, flogging, and often shooting out of hand, the Cossacks passed through the urban and rural areas of the empire, leaving a lasting legacy of hatred, bitterness and pain behind them. The merciless campaign of the Cossacks became part of revolutionary folklore as the counter-revolutionary terror unleashed by the government passed into collective memory. With so many thousands of nameless victims, it is easy to lose sight of the human tragedy that each one embodied. One case that found its way into the archives because the peasant involved had the courage to bring a complaint against the Cossacks gives a rare first-hand account of what it was like to be on the receiving end of a punitive expedition during the revolution. It is worth retelling also because it contains within it all the elements which within a matter of months would lead to extensive and prolonged mutinies in Cossack regiments.

At 11.00 am on 31 December 1905 a delegation of elders from several villages approached the house of Prince Kil'dishev, the land captain or official responsible for peasant affairs in Elatomskaia district. The delegation was led by Sharif Krymskii one of the elders. They asked the land captain to loan them grain to tide them over until the next summer's harvest. Krymskii takes up the story:

> When we had all expressed our most humble petition to the Gospodin Land Captain Prince Kil'dishev, then he the land captain began to swear at us with filthy words which are not used on paper and drove us away with threats to put us all in jail. When I said to him that we had come to ask him for bread because of hunger and not to hear him swear at us with unprintable words, he said that he had not sworn and asked the elders and other representatives if he had sworn. All the village elders and other representatives, the former with their symbols of office said 'Yes your excellency you swore.' After this he yelled 'There will be no bread for you.'[38]

There could well have been more going on here than a simple request for grain as related by Krymskii, Whatever the truth, Kil'dishev used his authority as land captain to send Cossacks to make an example of Krymskii. On night of 3 January 1906 twelve Cossacks arrived in Krymskii's village and began banging on the door and shouting:

> Is this the home of Sharif? I said that it was the home. But seeing that they were all drunk and hearing from them threats aimed at me, I immediately fled

from the danger of being beaten to death. Then there remained in my home my wife Khaeni Bikunevna and two small children . . . I heard yells from the house 'Give us your husband or we will beat you instead' and they beat my wife with their *nagaikas*. She fell to the floor and the children began to scream. But my wife who was pregnant at the time went out of her mind on account of the loss of her baby. She became mentally ill, tore her clothes and did not recognize her children.[39]

While a tragedy for the Krymskii family, this incident was only unusual for being investigated. In other respects, however, it is very revealing. The Cossacks were from a privileged service unit, the 30th Don Cossack Regiment, were broken up into a tiny group of twelve, were acting as enforcers for the local nobility and were drunk. No doubt Kil'dishev had provided them with ample quantities of vodka for the mission. When they could not get hold of Krymskii they beat his pregnant wife instead, causing her to have a miscarriage and a mental breakdown. Krymskii ended his petition with this comment: 'From all this your excellency it is possible to see that the army is summoned at the whim of influential persons and that the Cossacks will beat even pregnant women.'[40] This is what Cossack service to the throne and fatherland had been reduced to by the revolution. Their families and households were facing ruin so Cossacks could protect the property of the nobility. By 1906 revulsion was fast spreading through Cossack ranks.

Mutiny

The Cossack administrations had long been aware of the potential dangers of mobilizing regiments of the second and third turn. When the commander of the Astrakhan Cossacks, already worried about the effect of the mobilization of second turn Cossacks on their households, was informed about the imminent mobilization of regiments of the third turn, he protested that it would have a devastating effect. He suggested that the government mobilize Cossacks from the Don or Orenburg hosts instead. As can be imagined such suggestions were not well received by his colleagues in the Don or Orenburg.[41] Much more ominous, however, was the reaction of the six Don Cossack regiments mobilized in June 1905:

. . . deep unrest was noted in the six Cossack regiments mobilized at the end of the present time. The Cossacks loudly expressed their unhappiness at being designated for military-police service within the Empire . . .

At this time the whole regiment in full battle order made up of Cossacks from Khoperskii *Okrug* of the Don *Oblast'* declared in a telegram to the

Nakaznyi Voisko ataman that everyone, officers and men of the regiment without exception, refused service within the empire.[42]

This was an extraordinary act of defiance by men already under military law. The participation of all the regiments' officers underlined the depth and breadth of anger among the Cossacks at the mobilizations. Yet far from carrying out arrests, the Don ataman himself rushed to the regiments to pacify them and offer reassurance about their families' well being. In the Kuban, the 17th Plastun battalion refused to embark on ships carrying them for police service. The *Okhrana*, the secret police, reported that 'Officers are not only without influence over the Cossacks, but are clearly afraid of them.'[43] Another Kuban Cossack regiment issued an appeal to all the Kuban Cossacks:

> To the Kuban Cossacks
> We have been deceived with sops, we have been seduced by titles like 'faithful servants' and we have gloried in these. And so all the Russian people hate the Cossacks. From one end of Russia to the other curses fly in their speech: 'Bloodsuckers, traitors to the people's cause . . .' We are shamed because the butchers of the people stretch out their hands crimson with blood and say to us 'You are our friends.' Not true! We are flesh of the same flesh and bone as the people. Where the people are, so we are there. We must not go against the people, but be with them because the grief of the people is our grief, the needs of the people are our needs.[44]

Far from being isolated incidents these were part of an increasingly obvious trend in Cossack regiments in 1906. Mobilization confronted the Cossacks and their families with imminent destitution but their anger had more than economic causes. The belief that only war was sufficient reason to justify the mobilization of the regiments on privileged service was widespread among the Cossacks. That the government could quite legitimately point out that this was not true did nothing to alter the sense of moral outrage felt by most Cossacks. Once they actually began to carry out police functions, the path to mutiny was open and short.

From across the empire, reports were coming in that Cossack units were refusing to carry out orders or had gone over to the people. Officers who attempted to restore order found themselves ignored or even attacked:

> . . . unrest has began among the regiments on privileged service of the 2nd and 3rd turn which showed itself in the following: on 21st June past the 1st sotnia of the 41st Don Cossack regiment, garrisoned in Taganrog, refused to advance as ordered on the settlement of Golodaevka and Zolotaia Kosa of Taganrog *okrug* where peasant disorders were taking place. Then many

of the Cossacks of the *sotnia* who were in an unsober state began to smash the glass in the windows of their quarters. When the Commander of the regiment *Voisko* Elder Golubintov arrived for discussions with the Cossacks drawn up on the courtyard a metal pot was thrown from the second floor that wounded sotnik Markov who was accompanying the commander of the regiment. In view of such a mood among the Cossacks, the *sotnia* was left in Taganrog.[45]

Obviously the unfortunate Markov took the pot intended for the commander, but violence directed against senior officers indicated how alienated Cossack regiments had become. In Iuzovka one of the most turbulent towns in the empire, Cossack units openly fraternized with striking workers, refusing to disperse them and promising not fire on them. Even worse as far as the authorities were concerned was that 'when dragoons of the Lubenskaia Regiment were summoned, the Cossacks declared that they would fire on them if they touched the workers'. So bad had the situation become that the governor-general was authorized to open fire on the Cossacks.[46] In Perm the governor informed the Ministry of the Interior 'the 17th Orenburg Cossack regiment stationed in the gubernia is unreliable. Discipline is weak, the Cossacks fraternize with local workers . . . and the Cossack authorities can do nothing about it'.[47] All over the empire Cossack units were signalling in the most unmistakable fashion that they were no longer willing to carry out repression.

The shock that mutinies in Cossack regiments delivered to the authorities was compounded by the unrest that was spreading into the Cossack home territories. The most serious disturbances took place in the Don and Kuban. In the Kuban, the 2nd Urupskii Regiment mutinied in December 1905 and held out for fifty-three days.[48] In the upper Don, Ust-Medveditskaia Stanitsa and some of the surrounding stanitsas joined in a prolonged refusal to send any more of their members on active service. In Cossack assemblies in the stanitsas items for discussion were no longer restricted to communal affairs, but moved on to political issues and the *sbory* became the forum for political discussion. Speeches of the Cossack Duma deputies were read out, lists of demands were drawn up, and repeatedly complaints about mobilization for police service were raised. Communities worried about their members on service and what they were doing there. Whatever else did not function in tsarist Russia during the revolution, the postal service did. Letters from Cossacks on service described the wretched conditions they were forced to live in and their bitterness about what they doing. Equally letters from home told of the catastrophic harvest failure in the Cossack territories in 1906. Discontent at home and on service fuelled the mounting sense of grievance shared by all Cossacks. The authorities in the Don recognized the interplay of the two when they discussed the reasons for the revolt in Ust-Medveditskaia Stanitsa:

> . . . the uneasy mood of the Cossack population is maintained on the one hand by letters from the mobilized regiments received by the families of Cossacks on the Don with complaints about the burden of police service, the lack of attention to the needs of the Cossacks by the local military and civil authorities, the splitting up of Cossack units among the properties of the nobles and converting them into guards around their property, and on the other hand the immoveable need as a consequence of the almost universal failure on the Don of the grain and hay harvest.[49]

The third corner of the triangle of unrest was the activity of the Cossack Duma deputies. The deputies used their privileged position to press for solutions to the immediate problems confronting the Cossacks, particularly military service and impoverishment. The duma deputies inside and outside the Duma repeatedly raised the issue of police service. In a declaration to the State Duma, Cossack deputies accused the government of ignoring the plight of the Cossacks:

> The central government has completely ignored the economic side and has left the Cossack to his own resources. Even now it cannot renounce its previous view of the Cossack as military fodder and does not want to take acccount of his economic ruin or even physical degeneration.[50]

Duma members did not restrict themselves to speech making in St Petersburg. Duma member Kriukov for example told the Cossacks in Ust-Medveditskaia stanitsa that:

> . . . in the State Duma the Cossack party had fully established and factually demonstrated that the mobilization of the Cossack regiments, with the exception of the those formally in the Far East had been done at the demand of the Minister of Internal Affairs without an IMPERIAL order of mobilization to the governing senate . . .[51]

However, those from the Don and Kuban had their eyes fixed on broader horizons. They saw it as an opportunity to reverse the erosion of Cossack freedoms and radically rewrite the relationship between the *voiska* and the government. For the first time since the eighteenth century the re-establishment of the institutions of the *krug* or *Rada*, elected atamans, and authority over all internal matters were raised. Deputies from the Don wanted 'to give to the Don territory autonomy over all our local affairs and needs (economic and social) so that the resolution of these matters would be dependent upon an *Oblast' sbor* elected by the native population and a *voisko* ataman chosen from the people.'[52] These calls were echoed in resolutions of many stanista assemblies.[53] Similar demands were expressed by Kuban deputies and at the end of 1906 a *Rada* convened in Ekaterinodar.[54] Under the pressure of events, the long established subordination of the Cossack *voiska* to the central government was breaking down. Cossack ambitions like those of other groups in the empire were growing as the revolution made what had previously been set in stone suddenly look very fragile indeed.

In fact although no-one was aware of it at the time, the peak of the crisis had already passed by the summer of 1906. A combination of exhaustion, brutal repression and political concessions had done enough to stabilize the government and split the revolutionary movement. Although throughout 1907 many expected a resurgence of the movement, not least provincial governors who continued to demand more Cossacks much to the irritation of the War Ministry, the government was steadily recovering its nerve and seeking to regain the ground it had lost during the revolution.

Among the Cossacks as well the crisis peaked in the summer of 1906. There were no more mobilizations and in early 1907 the first demobilizations had began. As Cossack units started to return home in 1907, life resumed some semblance of normality. Somehow most Cossack farms managed to struggle on. A series of good harvests up to the First World War helped diffuse some of the tension. The government investigated the disturbances among the Don and Kuban Cossacks but wisely decided in nearly all cases to quietly drop them. No-one was prosecuted for the Ust-Medveditskaia revolt. Similarly, serving Cossacks who had been involved in mutinies escaped prosecution with very few exceptions. Even when the government initially intended to make an example of the Urupskii Regiment, it rapidly scaled back its plans. Of the 400 men facing court-martial, only thirty-nine were actually tried. The ringleader was sentenced to death, but unlike army mutineers and the Krondstadt sailors the death sentence was not carried out.[55] By 1910 it appeared that the revolution had been an unfortunate episode which was best forgotten. Nicholas continued to believe that the special relationship between the Cossacks and himself was as strong as ever.

Yet underneath the appearance of normality, changes were evident in the empire as a whole and in the Cossack *voiska*. Despite the reassertion of government power, its authority never recovered. The tsar's absolute monopoly of political power had been broken. The Duma, emasculated as it was, survived and it's mere survival challenged the fundamental principle that political power was a prerogative of the tsar alone. The mystique of the tsar, a vital element in the power structure, had been irreparably destroyed by Bloody Sunday and the repression in the countryside. The urban working class never again showed any sympathy or trust for the royal family. In the countryside government authority was reasserted to the extent it could put down armed revolts. But its legitimacy had been entirely eroded. Fear kept the countryside from a renewed revolutionary outburst. The political, social and industrial elites of the country found it impossible to work with Nicholas II. The only resource the throne really possessed was the loyalty of the military elites and the standing army. If these were lost, it had nothing else to draw on.

For the Cossacks the 1905 Revolution had been a traumatic experience. Thousands of men on privileged service had been called up, illegally in their view, their farms had faced ruin and they had been involved in a war of repression that had revolted them. The revolution had escalated long-term grievances and simultaneously expanded the parameters of what was politically conceivable. The whole relationship with the tsarist government had suddenly, albeit briefly, been available for negotiation.

The re-establishment of tsarist power from 1907 brought to an end the strife in the Cossack *voiska* and regiments. But none of the basic dilemmas of Cossack existence had been resolved. Military service was still driving Cossacks into penury and Cossacks continued to be used in a policing capacity. The revolution had offered briefly and in an aborted manner an alternative framework to the autocratic political order in which these problems could be resolved. At it's most extreme it raised the possibility of a reversal of the centralizing policy of the tsarist state by re-establishing Cossack autonomy; in effect restoring the constitutional position to what it had been before the reign of Peter the Great. Fortunately for the government the war had been short and was over before the revolution had began and enough of the armed forces had remained loyal to prevent its overthrow.

Notes

1 RGVIA, f.1, op.2, d.130, l.57.
2 Pronshtein, *Zemlia Donskaia*, p. 126.
3 Svatikov, *Rossiia i Don,* p. 329.
4 O'Rourke, *Warriors and Peasants*, p. 42.
5 O'Rourke, *Warriors and Peasants*, pp. 83–84.

6 RGVIA, f.1, op.2, d.154, l.109.
7 *Donskiia Oblastnyia Vedomosti*, 6 October 1881.
8 RGVIA, f.1, op.2, d.154, l.109.
9 RGVIA, f.1, op.2, d. 164, l.11.
10 RGVIA, f.1, op.2, d.137, l. 107.
11 RGVIA, f.1, op.2, d.137, l.107.
12 RGVIA, f.1, op.2, d.154, l.98.
13 RGVIA, f.330, op.61, d.154, l.2.
14 RGVIA, f.330, op.61, d.1948, l.58.
15 RGVIA, f.330, op.61, d.1948, l.58.
16 Svatikov, *Rossiia i Don*, p. 324.
17 Ermak, *Semeinyi i Khoziastvennyi Byt*, p. 104.
18 O'Rourke, *Warriors and Peasants*, p. 88.
19 Tabolina (ed.) *Rossisskoe Kazachestvo*, pp. 239–240.
20 RGVIA, f.330, op.61, d.1948, ll.7–10
21 O'Rourke, *Warriors and Peasants*, p. 87.
22 L.I. Futorianskii, 'Zemlevladenie i Zemlepol'zovanie', in Bondar', *Ocherki Traditsionnoi Kul'tury*, vol. 1, p. 349.
23 N.E. Bekmakhanova, *Kazach'i Voiska Aziatskoi Rossii v XVIII–Nachale XX Veka* (Moscow, 2002) pp. 273–274.
24 RGVIA, f.330, op.61, d. 1948, l.5.
25 W.C. Fuller, *Civil-Military Conflict in Imperial Russia 1881–1914* (Princeton, 1985) p. 95.
26 Pronshtein, *Zemlia Donskaia*, p. 123.
27 RGVIA, f.400, op.3, d.2876, l.156.
28 RGVIA, f.400, op.3, d.1328, ll.29–30.
29 RGVIA, f.400, op.3, d.1328, l.16.
30 Fuller, *Civil-Military Conflict*, p. 92.
31 RGVIA, f.400, op.3, d.1328, ll.36–37.
32 RGVIA, f.1, op.2, d.164, l.11.
33 RGVIA, f.400, op.3, d.2637, l.384–387.
34 RGVIA, f.400, op.3, d.2637, l.501.
35 RGVIA, f.400, op.3, d.2637, l.104.
36 RGVIA, f.400, op.3, d.2637, l.613.
37 RGVIA, f.400, op.3, d.2637, l.435.
38 RGVIA, f.330, op.50, d.1092, l.1
39 RGVIA, f.330, op.50, d.1092, l.1–2.
40 RGVIA, f.330, op.50, d.1092, ll.1–2.
41 RGVIA, f.400, op.3, d.2637, l.194.
42 RGVIA, f.400, op.3, d.2637, l.298.
43 I.A. Kutsenko, *Kubanskoe Kazachestvo* (Krasnodar, 1993) p. 144.
44 Kutsenko, *Kubanskoe Kazachestvo*, p. 145.
45 RGVIA, f.400, op.3, d.2819, l.99.

46 RGVIA, f.330, op.50, d.1230, l.3–4.
47 G. Iu Gorshkov, *Dorogi Orenburgskoro Kazach'ego Voiska* (Cheliabinsk, 2002) p. 20.
48 Kutsenko, *Kubanskoe Kazachestvo*, p. 151.
49 RGVIA, f.330, op.50, d.1233, l.4.
50 V.N. Sergeev and D. Iu Shapsugov, *Parlamentskaia Deiatel'nost Rossiiskogo Kazachestva (1906–1917)* (Rostov-na-Donu, 2003) p. 57.
51 RGVIA, f.330, op.50, d.1233, l.5.
52 Sergeev, *Parlamentskaia Deiatel'nost'*, p. 45.
53 Svatikov, *Rossiia i Don*, p. 471.
54 Tabolina, *Rossisskoe Kazachestvo*, p. 238.
55 Kutsenko, *Kubanskoe Kazachestvo*, pp. 152–153.

Part IV

The Cossacks in
the Soviet era

The bullets fired by Gavrilo Princip in Sarajevo in June 1914 set in motion events that would bring catastrophe to millions of people. The First World War and its aftermath would dominate world history for the rest of the twentieth century. Among the malign consequences of the war were Bolshevism and Nazism in the short term and the Second World War and the Cold War in the long term. Beyond purely politcal consequences the war profoundly coarsened human behaviour and drastically lowered the value of human life. The war laid bare the capacity of a modern state to kill while simultaneously dismantling the moral codes that had previously held that capacity in check.

The consequences of the war for the Russian Empire were particularly grave, culminating in the February Revolution of 1917. The revolution overthrew the autocracy and replaced it with a liberal democratic government. But there was no consensus among the population of the former empire concerning the subsequent direction of the revolution. The elite and popular visions of the revolution differed sharply. For the elite it was a means to see the war to a victorious conclusion and secondly to establish a liberal democratic state. For the people, however, the revolution was to bring the hated war to an end and secondly to transform power and property relationships in the town and country. In other words they wanted to transform the political revolution into a social one. To this initial conflict, ethnic and national ones were soon added, fragmenting further the limited cohesion of the post-February world.

The Provisional Government proved unable to deal with the growing political crisis. Even more corrosively it failed to stem the tidal wave of social hatred, welling up from the depths of the empire which threatened to turn the political conflict into a far more atavistic, bloodier settling of accounts. Pugavchev's raven was once more flying over Russia.

In these confused and fraught circumstances a new political force emerged led by Vladimir Ilych Lenin. Riding the wave of popular discontent, the Bolsheviks seized power in October 1917, establishing the first proletarian state in history. The men and women of the Bolshevik Party who organized the October Revolution believed that it was the opening of a new era in the history of humanity, indeed its final era. What had began in October in Petrograd would end with the liberation of all mankind. Few expected the path from Petrograd to universal salvation to be as long and as crooked as it turned out to be. But in October 1917 the party believed that they were beginning a transformation of world historical importance.

The Bolsheviks saw themselves as a political movement based on the values of the Enlightenment. Rationality, reason and science were filtered through Marx's teaching about society and history to produce a political party convinced that it, and it alone, had understood the fundamental laws on which society, all societies, operated. But the rhetoric of scientific socialism masked a world view that was essentially eschatological. Bolshevism was closer to a religious cult than a political party.[1] Standing on the threshold of the promised land of communism, any sacrifice in the present paled before the glorious future awaiting humanity just over the horizon. The fervour this vision generated empowered the Bolsheviks and their supporters, tapping deep seams of enthusiasm and self-sacrifice which are often forgotten, particularly now when the cynicism and corruption of the late Soviet regime are so well known. Through the civil war and beyond, the Bolsheviks revealed heroic endurance, an acceptance of intolerable burdens and an implacable will to succeed. A burning faith in the righteousness of the cause had a long tradition in the revolutionary intelligentsia, stretching from the Decembrists, through to the People's Will and then on to the Socialist Revolutionary Military Organization. Despite their Marxism, the Bolsheviks were the true heirs of these groups and their traditions. This heroic vision, however, had its darker side. Hand-in-hand with the willingness for self-sacrifice went an even greater willingness to impose sacrifices on others. For those who believed, the truths were so self-evident that the ends justified any means. Nor did a world view like this leave room for neutrality; those who were not for you were against you. 'Agreeing to differ' was not a phrase heard very often in Bolshevik discourse.

Millenarianism inspired the Bolsheviks, but this on its own did not make Bolshevism such a formidable force. Alongside its millenarianism, Bolshevism possessed a remarkable instinct for power: its exercise, maintenance and extension. Political pragmatism, deviations, retreats, ideological compromises gave Bolshevism tactical flexibility without reducing the fervour of its believers. Both aspects of Bolshevism existed in constant tension with each other; sometimes the millenarian predominated, sometimes the practical. If enthusiasm for the communist society of the future threatened the regime in the here and now, then pragmatism reasserted itself. If the compromises and retreats forced on the party by political circumstances threatened to become permanent, the visionaries ensured that such deviations were never accepted as a permanent state of affairs; a renewed drive towards the promised land depended only on a change of circumstances.

Where did the Cossacks fit into this world view? For most Bolsheviks, the Cossacks represented tsarist power in its crudest and most brutal form. Hostility to the Cossacks based on one crude stereotype of the Cossack as an incorrigible counter-revolutionary was deeply rooted in all levels of the party.[2] Sensitivity to Cossack history, an understanding of divisions among the Cossacks and an awareness of nuances in their political behaviour did exist in sections of the party, but it was easily overwhelmed by the gut prejudice that the Cossacks had always been counter-revolutionary and always would be. The Bolsheviks had very few members who were Cossacks and who might have been able to provide the party with a more sophisticated understanding of them. Party members who came from the Cossack territories, but were not Cossacks, such as S.I. Syrtsov, brought with them to the party a rancour based on concrete experience of the Cossacks to complement the more general, abstract dislike shared by the party as a whole.[3] Many so-called party experts on the Cossack question had not the slightest understanding of the Cossacks or their history. Often a few weeks spent in a Cossack *voisko* before the revolution was sufficient to establish expert status. Those few members who did have real, intimate knowledge of the Cossacks struggled to make their views known. When they were listened to, the party was able to exploit fault lines in Cossack society with great skill and effectiveness.

The tension that existed at the core of the party between its ultimate goals and the means of achieving them worked itself out in the Cossack territories in a particularly striking manner. The temptation to speed up the inevitable historical process of the Cossacks' disappearance was balanced by a pragmatic respect for the Cossacks as a military and political factor which far outweighed their numbers. Lenin himself embodied these tensions. In his millenarian mode he was capable of approving a policy of genocide against the Cossacks, but in his pragmatic mode a few weeks later he could lambast local officials for needlessly giving offence to Cossack tradition by forbidding Cossacks to wear traditional clothing or to use the name Cossack:

> Pay attention and be particularly cautious in the area of such petty features of everyday life which have absolutely no general political significance and only arouse the population. Be firm on basic questions, but meet the population halfway and make allowances for archaic survivals of custom.[4]

Bolshevik policy towards the Cossacks oscillated between these poles from the October Revoution up to the Second World War.

Notes

1 I. Halfin, *From Darkness to Light: Class, Consciousness and Salvation in Revolutionary Russia* (Pittsburg, 2002) pp. 17–18.
2 S.A. Kislitsyn, *Gosudarstvo i Raskazachivanie 1917–1945* (Rostov-na-Donu, 1996) p. 13.
3 Kislitsyn, *Gosudarstvo i Raskazachivanie*, p. 8.
4 GARF, f.1235, op.82, d.36, l.212.

8

The Cossacks and the February Revolution

The burden of the war fell heavily on the Cossacks as one would expect. Approximately 12.5% of the adult male population was subject to mobilization compared to 4.2% of the non-Cossack population.[1] They supplied a wholly disproportionate number of soldiers to the army over the course of the war. Numbering just over 4.2 million according to the census of 1913 or 2.4 per cent of the empire's population, they provided the army with approximately 368,000 men. The Don and Kuban gave over 100,000 men apiece.[2] Unlike the mobilizations during the 1905 Revolution, there were no protests or displays of dissent as stanitsas and *khutora* were emptied of men over the next three years.

This war was to be like no other the Cossacks fought. The fast moving campaigns of the summer and autumn of 1914 soon bogged down. Though the war in the east remained more mobile than in the west, there was little place for cavalry in this war and most Cossacks found themselves fighting in the trenches alongside peasant soldiers. They shared the misery, deprivation and death common to the entire army in the war. Standing shoulder to shoulder with peasant soldiers, Cossacks serving at the front, the *frontoviki*, also shared the increasing anger of peasant soldiers at its apparent futility and endless nature. Casualties in the war were high. 8,314 were killed, 6,453 were listed as missing in action and 30,032 were wounded. In total there were 44,799 Cossack casualties or approximately 12 per cent of those mobilized.[3]

The outflow of so many men obviously had a disastrous impact on the already fragile Cossack farms.[4] The absence of male labour once again thrust enormous burdens on to the female population who struggled to keep the farms going and feed their families. For all it was a difficult time, but for those who lost fathers, husbands and sons it was a time of unmitigated misery. Over the months and years that followed, thousands of Cossack families experienced this tragedy and many thousands more

EN RUSSIE

Comment la femme de l'Ataman cosaque Poltenko a organisé le transport des blessés

Figure 13 *How the Wife of Cossack ataman Poltenko organized the
evacuation of the wounded*

lived in fear of dreadful news from the front. Like their men on the
battlefields, families must have wondered when it was going to end. When
the end came it was in a way and manner that no-one had foreseen.

On 23 February 1917 women, standing in one of the endless bread
queues that had become common in Petrograd over the previous two
years, vented their frustration by smashing up the bakery. Coincidentally,
this day was also International Women's Day and several marches were
taking place to commemorate it. Protest and commemoration merged;

crowds swirled through the industrial districts of the capital, calling on workers to come out in support. With astonishing rapidity factory after factory struck and by the next day the city was in the grip of a general strike. Troops of the Petrograd garrison, called out to suppress the strikes, mutinied on 27 February, transforming a breakdown in public order into a revolution. The Russian political and military elites, judging Nicholas to be liability, urged him to abdicate. Long since rejected by the workers and peasants of the country, Nicholas now found himself completely isolated. Almost as if he was glad to be finally relieved of an unwanted burden, Nicholas readily agreed to abdicate. The Romanov dynasty born at the end of the Time of Troubles in the seventeenth century disappeared as a new time of troubles overwhelmed Russia in the twentieth.

The Cossacks as other peoples and groups within the empire now had to make sense of their lives in a radically altered context. The political, legal and administrative framework which had dominated their existence for the past 200 years vanished. The February Revolution confronted the Cossacks with the most basic existential questions. What role was there for a privileged military caste in a liberal democratic system which insisted on equality of rights and duties for all citizens? Could the Cossacks survive without the estate system which had attempted to regulate their existence since at least the time of Peter the Great? How would they define their relationship with the new government and the non-Cossack population who lived within their territories? Were they capable of responding as a community to the revolution or would they lose the capacity to make any collective response, developing new identities, individual and collective, from the choices thrown up by the revolution?

In the euphoria surrounding the February Revolution scarcely any Cossacks or for that matter scarcely any other people paid attention to these questions. Everything seemed possible for a few short weeks. But soon, insistently and in ever more violent tones these questions demanded answers. The revolution of course was only part of the backdrop to these matters. The war continued, sucking the lifeblood out of the Cossack communities, domestic economies and families. Far from ending the slaughter, the new government committed itself to an intensification of the war effort until final victory had been achieved. The February Revolution brought different opportunities and risks to each Cossack host, but there was nothing inevitable about the eventual outcomes. Which would become real and which would remain unrealized would depend on the unpredictable and unknowable course of events.

The Cossacks and Petrograd during the February Revolution

Petrograd was far removed from the Cossack territories, but Cossacks had a significant influence on the mounting strike movement in the city. By refusing to play the part scripted for them by the tsarist authorities, Cossack units in the capital encouraged the striking workers in the momentous first days of the revolution. There were Cossack units from the Don, Kuban and Terek hosts in Petrograd and its surroundings in February 1917, numbering approximately 3,200 men.[5] As ever their task was to support the police in maintaining order and dealing robustly with any public disturbance. When the strikes began the mounted police moved in resolutely to deal with the strikers. But already on the first day, the swelling strike movement had exceeded the capacity of the police to control it. Cossack units were summoned to provide extra muscle. Up to this point nothing particularly unusual had happened. All sides were acting out a script that was decades old. Workers struck, the police moved in to contain and disperse the strike movement while the Cossacks waited menacingly in the wings ready to put to flight the striking workers. The city authorities saw the strike movement as an irritation but no more and did not feel it necessary to inform the tsar.

Yet all was not going as planned. The scale of the strikes, the determination of the strikers and the inchoate but surprisingly effective organization escaped the notice of the city authorities. Even more disturbing was the behaviour of the Cossacks assisting the police. One Bolshevik worker at the head of a group of demonstrators remembered running into a Cossack patrol on the first day of the revolution. As the two groups faced off menacingly, the tension was suddenly broken when one Cossack winked at the workers and others broke into smiles[6]. This was no isolated incident. Time and again the Cossacks revealed their sympathies with the strikers in subtle but unmistakable ways. Reports from the secret police, the *Okhrana*, recorded similar incidents from all over the city. Nikolai Sukhanov who wrote by far the best eye-witness account of the whole February to October period described the unexpected behaviour of the Cossacks in the first days of the revolution:

> Unexpectedly the Cossack units displayed special sympathy with the revolution at various points, when in direct conversations they emphasized their neutraility and sometimes showed a clear tendency to fraternize.[7]

Confronting the strikers, the Cossacks on their horses did not charge them, laying into them with their sabres and whips as they were supposed to.

Instead they stood passively, allowing the crowd to press up against their horses and then to flow around and underneath them.

Word of what was happening passed through the hundreds of thousands milling around the city centre. As Cossacks and workers began to communicate in gesture and speech the barrier between the barracks and the street was crumbling and with it the regime itself. Intuitively the Cossacks and the strikers understood each other. Cossacks were greeted with cheers while the police received volleys of stones. Cossacks stood aside, passively watching the crowds attack and beat the police. Then on 25 February in one of the most famous incidents of the revolution, Cossacks moved from passivity towards the police to overt aggression. An eye witness account describes what happened as demonstrators moved into one of the main squares of Petrograd:

> Several small detachments of mounted Cossacks stood at different ends of the Square, but they showed no aggressive intentions towards the crowd. One of these detachments suddenly moved from one corner of the Square to the other – the crowd willingly made way and let the detachment pass; then it closed ranks again . . . The clatter of horseshoes on stone was heard – a new mounted detachment appeared from the direction of the Nikolaevskii Railroad Station – as I found out later on, this was a detachment of mounted police; in front of it rode an officer in a gray greatcoat, tightly laced with straps. The warning signal of a horn was heard. Then another . . . It was followed by the crack of a single shot and [then] a volley resounded. Only later did I learn that the first shot was fired by one of the Cossacks and that it killed Inspector Krylov, who was at the head of the mounted police detachment.[8]

The actions of the Cossacks exposed the vulnerability of the police who remained unflinching in their determination to crush the strikes. After the killing of Inspector Krylov there could be no mistaking the sympathies of the Cossacks. The alarmed city authorities, finally recognizing the magnitude of the crisis they were facing, ordered the rest of the garrison out on to the streets. What had began among the Cossacks, now manifested itself in a much more radical form among the ordinary soldiers of the garrison. Rather than shoot the strikers, they mutinied. The strike movement had become a revolution.

The behaviour of the Cossacks during the February Revolution came as a surprise to everybody, probably not least to the Cossacks themselves. There had been no forewarning of it. The city authorities while wary of the mass of soldiers who made up the garrison trusted the Cossacks absolutely. Generation of workers and students had been exposed to Cossack brutality and many had lumps taken out of their bodies by the

Figure 14 *Cossack Soldiers Demonstrating outside the Duma during the February Revolution*

wicked Cossack whip, the *nagaika*. February 1917 should have been no different. What had happened?

The most obvious explanation, but a partial one, was the war. All the Cossack units in Petrograd had served at the front and one of them had been withdrawn to Petrograd as late as January 1917. These were not men sitting out the war in a cushy birth in the capital. They were being given a brief respite before moving back to the front. The carnage of the war, the misery and deprivation alienated the Cossacks, like millions of other soldiers of all nationalities, from the societies that had sent them to war.[9] The self-evident truths with which they had gone to war had been shredded no less than human bodies. For all their martial traditions, weariness with the war was upon the Cossacks as much as any other frontline soldiers.[10] In February 1917 the Cossacks confronted men and women protesting about the bloody conflict into whose ravening maw they would soon return.

The war was not the only reason, however. The 1905 Revolution had not been forgotten by the Cossacks. The mutinies that had swept through the Cossack regiments in 1906 after months of carrying out repression awakened a revulsion in the Cossacks for this type of work. Although the mutinies petered out, the revulsion remained. Cossacks in 1917 must have seen the shades of 1905 looming before them.[11] In 1917, however, they rejected this role from the very beginning.

Without organization, without conspiracy, something in the Cossacks gave way and they passed from obedience to mutiny. The practical consequences of this mutiny were grave in their own right, forcing the city authorities to rely on the reserve units of the garrison whose loyalty they already doubted. Even so the loss of authority over three or four thousand men in a garrison of at least 300,000 should not have been more than an irritant to the authorities. In October 1916 when the 181st Infantry Regiment had mutinied, it was quickly suppressed. Yet the psychological impact of the Cossacks' action was out of all proportion to the numbers involved. For the workers the behaviour of the Cossacks was elating. All the eye-witness accounts of the February Revolution agree if not on the details of Cossack behaviour then certainly on the impact that behaviour had on the self-belief and confidence of the demonstrators.[12] The city authorities, on the other hand, were shaken from lethargy into the opposite and equally destructive behaviour: panic. The sureties on which the regime rested, and none were more sure than the Cossacks, had been shown to be worthless.

The February Revolution and the Cossack territories

The mythology of the tsarist regime had emphasized the unique fellowship between the Cossacks and the dynasty. Once Nicholas had made up his mind to abdicate the throne he had defended so stubbornly, he hesitated only once wondering what the Cossacks would say about his abdication. Most supporters of the revolution likewise cast nervous eyes towards the

Cossack territories with the same question in mind. In the event neither Nicholas nor the supporters of the revolution need have worried. The Cossacks reacted with indifference to the end of the dynasty.[13] Remarkably, decades of propaganda were shrugged off once the power that animated it had ceased to exist. The dynasty had long since exhausted any reserves of support among the Cossacks as it had among the overwhelming majority of the empire's population. The long-term economic crisis, the experience of the 1905 Revolution and the war itself had leeched away whatever vitality the connection between the Cossacks and throne had once possessed. What was left by 1917 was a desiccated husk which the Cossacks sloughed off without a backward glance.

The creation of a new order was a considerably more complex affair. The tsarist administration had essentially contained the conflicts over land, between ethnic groups, and within them. It had not solved or even ameliorated any of them. Once this restraint was removed these conflicts floated rapidly to the surface of political life. War and revolution, however, had infused them with a new urgency and encouraged a spirit of intransigence in which those who sought compromise were increasingly marginalized. Even as it made political conflict in the Cossack territories more acute, the revolution undermined all attempts to exercise any political authority. Power flowed away from central institutions down towards the grassroots: the stanitsa; the khutor; the town; the village; the regimental committee. At the national, provincial and local level, the fragmentation of power accelerated unstoppably after the February revolution.

The Cossacks were rather slow to organize after the February Revolution. Other non-Cossack groups took the initiative. As in the capital, it was the workers who initially took the lead after the fall of the tsar. Within two weeks of the revolution beginning in Petrograd, soviets had been set up in Rostov-na-Donu, Krasnodar in the Kuban and Vladikavkaz in the Terek. Although the soviets were initially working class organizations, very quickly as in the capital the large non-Cossack garrisons in the towns of the Cossack territories declared for them. The Rostov soviet now had 30,000 soldiers at its disposal while the soviets in Ekaterinodar and Vladikavkaz had ten and twelve thousand soldiers respectively.[14] The previously mute had not only found their voices, but had simultaneously been given the means to make those voices heard in unmistakable fashion. In February, however, the soviets in the Cossack territories, as in the capital, had no ambitions to rule.[15]

With the main social force in the Cossack territories uncharacteristically mute, power initially was exercised by sections of social activists particularly those who were engaged in organizations helping the war effort. These organizations naming themselves executive committees peacefully dissolved the tsarist administration and appealed to the population for calm.[16] In the Kuban and Terek essentially the same process was followed.[17] Events in the Cossack territories appeared to be mirroring those in the capital remarkably closely.

Conspicuously absent from this flurry of organizational activity were the Cossacks. In fact the first Cossack organization to be formed was in Petrograd by Cossack members of the Duma. They issued a call for an All Cossack Conference and appealed for delegates to come from the Cossack *voiska* and armies to Petrograd. When the Conference opened on 23 March there were delegates from all the European hosts, but, not surprisingly in the cirucmstances, fewer from the Far Eastern hosts.[18] The conference established a permanent executive committee in Petrograd and made plans for a second, more representative Cossack Conference to meet later. A combination of this central initiative and local fears that the Cossacks would soon find themselves under firmly established non-Cossack authorities spurred the Cossacks to organize themselves.

Small groups of Cossack officers and intelligentsia issued calls for Cossack stanitsas and regiments to send delegates to the various Cossack capitals.[19] Unlike the workers, peasants and soldiers, the Cossacks had aspirations to rule their territories immediately. Tradition provided them with a ready-made model of rule. The old Cossack assemblies which had once been the uncontested masters of the Cossack *voiska* appeared to answer both the needs and the spirit of the time. Elections were organized which, however limited, gave a degree of legitimacy to the new assemblies. By April 1917 the ancient Cossack assemblies had been refounded in the Don, Terek, Ural and Kuban territories. The Kuban Cossacks, reflecting their partial Zaporozhian ancestry, named their assembly the *Rada* while the other three had *krugs*.

In the Cossack territories east of the Ural mountains, assemblies were created and atamans elected even though these had never had either assemblies or elected atamans. The Ussuri Cossacks for example as early as 11 March had established an executive committee and issued a call for elections to a Cossack assembly.[20] Similarly the Orenburg and Semirech'e Cossack hosts also created *krugs* to exercise power within their territories. Although these Cossack hosts had never experienced any form of *voisko* wide democracy, they appeared to appropriate the tradition of Cossack democracy without any difficulty.

Legitimized by history and elections, these institutions confidently pushed aside whatever interim authorities had existed in their territories, proclaiming themselves the supreme authority. Each assembly proceeded to create an executive branch of government which again was drawn from Cossack tradition. Cossack atamans and elders under the control of Cossack assemblies once more ruled the Cossack territories. The remorseless and seemingly unstoppable institutional subordination of the Cossacks to the central authorities over the past two centuries was undone at a stroke.

The Cossack assemblies represented a rather broad range of opinion. Ranging from moderate socialists to a few die-hard monarchists, the centre of gravity appeared to reflect the liberal consensus of the post-February days.[21] Again this was largely in keeping with the state of affairs elsewhere in the country. The men elected to run the Cossack territories, the atamans and elders, were drawn from the upper sections of Cossack society. Ataman Kaledin in the Don was a general, ataman Filimonov in the Kuban was a colonel from the General Staff, while ataman Karaulov of the Terek Cossacks had been a member of the Duma. It was these men and their assistants who set the public image and tone of the Cossack hosts rather than the more diverse Cossack assemblies.

These men were far from unthinking reactionaries and had accepted the outcome of the February Revolution without duplicity. Yet they shared the conservative understanding of the revolution and were keener to stress duties than rights, order rather than freedom and certainly discipline over anarchy.[22] They perpetuated the widely held view of the Cossacks as among the most conservative sections of society, not separated by any great distance from overtly counter-revolutionary groups. In all probability the new Cossack governments believed the claims they made about Cossack society as models of liberty and responsibility. Their claims, however, largely reflected the notions of the Cossacks held by the Cossack elites during imperial times (without of course the newly rediscovered love of freedom). The centuries old suspicion that ordinary Cossacks had held for their elites was not as deep as the peasant hatred of the nobility. But it was real and it belied the glib formulations of a united, disciplined and responsible people so assiduously promoted by the Cossack elites.

The first task of the new Cossack assemblies was to define their relationship with the Provisional Government. The abject subservience of imperial times was replaced by a new, confident assertion of local rights.

The Don as always led the way for all the Cossack *voiska* formulating the new relationship:

> 1) The Don Cossack *voisko krug* assumes that Russia must be an undivided people's republic, with a single chamber, with the granting of national self-determination, and with the widest local autonomy for the separate parts of the state.
> 2) The Don *voisko* constitutes an indivisible part of the great Russian people's republic, possessing wide local autonomy with the right of legislation on local affairs not contradicting the general basic laws and with the right to independently manage the lands, depths and resources belonging to the Don *voisko* Cossack community.[23]

Interestingly, the *krug* already assumed that the future state would be a republic which speaks volumes about the irrelevance of the monarchy barely eight weeks since the abdication. The *krug* did not envisage nor even conceive of a future outside the new republican state, but the idea of extensive internal autonomy was already beginning to gain ground.[24] But at this stage even those groups with the most highly developed national consciousness such as the Finns were still looking at federal solutions within the framework of a liberal, democratic state.

The Provisional Government, normally very sensitive to pre-emptive claims of local autonomy, acquiesced to this unilateral assertion of self-rule. Already worried about growing anarchy in the country, the Provisional Government had no wish to pick a fight with the Cossack territories, regarding them as oases of stability in an increasingly chaotic situation.[25] The Cossack elites felt that they had established a working relationship with the Provisional Government, but within a matter of weeks they began to doubt whether any stable relationship was possible. Through the spring and summer of 1917 the Provisional Government lurched from crisis to crisis unable to impose itself on either the country or the army. The massive demonstrations of soldiers, sailors and workers at the beginning of July in Petrograd demonstrated the abject impotence of the government in the face of popular anger. The deaths of several Cossacks in the fighting to restore order only deepened the contempt the Cossack elites had for the Provisional Government. The funerals of these Cossacks became the occasion of a major patriotic demonstration by all those forces opposed to the course the revolution was taking.

The failure of the Provisional Government to take advantage of the post-July demoralization of the revolution forces to establish its authority led many on the right to look for a more authoritarian solution to the country's problems. The Cossack elites, particularly those of the Don, were one of the key constituencies in the new authoritarian trend, revolving around General Kornilov, popular war hero and Siberian Cossack. Ataman Kaledin of the Don was especially outspoken in his criticism of the Provisional Government. The leaders of all the Cossack *voiska* presented themselves and were perceived by outsiders as sharing a common platform against the revolution.[26]

The new Prime Minister Kerensky in a rather desperate move summoned a State Conference in August to promote the unity of the government. In reality the State Conference in Moscow turned into an embarrassing fiasco for Kerensky. Barely veiled threats of a military coup were made by speaker after speaker from the right. Kaledin's speech at the Conference caused a sensation with its overt attacks on the soviet system, the democratization of the army and the beginning of the agrarian revolution. It was an explicit rejection of the popular vision of the purposes of the revolution:

> In the menacing hour of grave ordeals at the front and complete internal collapse from the political and economic disorganization, the country can be saved from ultimate ruin only by a really strong government in the capable and experienced hands (cries from the right: 'Bravo, bravo!') of persons who are not bound by narrow party or group programs (cries from the right: 'Right!'; applause), who are free from the necessity of looking over their shoulders after every step they take to all kinds of committees and Soviets (applause from the right; cries: 'Right!'), who are clearly aware of the fact that the source of the sovereign power of the state resides in the will of the whole people and not in individual parties and groups (cries from the right: 'Bravo!' storm of applause). There must be a single power for the central and local levels. The usurpation of state power by central and local committees and by the Soviets must be immediately and abruptly brought to an end.[27]

At the end of August General Kornilov attempted to carry out a coup which disintegrated into a miserable shambles. The fallout from the unsuccessful coup had serious consequences for the Cossacks.

The prominent role taken by Kaledin and other Cossack atamans identified all the Cossacks indelibly with the counter-revolution even though the vast majority of the Cossacks were opposed to the Kornilov coup.[28] This identification was made all the easier because of the Cossacks' long history of repression on behalf of the tsarist state. When the Cossacks demonstrated support for the revolution or deviated from the image of the Cossacks so assiduously promoted by the Cossack elites these were dismissed as isolated or temporary aberrations caused by the extraordinary conditions. Few people grasped that the quantity of 'isolated' or 'temporary' aberrations was approaching the point of qualitative change. Unfortunately for the Cossacks, the speed of events was now exceeding the capacity of people to understand them. On 25 October 1917 the Bolsheviks began their seizure of power in the capital, opening a new chapter in the history of the Russian Revolution. Although the Cossacks were far from their main preoccupation, the Bolsheviks carried to power a wariness bordering on hostility to all Cossacks.

The disintegration of the Cossacks

The Bolsheviks were not alone in missing the transformation going on among the Cossacks. Even those much more attuned to the Cossacks failed to see or refused to believe what was happening. In the Cossack regiments the unthinkable was taking place. So long applauded by their own elites and by all those opposed to the revolution as models of traditional military discipline, the sovietization of Cossack regiments was steadily gathering pace.[29] The process had been began in February and had continued almost unnoticed. It was masked because Cossack officers had not been expelled from their regiments. Unlike the rest of the army, Cossack officers, particularly those of lower ranks, shared the same social background as the rank and file and often came from the same stanitsa or district. But this did not stop the radicalization of Cossack regiments which on the fundamental issues of the war and soviet power could no longer be distinguished from the rest of the army.

Symptomatic of the changes taking place in the Cossack regiments was the refusal of the 1st and 4th Don Cossack regiments to take the oath to the Provisional Government. Nor, like the rest of the Petrograd Garrison, did they show any enthusiasm to return to the front. These units had been involved in the February strikes in Petrograd and, having broken the habit of obedience, showed little inclination to return to their habitual subordination.

In May the *krug* in exasperation ordered these regiments to 'a) exactly and unconditionally fulfill the orders of the Provisional Government and to set out for the front as soon as ordered and b) to take immediately the oath to the Provisional Government'.[30] Under pressure from the *krug*, senior officers in the regiment and the regimental committees, the regiment passed a resolution indignantly denying that they had refused to obey orders 'which we are exactly and unconditionally carrying out'. The effect of this triumph was diminished by the admission that two *sotnias* of the regiment stationed around the Putilov factory, a Bolshevik stronghold, continued to refuse to take the oath.[31]

Through the spring and summer the breach between Cossack regiments and their ostensible leaders widened. Conferences of Cossack army units carefully organized to project the official Cossack policy of an unconditional restoration of authority by whatever means necessary broke down in chaos when ordinary Cossack soldiers dared to voice opposing opinions. At a conference of the Orenburg Cossacks, senior officers fulminated against the Bolsheviks, the soviets and the Provisional Government, but on the final day of the conference the facade of unity was destroyed when a Cossack from the ranks spoke out:

> Let not the Cossacks separate themselves from their brothers, he said, for we are united in spirit with them. Our soldier comrades are sometimes weak, but their hearts are sound. It is our duty to help them and not to embitter them against us. We must therefore cooperate with the Soviets. Only a union between the Cossacks and the common soldiers can save Russia. We Cossacks from the South-west front look upon the Russian soldiers as our comrades. They and we must stand and fall together.[32]

Even the Moscow State Conference which was the most carefully orchestrated piece of political theatre and the prelude to the Kornilov coup could not paper over the chasm now separating the Cossack elites and the rank and file. On the day after Kaledin's inflammatory speech a junior officer from a Cossack regiment warned Kaledin not to 'tear the Cossacks away from the people. Even in 1905 there were unknown martyrs among our Cossacks, and now you desire to set the Cossacks against the people'.[33] The storm of abuse from the right wing of the conference hall prevented him finishing his speech, but the officer had exposed the image of a unified Cossack community sharing one vision of the revolution for the fiction that it was.

Whatever the mood of the Cossack regiments, there was little obvious sign the revolution had brought any fundamental change in the attitudes of the Cossack populations, living in the Cossack territories. If anything it appeared that the perceived threat from peasant or native populations had actually hardened Cossack intransigence and made them even more determined to maintain their dominance within their homelands.[34] Congress held by peasants and indigenous peoples demanded a share of political power and a redistribution of land. Cossacks in the Don and the Kuban were not unsympathetic to the redistribution of church, noble or state land to the peasantry; generosity was easy when someone else was footing the bill. But the Cossacks were by far the biggest landholders in their territory, owning over 80% in the Don and Kuban. The Cossacks believed that they had paid for their land many times over, both in the initial conquest of the territory and subsequently through their military service. A Cossack congress on the land question stated bluntly:

> . . . all Cossack lands were neither gratuitously offered nor allocated to them by anyone, but were conquered by the Cossacks who more than once shed their blood for the inviolability and safety of the lands of the Russian state.[35]

To the non-Cossack population, Cossack lands had been part of the same privileged dispensation under which the nobility had received land. Cossack insistence that their land had been paid by the blood of earlier generations cut little ice with people whose lives had been blighted by poverty for generations. For indigenous peoples who had been displaced by Cossack settlement such justifications were galling in the extreme. Just how far apart the two sides were was apparent from the Don *Oblast'* Peasant Conference held in May. Although the *voisko* government participated in the conference, it refused absolutely to budge on the critical issue of the redistribution of Cossack land. After the conference one peasant delegate remarked 'Don't bother to speak to me about friendship between Cossacks and peasants.'[36]

Coping with a newly assertive peasantry was causing severe problems for the Cossack authorities, but a much more immediate problem was posed by the large cities and towns throughout the Cossack *voiska*. Most of these had large non-Cossack majorities who rejected the authority of the Cossack governments in which they had no representation and turned instead to the soviets. The large garrisons in every town were made up of non-Cossacks, mostly peasants, who were equally hostile to the Cossack governments. In all the major cities of the Cossack territories such as Rostov-na-Donu, Ekaterinodar and Orenburg, the Cossack governments' authority had little more substance than that of the Provisional Government. Even in Cossack cities such as Novocherkassk in the Don and Uralsk in the Urals, *voisko* authority was far more fragile than anyone realized.

The Cossack leadership struggled to contain these conflicts, but the crisis of authority had penetrated into the Cossack populations themselves. Some tensions had existed for decades if not centuries. The resentment felt by Cossacks who had kept true to the Old Faith could now be expressed freely, while divisions between different regions of the *voiska* often reflecting differences of wealth, power and status added to the fragmentation of identity. Most divisive of all was simmering resentment that most ordinary Cossacks felt for their own elites.[37] Rooted in the widely held beliefs that the elites had betrayed the interests of the host in return for noble status, it had never died even if it did not have the same explosive force as in the seventeenth and eighteenth centuries. The suspicion that the elites were pursuing interests of their own rather than those of the host corroded the political potential of the Cossacks *voiska* from the roots up.

The disorientation brought by the war and compounded by the revolution was not confined to the political sphere. As in other European countries, the very foundations of society seemed to be dissolving the longer the conflict continued. The tensions between the Cossack regiments and the political elites was also a generational conflict and an assertion of sons against their fathers. But even those Cossacks who were still too young to fight now began to contest traditional authorities and ways of doing things. The older generation was perplexed by the disrespect, the casual disregard of traditional ways and often downright hooliganism of children in their early teens. One Cossack *khutor* attempting to reassert discipline in the most traditional of ways asked the *voisko* authorities for permission to flog them. The authorities replied 'that their petition about punishing young hooligans with birches has been rejected by the Council of Elders of the *voisko* Small *krug*. Measures for combatting hooliganism must not be by thrashing with birches, but by other measures'.[38] Rather unhelpfully, it did not specify what other measures it had in mind.

Women in Cossack society had traditionally enjoyed a lot more status and freedom than peasant women, but much of that had depended on a veneer of compliance and subordination to male authority. Now many women openly flouted that authority, taking lovers and completely disregarding public opinion. One outraged stanitsa *sbor* demanded that the monetary assistance given to certain women whose husbands were at the front be removed on the grounds 'that these women have completely abandoned their husbands and are carrying on a dissolute way of life both before their husband's mobilization and just the same on his departure for service'.[39] Sholokhov also noticed the change in the behaviour of Cossack women, using Gregor's sister-in-law, Daria, to express in word and deed an overt rejection of sexual conformity. After a blazing row with her father-in-law about her behaviour, Daria lured him into the barn and to his horror attempted to seduce him:

> 'Don't you want to?' Daria panted. Opening her hands, she shoved the old man in the chest. 'Or perhaps you can't? Then don't judge me! Do you hear?'

Jumping to her feet, she hurriedly adjusted her skirt, brushed the chaff off her back and shouted into the frenzied old man's face:

'What did you beat me for the other day? Am I an old woman? Weren't you the same when you were young? My husband . . . ? I haven't seen him for a year! And what am I to do . . . lie with a dog? A fig for you! Here, take this!' she made an indecent gesture, and, her eyebrows working, went towards the door.[40]

Specific groups challenged the way of living that tradition had prescribed for them. But there was a more general malaise, spreading through society that was not confined to any particular section of society nor even to the Cossacks as a whole. Peasants, workers and soldiers were effected equally. A decline in civilized behaviour and a rejection of any type of authority whether traditional, legal or social was evident. Symptomatic of this and a partial cause was the unbridled illegal production and consumption of alcohol. The drinking orgy that accompanied the October Revolution in Petrograd was probably more dangerous to the Bolsheviks than any counter-revolutionary threat of the time. But it was country wide phenomenon. By the summer of 1917 the authorities in the Don regarded the abuse of alcohol as one of the most urgent problems they faced:

Secret distilling within the borders of the *Oblast* of the Don *Voisko* is growing progressively worse with each day, spreading wider and wider with unbelievable speed. Whole settlements have been overcome by it and in several places this evil has cobbled together permanent dens. Under the influence of the events of the present time and thanks to the disorganization of the local authorities, alcohol is produced openly and on an extraordinarily wide scale. It threatens the moral and cultural foundations of public wellbeing. Therefore according to the recommendation of the Don commission the most urgent task of the present is the taking of the most decisive measures for the suppression at the root of this evil.[41]

All local authorities were to do all they could to combat this problem. Senior military officers entrusted with guarding the huge government alcohol warehouses had little confidence in their ability to protect them. They saw them as a standing temptation both to the soldiers stationed there and the surrounding population. Above all they feared the looting of the warehouses would provide the pretext for an outbreak of the murderous type of riot known as '*bunt*' or in its anti-semitic variant pogrom. *Okrug* ataman of Donetskii *Okrug* asked for permission to destroy the alcohol stocks and his reasons were a telling comment on the state of the country in summer of 1917:

I have come to this conclusion from the following positions:
1) The guarding of aforementioned wine has been entrusted to the 2nd reserve regiment and has been fulfilled by them reasonably correctly, but I have to take into account that in many places in Russia there have been instances of looting of the wine warehouses and drunken pogroms. Although the 2nd reserve regiment has not given any cause up till now to assume something similar from its side, nevertheless we should not close our eyes to the fact that the wine warehouse represents a great temptation to both the local population and to the soldiers who are gathered in rather large numbers in Kamenskaia Stanitsa and its surrounds.[42]

Conclusion

The February Revolution promised initially to offer a solution to all the problems that had plagued the Cossacks in the last decades of tsarist power. Solutions to the economic woes, the burden of military service and the lack of political freedom could now be sought far beyond the straightjacket of what was acceptable to the tsarist authorities. A wide degree of self-rule, almost home rule, but still within the framework of an overarching Russian state was the preferred solution of all the Cossack hosts. Yet such solutions unravelled very quickly. The Provisional Government could not provide the necessary stable framework to make this viable. Even if it could, the demands of the non-Cossack populations who were a majority in all the Cossack *voiska* made a political agenda established and controlled exclusively by the Cossacks inherently unstable. After the failure of the Kornilov Coup and especially after the October Revolution, the Cossack elites began to lose faith in an all Russian solution to the political crisis engulfing the country.[43] However, there was as yet no obvious alternative. All the Cossack elites assumed as well that they presided over a united society who were still following the precepts which tsarist propaganda had trumpeted: order; discipline; submission to hierarchical authority. Where the elites led, the rest of the society would follow. Yet the evidence suggested that the relationship between elite and society was far more complex than this simple formulation allowed and was becoming more complex all the time. Cossack society was fragmenting in 1917. What collective response it would make, if any, to the new demands put upon it by its elites remained to be seen.

What was obvious already, however, was brutalization of all forms of human interaction in Russia by late 1917. The disintegration of civilized codes of behaviour developing since the start of the war presaged a much more destructive descent into barbarism after the October Revolution on all sides. War accustomed people to violence on a previously inconceivable scale even if for the most part it was directed at an external enemy. The February Revolution offered the possibility that peaceful solutions could be found to the myriad conflicts held in check by the tsarist state. Eight months of revolution though had failed to find any solutions to these conflicts and had, on the contrary, brought them to a new pitch of intensity. The attempted coup of Kornilov and then the October Revolution signalled a growing determination to solve these problems through violence. The world war, however, had increased the capacity for violence exponentially while making its use much more acceptable. How swiftly that capacity and acceptance could be switched from world war to civil war would become apparent to the peoples of the former Russian Empire all too swiftly.

Notes

1 V.P. Trut, *Kazachestvo v Rossii v Periode Pervoi Mirovoi Voiny* (Rostov-na Donu, 1999) pp. 5–6.

2 Tabolina, *Rossiiskoe Kazachestvo*, p. 22. N.V. Ryzhkova, *Za Veru, Otechestvo i Drugi svoia: Donskie Kazaki v Velikoi Voine 1914–1917* (Rostov-na-Donu, 1998) p. 15.

3 Trut, *Kazachestvov Rossii*, p. 72.

4 Trut, *Kazachestvov Rossii*, p. 26.

5 V.P. Trut, *Kazachii Izlom: Kazachestvo Iugo-Vostoka Rossii v Nachale XX Veka i v Period Revoliutsii 1917 goda* (Rostov-na-Donu, 1997) p. 72.

6 L. Trotsky, *The History of the Russian Revolution* (3 vols, London, 1932) vol. 1, pp. 127.

7 N.I. Sukhanov, Th*e Russian Revolution 1917: A Personal Record*, trans. J. Carmichael (Princeton, 1954) p. 15.

8 R.P. Browder and A.F. Kerensky, *The Russian Provisional Government 1917* (3 vols, Stanford, 1961), vol. 1, pp. 32–33.

9 Trut, *Kazachestvov Rossii*, p. 50.

10 See for example, M.D. Mashin, *Orenburgskoe Kazach'e Voisko* (Cheliabinsk, 2000) pp. 188–189.

11 Trut, *Kazachestvov Rossii*, p. 49.

12 Sukhanov, *The Russian Revolution 1917*, p. 19.

13 G. Ianov 'Donskiia Nastroeniia ko Vremeni Revoliutsii' in *Donskaia Letopis': Sbornik Materialov po Noveishei Istorii Donskogo Kazachestva so Vremeni Russkoi Revolutsii 1917 goda* (3 vols, Belgrade, 1923) vol. 1, p. 68.

14 V.N. Sergeev, *Politicheskie Partii v Iuzhnykh Kazach'ikh Oblastiakh Rossii 1917–1920* (3 vols, Krasnodar, 1992) vol. 1, pp. 39, 56, 71.

15 N.V. Zvezdova, *Vremmenoe Pravitel'stvo i Kazachestvo* (Rostov-na-Donu, 2003) p. 55.

16 G. Ianov, 'Revoliutsiia i Donskie Kazaki' in *Donskaia Letopis*', vol. 2, pp. 20–24.
17 Zvezdova, *Vremennoe Pravitel'stvo*, p. 54.
18 Sergeev, *Parlamentskaia Deiatel'nost' Rossiiskogo Kazachestva*, p. 77.
19 See for example, K. Kakliugin, 'Organizatsiia Vlasti na Donu v Nachale Revoliutsii' in *Donskaia Letopis*', vol. 2, p. 89.
20 S.N. Savchenko, *Ussuriiskoe Kazach'e Voisko v Grazhdanskoi Voine na Dal'nem Vostoke (1917–1922)* (Khabarovsk, 2002) p. 32.
21 Astapenko, *Istoriia Kazachestva Rossii*, vol. 3, p. 15.
22 N.M. Mel'nikov 'A.M. Kaledin(Lichnost'i Deiatel'nost). Vospominaniia' in *Donskaia Letopis*', vol. 1, p. 16.
23 *Postanovlenie Donskogo Voiskovogo Kruga: Pervyi Sozyv, 26 Maia-18 Iunia 1917 g* (Novocherkassk, 1917/1918) p. 2.
24 Iu. D. Grazhdanov, *Vsevelikoe Voisko Donskoe v 1918 godu* (Volgograd, 1997) p. 28.
25 Zvezdova, *Vremmenoe Pravitel'stvo*, p. 95.
26 Mel'nikov, 'A.M. Kaledin' in *Donskaia Letopis*', vol. 1, p. 23.
27 Browder, *The Russian Provisional Government*, vol. 3, p. 1480.
28 Trut, *Kazachii Izlom*, p. 105.
29 Ianov, 'Revoliutsia i Donskie Kazaki', in *Donskaia Letopis*', vol. 2, p. 16.
30 *Postanovlenie Donskogo Voiskogo Kruga: Pervyi Sozyv, 26 Maia-18 Iunia 1917 g* (Novocherkassk, 1917) p. 6.
31 GARF, f.1255, op.1, d.4, l.23.
32 M. Philips-Price, *My Reminiscences of the Russian Revolution* (London, 1921) p. 120.
33 F.A. Golder, *Documents on Russian History 1914–1917* (Boston, 1964) p. 507.
34 K. Kakliugin, 'Organizatsiia Vlasti na Donu v Nachale Revoliutsii' in *Donskaia Letopis*', vol. 2, pp. 104–105.
35 Browder, *The Russian Provisional Government*, vol. 2, p. 596.
36 V. Danilov and T. Shanin (eds) *Filipp Mironov: Tikhii Don v 1917–1921* (Moscow, 1997) p. 8–9.
37 Ianov, 'Donskiia Nostroeniia' in *Donskaia Letopis*', vol. 1, p. 65.
38 GARF, f.1255, op.1, d.4, l.197.
39 GARF, f.1255, op.1, d.4, l.178.
40 Sholokhov, *And Quiet Flows the Don*, pp. 360–361.
41 GARF, f.1233, op.1, d.39, ll.41–42.
42 GARF, f.1255, op.1, d.39, ll.60–61.
43 Kislitsyn, *Gosudarstvo i Raskazachivanie*, p. 11.

9

The Cossacks and the civil war

All the Cossacks hosts from the Don to the Ussuri refused to recognize the Bolshevik seizure of power and declared themselves the sole authority within their own territories. Most of them were unambiguously hostile, following the lead of the Don *krug* which declared 'Henceforth, until the creation of a lawful all Russian state government, complete executive authority within the borders of the *oblast'* belongs to the *voisko* government.'[1] Only the Ural Cossack government, more isolated and vulnerable than other Cossacks hosts, did not link its assumption of sole power with an overt call for the overthrow of the regime, hoping that this would at least delay the start of any armed conflict. The Bolsheviks, already suspicious of the Cossacks, saw the actions of the Cossack *voiska* as hostile acts and responded in kind.

Quite rightly the Bolsheviks regarded the Don as the most immediate threat to their rule and directed all their efforts to crushing what they constantly referred to as a 'mutiny'. In December the Bolsheviks put together a makeshift army of Red Guards and sailors and sent them off to the Don to crush the Cossack government.[2] Although the central government did not have the capacity to direct expeditions against the other Cossack *voiska*, supporters of soviet power within them and in the adjacent areas began to attack them on their own initiative The Saratov Soviet, for example, demanded the dissolution of the Ural Cossack government and organized military forces to attack them.[3]

Simultaneously, the Bolsheviks mounted a propaganda offensive to divide the Cossacks internally and above all to neutralize the *frontoviki*. The Decrees on Peace and Land issued within twenty-four hours of coming to power could not have been better calculated to disarm any suspicions the *frontoviki* might have had about the new government. The Decree on Land nationalized all land but it specifically stated that the land of 'ordinary Cossacks shall not be confiscated'[4]. This was followed up on 9 December with a specific appeal by the Council of Ministers to the Cossacks not to believe the *voisko* governments, but to put their trust in the new Soviet government which would deliver peace, freedom and prosperity:

> Brother Cossacks!
> They are deceiving you. They are stirring you up against the rest of the people. They say to you that the Soviet of workers, soldiers and peasant deputies are your enemies, that the soviets want to take your Cossack land, your Cossack 'freedom'. Don't believe them, Cossacks. They are lying to you. They are criminally deceiving you. Your own generals and nobles are deceiving you in order to hold you in darkness and slavery.[5]

Several other similar appeals were issued over the next few weeks. On 22 December the Soviet government enacted a decree which ended centuries of compulsory military service:

> The Council of People's Commissars has decided:
> 1) To abolish compulsory military service and to replace constant service with short training courses in the stanitsas.
> 2) To equip and supply Cossacks called for service at the state's expense.
> 3) To abolish the weekly duties of Cossacks relating to the stanitsa administration, winter duties, reviews and camps.
> 4) To establish complete freedom of movement for the Cossacks.[6]

The Bolsheviks were greatly helped by the Cossack Section of the Soviet which had been established shortly after the October Revolution on the 4 November 1917. The Cossack Section was made up of radical Cossacks who provided invaluable advice to the new government on how to address the Cossacks.[7] The volley of appeals and decrees issued by the new regime were precisely targeted to allay Cossack fears and to remove the grievances stemming from military service. In this the decrees were stunningly successful. The *frontoviki's* cautious trust in the new government was immediately confirmed while most Cossacks in the home territories saw no specific or immediate threat to their way of life from the new government. Few seemed to notice that the government could not simultaneously give land to the peasants and protect Cossack landholdings or that a completely bankrupt state was in no position to finance anything at all.

The simmering internal conflicts within the Cossack *voiska* boiled over with the Bolshevik seizure of power. Workers and peasants in the Cossack homelands refused to recognize the Cossack breakaway governments and proclaimed their loyalty to the Soviet government. Most of the large towns in effect seceded from the Cossack *voiska*.[8] The *voiska* governments did attempt to broaden the base of their support by including representatives of workers and peasants, but it was too little, too late. What might have worked a few months earlier was already hopelessly out of date. The fragmentation of power deepened as independence movements developed among native peoples living in nominally Cossack territories. In the Terek for instance the non-Cossack people rejected the Terek-Dagestani government which they were supposedly a part and opted for Soviet power instead.[9] In the Cossack hosts east of the Urals, there was not even the semblance of state power as none of the hosts were capable of establishing any control over the vast territories of Siberia and the Far East. Contrary to the image of bulwarks of order in a sea of chaos, the Cossack territories were being inundated by that same sea.

The intensification of the struggle for power caused by the October Revolution made it increasingly likely that it would be force that decided the outcome. Here at least, the Cossack governments felt that they possessed some aces. The number of Cossack regiments and their relative cohesion gave the Cossacks a significance out of all proportion to their numbers. With the collapse of all other military units, the importance of the Cossacks was even more marked. The *voiska* governments still clung to the belief that the Cossack regiments had been fundamentally unchanged by war and revolution, desperately hoping that any manifestations of revolutionary behaviour were only temporary. Once back among their own people and on their own territory, the elites hoped that traditional Cossack values would reassert themselves.[10]

The three months from October 1917 to January 1918 became a period of bitter disillusionment for the Cossack governments. Cossack regiments in the capital, like the rest of the garrison, welcomed the October Revolution believing that it had established Soviet power rather than the dictatorship of the Bolshevik Party. Expressing solidarity with the revolution, Cossacks from the 4th Don Cossack regiment and the 5th Kuban Division arrested the members of the Union of Cossack Armies which was the mouthpiece of the Cossack governments in the capital.[11]

Events soon showed that, even removed from the fevered atmosphere of Petrograd, the *frontoviki* were committed to the Soviet regime. As Cossack regiments began to arrive back in their native *voiska* their hostility to their own governments was unmistakable. In the Don, report after report noted the Bolshevization of Cossack regiments:

> Units of the fifth division are extremely Bolshevik minded and very little reliance can be placed on them. Exactly the same mood is in the 35th Don Cossack regiment which has passed a resolution that it will not move against the Bolsheviks until the real reasons [for fighting] are clear to them.[12]

Returning Kuban Cossacks blamed the Kuban government for the developing conflict and threatened an armed revolt.[13] Ural Cossacks, returning to Uralsk, simply went on a week long rampage fuelled by drink looted from the wine warehouses.[14] When the Ussuri Cossacks finally arrived home in March 1918 they refused to recognize the Cossack government and declared for Soviet power.[15] The returning *frontoviki* in all the *voiska* blamed their own Cossack governments for initiating armed conflict. Several *frontoviki* set up alternative governments in their *voiska* which provided yet another locus of power. Even those soldiers who had no desire to fight for the Bolsheviks showed little inclination to fight for the Cossack governments.

The mood among the Cossacks in the stanitsas was more difficult to read. There had been few signs of overt sympathy for the Bolsheviks or the Soviets although whether this was an informed decision or simply ignorance was a moot point. As far as we can tell, the Cossacks in the home territories did not see the Soviet regime as an imminent threat to their way of life. Certainly there had been nothing so far in either the words or deeds of the Bolsheviks which would seem to justify a bloody civil war. Writing in 1919, an anti-Bolshevik Cossack ruefully summarized the most widely held feeling immediately after the October Revolution:

> However there was no desire to participate in the struggle and the question was often heard 'How do we know who to support? Kaledin or the Bolsheviks?' But the Cossacks gave this question a particular meaning. What strictly concerned them was who would be victorious and which would be the least dangerous policy to support. They themselves had no interest in the direction of either Kaledin's policy or that of the Bolsheviks.[16]

Bolshevism was at most a distant threat; something located in the cities that would have little relevance for their lives. Even in those parts of the Cossack territories where antagonism between Cossack and non-Cossack was most acute, the Bolsheviks appeared to be largely irrelevant to these local quarrels. In the Terek for example an ethnic war erupted between the Cossacks and the native peoples in which Soviet power, initially at least, had little part. Three Cossack stanitsas were ethnically cleansed in 1918 and over 4,000 people driven from their homes.[17] If the Bolsheviks and their opponents were going to fight, the overriding concern of most Cossacks was to stay out of the conflict and not get dragged in on someone else's coat-tails.[18]

A reluctance to be drawn into a wider struggle lay at the root of hostility of the Cossacks to the numerous anti-Bolshevik organizations set up on the Cossack territories to spearhead the counter-revolution. The Volunteer Army, which became the core of the White movement in southern Russia, attracted particular hostility from the Don Cossacks. Like Admiral Kolchak's movement in Siberia, the Volunteer Army was unambiguously committed to the destruction of the Bolsheviks and the re-establishment of a unitary Russian state. Neither of these ideas had much appeal to the Cossacks. Later on the Cossacks would fight alongside and sometimes as part of the White armies; but there was no identity of interest between them and the mutual hostility and suspicion evident at the very beginning continued until the end. The connection between what was happening on the local level in the Cossack territories and what was happening at the national level was not made. Only the experience of civil war would hammer this lesson into Cossack consciousness. As the regime in Petrograd changed in October, the majority of Cossacks seemed to have far more pressing problems than the new government in the distant capital.

When the Cossack *voiska* seceded from Russia they had envisaged only a temporary separation, but the cutting of the umbilical cord to Russia had profound consequences. For some Cossack hosts it marked the beginning of the end of their identity as Cossacks; for others it marked the beginning of the elevation of Cossack over all other identities. Practically, the Cossack governments now took over all the functions that had been the responsibility of the central state: foreign affairs, defence, finance, posts and telegraphs and so on. Assuming the functions of independent states, particularly in the Don and Kuban, made the notion of a permanent separation from Russia much less whimsical. Related to this was a subtle shift in emphasis in the rhetoric of identity. Among all sections of Cossack society references to a Russian motherland and a Russian identity slipped out of usage to be replaced with an increasing emphasis on the Cossack homeland as the motherland or *rodina* and a Cossack identity as the primary one became evident. An appeal from Novocherkassk stanitsa *sbor* appealed to Cossacks from its stanitsa to take part in the anti–Bolshevik struggle. The *sbor* resolved:

> To request the commanders of military units to declare immediately to Cossacks of our stanitsa that Cossacks forgetting their duty to their native Don (*rodnoi Don*) that they will be acting in the interests of the enemies of the Don: the *sbor* resolved to exclude them as citizens of the stanitsa and where necessary expel them beyond the borders of the *voisko*.[19]

Strikingly absent is any mention of Russia as homeland or something to which a duty is owed. Appeals from other stanitsas and from ataman

Kaledin all dropped any mention of Russia and replaced it with the appeals to the Don as homeland.[20] From now on, all the Cossacks in the Don and the Kuban, whether they fought with or against the Bolsheviks, exhorted each other in the in the name of the Cossacks and their Cossack homelands. This did not signify a seamless or clear transition to nationalism for either of them, but it did show far reaching changes were already taking place in Cossack understanding of themselves under the pressure of extraordinary events. Those events had still barely touched the Cossacks by the end of 1917.

When the Cossack governments attempted to mobilize the Cossacks to defend their territories, it became clear that few Cossacks were willing to fight. As the internal threat from the non-Cossack population became more menacing and the external threat from outside forces pressed harder, the Cossack governments, leaders of the most militarized communities in the empire, found themselves virtually without armed force. In Novocherkassk the government in its desperation attempted to despatch military choirs to the front.[21] Already by December the Terek Cossack government had collapsed and its leader, ataman Karaulov, had been shot. In the first three months of 1918, one by one, the remaining Cossack *voiska* began to collapse through a combination of external pressure, internal revolt and the indifference or hostility of the Cossack population.

Instead of being springboards for anti-Bolshevik offensives, the Cossacks had permitted pro-Soviet forces a virtually uncontested takeover of their homelands. How can we explain this? To many at the time it offered confirmation that the Cossacks were nothing more than an artificial construct of the tsarist regime. Once that regime vanished, the Cossacks like all the other estates, the nobility, clergy, the merchants, simply unravelled. Any separate identity or capacity for a collective articulation of their interests was an illusion, assiduously fostered by the Cossack elites. Not surprisingly the attempt to turn illusion into reality foundered at the first test. Cossacks seemed to have shed their collective identity and joined the general retreat into localism that was taking place all over the country.

However, there is another explanation. Cossack action could be interpreted as a combination of war weariness, political optimism about the intentions of the new regime and suspicion of their own elites. Most Cossacks had had more than enough of the war. What they wanted more than anything else was for the safe return of absent husbands, fathers, brothers and sons and a chance to rebuild their shattered domestic lives and economy. Within twenty-four hours of coming to power the

Bolsheviks had issued decrees on peace and land which gave the Cossacks the longed for peace without any apparent threat to their land. No wonder most Cossacks saw little threat to their way of life from the Bolsheviks. Their own elites on the other hand appeared to be following policies that would lead inevitably to civil war even as the world war continued. In these circumstances it is hardly surprising that most Cossacks hoped to opt out of the struggle. Few Cossacks were willing to die to save the political trappings of an independent state which had only been resurrected a few months earlier. How they would react to a direct threat to their interests was still unknown. One change, however, had become discernible particularly in the post-October period. Cossack elites and rank and file had began to radically refocus their identities. Some simply abandoned their Cossack identity. Others no longer spoke so much about Russia or their Russian identity. The focus of their loyalty began shrink to their own territories and to their identity as Cossacks. The consequences of this likewise remained an unknown quantity in early 1918.

First contact: the Cossacks and Soviet power

The 'triumphal march' of Soviet power from October 1917 to March 1918 testified to the popularity of the Soviet form of government among the overwhelming majority of the population of the former empire. During these six months all organized anti-Soviet forces imploded spectacularly and those, such as the Volunteer Army, which were still in existence had been driven from any strategically important positions. The very ease and extent of the Bolshevik triumph, however, left them presiding over vast territories with the barest skeleton of a central administration and with local administrations that, although nominally part of the Soviet regime, were in effect independent satrapies staffed by ambitious, ruthless men who frequently had scores to settle. The general population now began to fulfill the promises of the October Revolution, seizing control of factories and land. Inevitably much property confiscated in the name of the revolution was simply appropriated by criminal gangs. Revolutionary violence often merging into criminal violence spread uncontrollably across the country which the regime in Petrograd had no means of containing let alone reversing. It was to remain a severe problem throughout the civil war.

Soviet power had been established in all the Cossack *voiska* by early 1918, but the power of the new authorities was fragile in the urban areas and non-existent in the rural ones. The large ill-disciplined local militias that were at the disposal of these proved effective enough at crushing overt protests, but were hopelessly unsuited to establishing any sort of stable rule. Their brutality constantly undermined all attempts by local or central officials to construct some semblance of order out of the chaos. The non-Cossack population moved to settle accounts with the Cossacks, seizing land and property; protests about the exemption of the land of ordinary Cossacks were given short shrift and denounced as counter-revolutionary. Any remaining restraints on the exercise of violence snapped, permitting one violent act to breed the next one.

Cossack populations intermingled with or living close to non-Cossack ones were most acutely exposed to the pent up wrath of peasants, *inogorodnie*, and native peoples. In the Terek the ethnic war between Cossacks on the one hand and Chechens, Ingush and Ossetians on the other continued unabated.[22] In the Don and Kuban power passed from previously dominant Cossack assemblies, from which non-Cossacks had been excluded, to soviets in which they ruled the roost. Although Cossacks were theoretically entitled to participate, they were now second-class citizens with the onus of proving that they were not counter-revolutionary. An account from one stanitsa in the Don described the changed fortunes of the Cossacks:

> A Sovdep was created in which the Cossacks made up about half the number. In the beginning they attempted to make up an opposition and to vote against several decrees which touched directly on the interests of the Cossack population. But the threatening cries of 'c[ounter]-revolutionaries', 'Kadets' and so on and the threat of arrest sharply discouraged them from real opposition. The Cossacks decided to evade their obligations and stay at home. In this way all power in the stanitsa was transferred to the *inogorodnie* population.[23]

Information about the period immediately following the establishment of Soviet power in the Cossack territories is scarce, hardly surprising in the circumstances. But later accounts all noted this reversal of the previous power relations and the accompanying violence as widespread in 1918 in the Cossack territories.

In areas of the Cossack territories that were overwhelming or pre-dominantly Cossack, the Soviet authorities found it extremely difficult to establish any foothold at all. Suspicious of the Cossacks, they immediately demanded the dissolution of the Cossacks' own administration and its replacement by a Soviet one. Most Cossack communities simply ignored these orders, but if forced to comply did so in ways that were meaningless as one community later described.

Only in March after a series of categorical demands and the arrival of delegates from the *Okrug* conference did the *sbor* decide to accept the inevitable and elect a soviet. But there and then it was decided to re-elect the previous type of administration, changing the ataman into the chairman of the soviet, his assistants into comrades and the *pisar'* into the secretary of the of the soviet.[24]

Even in stanitsas where there was a genuinely Soviet administration, those running it found themselves torn between their own community and the demands of regional representatives of Soviet power. Incessant demands to arrest counter-revolutionaries became entangled in the dense web that connected all Cossacks to their own community. The dilemmas facing Cossack supporters of Soviet power were caught by a contemporary observer:

> Almost everybody knew one another from childhood and almost all were related to one another. To arrest a counter-revolutionary meant to put in prison the husband of your aunt. To confiscate the property of another meant to rob the god-father of your sister.[25]

The lack of control over Cossack communities fed the paranoia of Soviet authorities who were convinced that they were dealing with hotbeds of counter-revolution. Frustrated by the policy of passive resistance and increasingly aware of the fragility of their position, local officials fell back on terror to bolster their authority. Motorcades were despatched around the countryside to carry out shootings and confiscations which were often little more than looting expeditions. The ferocious reality of Soviet power was coming home to the Cossacks.

Punitive expeditions entered Cossack stanitsas, rounding up anyone suspected of counter-revolutionary activity. Whereas Cossack officials had been restrained by their ties to the local community, the personnel of punitive expeditions were mostly non-Cossacks and had every intention of using exemplary violence. In February 1918, Velikokniazhskaia Stanitsa was visited by punitive detachment:

> Late in the night the Bolsheviks entered the stanitsa and immediately began their savage reprisals against the inhabitants. Straight away they arrested the two Proskuriakovoi students whose two brothers had left with the partisans. Their father, a priest and social activist who was very popular among the Cossacks, succeeding in escaping arrest and hid himself. The Bolsheviks gave him two hours at the end of which they would shoot his children if he did not appear. The priest appeared within the time, but only to see the corpses of his two children who had already been shot. He himself was killed on the exact same spot.[26]

These cavalcades projected dread before them and left mangled communities, stunned by the brutality of what they had experienced, in their wake. Rumour magnified the terror, creating a fraught atmosphere of imminent peril.

By the spring of 1918, Soviet power was unmistakably becoming the dictatorship of the Bolshevik party. The refusal to enter a coalition with any other socialist party, the dispersal of the Constituent Assembly and the unstinting use of terror against all real or imagined opponents breathed new life into the anti-Bolshevik struggle that had been almost moribund since October. Opposition to the Bolsheviks flared up in urban and rural areas, giving new hope to the anti-Bolshevik movements still in existence. The opposition, however, was local, uncoordinated and dispersed, and the Bolsheviks were becoming far more accustomed to deploying terror as a first resort or even pre-emptively. Cossack revolts against Soviet power joined the hundreds of other spontaneous revolts taking place independently in the spring of 1918.

In nearly all cases Cossack revolt was set off by the activity of punitive expeditions. Armed resistance in the Urals burst out after 500 Red Guards from the Orenburg Soviet descended on Iletskaia Stanitsa, deposed the local administration, shot one officer and began to systematically loot the stanitsa. The Iletskaia Cossacks fought back and wiped out the Red Guards and almost immediately their example was followed across the Ural *Voisko*.[27] In the Don, risings began to break out from March 1918. On the 8th March Cossacks from Luganskaia Stanitsa held up a train carrying Cossack prisoners and freed them. The next day Cossacks from Kholmilovskaia Stanitsa drove off a punitive detachement. But it was the rising of Suvorovskaia Stanitsa in mid-March which tied the disparate revolts together and initiated a general rising against Soviet power as opposed to rebelling against specific acts of its agents.[28] Revolts among the Kuban Cossack began at the beginning of April.[29]

Cossack revolts initially had much in common with peasant ones. They began through one community on its own taking action to ward off a threat or in retaliation for what they had suffered. But differences in the structure of Cossack and peasant communities produced very different types of revolt. All Cossack communities possessed large numbers of men with military experience. Although, as a result of the war, so did peasant ones, the distribution of military experience among the Cossacks was much more widespread. Officers of all ranks were liberally scattered through the Cossack settlements. The training of these men conditioned them to think beyond their immediate environment or forthcoming action and consider the wider picture. They were also accustomed to organizing and leading men in battle. The convention that men from the same stanitsa served in the same regiment provided Cossack units with an already existing cohesion that all other military units had to develop from scratch. Once mobilized and determined to fight, Cossack units were technically far superior to any that they were likely to face. But it was this determination to fight that had been so signally lacking a bare few weeks earlier.

By the spring of 1918 a very different type of mobilization was taking place. This mobilization emanated directly out of the stanitsas themselves. In effect a grass-roots mobilization was taking place – a horizontal as opposed to a vertical one. Not only the Don, but the Kuban, Terek, Ural and Orenburg Cossacks mobilized themselves in this way. The Cossacks in the Upper Don for example immediately the rising had began proclaimed a general mobilization of all men between seventeen and forty.[30] As we have seen, the Cossack administration based around the stanitsa had shrugged off all attempts by the Soviet authorities to penetrate it. Faced with a dire threat, stanitsa *sbory* surged into action, summoning the inhabitants of the stanitsa and its satellite settlements to decide on what action to take. In Migulinskaia Stanitsa in the upper Don region, news came of the approach of a punitive expedition:

> The news put an end to any doubts and the *sbor* unanimously decided to forestall a bloody battle and to disarm the red guards. To do this it was decided to proclaim a general mobilization of everyone from 20 to 55 years . . . a military staff of the stanitsa council, or as it called itself a military section, was formed in the *sbor*. Two officers and two ncos who were in the staff were elected commander of the unit and its chief of staff. These men were granted full authority and commissioned to lead military operations.[31]

Cossack stanitsas had a long tradition of cooperating with each other especially in times of crisis. Riders were sent to all the neighbouring stanitsas appealing for help. Nor was this unique to the Don. The Cossacks of Iletskaia Stanitsa immediately despatched messengers to other Ural stanitsas appealing for support.[32] Once the process had started, it took on a momentum of its own. Soviet punitive detachments no longer confronted isolated, defenceless communities, but proper military units numbering initially hundreds and then thousands of men fighting in defence of their homes and communities.

The resurgence of the Cossack *voiska*

In the spring of 1918 the triumphal march of Soviet power ground to halt and then rapidly reversed. Strikes in the cities, peasant and Cossack risings dramatically exposed how isolated the Bolsheviks had become since the heady days of October. The struggle for Soviet power had also become internationalized in the spring of 1918. The Treaty of Brest-Litovsk in March 1918 allowed the Bolsehviks to fulfill their promise of peace, but at a stunning cost. All of Ukraine, the Baltic States and large parts of the Don territory, up to the borders of the Kuban, came under German occupation. Despite having done all they could to bring the Bolsheviks to power in 1917, the Germans were determined to root them out of any areas they controlled. German power provided a shield behind which the anti-soviet movements could reorganize in the western parts of Russia. The revolt of the Czechoslovak Legion on the Trans-Siberian Railway brought Bolshevik power crashing down east of the Ural Mountains. The Soviet regime in matter of weeks had shrunk from a transcontinental power to the historic heartland of the old Muscovite state. The enemies of Soviet power now appeared ready to overwhelm it and establish a very different kind of state. Beleaguered on all sides, the apocalyptical struggle that the Bolsheviks had talked about for so long was now upon them. Far from cracking under the enormous pressure, however, the Bolsheviks were energized by the dire situation they had created for themselves. The threat of defeat unleashed the potential that had always existed in Bolshevism for unrestrained, unlimited violence consciously directed by the state.

The Cossack *voiska* that reconstituted themselves in the European part of Russia were much more ruthless organizations than those that had existed before. The belated attempts to extend olive branches to the non-Cossack population were not repeated. Peasant communities were now subjected to a vicious war that amounted to an early form of ethnic cleansing. In Siberia and the Far East an even more brutal form of power developed which became known as the '*atamanshchina*' that is the rule of the atamans. Simultaneously, the new Cossack states were much harsher in their attitudes to the Cossack population. They were equally ready to use violence against their own people, usually, but not always, in a more restrained and limited manner.[33] On all sides the conflict now recognized no distinction between civilian and soldier, young and old, man and woman.

The brutalization of the conflict was evident from the beginning of the Cossack revolt. The leader of the Don Soviet Government, Ensign Podtelkov and an entourage of around seventy of the most committed Cossack supporters of Soviet power found themselves cut off amidst a hostile population. Podtelkov and his companions attempted to break through to Soviet lines but were caught and disarmed by Cossacks taking part in the rising. A people's court was arranged which sentenced Podtelkov and his assistant Krivoshlykov to death by hanging and the remaining Cossacks to death by shooting.[34] The killing of seventy prisoners by their captors was an unremarkable event in the civil war, hardly worthy of note. But for the Cossacks it represented a radical departure from previous norms, violating a powerful taboo preventing Cossack communities using lethal violence against one of their own. That taboo had been broken irreparably by the summer of 1918.

The new Cossack governments continued to pay lip-service to the eventual restoration of a lawful Russian government, but increasingly emphasized independence and state building in the Cossack territories.[35] Other Cossack *voiska,* such as the Terek, the Ural and Orenburg did not contemplate independence as local circumstances did not offer the slightest chance of success. Instead powerful regional movements developed which sought sufficient autonomy to guarantee their way of life.

In Siberia and the Far East, the cohesion of the Cossacks was not sufficient to allow even this regional movement to develop. Instead the *voiska* there acted very much like peasant communities, responding to events as they affected their community and rarely transcending these boundaries. Some *voiska* even abandoned their Cossack identity altogether merging with the wider peasant community. In March 1918, a conference of the Transbaikal Cossacks abolished the Host and even the name 'Cossack'. The Amur Cossacks agreed a month later to amalgamate with surrounding peasant communities and, for all practical purposes, ceased to exist.[36] Cossack identity was becoming simultaneously stronger and weaker. Among those *voiska* who had never seen themselves as the creation of the central government, identity was now being expressed in either national or regional terms. For other hosts, always much more subject to government manipulation, 'Cossackness' no longer'appeared the defining feature of their identity.

In the European *voiska,* the new governments set about organizing the institutions of a state. First and foremost were the creation of armies. The mobilizations that had taken place in the spring were largely local affairs, but the new Cossack governments rapidly took over this effective but unsystematic mobilization and imposed a central one. The response of the Cossacks to this mobilization showed just how far and fast attitudes had shifted since October when hardly any Cossacks were willing to fight. Now in the Don and Kuban regular armies were created; by the summer the Don could boast a field army of almost 40,000.[37] The Kuban army merged with the Volunteer Army as a result of an agreement between the Kuban government and General Denikin, its leader, although neither the Kuban Cossacks nor their government showed much enthusiasm for Volunteer Army's ultimate objectives.[38] These were not armies of guerillas or partisans but units capable of meeting the newly formed Red Army head on. Again in the Urals and Orenburg matters were not so clear cut. Constantly shifting front lines and rears emphasized the local nature of the struggle. Rather than full scale encounters between regular armies, a savage guerilla war developed on the Ural and Orenburg territories.[39] The priority the Bolsheviks gave the different Cossack *voiska* likewise reflected these differences. The Don and the Kuban became the focus of the state's efforts while the other *voiska* were much more the responsibility of local soviet authorities. This in itself tended to emphasize either the national or regional nature of the struggle.

How did ordinary Cossacks respond to these momentous changes? It is not possible to gauge their attitudes simply from appeals and counter-appeals addressed to them. General Krasnov, the new ataman of the Don, made ringing declarations about the independence of the Don, but this did not mean that all Cossacks were committed to fight for independence or trusted the new governments unambiguously. Nevertheless, the successful raising of large armies showed at the very least that the bulk of the Cossacks had accepted that they could not stay out of this struggle. Still at issue, however, was precisely what sort of a struggle it was. For the Don and Kuban elites it was a struggle for national independence; for the Volunteer Army it was a struggle for Russia one and indivisible; for the Soviet side it was a struggle to liberate the oppressed of the earth. Ordinary Cossacks moved between these options-many fighting on different sides. 1918 would be a year of fluid loyalties. Those Cossacks who had experienced Bolshevik power in its harshest form, such as those of the lower Don, were more resolutely committed to a long term struggle for independence. Those who had not been so scarred by the experience of soviet rule still tended to believe that some accomodation with the Bolsheviks was possible. What was very evident was the absence of any desire to fight for a unitary Russian state.

The rapid collapse of Soviet power in the spring of 1918 was followed by a sudden stiffening as the Soviet regime implemented draconian measures to ensure its survival. The disbanding of the Red Guards and the formation of the Red Army signified the increasing professionalization of the conflict. The proclamation of the Red Terror, after the attempted assassination of Lenin, extended the war into the civilian population. Through the summer and autumn of 1918 heavy fighting took place continuously in the Cossack territories. Although the Don and Kuban had been mostly cleared of Soviet forces by late summer, the Bolsheviks continued to fight hard to recover their position.

All the Cossack *voiska* were conducting separate campaigns, unable to support each other even if they had wished. By the autumn Cossacks had been fighting continuously since the rebellions of the spring. Without any end to the fighting in sight, exhaustion and demoralization set in.[40] The Soviet state appeared to have endless human and material resources which no amount of defeats or setbacks seemed able to diminish. In all the major theatres of the war, the Don, Kuban and Urals, ordinary Cossacks began to despair of the fighting ever ending. At this moment Bolshevik strategy once more displayed the same acute awareness of Cossack needs and desires as it had the previous October. Cossacks were bombarded with propaganda, appealing to them to stand with their brother workers and peasants. The Soviet regime had no quarrel with ordinary Cossacks, simply their leaders who were tools of international capital:

> Brother Cossacks! We believe that they majority of you have been deceived by the old regime and that you are the unwilling accomplices of the hangmen of the people. But by heeding the voice of conscience you will fight against the hangmen. Leave their ranks and join us for the common struggle against the enemies of the people.[41]

Combining easily with demoralization, these appeals sapped the will of the Cossacks to fight.

The Don remained the key front throughout the civil war. The Bolsheviks knew that once the Don Cossacks had been defeated and their land occupied the civil war would to all intents and purposes have been over. It was on this front that events were running most strongly in the Bolsheviks' favour. On their own initiative Cossacks began to negotiate cease-fires with their opposite numbers. In return for promises to respect the Cossack way of life nor to molest Cossacks, Cossacks in the upper Don began to drift away from the frontlines. By the end of the year this process had become unstoppable. Gaping holes opened up in the Cossack frontlines through which Bolsheviks forces poured.[42] Once sufficient numbers of Cossacks had lost the will to continue the fight, no amount of coercion could keep them in the field.[43] A decree of the *krug* threatening 'to punish the traitors with the full severity of the law, applying to the traitors the penalties laid down for treason' failed to hold the army together.[44] The much shrunken Cossack army retreated southwards. At the same time the defeat of Germany removed a critical stabilizing factor for the whole anti-Bolshevik struggle. Everywhere Bolshevik forces shifted on to the offensive, driving their enemies before them.

The genocide of the Cossacks

Reports from Bolshevik officials towards the end of 1918 were brimming with confidence and optimism at the imminent defeat of all the anti-Soviet Cossack forces. The Red Army was driving hard towards the capital of the Don, Novocherkassk, while further east Uralsk and Orenburg were poised to fall. The Volunteer Army was still bogged down in the Kuban, far from any strategic centre and no threat to Bolshevik power. Unceasing military pressure and deft political propaganda had opened up old divisions and resentments in Cossack society with startling results. Nothing appeared to stand in the way of victory and an early end to the civil war.

The Bolshevik leadership uplifted by the successes of the Red Army turned their attention to the consolidation of Soviet rule in the newly reconquered Cossack homelands. Above all they were determined not to repeat the mistakes that had led to its collapse earlier in the year. The party, however, at local and national level was divided on what precisely those mistakes were.[45] Some party members on the ground argued for a continuation of the policies that had given such spectacular results that autumn. Many believed that the Cossacks were ready to welcome the Bolsheviks as liberators from the counter-revolution and that as long as the Red Army maintained its discipline and Soviet officials showed respect for Cossack sensibilities, victory was certain. One party official wrote:

> If we are able, and we must be able, to raise still further the consciousness of the Red Army men then our imminent victory over the counter-revolution will be secure and as well we will secure an internal spontaneous revolt against the *krasnovshchina*. And so the Red Army's movement forward will be not through a country of enemies but through a country of close friends united by blood and belief.[46]

Repeatedly through the civil war Bolshevism demonstrated its capacity for pragmatic adaption to a multitude of local circumstances just as these officials were doing with the Cossacks. Pragmatism, however, was not the only strain contained within Bolshevism. Millenarianism existed in constant tension with it and now flushed with military success, the millenarians within the party proposed a radically different solution to the Cossack problem.

The Cossacks, they argued, were perpetual opponents of Soviet power. From the Don to the Ussuri the Cossacks were at the core of all

Figure 15 *Decossackization 1919*, by Dmitrii Shmarin, 1995

anti-Bolshevik movements. Attempts to exploit divisions within Cossack society were fundamentally misconceived since Cossack opposition to Soviet power did not derive from their class position, but from their being Cossacks.[47] Given that Cossacks were by their nature enemies of Soviet power, it followed that their resistance would only end when they ceased to be Cossacks. A successful solution to the Cossack problem, therefore, did not depend on applying different policies to rich, middle or poor Cossacks; on the contrary it demanded one policy for all Cossacks, regardless of socio-economic status or political loyalties. Such a policy must have as its goal the elimination of the Cossacks as a distinct group through the destruction of their culture and way of life or through their physical extermination. One party member who advocated this approach wrote to the Chairman of the Central Committee Sverdlov at the end of September 1918:

> Our direct acquaintance with the political essence of the civil war taking place on the Don which began at the same time as our arrival in Velikokniazhevskaia Stanitsa has led us to be convinced first and foremost that this war has the character not so much of a direct class struggle so much as one of communal antagonism between Cossacks and peasants. The example of other parts of the Russian countryside do not correspond with this. The struggle in the Don *oblast'* has developed not as a struggle between wealthy kulaks and the poor, but as a struggle between citizens 'brothers' Cossacks on one side and 'louts' 'fugitives' *inogorodnie*, on the other. This has caused the almost universal uprising of the Cossacks which is raging over all the peasants without exception and has compelled the peasants to cling on to their homes with unbelievable stubborness and to stand firm for Soviet power. As a consequence the conviction has spread among the Cossacks that it is necessary to exterminate the *inogorodnie* to a man (the Don for the *Dontsi*) which in its turn has forced the peasantry and Soviet armies to begin to think about the necessity of a universal extermination of the Cossacks.[48]

These were the choices that the Bolshevik leaders pondered at the end of 1918 as the reconquest of the Cossack territories approached completion. Both the pragmatic and millennial option conformed equally well to the Bolshevik tradition. But the party leadership had increasingly began to share the 'Cossack phobia' of some of the ordinary party members.[49] No record has yet been discovered of the debates that must have gone on within the party leadership as they discussed the Cossack problem, but the outcome of the discussions is not in doubt.

On 24 January 1919 the Orgbiuro issued a secret circular to all party, military and Cheka organizations in the Cossack territories. The Circular had been drawn up primarily with the Don in mind, but nothing in it indicated that it was to be limited to the Don Cossacks; all Cossacks fell within its capacious scope. It is worth quoting that circular in full.

24 January 1919
Circular. Secret.

The latest events on different fronts in the Cossack regions-our advance into the interior of the Cossack settlements and the disintegration among the Cossack hosts-compels us to give instructions to party workers about the character of their work during the reestablishment and strengthening of Soviet power in the said regions. It is necessary to recognize, based on the experience of the civil war with the Cossacks, that the most merciless struggle with all the upper layers of the Cossacks through their extermination to a man is the only correct policy. No compromises or halfheartedness whatsoever are acceptable. Therefore it is necessary:

1. To carry out mass terror against wealthy Cossacks, exterminating them to a man; to carry out merciless mass terror in relations to all Cossacks who have taken part in any way directly or indirectly in the struggle with Soviet power. Against the middle Cossacks it is necessary to take all those measures which give a guarantee against any attempt on their part [to join] a new attack on Soviet power.

2. To confiscate grain and force [them] to gather all surpluses in designated points; this applies both to grain and all other agricultural products.

3. To take all measures assisting the resettlement of newly arrived poor, organizing this settlement where possible.

4. To equalize newly arrive *inogorodnie* with the Cossacks in land and in all other relations.

5. To carry out complete disarmament, shooting those who after the time of handing over are found to have arms.

6. To give arms only to reliable elements from the *inogorodnie.*

7. Armed detachments are to be stationed in Cossack stanitsas henceforward until the establishment of complete order.

8. To order all commissars appointed to this or that Cossack settlement to show maximum firmness and to carry out the present orders unswervingly.

TsK imposes the obligation on Narkomzem to work out quickly practical measures concerning the mass resettlement of poor on Cossack land to be carried out through the corresponding Soviet institutions.

Central Committee RKP[50]

The leadership in their millenarian outlook probably believed that they were doing no more than speeding up an historically inevitable process. In their eyes the Cossacks were an anachronism doomed to disappear in the new Communist society just as peasants would eventually do so.[51] Unlike peasants who were too numerous, for the present, to be despatched immediately into non-existence, the Cossacks were sufficiently small to make it possible to contemplate such a step. The direct military threat the Cossacks presented to the regime made it necessary. The Bolsheviks had been in power barely a year when they took this decision; in twelve months their ambition to use state violence and their capacity to carry it out had grown exponentially.

Revolutionary tribunals were set up in every Cossack stanitsa through which the Red Army passed. Immediately they began their work of selecting Cossacks for extermination. Local officials were given no supplementary guidance on how to discern a wealthy Cossack from a middle or poor one or what constituted direct or indirect participation in the anti-soviet struggle. Brutally clear, however, was the repeated injunction to interpret the decree in the harshest possible way. The Bolshevik leadership conceived of their violence as an abstract, impersonal force of history, but the sheer physicality of it was hideous. The tribunals worked without regard for evidence, due process or any right of appeal. One horrified eye-witness described the operation of the tribunal in Khoperskaia Stanitsa:

> The point is that the tribunal heard around 50 cases a day and so it is possible to judge how attentively they heard the cases. Death sentences were handled out in bundles. Moreover often those who were shot were completely innocent old men, old women and children. Well known cases were the shooting of an old man of 60 for an unknown reason: a young girl of 17 denounced by one of the wives out of jealously despite the fact that it was well known that this girl had never taken any part in politics. They were shot on suspicion of speculation, spying. It was sufficient for the mentally unbalanced Detkin to declare in the meeting of the revtribunal that the condemned was well known to him as a counter-revolutionary for the tribunal without any other evidence to sentence the person to be shot . . . The shootings were carried out during the day in view of all the stanitsa, 40 or 50 at a time. Moreover the condemned were led to the place of shooting with mocking, with whoops and cries. At the place of shooting the condemned were stripped naked in front of all the inhabitants. The women, covering their nakedness with their hands, were mocked and forbidden to do this. All the shot people were buried in shallow graves close to the mill not far from the stanitsa. The result of this was that a pack of dogs gathered around the mill and fell evilly on the deceased inhabitants and the dragged the arms and legs of the executed through the stanitsa.[52]

The writer of this report was not anti-Bolshevik, but a member of the party appalled at what was happening. Other party members filed similar reports. In a few short weeks approximately 8,000 Cossacks were executed by revolutionary tribunals in the upper Don territory.[53] In the Urals thousands more Cossacks were shot.[54]

Through physical extermination of anyone who might conceivably pose a threat to them, the Bolsheviks sought to remove an immediate threat. Just as important, though the regime wanted to destroy any capacity the society had to regenerate itself in the future. Terror served as starting point for this, but it was supplemented by a series of measures designed to cut the invisible nexus that tied one Cossack to another and each to the land of their birth. By insisting on the confiscation of all 'surpluses', another word with a very elastic definition in the Bolshevik dictionary, the survivors would be kept at semi-starvation or starvation level and utterly dependent on the state for their survival. Importing thousands of non-Cossack settlers on to Cossack land would destroy the economic basis of their way of life as well as providing a hostile population to keep them in permanent subjection. Subjected to such relentless pressure not only would a large percentage of the community be physically exterminated, but its very identity as a distinct community would be broken and lost.

The Bolsheviks were also beginning to experiment with the idea of mass deportations of Cossacks. The Circular specifically mentioned 'mass resettlement of poor on Cossack land' which carried within it the implication of eviction and deportation. The Party organization in the Don, discussing the implementation of the Orgburo order, decided 'To Take all measures towards the deportation of Cossacks, with the exception of Red Cossacks, from a 50 kilometre strip on both sides of the railway and to resettle armed supporters of Soviet power from the poor.'[55] Deportation was also seriously considered for the Ural Cossacks at the same time.[56] The demands of the civil war, however, prevented any implementation of these plans. Yet this was not a passing phase of Bolshevik policy brought on by the exigencies of the civil war. Thousands of Terek Cossacks were deported at the end of 1920, providing valuable experience for the regime in the practicalities of deporting large numbers of people.[57] It would of course become an established practice of the regime under Stalin, but it was first used under Lenin.

For all its ruthless logic, the new Bolshevik policy had one flaw. Its implementation was premised on a society that had already been defeated and was defenceless before the overwhelming power of the state. The Cossacks had been battered by five years of fighting, but they were far from defeated. Those Cossacks that had opened the front to the Bolsheviks had not been defeated, but had negotiated in good faith. Now faced with betrayal and imminent destruction, the Cossacks of the upper Don used the same cultural resources that had made possible a successful rebellion the previous spring: the stanitsa and the Cossack military tradition.

In early March 1919 the revolt began in Veshenskaia Stanitsa. Neighbouring stanitsas immediately joined and within days all of the upper Don was in rebellion.[58] Soviet forces who had days earlier confronted only terrified, defenceless citizens were bewildered to find themselves up against armies that had seemingly materialized out of the ether. The rebellion stopped the advance of the Red Army in its tracks. Once the momentum of the advance stalled, confusion and fear replaced the elation which had recently been so evident. The example of Soviet officials taking to their heels, with the staff of the revolutionary tribunals foremost, did little to improve moral among soviet forces.

The Army of the Don seemingly heading for inevitable defeat rallied as news filtered through about the rising in the Northern Don. Bolstered by the Volunteer Army, the Army of the Don moved onto the offensive. Already unnerved by the Cossack rising in the upper Don and the headlong flight of many officials, the Red Army collapsed completely. In a matter of days, the whole strategic shape of the war had shifted. From imminent victory, the Bolsheviks now faced an invigorated foe, advancing on all fronts. A few weeks later a Bolshevik official looking back on the wreckage of the Soviet advance into the Don wrote:

> From the military point of view the Cossacks are excellent material. From early childhood they are accustomed to master weapons and are good cavalry. This gives them the possibility of organizing battle worthy military units. . . . All these conditions made it possible for the rebel Cossacks to rally immediately and quickly create military units out of the crowds of rebelling Cossacks. They also made possible the creation of a battle hardened army which has nothing in common with the kulak rebellions which we have seen in central Russia.[59]

Too late, the Bolshevik leadership realized the catastrophic error they had made in January and belatedly attempted to undo it. A week after the beginning of the rebellion in the Northern Don a meeting of the Central Committee which included Lenin, Trotsky, and Stalin discussed the Cossack rebellion. The Central Committee resolved:

> In view of the clear split between the northern and southern Cossacks in the Don and in so far as the northern Cossacks might join with us, we resolve to suspend the carrying out of measures against the Cossacks in order not to prevent their disintegration. The same is accepted in regard to the Orenburg and Ural [Cossacks] with the qualification excluding the antagonism between the North and the South which does not exist in the Urals.[60]

There was no word of regret or even overt mention of what had taken place. Physical extermination had become 'the carrying out of measures against the Cossacks'. There was nothing to indicate that thousands of human beings had lost their lives in an indiscriminate orgy of killings. Bolshevik policy once more reverted to its pragmatic mode but not surprisingly there were few now who would place any trust in the Bolsheviks or their promises. Whatever sympathy had existed among the Cossacks had vanished to be replaced by an unwavering commitment to drive out all Bolsheviks for good. For the first time since the revolution began, all sections of Cossack society shared broadly the same goals.

The Moscow march

The revolt of the upper Don in 1919 initiated a wave of anti-Bolshevik successes that would culminate in Moscow campaign of the summer of that year. The Volunteer Army had completed the conquest of the Kuban and returned to the Don as the rising in the north began. Denikin's position was strengthened by British insistence that he be recognized as the commander of all anti-Bolshevik forces in southern Russia. Krasnov, much weakened by the defeat of Germany, reluctantly agreed to subordinate the Don Army to Denikin. After fifteen desperately difficult months, the Volunteer Army was poised to take the struggle out of the Cossack periphery into the heartland of the Bolshevik state. With large Bolshevik forces still tied up with the fight against Admiral Kolchak, the constellation of forces had never been so favourable to those seeking to overthrow the Bolsheviks nor would it be again. All sides sensed that the critical moments of the civil war were fast approaching.

Denikin's offensive rolled forward in three separate thrusts: through Ukraine, north out of the Don and along the Volga. City after city fell as Bolshevik forces collapsed. Tsaritsyn, the Red Verdun, surrendered, opening the way to link up with the Orenburg and Ural Cossacks for the first time. By mid-summer the combined Volunteer and Don armies were deep into Soviet territory, ready for the final push towards Moscow. Celebrating the fall of Tambov, Denikin issued his Moscow directive and his forces moved swiftly northwards with the capital firmly in their sights.

Cossacks who constituted the overwhelming majority of the anti-Bolshevik forces were fighting outside the borders of their own homelands for the first time since the civil war began. Despite appearances, however, Cossack enthusiasm for the common anti-Bolshevik struggle was no greater than it had been earlier.[61] Tension between the Cossack elites and the leadership of the Volunteer Army had been reduced but not eliminated by the removal of Krasnov as ataman. The unwavering commitment of the Volunteer Army to 'Russia One and Indivisible' struck few chords with the Cossacks. Only a recognition that on their own the Cossacks could neither defeat nor keep out the Bolsheviks from their homelands persuaded them to go north. Speed, and above all, success were necessary to keep the Cossacks committed to the cause. As long as the advance was successful, the tensions between the various elements of the White cause could be contained.

Even though the Bolsheviks were forced to divide their forces to meet the threats from the east and the south, they still possessed overwhelming superiority in numbers. Only in cavalry did the anti-Bolshevik forces have superiority, thanks of course to the Cossacks. The unbroken, densely fortified frontline of the First World War had reduced the cavalry to insignificance. The frontlines of the Russian civil war, however, were broken and shallow, allowing easy penetration deep into the rear. In this war cavalry were no anachronism, but potentially a war winning weapon and there were no cavalry like the Cossacks. Concentrated into large cavalry armies, Cossack cavalry spearheaded the White offensives, punching holes in the Red frontlines and bringing chaos to the rear areas. Moving swiftly, Cossack cavalry armies operated at will deep in enemy territory. Raids by Generals Mamontov of the Don Cossacks and Shkuro of the Kuban Cossacks became legends of the civil war. Now indeed the Bolsheviks were made to pay for their treatment of the Cossacks.

All summer and into autumn the White offensive moved ever closer to Moscow. Cities on the approach to Moscow fell in succession and by October the Whites were at Orel less than 200 kilometres from the capital. The fighting had been heavy and was getting heavier as it drew nearer to Moscow. The industrialized cities of the north had little sympathy with the Whites whatever their quarrels with the Bolsheviks. The peasantry who had suffered enormously at the hands of the Bolsheviks showed even less enthusiasm for the Whites who they believed, with good reason, were fighting for the return of old regime. With no possibility of popular support, victory depended on Bolshevik collapse. But even as the Whites approached Moscow, the Bolsheviks' determination to hold on to power and to defeat the Whites never wavered. Concentrating their forces in front of the capital, they readied themselves for a counter-offensive just as the Whites were coming to the end of their strength. The heavy fighting of the summer had exhausted their reserves at the point when their goal appeared to be within their grasp. When the Bolshevik counter-offensive struck in

October, the White front deflated rapidly. Soon the Whites were in headlong retreat. Only once the fighting re-entered the Cossack territories did the retreat slow down. But there could be no doubting the final outcome. Bolshevik resources were now so overwhelming while that of the Cossacks were so reduced that it was only a matter of time before victory.

All the Cossack *voiska* collapsed in early 1920. With the defeat of the Don and Kuban Cossacks, any direct threat to the regime was eliminated. The Urals and Orenburg *voiska* succumbed at the same time while the hosts of the Far East had long ceased to be anything more than an irritant to the Bolsheviks. Organized, centrally directed resistance of the Cossacks to the Bolsheviks came to an end, but thousands of Cossacks continued to fight on as individuals and as members of the innumerable gangs operating on all the Cossack territories.

Conclusion

The civil war had been a horrendous experience for the Cossacks. The Cossack homelands particularly those of the North Caucasus and the Urals had been the main battlegrounds of the civil war. Invasion, occupation and rebellion had followed in relentless cycles. The hosts of Siberia and the Far East had been destroyed while the vibrant, self-conscious communities that had existed in the European part of Russia had been eviscerated. In the Don and Ural *Voiska* the Cossack population was approximately half of what it had been in 1917. In the Don, for example, possibly as many as 1.3 million Cossack men, women and children lost their lives during the civil war.[62] Losses caused by the First World War paled into insignificance compared to those killed in the civil war. Some indication of the scale of the killing can be gauged from the losses of two stanitsas in the Upper Don. Seventeen men had been killed as a result of the First World War in Eryzhinskaia but 320 had been killed in the civil war; the respective figures for Annenskaia were 22 and 413.[63] Economic losses were on a commensurate scale. Only the Kuban had escaped with significantly lower human and material losses.[64] It would become the centre of gravity for the Cossacks under the new regime.

Paradoxically, even though the conflicts of 1917 to 1920 destroyed or severely weakened Cossacks, the revolutionary process had crystallized Cossack identity into new forms. The February Revolution destroyed the political structure which had constrained and defined Cossack identity for the previous 200 years. All the Cossack *voiska* took the opportunity to redefine their relationship with the new central government. They recognized the overarching authority of the state, but beneath it they carved out self-governing enclaves. The October Revolution replaced a benign central authority with one that was implacably imposed to the Cossacks in the long run. Although most Cossacks did not discern this immediately, the experience of Bolshevik rule offered ample proof of it. But Cossacks now confronted a dilemma. If the central state was hostile to them what political structure was available to them.

For the hosts of the Urals and east of the Urals, the brutal truth was that there was no structure available to them. Scattered and isolated by the vast expanses of Siberia and the Far East, these Cossack communities responded largely as individual settlements, trying to ward off outside interference in their way of life. Attempts to move beyond this produced only the *atamanshchina* and levels of psychopathic violence, shocking even by the depraved standards of the civil war. West of the Urals, the mobilization of the communities took more constructive forms. Among the Orenburg and Ural Cossack, regional movements developed which sought to preserve their way of life under the auspices of a benign central state. But as with the *atamanshchina* this too led into a dead end as the central state resolutely sought their destruction. Continued existence for the Cossacks depended on a life outside the Russian state. Only for the Don and Kuban was this a real possibility.

Their history, their attachment to their native lands and their institutional resources contained the potential for the transition to nationhood. Strangely enough, it was a senior party member on the Don who put his finger on the key source of Cossack identity:

> Neither stripes, nor the word 'Cossack' or 'stanitsa' have made the Cossack a Cossack. It is their way of life. And it necessary to pay particular attention to this. It is necessary with skilful propaganda to reveal all the dark sides of the Cossack past (of which there are a great many) and to show through the practice of Soviet construction the bright sides of the new life. And then the Cossacks will cease to be Cossacks.[65]

Perhaps not so strange: the party member in question was V.V. Trifonov a Cossack from Novocherkassk stanitsa. Turning this potential into reality, however, required a cataclysmic shock. Not even the civil war on its own could suffice to drive the Don and Kuban Cossacks down the road towards nationhood. It was the realization that the regime was targeting them for immediate destruction rather than some long drawn out campaign of attrition that galvanized the Cossacks. The Don and Kuban elites were already thinking of independence by October 1917. The bitter experience of Bolshevik rule in 1918 and 1919 convinced most ordinary Cossacks that there was no other way for them. Not surprisingly this nationalism was inchoate and not fully developed. Decades of work would have been necessary to consolidate the nascent national identity of the Don and Kuban Cossacks. But the political mobilization of the community had taken place in 1918 and 1919 which put the Cossacks firmly on the road to independent nationhood. Nations and nationalisms are contingent and are subject to the ebb and flow of events; the Don and Kuban were no exception to this rule. The same revolutionary processes that had brought them to the brink of independent nationhood ultimately dashed any possibility that it would be realized.

Notes

1 *Postanovleniia Bol'shogo Voiskogo Kruga voiska Donskogo tret'iago sozyva. 2–13 Dekabria 1917 godu* (Novocherkassk, 1917).

2 A.V. Venkov, *Antibolshevistskoe Dvizhenie na Iuge Rossii na Nachal'nom Etape Grazhdanskoi Voiny* (Rostov-na-Donu, 1995) p. 93.

3 N.I. Fokin, *Final Tragedii: Ural'skie Kazaki v XX veke* (Moscow, 1996) pp. 95–97.

4 Y. Akhapkin, *First Decrees of Soviet Power* (London, 1970) p. 26.

5 T.V. Tabolina (ed.), *Vozrozhdenie Kazachestva 1989–1994* (Moscow, 1994) p. 232.

6 Tabolina, *Vozrozhdenie Kazachestva*, p. 238.

7 Trut, *Kazachii Izlom*, p. 135.

8 Sergeev, *Politicheskie Partii*, vol. 2, pp. 96–98.

9 Astapenko, *Istoriia Kazachestva*, vol. 3, pp. 315–316.

10 Trut, *Kazachii Izlom*, p. 145.

11 GARF, f.1255, op.1, d.57, l.2.

12 GARF, f.1255, op.1, d.57, l.2.

13 Trut, *Kazachii Izlom*, p. 140.

14 Fokin, *Final Tragedii*, pp. 86–89.

15 Savchenko, *Ussuriiskoe Kazach'e Voisko*, p. 76.

16 *Donskaia Volna*, 12 May 1919.

17 RGASPI, f.64, op.1, d.247, ll.104–6.

18 Trut, *Kazachii Izlom*, p. 173.

19 GARF, f.1255, op.1, d.156, l.243.

20 *Donskaia Volna*, 18 June 1918. Golubunskaia Stanitsa declared that 'we from the youngest to the oldest will stand in defence of our NATIVE FATHER, THE QUIET, GREY DON'. GARF, f.1255, op.1, d.56, l.258. (Capitals in the original.)

21 *Postanovleniia Chastnogo Soveshchaniia Deputatov Voiskovogo Kruga Voiska Donskogo 3 Ianvaria-5 Fevralia 1918* (Novocherkassk, 1918) p. 4.
22 RGASPI, f.64, op.1, d.247, ll.3–4.
23 *Donskaia Volna*, 10 February 1919.
24 *Donskaia Volna*, 12 May 1919.
25 *Donskaia Volna*, 2 September 1919.
26 *Donskaia Volna*, 10 February 1919.
27 Fokin, *Final Tragedii*, pp. 126–134.
28 G. Ianov, 'Don pod Bolshevikami Vesnoi 1918 goda i Vosstanie stanits na Donu' in *Donskaia Letopis'*, vol 2, pp. 22–23.
29 Kutsenko, *Kubanskoe Kazachestvo*, p. 328.
30 Ianov, 'Don pod Bolshevikami', in *Donskaia Letopis'*, vol. 2, p. 26.
31 *Donskaia Volna*, 12 May 1919.
32 Fokin, *Final Tragedii*, p. 129.
33 Grazhdanin, *Vsevelikoe Voisko Donskoe*, p. 96.
34 *Donskaia Volna*, 29 June 1918.
35 K. Kakliugin, 'Donskoi Ataman P.N. Krasnov i ego Vremia' in *Donskaia Letopis'*, vol. 3, pp. 70–71.
36 Astapenko, *Istoriia Kazachestva Rossii*, vol. 3, p. 406.
37 V. Dobrynin 'Vooruzhennaia Bor'ba Dona c Bolshevikami' in *Donskaia Letopis'*, vol. 1, p. 103.
38 Tabolina, *Rossisskoe Kazachestvo*, p. 256.
39 Fokin, *Final Tragedii*, pp. 173–176.
40 Kislitsyn, *Gosudarstvo i Raskazachivanie*, p. 20.
41 GARF, f.1235, op.82, d.10, l.193.
42 Dobrynin, 'Vooruzhennaia Bor'ba Dona', in *Donskaia Letopis'*, vol. 1, p. 111.
43 Kislitsyn, *Gosudarstvo i Raskazachivanie*, p. 20.
44 GARF, f.1235, op.82, d.15, l.286.
45 Holquist, *Making War, Forging Revolution*, pp. 173–174.
46 GARF, f.1235, op.82, d.15, ll.67–68.
47 Holquist, *Making War, Forging Revolution*, pp. 174–178.
48 RGASPI, f.71, op.34, d.2158, l.89. *Inogorodnie* were peasants who migrated into the Cossack territories after 1861.
49 Kislitsyn, *Gosudarstvo i Raskazachivanie*, p. 22.
50 RGASPI, f.17, op.4, d.7, l.5.
51 Kislitsyn, *Gosudarstvo i Raskazachivanie*, p. 7.
52 GARF, f.1235, op.83, d.8, ll.43–52.
53 This figure is based on an estimate by *Nezavisimaia Gazeta*, 23 April 1992.
54 Fokin, *Final Tragedii*, p. 218.
55 RGASPI, f.17, op.65, l.35, l.215.
56 Kislitsyn, *Gosudarstvo i Raskazachivanie*, p. 27.
57 RGASPI, f.64, op.1, d.247, ll.15–16.
58 Dobrynin, 'Vooruzhennaia Bor'ba Dona', in *Donskaia Letopis'*, vol. 1, p. 118.

59 RGASPI, f.17, op.65, d.35, l.30.
60 RGASPI, f.17, op.2, d.11, l.104.
61 Kislitsyn, *Gosudarstvo i Raskazachivanie*, p. 31.
62 Grazhdanin, *Vsevelikoe Voisko Donskoe*, p. 96.
63 GARF, f.1235, op.82, d.15, l.121.
64 Ia. A. Perekhov, *Vlast' i Kazachestvo: Poisk Soglasiia* (Rostov-na-Donu, 1997) p. 29.
65 RGASPI, f.17, op.65, d.34, l.89.

The Cossacks under Soviet power

By early 1920 the Red Army had won the civil war. True, General Wrangel with the last of the White forces was holding out in the Crimea and a bitter war with Poland was to break out almost immediately, but incontestably the Bolsheviks had triumphed. Other regimes might have been dismayed or daunted by the prospect before them as they surveyed the wreckage of the former empire: not the Bolsheviks. If anything, victory sent a surge of adrenalin flowing through them, fuelling their ambitions to build their version of paradise not just in Russia but throughout the world. Domestic and international circumstances suddenly appeared to come together to make everything possible. War Communism which had began as an ad hoc response to the collapse of industrial production and the shortage of grain in 1918 had coalesced into fully blown system by 1920. Resting on the nationalization of industry, the abolition of the market and the seizure of grain from the peasantry, it projected a vision and a path to the future socialist society. The international prospects appeared equally bright as the Red Army swept deep into Poland, holding out the tantalizing possibility of reaching the German border and linking up with the revolutionary movement in Germany.

One year later euphoria had been replaced by dismal reality. The Red Army had been driven out of Poland, ending any prospect of European wide revolution. At home, the situation was catastrophic. The largest peasant revolt in history was underway, embracing Siberia, the North Caucasus, the Ukraine and parts of the central provinces. Peasant revolt was bad enough, but not entirely unexpected. Far worse was the rejection of the Bolsheviks by their key constituencies. Strikes broke out in Petrograd and other major cities, and, most crushingly of all, the sailors of Krondstadt, the 'pride and glory of the revolution', had risen in revolt against the Bolshevik regime.

Under more pressure than at any time in the civil war, Lenin recognized the necessity of changing course. Once more it was time for pragmatism to assert itself over utopianism. The result was the New Economic Policy which denationalized much of what industry was left, legalized private trade and replaced requisitioning with taxation, leaving peasants to dispose of any surplus on the market. On the political front, however, there were absolutely no concessions; on the contrary, the dictatorship of the party was even more tightly enforced. The Krondstadt rebels were crushed, merciless pacification campaigns were undertaken in the countryside to defeat the peasants, and even within the party the room for discussion was drastically reduced with the ban on factions.

The Cossacks in emigration

The experience of civil war had convinced tens of thousands of Cossacks that they could expect little mercy from the victorious Bolsheviks. Like defeated Cossack rebels in earlier centuries, the only option was to leave Russia in the hope of a better life elsewhere. Cossacks of the Ural, Orenburg and Far Eastern hosts trekked east towards the Chinese border while those of the Don, Kuban and Terek found refuge of a sort in Europe. From these initial havens, Cossacks gradually dispersed across the globe finding homes in Brazil, the USA, Australia as well as various European countries. The fate of the exile communities reflected that of the Cossacks who remained behind. The Don, Kuban and Terek Cossacks were able to keep their distinct identities alive much longer in exile than the hosts of the Urals and those further east. The numbers of exiles from the Don, Kuban and Terek were greater than other hosts and the continuing existence of their communities in their native land helped sustain them in exile. The small number of exiles from other Cossack communities and the dissolution of their native *voiska* left them adrift with little to sustain their identity as a Cossack.

The great bulk of Cossack exiles left on board ships from the Crimea in November 1920. Unlike the evacuation from Novorossiisk in March of the same year, the evacuation from the Crimea was properly planned and carried out. Approximately 50,000 Cossacks mostly men of the Army of the Don and the Volunteer Army went into exile from the Crimea; 28,000 were from the Don and 18,000 from the Kuban.[1]

The Cossacks were carried under French protection to a number of camps in Turkey and on islands in the Aegean Sea of which Lemnos was the most important. Conditions in the camps were miserable. Shelter, food, fuel and medicine were all in short supply which contributed to frequent outbreaks of stomach problems and a few outbreaks of cholera. Even more debilitating than the wretched living conditions was the uncertainty over the future. What would become of these Cossacks? The French who were responsible for them rapidly lost interest. The numbers of Russian exiles including the Cossacks was far greater than they had anticipated and they desired to wash their hands of them as quickly as possible. In March 1921 the French announced that they were cutting their links with all the Crimean exiles, offering them the choice of returning to the Soviet Union, emigrating to Brazil or taking their chances on their own.

Fortunately for the Cossacks, Bulgaria, Yugoslavia and Czechoslovakia offered them new refuges. In 1922 the Cossacks took ship again to their new homes. Most of the Don Cossacks went to Bulgaria while those from the Kuban settled in Serbia. In more permanent places of exile the Cossacks began to reconstruct their lives as best they could. Political, social and cultural organizations were formed to help protect their interests and preserve their cohesion. Archives were collected, newspapers produced and many accounts of the Cossack civil war experience were published. Belgrade and later Prague became important centres of the Cossack diaspora. Most Cossacks still wished to return to their homelands. Some took advantage of the various amnesties the Bolsheviks offered while others clung to the hope of returning to a non-Bolshevik Russia. Both groups were destined for tragedy.

The Cossacks and the Bolsheviks after the civil war

The Cossacks were one of many minorities who had fought against the Bolsheviks and now found themselves under the power of the new regime. Bolshevik policy towards ethnic and national minorities, in many ways sophisticated and enlightened, sought to depoliticize their national or ethnic aspirations while preserving or even promoting their cultural identity.[2] The Bolsheviks, and Lenin in particular, had an abhorrence of Great Russian chauvinism. During the civil war, the Bolsheviks had considered different schemes for administering the Cossack territories which suggested that their thinking on the exact status of these regions had been rather fluid. The various Cossack Soviet Republics that appeared in early 1918 and indeed the appearance of Cossack in the official title of the Soviet gave the impression that they were willing to consider some recognition of a collective identity for the Cossacks. By the end of the civil war, however, the regime had set its face against any recognition of Cossack identity even in its limited Soviet version. But Bolshevik policy towards the Cossacks had already evolved in much more radical directions than simply withholding recognition from them. The goal of Bolshevik policy was the destruction of the Cossacks through the elimination of their way of life and suppression of their culture.

With the civil war barely over in the Don and still continuing in the Kuban, the *First All-Russian Conference of Toiling Cossacks* met in Moscow at the end of February 1920. Many of the Bolshevik leaders including Lenin participated.[3] Mikhail Kalinin, a leading Bolshevik and future President of the USSR, speaking at the Conference appeared to hold out an olive branch of sorts to the Cossack population:

> Many Cossacks think that Soviet power, now appearing on the Don, is immediately setting about building communism which in their opinion amounts to the smashing and mangling of the entire Cossack way of life and turning their lands into a communist paradise. Or as they say to decossackizing. Soviet power is of course morally obliged to decossackize the Cossacks and they will be decossackized, but in what sense? To decossackize does not mean to remove or cut off the red stripes from their trousers – a mundane adornment which the whole Cossack population is accustomed to wear. Decossackization does not consist of this, but rather in the fact that railroads will be built in the Cossack territories, Cossack women will be raised to a higher cultural level, that the peculiar military obligations will be removed from the Cossack population. . . . If you only think of what constitutes the essence of decossackization then you will see that it must be welcomed by the whole Cossack population.[4]

Kalinin was pointing out to the Cossacks the road by which all national groups within the new Soviet realm would eventually abandon their original identity for a new Soviet one. This would be an organic, completely unforced abandonment of one identity and its replacement with another. By raising living standards and educational levels while still not forcing anyone to abandon traits or customs specific to them, people would in time voluntarily let go of them, recognizing them as remnants of an archaic and no longer relevant historical epoch.

In reality, however, the Conference was in no mood to make concessions to the Cossacks. It brusquely dismissed any hopes of official recognition of a collective identity for the Cossacks in its key resolution:

> The Cossacks are by no means a separate people or nation, but are an indivisible part of the Russian people. Therefore there can be no question of a separation of the Cossack territories from the rest of Soviet Russia – a goal

to which the Cossack elites, closely joined by the nobles and bourgeoisie had been striving.

The labouring Cossacks stigmatize any attempt to tear away the Cossacks from the common cause and life of the toiling Russian people as clearly hostile to its interests and to the interests of the Revolution and will be mercilessly fought with.[5]

This resolution established the fundamental principle on which the regime's policy to the Cossacks was based. Alone among the kaleidoscope of peoples that made up the former tsarist empire, the Cossacks were to be denied any recognition of their collective identity and were warned that any attempt to promote it would be ruthlessly crushed. The Conference immediately began to apply this principle in practice. The Cossacks were denied any special representative institutions in the new state structure:

The First All Russian Conference of Toiling Cossacks decrees:
1) To recognize that Soviet power in the Cossack territories must be built on the common basis of the Constitution of the RSFSR.
2) No separate Soviets of Cossack deputies whatsoever must be created.[6]

Bolshevik policy in the immediate aftermath of the civil war set out to dismantle the institutional, economic and even psychological props which had sustained Cossack identity. Local authorities did not wait for central government approval before beginning the attack on the Cossacks. In February 1920 before the resolutions of the Conference, the Siberian *Oblast* biuro resolved:

1) In the interests of the complete merger of the Cossacks with the whole population, the *oblast* biuro believes that Cossacks must participate in the common work of soviet construction, and not isolate themselves in Cossack branches or sections.
2) To publish a decree liquidating the Cossacks as an estate and annulling privileges linked with the estate duty of the Cossacks.
In the light of this it is necessary to rename stanitsas and *khutora* into villages and settlements . . . .
4) To give a decree to local *ispolkoms* and *gubkoms* not to leave separate stanitsa jurisdictions but to include them in the general structure of urban organs of adminstration.[7]

In March 1920 the Council of Ministers issued a decree *Concerning the Construction of Soviet Power in the Cossack Territories* which gave legal force to the resolutions passed by the Conference and the measures already taken on the by local authorities in the Cossack territories.[8]

The administrative institutions which had made the Cossacks such formidable foes in the civil war were abolished and replaced with Soviet ones which were exclusively under the control of non-Cossacks since Cossacks were banned from them on account of their role in the civil war. Cossack communities now had no say in the running of their territories and were defenceless before the local organs of state power. Most of the personnel in the local administrations had built their careers in the bitter struggle against the Cossacks and harboured a deep enmity towards them.

In October 1920 the attack on institutional props of the Cossack way of life continued with the *Law on Land Tenure in the Former Cossack Voisko* which abolished any specific Cossack claim to land. Land was to be divided on an equal basis with all the inhabitants of the Cossack territories.[9] As well as paying its debts to the non-Cossack population, the law deprived the Cossacks of all the economic resources which they had used to sustain an independent administration and various other forms of communal autonomy.

Even these measures, however, were not deemed sufficient. The Bolsheviks wanted to break the concept of a Cossack homeland in the mind of the Cossacks. They understood how important this was to the Cossacks who routinely identified themselves as *Dontsi, Kubantsi, Tertsi* or *Uraltsi* and how potent a factor this had been in mobilizing the Cossacks in defence of their homeland. The former Cossack *voiska* lost their administrative unity and were broken up into many different jurisdictions. Parts of the Terek and Kuban were hived off to the new mountain republics in the Caucasus, parts of the Don became part of Tsaritsyn *oblast* while other parts were given to Ukraine. The Ural and Orenburg Cossacks even found themselves divided between different republics.

Dismantling Cossack identity through a series of legal and administrative measures and waiting for the historical evolution of a new identity proved too slow for many Bolshevik leaders and activists. The hatreds of the civil war easily overcame any more moderate inclinations.[10] Throughout 1920 the regime continued to follow a policy of extraordinary brutality towards the Cossack areas. Unlike 1919 when the Don suffered most acutely, Bolshevik vengeance shifted to the Terek in 1920. Fittingly, it was Stalin, then in the Caucasus, who laid aside the mask of gradualism to reveal the essence of Bolshevik decossackization in a telegram he sent to Lenin in October 1920:

> Stanitsas and auls which conceal whites will be exterminated: the adult population will be shot; property will be confiscated; all people offering any assistance to the whites will be subject to shooting. The majority of those in

the detachments of the whites have relatives remaining in the towns and stanitsas – these have all been registered by us. In case of continuing insubordination and attacks by the whites, all the adult relatives of those fighting against us will be arrested and shot, their property confiscated and the children deported to Central Russia. In case of mass uprisings in separate stanitsas and towns we will be forced to carry out red terror in these places. For every red army man or soviet worker killed one hundred people belonging to the bourgeois strata will pay for that life.[11]

The comprehensive nature of the measures the Bolsheviks undertook against the Cossacks immediately following the civil war belied the dismissal of any separate Cossack identity so confidently proclaimed by the *First All-Russian Conference of Toiling Cossacks* and enthusiastically endorsed by the regime. They were a tribute in a wholly negative way to the strength of Cossack collective identity and to the hatred that they regime harboured towards them. No other group in the first years of the regime suffered such a wide ranging and persistent attack. Extermination, deportation and confiscation of property were combined with legal, administrative and cultural attacks to eradicate not just large numbers of Cossacks physically, but the very idea of Cossack as a badge of identity for subsequent generations.

The Cossack territories after the civil war

The conquest of the Cossack territories in 1920 did not bring peace or stability. Much like the situation in the country at the end of the Time of Troubles in the seventeenth century, Moscow's authority remained very unstable. Large numbers of armed gangs continued to roam the countryside, attacking Soviet outposts and personnel, avoiding the Red Army and Cheka detachments, dispersing when the pursuit got too hot and reforming when the hard pressed Soviet units were directed elsewhere. Many stanitsas refused to reconcile themselves to Soviet power and continued to raise rebellions and rally surrounding stanitsas. Even a year after the end of the civil war, Soviet authority remained fragile, vulnerable and weak. The Kuban Cheka reported on one of the numerous rebel bands operating in April 1921:

In Rozhdestvenskii and Sengileiskii districts the mood of the bands is bellicose. The bandits have gone on to the offensive . . . A mobilization of all the men from 18 to 45 was carried out. Many Cossacks have willingly joined the bands. The rebellious stanitsas have created links between themselves. When the stanitsas were occupied by us, the male population fled with the bandits. The approximate number of bandits is more than a thousand. They are poorly armed.[12]

All over the Cossack territories many large groups were operating. They, at least, provided a target for Soviet forces to track and pursue. But these large gangs were the tip of the iceberg. Hundreds of smaller armed groups operated with impunity and the authorities could do little more than register their existence: The Don Cheka wrote ' . . . we ought to note that in almost every *volost* petty bands of up to 10 people are operating. These do not have any political aims. The only reason for the appearance of such bands we should note is the poor food supply and economic situation.'[13]

The last report hinted at the reason for the continuing unrest in all rural areas in the early 1920s. The food shortages more than anything else provoked hundreds of thousands to take up arms against the Soviet state between 1920–23. It was not natural disaster that caused the catastrophic collapse of the food supply in the most grain productive areas, but the activities of the food procurement squads. These descended hot on the heels of the victorious Red Army with one aim: to extract as much grain as possible for the hungry cities of the north.[14] Technically, they were supposed only to confiscate surpluses from wealthy peasants or kulaks. In reality they had no time for such nicities and took everything they could get their hands on, regardless of social categorization. Cossacks and peasants alike watched helplessly as the squads stripped their farms of grain, livestock and tools. Frequently they helped themselves to clothes and household items as well, confirming to all, the criminal nature of the whole enterprise. A visit from one of the procurement squads left stanitsas, *khutora* and villages facing starvation and seething with anger. A report from the Kuban that could have come from anywhere in the Soviet countryside in the early 1920s noted:

> In May the political condition of the province has sharply worsened. The middle and poorest peasantry have far from fulfilled their delivery quotas even under intense pressure. This has created mass unrest . . . The peasants say they have seized all the grain from us and say we have no hope for the new harvest since the winter wheat has shrivelled up . . .[15]

Any protest or attempt to resist brought down savage reprisals individually and collectively by punitive squads. Occasionally, the grain requisitioning detachments suffered retribution: not always from angry peasants. One such detachment had the bad luck to be at work when Cossack Red Army cavalry units under the command of the maverick Cossack commander Philip Mironov ran across them:

... the latter arrested the senior procurement workers, flogged them mercilessly with their whips, broke into their apartments and seized all their goods and distributed the property of the procurement workers on the streets. And in full view of the peasantry said to the procurement workers that they were carrying out procurement incorrectly, clearly inciting the peasants not to give any grain to procurement workers.[16]

Doubtless the Cossacks explained the mistakes of the procurement workers to them in language a good deal more colourful than that recorded by the Cheka, but it was an indication of how explosive the issue of grain procurement had become in late 1920 and early 1921.

When the conflagration that Bolshevik policies had been so assiduously stoking burst out, it was on a scale that stunned the leadership. Control over vast spaces of the Eurasian landmass was lost to the regime for months at a time. Peasant detachments waged a brutal insurgency against the Soviet state and its institutions especially the grain procurement agencies and the Cheka. Needless to say the Cossack territories participated fully in this revolt. Cossack revolt unlike the civil war merged with the wider peasant revolt and often former enemies found themselves fighting side by side against the regime.[17] Cossacks used the same structures and the same methods to fight the regime as they had in the civil war:

On 17th April former officers with several bandits, in all around 8–10 people, appeared in the aforementioned stanitsas and sounded the tocsin for a pre-arranged *sbor* of the counter-revolutionary Cossacks to start an uprising. Immediately at the sound Cossacks of various ages began to gather armed with rifles . . .[18]

In this particular revolt in the Kuban over 2,000 Cossacks were mobilized into two cavalry regiments. Of the 2,000 Cossacks, the Cheka reported that by the time the revolt was crushed over 700 had been killed and another 700 wounded.

Despite the scale of the revolt which seemed to be on a par with the civil war, the myriad revolts lacked elements critical to the success of those that had taken place earlier. Above all, there were no longer any coordinating centres or regular anti-Bolshevik armies in the field. These weaknesses ultimately doomed Cossack and peasant alike to defeat.

The regime was by now utterly ruthless in its suppression of any direct challenge to its authority. When five Terek Cossack stanitsas revolted in autumn 1920, Stalin's friend and compatriot, Sergo Ordzhonikidze, showed just how far the Soviet state had come in the art of mass repression. The staccato order barked by Ordzhonikidze in 1920 still echoes with the pitiless determination of the Bolsheviks to crush their opponents by any means almost ninety years later:

> First – Kalinovskaia Stanitsa, burn it. Second – Ermolovskaia, Zakan Iurtovskaia, Samashkinskaia, Mikhailovskaia. – Give them to the poorest, landless population, above all the mountain Chechens who have always been loyal to Soviet power. For this load all the male population between 18 to 50 of the aforementioned stanitsas into trains and send them under guard to the north for heavy, forced labour. The elderly, women, children – deport them from the stanitsas . . .[19]

However, some of the Bolshevik leadership, including Lenin, were beginning to have doubts about the savagery of the war against the peasantry: if not its morality then at least its effectiveness. By 1921 Lenin was convinced that the survival of the regime was at stake if Bolshevik policy continued on its present course. The New Economic Policy (NEP) was the recognition that the party had to call a halt. The combination of unlimited repression with economic concessions would, it was hoped, draw the sting of peasant rebellions. But a new ally now came to the Bolsheviks' aid: famine.

The dislocation caused by seven years of war made famine a possibility, but Bolshevik policies in the post-civil war period made it a certainty. The Cossack territories were among the worst hit areas and, unlike the 1890s, there was no sympathetic government to bale them out. The Cossacks were familiar with lean years, but famine was a horrifying new experience. By 1922 officials in the Cossack territories were besieged by the starving. From the Kuban they reported 'because of hunger women of the poorest families with children at their breast and adolescents are appearing more and more often at the volost executive committees, demanding the handing over of foodstuffs to them'.[20] From the Don their counterparts filed similar reports:

> The *okrug* is suffering a severe production crisis, worsening the counter-revolutionary mood of the population. In many places of the *okrug*, crowds of people arrive at the stanitsa and *khutor* executive committees with demands for the handing out of food. They later direct them to the *okrug* executive committees which in the absence of any foodstuffs refuse this demand . . . in many places skeletons are lying on the grass.[21]

In 1922 the Cossack territories of the North Caucasus, the Urals and Siberia were part of one of the greatest famines in European history. Hunger deepened to starvation, trailing in its wake typhus, cholera and other famine diseases. Livestock died in their hundreds of thousands for lack of food. From Stavropol the authorities reported that 'around

500,000 of the peasant population including children are estimated to be starving' while from the 1st Don Okrug: 'the number of starving has reached 475,900 people of whom 75,000 are children. Cases of cannibalism are becoming more frequent. Epidemic diseases are spreading.'[22] In the Cossack stanitsas of the Urals the death rate from starvation claimed 30–40 per cent of the population.[23]

It is impossible to separate the Cossack victims of famine from the non-Cossack ones. The local authorities in the Cossack territories were completely overwhelmed by the catastrophe and they could not count the numbers of dead, let alone establish their identity. There were no emergency supplies, Moscow continued to extract grain in spite of all the warnings and only the American relief agencies working in the country offered any help at all. The famine undermined the most fundamental norms of human life: mothers abandoned their children; killing for cannibalism was reported, as was the eating of corpses.[24] Only a better harvest in 1923 brought some relief.

Although NEP had been introduced in 1921, it took at least two years for the Cossack territories to feel any benefits from it. Nevertheless when it began to take effect, it did bring some respite from the terrible violence and famine of the previous years.[25] In retrospect, NEP has been viewed as a golden age of cooperation between the regime and the rural population, but the evidence from the Cossack territories at least suggests that it was still a time of acute difficulty. As far as the Cossacks were concerned, NEP was flattered by being framed by famine at its start and by collectivization at its end. The taxes which replaced requisitioning were heavy, particularly in the context of a post-famine society and the Soviet state was every bit as ruthless as the tsarist one in extracting its due. Those who failed to make the payments were arrested, imprisoned and had property confiscated. From Stavropol the authorities reported 'Only 60% of the population have paid their taxes without difficulty, but the remaining part could only pay them by selling their livestock and other possessions which have damaged their household.'[26]

The authorities interpreted the refusal to pay as an act of political disobedience, but for Cossacks and peasants the threat of hunger was constant throughout the rest of the 1920s. Hunger was not universal as it had been in 1921–23, but the fear of it was. The authorities reported as late as the summer of 1925 that large numbers of people in the Cossack areas still faced starvation.[27] Amidst all the misery, however, at least one group of Kuban Cossacks had not lost their sense of humour. Thirty-four Cossacks arrested for 'malicious' non-payment of taxes taunted their jailers with their choice of songs as the Cheka report dutifully recorded: 'Sitting in prison they sang religious songs and 'God Save the Tsar' the whole time.'[28] The latter was the old tsarist national anthem.

The partial respite that NEP offered was complemented by an apparent softening of the regime's hostility to the Cossacks in the mid-1920s. The passing of the immediate post-civil war crisis and the famine contributed to the lifting of the siege mentality and fostered the search for alternative ways to deal with problem groups. In a muted echo of tsarist times, the regime felt that attracting the Cossacks into service might be mutually beneficial. From late 1922 a number of developments took place which suggested that the regime might be reverting to the alternative method of 'decossackization' laid out by Kalinin in February 1920. Amnesties were offered to rank and file members of the anti-Bolshevik Cossack armies: both those who had remained behind and those who had emigrated. Between autumn 1922 and the beginning of 1925 over 30,000 emigres took the opportunity to return to their homelands.[29] Under the amnesty Cossacks could participate in Soviet elections and institutions and even join the party. Cossacks were once more allowed to serve in the Red Army.

A major discussion of the Cossack question took place at a special party plenum in April 1925. The plenum reviewed Bolshevik policy concerning the Cossacks since the October Revolution and discussed ways of moving forward. Perhaps the most remarkable feature of the plenum was the frankness with which leading Bolsheviks discussed their attitudes to the Cossacks. It was quite clear that the party regarded the Cossacks as a conquered people to be exploited for the good of the metropolis. Mikoian, one of Stalin's close circle, did not attempt to disguise the ferocity of Bolshevik policy towards the Cossacks and their homelands:

> We occupied the Cossack regions of the North Caucasus and all these years right up to the last few months we ruled as conquerors in a vanquished country. . . . We shot as many Cossacks as Georgians. Only the Georgians could cry out to the whole of Europe and the Mensheviks started bellowing, but the Cossacks could not cry out and even if they could no one would have believed them. We shot no fewer in the North Caucasus than we did in the Transcaucasus. We were even forced to shoot no small number in the past year of peace. But now there are few gangs left. We gunned down Cossacks officers leading the political gangs. Now we have no gangs and now the Cossacks pick, discuss and vote.[30]

Later in his speech, he would again make explicit reference to the colonial relationship that existed between the metropolis and the Cossack 'colonies':

Our territory is a colony. We say: let it be a colony – we understand this – for the agrarian economy. It is necessary to invest for socialism. But in so far as one colonizes skilfully, one must invest skilfully otherwise the cow will not give more milk. To this extent it is necessary to invest in order to continue to take and undoubtedly it is necessary to take with skill.[31]

The Plenum heard, however that these harsh policies were not having the desired result. The Kuban and Don Cossacks, who had recently been allowed to participate in local elections for the first time, promptly reelected the old stanitsa administrations much to the fury of the local party. Much more worrying, however, was not just that the crude polices of the regime appeared to be having little success in undermining Cossack identity, but that they were actually reinforcing that identity so that 'the Cossacks as a social, estate/group continue to be preserved artificially'.[32] The Plenum decided that a softening of the party line was appropriate. Local officials were called on to be tactful in their dealings with Cossacks, take account of their sensibilities and try to attract more Cossacks into the administration.

The mid-1920s, however, marked the high point of NEP and not coincidentally the high point of the attempts to win over the Cossacks. Extracting grain through taxation had been more successful than the outright confiscation of War Communism, but grain procurement remained a constant source of anxiety for the party and resentment at what the party perceived as peasant malevolence towards the regime increased sharply as the decade wore on. Most party members felt that construction of socialism was a hostage to peasant whim at best and political enmity at worst. Looked at from the side of the Cossacks and the peasants, the taxes were set at such high levels that they threatened the survival of the farm and family for the next year. Mikoian in his speech to the 1925 plenum admitted that in the Cossack territories of the North Caucausus 'The sown area is only about 49% of the best peace time year. We will only achieve the peace time level in another five years if we proceed at the present tempo.'[33] With agricultural production still way below its 1914 level and a society barely a couple of harvests since famine, the reluctance to hand over taxes was understandable. Resistance to the tax collectors and harsh punitive measures pursued each other in a vicious cycle well before the launch of collectivization:

Perversions in methods of grain procurement – mass searches, arbitrary arrests, coarse behaviour and incidents of violent seizure of all grain surpluses (leaving only 15 pounds per head until the new harvest) continue to take place in the Kuban, Don, Terek and Maikop *okrugs*. Administrative excesses have been permitted in a series of cases against middle peasants which have aroused among the latter (particularly among the Cossack part of the middle peasantry) criticism and resentment at the measures of Soviet power and have deepened the anti-Soviet mood. Mass searches in the majority of cases do not give positive results. Thus according to 7 village soviets in Semikarakkorskii district (Donskoi *Oblast'*) of more than 200 searches carried out in a short time, 159 did not produce any results.[34]

The quantities of grain needed to finance the importation of machinery were so high that they made the return of famine a certainty. Peasants including the Cossacks fought to save their families from starvation and their way of life as they had done in the civil war. Cossack women, just like peasant women, were prominent in defending their grain from the requisitioning squads.[35] But the regime was incomparably stronger at the end of the 1920s than it had been at the beginning. Collectivization and dekulakization would break the resistance of the peasantry and allow the state to exact unlimited quantities of tribute from them.

Collectivization and dekulakization

The storm of violence unleashed by collectivization consumed the Cossacks as living, vital communities capable of reproducing themselves. The North Caucasus, the heartland of the Cossacks, was one of the first areas singled out for 'complete collectivization' which in practice meant party officials achieving 100 per cent collectivization in the shortest possible time. The only way that such a target could be achieved without preparation, consultation or planning of any kind was through unlimited coercion. Cossacks were summoned to mass meetings in which they 'volunteered' to give their land and livestock and enter the collective farm. The local party boss spelt it out to the Cossacks of one Kuban stanitsa 'whoever doesn't go into the kolkhoz will be going to Solovki'.[36] Solovki was one of the most notorious camps in the Gulag. Intimidation on a huge scale was necessary to create the sham votes. This level of intimidation, however, paled before the shocking, preemptive violence used during 'dekulakization.'

Stalin and his inner circle did not wait for opposition to manifest itself before striking. His demand for the 'liquidation of the kulaks' as a class on 7 November 1929 was the start of the dekulakization campaign. Each area was given a quota of kulaks to be arrested and deported with their families. These quotas were minimums and local authorities were expected not only to reach them but to exceed them. Twenty thousand households were to be deported from the North Caucasus, the heartland of the former Cossack territories, in the first instance.[37] Although the area contained large numbers of non-Cossacks, it was obvious that Cossacks would form a large percentage of the deportees. Cossacks were particularly vulnerable to the charge of being a kulak because of the party's deep-rooted suspicion of them and their history.[38] Despite the 1925 Plenum, local administrations remained as hostile as ever to the Cossacks. As in the civil war, it was very easy to elide Cossack and kulak. Cossacks fell into nearly every definitional category of kulak issued to activists:

> 1. To subject to deportation the counter-revolutionary, socially dangerous kulak element who have been discovered disrupting political and economic campaigns in the village, who have participated in armed struggle against Soviet power particularly the following categories:
> a) kulaks – those who were active white guards in the past, Cossack ideologues and authorities, former white officers, members of punitive detachments, returned emigres, former white-green bandits, those who have officer sons in emigration.[39]

The Cossacks were the only group to be singled out by name, but even the categories that did not specifically mention them could have been drawn up with them in mind. Under the expansive definition provided by the party, there could be hardly any Cossack who did not fall under one or other category of kulak. For activists under enormous pressure to meet their quotas the Cossacks offered perfect targets.[40]

Dekulakization was not a single campaign in the Cossack territories, but extended in waves until 1933. Production in the farms fell off sharply compared with pre-collectivization days and became progressively worse. In 1932 the total grain harvest in the North Caucasus was only half what it had been in 1931.[41] This set off a frenzied search for scapegoats and a new wave of deportations. By 1932 the authorities had moved from deporting individual households to whole communities. Those communities who failed to meet delivery quotas were included on a black list and warned that future failure would result in mass deportations. In December 1932 the local party under the guidance of Stalin's close companion, Kaganovich, imposed this terrible fate on Poltavskaia Stanitsa in the Kuban:

> In view of the fact that Poltavskaia Stanitsa in spite of all the measures taken continues to maliciously sabotage all the economic activities of Soviet power and is clearly under the thumb of the kulaks we have to recognize the necessity of deporting all the inhabitants of the stanitsa from the district with the

exception of those who can prove their loyalty to Soviet power in the civil war and in the struggle with the kulaks.[42]

Two other stanitsas, Medvedovskaia and Urupskaia were deported alongside Poltavskaia. The three stanitsas had a combined population of 47,500 people of whom 45,600 were deported.[43] Less than 2,000 people had been able to prove their loyalty to the regime's satisfaction.

The secret police accounts of the deportations give the impression that in nearly all cases the deportations were carried out in an exemplary manner with hardly any excesses. The worst that happened was that the children did not have enough warm clothes for the winter. Given the nature of Stalinist society it is hard to find alternative views. However, Mikhail Sholokhov, the author of the epic *And Quite Flows the Don*, provided a description of the shocking brutality of the dekulakization process. Sholokhov witnessed the deportation of over 1,000 Cosssack families from Veshenskaia Stanitsa in the Upper Don and was so appalled by what he had seen that he wrote to Stalin to protest. The families who had been selected for deportation were thrown out of their homes immediately despite it being the depths of winter. Their houses were sealed and the local population were forbidden to shelter any of the deportees even though there would be no transport for several weeks:

> It was officially and most strictly forbidden for any of the remaining *kolkhozniki* to allow any of the evicted people into their homes to spend the night or warm themselves. They were forced to live in sheds, cellars, on the streets, in gardens. The population was warned: whoever lets in an evicted family will themselves be deported with their families. And people were deported only because some *kolkhoznik* moved by the howls of the freezing children let in his evicted neighbour to warm himself. Day in day out, 1090 families in 20 degrees of frost lived on the streets twenty four hours a day. In the day, like ghosts, they hung around their boarded up houses and by night they sought refuge from the cold in sheds and in barns. But according to the law passed by the *kraikom*, it was impossible for them to spend the night there. The chairmen of the soviets and the secretaries of the cells sent patrols through the streets who combed the sheds driving the families of *kolkhozniki* who had been thrown out of their homes onto the streets.
>
> I saw such things that I will remember until I die. In Volokhovskii *Khutor* in Lebiazhenskii *kolkhoz* at night in a cruel wind, in frost, when even the dogs were hiding from the cold, the families who had been thrown out of their homes had lit fires in the lanes and were sitting around the flames. The children were wrapped in rags and lay on the earth, thawing out by the fire. The unending cries of the children hung like curses. Is it possible to mock people in this way?[44]

Many people had paid with their lives for much smaller acts of courage, but Sholokhov had some protection as writer of international reputation and a certain regard that Stalin had for him. Sholokhov did not suffer any repercussions for speaking out and Stalin even took time to reply personally. Stalin's answer was a chilling combination of indifference, cruelty and breezy bonhomie:

> Dear Comrade Sholokhov,
> I thank you for your letters as they reveal defects of our party-soviet work and reveal how sometimes our workers wishing to restrain the enemy accidentally beat friends and prove themselves sadists. But this doesn't mean that I agree in everything with you. You see only one side and you see it quite sharply. So we don't make mistakes in policy (your letters are not literature, but purely political) it is necessary to take an overview; it is necessary to be able to see the other side. And the other side consists of the fact that the esteemed grain producers of your region (and not only of your region) are carrying out an 'Italianka' (sabotage!) and had no objection to leaving the workers and the Red Army without grain. The fact that the sabotage was quiet and outwardly inoffensive (without bloodshed) – this circumstance does not change the fact that the esteemed grain producers were as a matter of fact carrying on a quiet war with Soviet power. A war of attrition, dear comrade Sholokov . . .
> Well, so long, shake Your hand.
> Yours I. Stalin.[45]

Calculating how many Cossacks were deported from their homes in the period 1930–33 is almost impossible. The authorities classified all deported Cossacks according to which ever sub-species of kulak they happened to fall. Where whole communities were deported such as Poltavskaia in the Kuban, it is clear that all the deported were Cossacks. But when only a percentage of a community was deported, the specifically Cossack element was not recorded. From the Kuban alone in the course of 1932/33 over 100,000 people were deported and undoubtedly a high percentage of these were Cossacks.[46] Large numbers of Cossacks, like their peasant counterparts, jumped before they were pushed. They sold off whatever they could and then disappeared into the cities and towns, hoping to lose themselves there. The authorities were outraged at yet another proof of kulak perfidiousness, but they could only guess at the numbers involved.

The disruption and dislocation of communities intensified with the onset of a new famine in 1932. Warnings about famine in the North Caucasus had been sounded since 1930 when the chaos caused by collectivization had barely began. The increasing failure of many *kholkhoz* in the North Caucasus to meet their grain procurement targets in 1932 had less to do with malicious sabotage as the regime claimed, but the appalling realization of the communities that they were going to starve. In spite of this and of the warnings of local party and state activists, the party leadership demanded that all procurement targets be met and on time. Local officials were left in no doubt of the consequences of the failure to comply:

> Non-fulfilment of the plan on time in the lagging regions means non-fulfilment of the whole district plan which means the failure of the district plan. Leadership of these lagging regions will be subjected to the very strictest of party investigations right up to expulsions from the party.[47]

Expulsion from the party in these circumstance invariably meant being handed over to the NKVD. Even so many thousands of local party workers tried to moderate the policy of the centre as the results of that policy became ever more obvious. Of the 120,000 party workers in the territory 40,000 were expelled for 'kulak sabotage' while another 30,000 fled the territory rather than carry on with the disastrous requisitioning policy.[48]

The 1932/33 famine was even worse than the one of the early 1920s. Reports poured in of the desperation of the starving. People were reduced to eating dogs, mice, cats as well as animals that had died of disease. Cannibalism and the stealing of corpses for food were also reported just as they had been in the previous famine.[49] So many died that the dead completely overwhelmed the living. From Shkurinskia Stanitsa in the Kuban the authorities reported that 'as a consequence of the significant death rate amongst the population, corpses have been thrown into the cemetery, into houses or into sheds. In the cemetery up to hundred corpses are lying on the ground'.[50] This example could be multiplied many times over. What made matters worse were the actions of the state. Far from alleviating famine or allowing outside relief agencies in as had happened in the 1920s, the state exacerbated the famine by blockading afflicted territory and preventing people seeking aid outside the region. Denouncing the exodus of the people 'as organized by the enemies of Soviet power' to discredit the *kolkhoz* and the Soviet system, an order from Stalin himself forbade the movement of famine stricken people in early 1933:

> The CC and the Council of Ministers orders the *kraikom*, the *krai* executive committees and the OGPU of the Northern Caucasus not to allow the mass exodus of peasants from the north Caucasus to other regions or the entry from Ukraine into the borders of the territory.[51]

Between June 1932 and December 1933 at least 350,000 people or 4 per cent of the population of the North Caucasus died from famine or famine related illnesses. Stanitsa, *kolkhozes* and villages were emptied of people.[52] As always the old and the young died in largest numbers, amputating the past and the future of the communities.

After the frenzied years of the early 1930s, the mid-1930s saw a partial relaxation of the pressure on what was left of the Cossacks. As the international situation became more threatening, the regime began to make overtures to the Cossacks just as they had done ten years earlier. Characteristically, the state saw an advantage for itself in raising military units drawing on the old Cossack traditions. An editorial in *Pravda* in February 1936 commenting positively on the Cossack military tradition signalled a change in the regime's tone. Shortly afterwards the Red Army began to raise Cossack divisions once again and even provide them with the old Cossack uniforms. A parade of Cossack units was given official sanction to be held in Rostov-na-Donu. But even as these partial concessions were being granted, new storm clouds were gathering.

In 1937 the Great Terror which had been steadily building over the previous three years broke in all its fury. Although neither peasants nor Cossacks were the primary target of the purge, they still suffered grievously. Particularly hard-hit were Cossack officers in the Red Army and emigres who had returned under the various amnesties.[53] In the hysterical atmosphere of 1937 it was inevitable that the secret police would turn its attention to the former Cossack areas. The NKVD discovered counter-revolutionary plots in all the former Cossack territories, providing an excuse to arrest, shoot or deport yet more Cossacks. A typical plot was unmasked by the Orenburg NKVD:

> Anti-soviet elements among the Cossacks, former Cossack 'authorities' have noticeably stepped up their counter-revolutionary work, attempting to wreck and discredit the measures taken by the party and government in relation to the Soviet Cossacks in eyes of the broad masses.[54]

In July 1937 a new directive of the NKVD ordered the arrest of former kulaks, Whites, bandits, anyone who had held office under the old regime and any emigres who had returned under amnesty in the 1920s. Again the decree specifically mentioned among others 'active participants of Cossack-Whiteguard rebel organizations which are presently in the process of being liquidated'.[55] On the basis of this decree alone more than 500,000 people were arrested of whom 239,252 had been shot by 1 January 1938.[56] There is no way of telling how many of these unfortunate people were

Cossacks, but it seems a safe guess that they had a large representation among the 'enemies of the people'.

The Second World War

When the invasion began there were already thousands of Cossacks in the Red Army and thousands more were conscripted after the war had begun. Several Cossack cavalry divisions were raised from the North Caucasus, the Urals and Orenburg.[57] These cavalry divisions proved surprisingly effective in the conditions of the Eastern Front, particularly when they were used to harry retreating German forces. Cossack guards divisions took part in all the great battles of the war, including, Moscow, Stalingrad and Berlin.

For some Cossacks, as for millions of Soviet citizens, the war provided an opportunity for revenge on the regime which had inflicted so much suffering on them. Emigre Cossacks persuaded the Germans to allow them to recruit a Cossack army to fight alongside the Germans. The occupation of the Don and parts of the Kuban in 1942 by the Germans raised the prospect of the re-establishment of the Cossack *voiska* as German protectorates. It also offered the chance to recruit more Cossacks to the cause. But the return home was to be short-lived.

In September 1942 a Cossack administration was reestablished in Novocherkassk and a former colonel of the Don Army, S.V. Pavlov, was elected ataman. As in the civil war, the Cossack government immediately announced the resurrection of the Don Cossack Republic, albeit under the auspices of the occupying power:

> In 1918 the Great Don *voisko* had reestablished its sovereignty broken by Peter the First in 1709. It expressed its statehood in the Don Constitution and for three years (1918–1920) defended its ancient territory from invading Soviet armies . . .
>
> The Don *voisko* declares the reestablishment of its independence and the recreation of it statehood under the Basic Laws of the Great *Voisko* of the Don.[58]

However, the tide of the war was turning against the Germans. Within weeks of this declaration, the Kuban and the Don itself had to be abandoned. The anti-Soviet Cossacks retreated with the Germans, abandoning once more their native *voiska*. In late 1944 these Cossacks were transferred to Northern Italy where they remained until 1945 when they crossed the Alps in Austria to the town of Lienz. There they surrendered to the British.

These Cossacks were now to share the fate of tens of thousands of their compatriots who had remained in the Soviet Union. Stalin demanded that all Soviet citizens and even those who had never been Soviet citizens but were members of the anti-Soviet forces be handed over. The latter category included thousands of Cossacks who had left at the end of the civil war. Although the British were fully aware of the likely fate of these Cossacks, they agreed to Stalin's demands. Stalin after all was their ally and, more to the point, thousands of British Pows had fallen under Soviet jurisdiction at the end of the war. Separating the officers from the men, British soldiers beat men, women and children on to the trains taking them to their deaths or the Gulags. Many were executed immediately they came into the custody of the NKVD while the remainder were sent to the camps. The leaders including heroes of the civil war such as Don ataman Petr Krasnov and the Kuban cavalry leader General Shkuro were brought to Moscow, tried and executed.

Conclusion

The twenty-five years between the end of the civil war and the Second World War were years of unmitigated tragedy for the Cossacks. The civil war had destroyed the hosts of the Far East and those of the Urals and Orenburg. But those of the Don, the Terek and above all the Kuban had survived. Even the destruction of their institutional autonomy, the expropriation of their land and the suppression of their culture immediately after the civil war did not destroy them. In the mid-1920s it seemed that the worst was over and that in the relatively benign conditions of NEP the slow process of reconstruction might begin. It is impossible to know what would have emerged had NEP continued indefinitely, but its termination in the late 1920s became the final act in the Cossack tragedy. Collectivization and dekulakization destroyed any possibility of collective survival for the Cossacks. The loss of their farms and the way of life that was woven around them was a mortal threat to Cossack existence. But the deportations of the anti-kulak campaigns of 1930–33 struck at the last bastion of Cossack identity: its human capital.[59] The deportations eviscerated individual families and communities. The powerlessness of communities to defend their neighbours and their families from the appalling violence unleashed on them, even to offer basic charity to their unfortunate neighbours, broke a unified, coherent sense of identity. Cossack identity would survive in fragments and isolated pockets throughout the remainder of the Soviet period, but the Cossacks as members of a distinct communities capable of reproducing themselves generation after generation had ceased to exist. As one historian of the Cossacks wrote 'only the old songs still heard at family celebrations recalled the fact that once, here on the territory of *Batiushka* Iaik lived, toiled and struggled a particular *voisko*'.[60] Although Fokin wrote of the Ural Cossacks his words stand equally well as an epitaph for all the Cossack hosts.

Notes

1 O.V. Ratushniak, *Donskoe i Kubanskoe Kazachestvo v Emigratsii (1920–1939)* (Krasnodar, 1997), p. 21.
2 T. Martin, *The Affirmative Action Empire: Nations and Nationalism in the Soviet Union 1923–1939* (New York, 2001) pp. 9–10.
3 Perekhov, *Vlast' i Kazachestvo* (Rostov-na-Donu, 1997) p. 16.
4 M.I. Kalinin, *Rech' na Pervom Vserossiiskom S'ezde Trudovykh Kazakov* (Moscow, 1920) p. 17.
5 GARF, f.1235, op.85, d.2, ll.3–4.
6 GARF, f.1235, op.85, d.2, ll.25–26.
7 V.I. Shishkin (ed.) *Sibirskaia Vandeia 1919–1920* (2 vols, Moscow, 2000) vol. 1, p. 18.
8 Tabolina, *Vozrozhdenie Kazachestva*, p. 248.
9 The law did indeed establish a rough parity in landholdings between the Cossack and non-Cossack populations. RGASPI, f.17, op.85, d.278, l.36–44.
10 Perekhov, *Vlast' i Kazachestvo*, p. 24.
11 RGASPI, f.85, op.11, d.131, l.11.
12 A. Berelovich and V. Danilov (eds) *Sovetskaia Derevnia Glazami VchK-OGPU-NKVD 1918–1939: Dokumenty i Materialy v 4 tomakh* (Moscow, 1998). vol. 1, p. 418.
13 RGASPI, f.65, op.1, d.131, ll.72–75.
14 F. Kamnnskii, *Kazachestvo Iuzhnogo Urala i Zapadnoi Sibiri v Pervoi Chetverti XX Veka* (Magnitogorsk, 2001) p. 107.
15 RGASPI, f.65, op.1, d.132, l.17.
16 RGASPI, f.65, op.1, d.132, l.1.
17 Kislitsyn, *Gosudarstvo i Raskazachivanie*, pp. 45–46.
18 RGASPI, f.65, op.1, d.132, ll.13–14.
19 RGASPI, f.85, op.11, d.131, l.11.
20 RGASPI, f.65, op.1, d.132, l.17.
21 RGASPI, f.65, op.1, d.131, ll.72–75.
22 Berelovich, *Sovetskaia Derevnia*, vol. 1, pp. 559, 571.
23 Kamnnskii, *Kazachestvo Iuzhnogo Urala*, p. 124.
24 Berelovich, *Sovetskaia Derevnia* vol. 1, p. 592. 'In the First Donokrug several cases of cannibalism and the eating of corpses have been recorded.'
25 Perekhov, *Vlast' i Kazachestvo*, p. 76.

26 Berelovich, *Sovetskaia Derevnia*, vol. 2, p. 171,
27 Berelovich, *Sovetskaia Derevnia*, vol. 2, pp. 315–329.
28 Berelovich, *Sovetskaia Derevnia*, vol. 2, p. 161.
29 Perekhov, *Vlast' i Kazachestvo*, p. 70.
30 RGASPI, f.17, op.2, d.179, ll29–31.
31 RGASPI, f.17, op.2, d.179, l.74.
32 RGASPI, f.17, op.2, d.179, l.57.
33 RGASPI, f.17, op.2, d.179, ll.30–31.
34 Berelovich, *Sovetskoi Derevnia*, vol. 2, pp. 754–755.
35 N.S. Shibanov, *Kazach'ia Golgofa* (Cheliabinsk, 2004) pp. 43–47.
36 Berelovich, *Sovetskaia Derevnia*, vol. 3, p. 86.
37 Danilov, *Tragediia Sovetskoi Derevni*, vol. 2, p. 100.
38 Kislitsyn, *Gosudarstvo i Raskazachivanie*, p. 60.
39 Danilov, *Tragediia Sovetskoi Derevni*, vol. 2, p. 101.
40 Kislitsyn, *Gosudarstvo i Raskazachivanie*, p. 63.
41 E.N. Oskolkov, 'Sud'by Krest'ianstva i Kazachestva v Rossii: Raskrest'ianivanie
    i Raskazachivanie' in V.N. Ratushniak (ed.) *Problemy Istorii Kazachestva*
    (Volgograd, 1995) p. 159.
42 Danilov, *Tragediia Sovetskoi Derevni*, vol. 3, p. 585.
43 Danilov, *Tragediia Sovetskoi Derevni*, vol. 3, p. 29.
44 Danilov, *Tragediia Sovetskoi Derevni*, vol. 3, pp. 717–720.
45 Danilov, *Tragediia Sovetskoi Derevni*, vol. 3, p. 720.
46 Oskolkov, 'Sud'by Krest'ianstva i Kazachestva v Rossii'in Ratushniak, *Problemy
    Istorii Kazachestva*, p. 160.
47 Danilov, *Tragediia Sovetskoi Derevni*, vol. 3, p. 599.
48 Oskolkov, 'Sud'by Krest'ianstva i Kazachestva' in Ratushniak, *Problemy Istorii
    Kazachestva*, p. 160.
49 See for example, Danilov, *Tragediia Sovetskoi Derevni*, vol. 3, p. 648.
50 Danilov, *Tragediia Sovetskoi Derevni*, vol. 3, p. 664.
51 Danilov, *Tragediia Sovetskoi Derevni*, vol. 3, p. 635.
52 I.I. Alekseenko, 'Kollektivizatsiia i Kazachestvo Kubani v 1929–1933' in
    Ratushniak, *Problemy Istorii Kazachestva*, p. 246.
53 Kislitsyn, *Gosudarstvo i Raskazachivanie*, p. 67.
54 Danilov, *Tragediia Sovetskoi Derevni*, vol. 5, p. 81.
55 Danilov, *Tragediia Sovetskoi Derevni*, vol. 5, p. 331.
56 Danilov, *Tragediia Sovetskoi Derevni*, vol. 5, p. 387.
57 Kislitsyn, *Gosudarstvo i Raskazachivanie*, p. 68.
58 K.M. Mikhailovich, *Protiv Stalina: Vlasovtsy i Vostochnye Dobrovol'tsy vo Vtoroi
    mirovoi voine* (St Petersburg, 2003) p. 31.
59 Kislitsyn, *Gosudarstvo i Raskazachivanie*, pp. 65–66.
60 Fokin, *Final Tragedii*, p. 313.

Epilogue: The return of the Cossacks?

After the Second World War, the Soviet state ceased to persecute the Cossacks. In truth, there was little left to persecute. Cossack customs, traditions, and history survived only in private. Family gatherings or small circles of close friends provided the only forum to have unfettered celebrations and discussions about the past. And the regime was keen to keep it that way. A sanitized version of Cossack history and culture was permitted by the authorities. The regime was happy to sponsor Cossack ensembles preforming traditional dances and songs, but was deeply suspicious of anything that tried to go beyond this Disneyesque version of the Cossack past.[1] There was no place for Cossack organizations or public commemorations under party auspices, let alone ones free of party control.

The guiding principles of the regime's policy towards the Cossacks remained those that had been first formulated at the *First All Russian Conference of Toiling Cossacks* in February 1920 which rejected a separate identity and separate organizations. The academic sphere remained as tightly controlled as the public. Historians of the Cossacks had to ensure that their work fitted squarely within the framework of the official ideology of the regime. Intimations that the Cossacks were anything more than a rather reactionary branch of the peasantry were not tolerated. Official sensitivity became more acute the closer one came to the Soviet period. Anything that strayed outside these limits or even attempted to push the boundaries of what was permissible very quickly ran up against official disapproval.

Attempts by specialists to share information, to establish journals or even organize a conference on the Cossacks were blocked. There was not a single academic conference devoted to the Cossacks in the revolutionary period in the sixty years following the civil war. When a leading academic attempted to convene a conference on Cossack history in 1978, the party authorities in Rostov-na-Donu firmly rebuffed his attempts, explaining that such a proposal was 'dubious in ideological and political terms'.[2]

Neighbouring authorities proved no more accommodating. It took two years before permission was finally granted and the conference held.

Only under Mikhail Gorbachev and his policies of *perestroika* and *glasnost* did anything more ambitious become possible. Even then, public commemorations or organizations had to remain very low key. Provincial party and state organizations had little enthusiasm for *perestroika* and *glasnost*, finding it hard to accept even the partial ending of their monopoly over all public life. The first independent organizations devoted to the Cossacks were founded by members of the intelligentsia and were informal clubs and societies for the study of Cossack history and traditions. In 1989 for example in Rostov a literary circle 'Sholokovskii Krug' was formed, bringing together about 40 writers, poets, journalists and academics. The same year the writer Vitislav Khodarev formed a circle for the study of the Terek Cossacks in Stavropol. All over the former Cossack territories similar organizations were being formed. A few even took the bold step of issuing a journal to publicize their deliberations. Even so, right up to the end of the 1980s, few Cossack organizations felt it prudent to stray beyond these rather narrow limits.

At the start of the new decade, however, the nature and profile of Cossack organizations were transformed. The increasingly obvious crisis of legitimacy within the Soviet Union emboldened all who wanted to express their anger at what they and their people had suffered under Soviet power. In 1990 explicitly political organizations were established for the first time. In Moscow a group of intellectuals set up the *Union of Cossacks* which proclaimed itself as a focal point for all Cossack organizations and individuals. On 30 June an appeal was issued for Cossacks everywhere to recreate their traditional organizations:

> Brother Cossacks! We call upon you to create your *krugs* in *oblasts*, districts, towns, stanitsas and *khutora*. Unify these with already existing organizations. Recreate Cossack spiritual values in your stanitsas and *khutora*, reestablish or build anew churches in all their beauty since their must be a place where our children can be raised in pristine beauty together with the word of God. Bring up your children in the venerable traditions of the Cossacks: respect for elders, love of the motherland, moral purity in the family and faithful service to the FATHERLAND.[3]

This set off a flurry of activity in all the former Cossack territories. In October 1990 the *Rada* of the Kuban Cossacks was reformed and was followed a month later by the Don Cossack *krug*. Other Cossack *voiska* quickly followed suit. Both central and local organizations were united in demanding recognition by the state of the injustices that the Cossacks has suffered under Soviet power and recognition of their existence as a separate people. The declaration issued by the Council of Cossacks in Krasanodar in the Kuban at the end of November was a robust formulation of Cossack demands:

> In the interests of Russia we demand the urgent introduction of measures by the state directed towards the rebirth of the Cossacks. The basis of the these must be:
> 1. The abandonment of stereotypes, spawned by Trotskyism and neo-trotskyism, depicting the Cossacks as a reactionary force; official recognition of the criminal policy of genocide against the Cossacks.
> 2. Recognition of the Cossacks as an authentic ethnos, possessing equal rights with others peoples in national self-expression.[4]

The Soviet regime's belief in its own legitimacy imploded unstoppably through 1990 and into 1991. Abandoning any attempt to deny or justify earlier crimes against individual peoples, the Supreme Soviet, in April 1991, issued a decree *On the Rehabilitation of Repressed Peoples*:

> Article 1. To rehabilitate all repressed peoples of RSFSR, recognizing the unlawful and criminal acts of repression against these people.
> Article 2. Repressed peoples (nations, nationalities or ethnic groups or other historically formed cultural-ethnic communities of people, for example the Cossacks) are those against whom a policy of slander and genocide was carried out at the state level against their national symbols or other distinguishing features. This was often accompanied by their forced resettlement, the abolition of national-state institutions, the redrawing of national-territorial borders, and the establishment of a regime of terror and violence in places of special settlement.[5]

This remarkable *mea culpa* of the Soviet regime swept away any restraints on the organizations or even the aspirations of repressed peoples; nothing now was beyond the pale. Far from re-establishing trust in the regime, however, the decree set off an avalanche of new accusations of crimes against humanity by individuals, groups and peoples.

As in earlier repressive legislation, the Cossacks were again singled out, which removed any possibility of local authorities arguing that the Cossacks were not a people and therefore were not covered by the decree. In July of the same year a specific decree was issued *On the Rehabilitation of the Cossacks*. The first article of the new decree declared all repressive measures taken against the Cossacks since 1918 illegal. Subsequent articles ordered the rehabilitation of individual Cossacks who had been repressed and allowed Cossacks to re-establish their traditional forms of self-government. The decree even restored the old Cossack forms of land ownership, usage and management although it qualified the last point 'without infringing on the rights of other citizens living in a particular place who are not Cossacks'.[6] Quite how the Cossacks were to have their lands returned to them without infringing on the rights of people living on that land was left unanswered.

The ignominious collapse of the Soviet Union at the end of 1991 and the emergence of the Russian Federation as its main successor removed any lingering hostility to the Cossacks at the state level. The new state was keen to emphasize the rupture with the Soviet Union not just through free elections, but by showing its continuity with the pre-Soviet Russian state over the centuries. One way of doing this was to re-establish its relationship with the traditional symbols of Russian national identity. The Orthodox Church was an obvious candidate; the Cossacks were another. The state actively courted Cossack organizations, hoping to use them as symbols of Russian patriotism and possibly as some form of counter-weight to the spreading ethnic conflict within the Federation and outside of it. Newly installed President Boris Yeltsin issued a decree confirming the recent Soviet laws rehabilitating the Cossacks and ordering government institutions to actively support the Cossacks in their attempts to recreate their organizations.[7]

Cossack organizations, like the Orthodox Church, were only too happy to cooperate with the new nationalistic state. They have become representative of an overt, aggressive form of Russian nationalism, constantly emphasizing past Cossack service to the Russian state, particularly the Cossacks role in the subjugation of the peoples of the steppe which is usually dressed up as the defence of the state's borders. Given the present condition of Russia's relationship with peoples of the North Caucasus, it is not surprising that the state and the Cossacks have become such enthusiastic bedfellows. Rather than just one of many groups clamouring for the attention of the state, the Cossacks now appear to enjoy a kind of 'most favoured status'. In 1995 the state established a register for all Cossacks willing to carry out military service. A year later it recreated the tsarist department responsible for the Cossacks: *Glavnoe Upravlenie Kazachikh Voisk*. The parallels with the old *soslovie* arrangements are obvious.

Soslovie, however, are not peoples nor are administrative organizations. Despite the undoubted success of Cossack organizations in covering the former Cossack territories with traditional Cossack forms of administration and transforming their relationship with the state, recreating a

Cossack people has proved much more problematic. Not the least of the problems is that some parts of the former Cossack homelands are now outside the borders of the Russian Federation. Ukraine and Kazakhstan, for example, all have Cossack land within their national boundaries. The latter state in particular is hostile to the Cossacks which is only to be expected given the past role of the Cossacks in the conquest of the steppe and the overt Russian nationalism of new Cossack organizations.

Even within the Russian Federation, and in a much more benign atmosphere, the work of recreating peoples and homelands has proved difficult. The Cossacks were already a minority of the population in their historical heartlands in the North Caucasus before the revolution. With the enormous demographic losses and changes of Soviet times, the Cossacks have shrunk to tiny minorities. The number of Cossacks who have remained living in their historical homelands are now outnumbered many times by the non-Cossack population which makes any attempt to create Cossack autonomous area quixotic to say the least.

More fundamental still is the matter of just who or what a Cossack is in the twenty- first century. Cossack organizations typically argue that anyone who is descended from Cossacks or works for the fulfilment of their aims can be considered a Cossack. The Union of Cossacks offered a broad definition:

> Members of the Union of Cossacks can be Soviet and foreign citizens, descendants of Cossack families, natives of traditional Cossack regions and migrants from them; also persons, interested and sharing in practical activity linked with the Cossacks, who wish to restore the originality of Cossack ethnic formations, their history and culture and who are actively assisting these and who acknowledge the rules of the present code and pay their membership dues.[8]

What are missing, however, are the living communities in which the history, traditions and culture of a particular people are passed on. The few that survive will be hard put to pass Cossack culture on to their own children particularly when it has to compete with the ubiquitous mass cultures of the modern world. Whether they can act as some sort of platform for the recossackization of the Cossack *voiska* seems doubtful.

My own belief, for what it is worth, is that the neither the Cossacks nor the Cossack homelands can be recreated in any meaningful sense. The Cossack communities that survived the collapse of the tsarist state did so because they had an identity that was autonomous from the state. In the conditions of the civil war, Cossack identity became ever more sharply defined, creating on the Don and Kuban the potential for independent nations. Defeat in the civil war closed off that option. For the Soviet state this was not enough. It wanted to eradicate the Cossacks as a separate people and destroy the traditions and memory of the Cossack communities. By the end of the Second World War it had largely succeeded. Trying to recreate the ties that bound the Don and Kuban Cossacks, let alone the other Cossack hosts, to their communities and to their *voiska* fifty years after they have been severed and where the wider political, social and economic landscape had been irrevocably transformed seems to me to be an impossible task. The Cossacks have now joined the succession of peoples who mastered the steppe for a time before being replaced by new peoples. Like the Scythian burial mounds, the Cossacks have become part of the history of the steppe. That history is moving on, but the Cossacks are no longer part of the story.

Notes

1 Kislitsyn, *Gosudarstvo i Raskazachivanie*, p. 74.
2 A.I. Kozlov, 'Problemy Istorii Kazachestva' in A.I. Kozlov (ed.) *Problemy Istorii Kazachestva XV—-XXvv* (Rostov-na-Donu, 1995) p. 5.
3 Tabolina, *Vozrozhdenie Kazachestva*, pp. 294–295.
4 Tabolina, *Vozrozhdenie Kazachestva*, p. 306.
5 Tabolina, *Vozrozhdenie Kazachestva*, p. 257.
6 Tabolina, *Vozrozhdenie Kazachestva*, pp. 262–63.
7 Tabolina, *Vozrozhdenie Kazachestva*, pp. 264–267.
8 Tabolina, *Vozprozhdenie Kazachestva*, p. 298.

Bibliography

Archives used

Gosudarstvennyi Arkhiv Rossiiskoi Federatsii (GARF).
Rossiiskii Gosudarstvennyi Arkhiv Sotsial'no-Politicheskoi Istorii (RGASPI).
Rossiiskii Gosudarstvennyi Voenno-Istoricheskii Arkhiv (RGVIA).

Published works

Donskaia Letopis': Sbornik Materialov po Noveishei Istorii Donskogo Kazachestva so Vremeni Russkoi Revolutsii 1917 goda (3 vols, Belgrade, 1923).
Postanovleniia Donskogo Voiskovogo Kruga: Pervyi Sozyv, 26 Maia-18 Iunia 1917 g (Novocherkassk, 1917/1918).
Postanovleniia Bol'shogo Voiskogo Kruga voiska Donskogo tret'iago sozyva, 2–13 Dekabria 1917 godu (Novocherkassk, 1917).
Postanovleniia Chastnogo Soveshchaniia Deputatov Voiskovogo Kruga Voiska Donskogo 3 Ianvaria-5 Fevralia 1918 (Novocherkassk, 1918).
——, A Relation Concerning the Particulars of the Rebellion Lately Raised in Muscovy by Stenko Razin: Its Rise, Progress and Stop; Together with the Manner of Taking that REBEL, the Sentence of Death Passed upon Him and the Execution of the Same (London, 1672).

Abaza, K.K. Kazaki: Dontsy, Uraltsy, Kubantsy, Tertsy (St Petersburg, 1890).
Abdirov, M.Zh. Istoriia Kazachesva Kazakhstana (Almaty, 1994).
Abramovskii, A.P. (ed.) Orenburgskoe Kazach'e Voisko: Kul'tura. Byt. Obychai (Cheliabinsk, 1996).
—— (ed.) Orengurgskoe Kazach'e Voisko: Istoriia i Sovremennost' (Cheliabinsk, 1993).
Ackerman, R. Characteristic Portraits of the Various Tribes of Cossacks (London, 1820).
Akhapkin, Y. The First Decrees of Soviet Power (London, 1970).
——, Emperor of the Cossacks: Pugachev and the Frontier Jacquerie of 1773–1775 (Lawrence, KN, 1973).

Aleksandrov, K.M. *Protiv Stalina: Sbornik Statei i Materialov* (St Petersburg, 2003).
Aleksenko, I.I. 'Kollektivizatsiia i Kazachestvo Kubani v 1929–1933' in Ratushniak, *Problemy Istorii Kazachestva*.
Andreev, I.A. *Materialy dlia Istorii Voiska Donskogo* (Novocherkassk, 1886).
Anisimov, E. *Dyba i Knut: Politicheskii Sysk i Russkoe Obshchestvo v XVIII Veke* (Moscow, 1999).
Arefin, A.M. *Donskoe Kazachestvo Prezhde i Teper'* (Moscow, 1907).
Astapenko, G. *Byt, Obychai, Obriady, i Prazdniki Donskikh Kazakov XVII–XX Vekov* (Rostov-na-Donu, 2002).
Astapenko, M. *Donskie Kazaki 1550–1920* (Rostov-na-Donu, 1992).
——, *Istoriia Kazachestva Rossii* (3 vols, Rostov-na-Donu, 1998).
Avrich, P. *Russian Rebels 1600–1800* (New York, 1972).
Auskii, S. *Kazaki: Osoboe Soslovie: Dokumenty, Karty, Fotografii* (St Petersburg, 2002).
Babychev, D.S. *Donskoe Trudovoe Kazachestvo v Bor'be za vlast' Sovetov* (Rostov-na-Donu, 1969).
Barber, J. and M. Harrison *The Soviet Home Front 1941–1945* (London, 1991).
Barfield, T. *The Perilous Frontier: Nomadic Empires and China 221 BC to AD 1757* (Oxford, 1989).
Baron, S.H. (ed.) *The Travels of Olearius in Seventeenth Century Russia* (Stanford, 1967).
Barrett, T.M. 'Line of Uncertainty: The Frontier in the North Caucasus', *Slavic Review,* 54, 3 (1995), pp. 578–601.
——, *At the Edge of Empire: The Terek Cossacks and the North Caucasus Frontier, 1700–1860* (Boulder, Colorado, 1999).
Benkendorff, K.K. *The Cossacks: A Memoir* (London, 1849).
Bekmakhanova, N.E. *Kazach'i Voiska Aziatskoi Rossii v XVIII–Nachale XX Veka* (Moscow, 2002).
Berelovich, A. and V. Danilov (eds), *Sovetskaia Derevnia Glazami VchK-OGPU-NKVD Dokumenty i Materialy* (3 vols. Moscow, 2000 ongoing).
Bezotosnyi, V.M. *Donskoi Generalitet i Ataman Platov v 1812 gody* (Moscow, 1999).
Bezotosnyi, V.M. *et al.* (eds) *Otechestvennaia Voina 1812 goda: Entsiklopediia* (Moscow, 2004).
Blagovo, V.A. and S.A. Sapozhnikov (eds) *Donskaia Armiia v Bor'be s Bolshevikami* (Moscow, 2004).
Bondar', N.I. *Traditsionnaia Kul'tura Kubanskogo Kazachestva: Izbrannye Raboty* (Krasnodar, 1999).
—— (ed.) *Ocherki Traditsionnoi Kul'tury Kazachestv Rossii* (2 vols, Moscow, 2002).
Bondarev, V.P. and A.G. Masalov *Terskoe Kazach'e Voisko iz Veka v Vek 1577–2003* (Vladikavkaz-Stavropol', 2003).
Bracewell, C.W. *The Uskoks of Senj: Piracy, Banditry and Holy War in the Sixteenth Century Adriatic* (Ithaca, 1992).
Bronevskii, V. *Istoriia Donskogo Voiska* (3 vols, St Petersburg, 1834).

Browder, P. and A.F. Kerensky (eds) *The Russian Provisional Government: Documents* (3 vols, Stanford, 1961).

Bussow, C. *The Disturbed State of the Russian Realm*, trans. and ed. G.E. Orchard (Montreal, 1994).

Butt, V.P *et al.* (eds) *The Russian Civil War: Documents from the Soviet Archives* (London, 1996).

Bykadorov, Is.F. *Istoriia Kazachestva* (Prague, 1930).

Campenhausen, P.B. von. *Travels through Several Provinces of the Russian Empire with an account of the Zaporog Cossacks* (London, 1808).

Carpenter, D. *The Struggle for Mastery: Britain 1066–1284* (Harmondsworth, 2003).

Chevalier, P. *Histoire de la Guerre des Cossaques contre le Pologne* (Paris, 1663).

——, *A Discourse of the Original Country, etc of the Cossacks* (London, 1672).

Chernisyn, S.V. 'Donskoe Kazachestvo' in Bondar', *Ocherki Traditsionnoi Kul'tury.*

Chynczewska-Hennel, T. 'The National Consciousness of Ukrainian Nobles and Cossacks from the End of the 16th to the Mid 17th Century,' *Harvard Ukrainian Studies*, X, 3–4 (1986), pp. 377–392.

Chistiakova, E.V. and V.M. Solov'ev, *Stepan Razin i ego soratniki* (Moscow, 1988).

Christian, D. *A History of Russia, Central Asia and Mongolia, Vol I. Inner Asia from Prehistory to the Mongol Empire* (Oxford, 1998).

Cresson, W.P. *The Cossacks: Their History and Country* (New York, 1919).

Danilov, V. and T. Shanin (eds) *Filipp Mironov: Tikhii Don v 1917–1921 gg* (Moscow, 1997).

Danilov V. *et al.* (eds) *Tragediia Sovetskoi Derevni: Kollektivizatsiia i Raskulachivanie: Dokumenty i Materialy 1927–1939* (5 vols, Moscow, 2000).

Darnfort, L.M. *The Macedonian Conflict: Ethnic Nationalism in a Transnational World* (Princeton, 1996).

Davies, N. *God's Playground: A History of Poland* (2 vols, Oxford, 1981).

——, *Heart of Europe: A Short History of Poland* (Oxford, 1984).

Dawson, C. (ed.) *Mission to Asia* (Toronto, 1998).

Dobrynin, V. 'Vooruzhennaia Bor'ba Dona s Bolshevikami' in *Donskaia Letopis'*, vol. 1.

Druzhinin, V.G. *Raskol na Donu v kontse XVII veka* (St Petersburg, 1889).

Dubrovin, N.T. *Pugachev i ego Soobshchniki* (St Petersburg, 1884).

Dulimov, E.I. and I.I. Zolotarev *Samoupravlenie Kazakov: Istoriia i Sovremennost'* (Rostov-na-Donu, 1998).

Dunning, C.S. *A Short History of Russia's First Civil War: The Time of Troubles and the Founding of the Romanov Dynasty* (Pennsylvania, 2004).

Efimenko, A.Ia. *Istoriia Ukrainskago Naroda* (St Petersburg, 1906).

Efremov, A.I. *Les Cosaques du Don* (Paris, 1919).

Engel, B.A. *Between the Fields and the City: Women, Work, and Family in Russia, 1861–1914* (Cambridge, 1994).

Ermak, G.G. *Semeinyi i Khoziaistvennyi Byt Kazakov Iuga Dal'nego Vostoka Rossii: Vtoraia Polovina XIX–Nachalo XX Veka* (Vladivostok, 2004).

Ermolin, A.P. *Revoliutsiia i Kazachestvo* (Moscow, 1982).

Felitsyn, N.N. *Kubanskoe Kazach'e Voisko, 1688–1696* (Voronezh, 1888).

Field, C. *The Great Cossack: The Rebellion of Sten'ka Razin* (London, 1946).

Firsov, N.N. *Pugachevshchina: Opyt Sotsiologo-Psikhologichesoi Kharakteristiki* (St Petersburg, 1907).

Fisher, A. *The Crimean Tatars* (Stanford, 1978).

Fletcher, G. *Of the Russe Commonwealth* (London, 1591).

Fokin, N.I. *Final Tragedii: Ural'skie Kazaki v XX veke* (Moscow, 1996).

Franklin, S. and J. Shepard, *The Emergence of Rus 750–1200* (London, 1996).

Fuller, W.C. *Civil-Military Conflict in Imperial Russia 1881–1914* (Princeton, 1985).

Futorianskii, L.I. *Bor'ba za Massu Trudovogo Kazachestva v Periode Pererastaniia Burzhuazno-Demokraticheskoi Revoliutsii v Sotsialistisheskuiu* (Orenburg, 1972).

——, 'Zemlevladenie i Zemlepol'zovanie' in Bondar', *Ocherki Traditsionoi Kultury*, vol. 1, pp. 346–364.

Gajecky, G. *The Cossack Administration of the Hetmanate* (2 vols, Cambridge, Mass., 1978).

Gatagova, L.S. (ed.) *TsK RKP(B)-VKP(B) i Natsional'nyi Vopros 1918–1933* (Moscow, 2005).

Geary, P. *The Myth of Nations: The Medieval Origins of Europe* (Princeton, 2002).

Glushchenko, V.V. *Kazachestvo Evrazii* (Moscow, 2000).

Golden, P. *Khazar Studies: An Historico-Philosophical Inquiry into the Origins of the Khazars* (Budapest, 1980).

——, 'The Peoples of the South Russian Steppes' in Sinor, *The Cambridge History of Early Inner Asia.*

Golder, F.A. (ed.) *Documents on Russian History 1914–1917* (Boston, 1964).

Gordeev, A.A. *Istoriia Kazakov: Zolataia Orda i Zarozhdenie Kazachestva* (Moscow, 1992).

——, *Istoriia Kazakov: So Vremeni Tsarstvovaniia Ioanna Groznogo do Tsarstvovaniia Petra I* (Moscow, 1992).

——, *Istoriia Kazakov: So Vremeni Tsarstvovaniia Petra Velikogo do Nachala Velikoi Voiny 1914 goda* (Moscow, 1992).

Gordon, L. *Cossack Rebellions* (New York, 1983).

Gorbunov, B.V. *Riazanskoe Kazachestvo v 15–18 v.v.: opyt istorikoetnograficheskogo issledovaniia* (Riazan, 1994).

Gorshkov, G.Iu. *Dorogi Orenburgskogo Kazach'ego Voiska* (Cheliabinsk, 2002).

Grazhdanov, Iu.D. *Vsevelikoe Voisko Donskoe v 1918 godu* (Volgograd, 1997).

Grekov, A.M. *Ocherki Ekonomicheskago i Khoziiastvennago Byta Naseleniia Donskoi Oblasti* (Taganrog, 1905).

Groushko, M.A. *Cossack: Warrior Riders of the Steppes* (London, 1992).

Gubarev, G.V. and A.I. Skrylov (eds) *Kazachii Slovar'-Spravochnik* (3 vols, Cleveland 1968 and St. Anselm 1968 and 1970: facsimile edition, Volgograd, 1992).

Gumilev, L.I. *Ot Rusi do Rossii* (Moscow, 2000).

Halfin, I. *From Darkness to Light: Class, Consciousness and Salvation in Revolutionary Russia* (Pittsburgh, 2000).

Hanover N. *Abyss of Despair*, trans. A. Mesch (New Brunswick, 2002).

Harris, J. (ed.) *Farewell to the Don: The Journal of Brigadier H.N.H. Williamson* (London, 1970).

Hellie, R. *Slavery in Russia 1450–1725* (Chicago, 1982).

Herodotus, *The Histories*, trans. R. Waterfield (Oxford, 1998).

Hildinger, E. *Warriors of the Steppe: A Military History of Central Asia 500 BC to 1700 AD* (Cambridge, Mass., 2001).

Hindus, M. *The Cossacks: The Story of a Warrior People* (London, 1956).

Hobsbawn, E.J. *Nations and Nationalism Since 1780: Programme, Myth and Reality* (Cambridge, 1990).

Holderness, M. *New Russia* (London, 1823).

Holquist, P. 'From Estate to Ethnos: The Changing Nature of Cossack Identity in the Twentieth Century' in N. Schleifman (ed.) *Russia at a Crossroads: History, Memory and Political Practice* (London, 1998).

——, '"Conduct Merciless Mass Terror" DeCossackization on the Don 1919' *Cahiers du Monde Sovetique*, vol. 38 (1–2), pp. 127–162.

——, *Making War, Forging Revolution: Russia's Continuum of Crisis 1914–1921* (Cambrdige, Mass., 2002).

Hrushevsky, M. *Istoriia Ukrainskago Kozachestva do Soedineniia s Moskovskim Gosudarstvom* (St Petersburg, 1913).

——, *History of Ukraine-Rus', Volume Seven: The Cossack Age to 1625*, trans. B. Struminski (Edmonton, 1999).

——, *History of Ukraine-Rus', Volume Eight: The Cossack Age, 1626–1650*, trans. M. Olynyk (Edmonton, 2002).

——, *History of Urkraine-Rus', Volume Nine, Book One: The Cossack Age, 1650–1653* (Edmonton, 2005).

Iakushkin, E.I. *Iuridicheskie Poslovitsy i Pogovorki Russkogo Naroda* (Moscow, 1885).

Ianov, G. 'Revoliutsii i Donskie Kazaki' in *Donskaia Letopis'*, vol. 1.

——, 'Don pod Bolshevikami Vesnoi 1918 goda i Vosstanie Stanits na Donu' in *Donskaia Letopis'*, vol. 2.

Ivantsova, Zh.A. (ed.) *Kubanskoe Kazachestvo: Tri Veka Istoricheskogo Puti: Materialy Mezhdunarodnoi Nauchno-Prakticheskoi Konferentsii* (Krasnodar, 1996).

Janke, A.E. 'Don Cossacks and the February Revolution', *Canadian Slavonic Papers*, 10, no. 2. (1968) pp. 148–165.

——, 'The Don Cossacks on the Road to Independence', *Canadian Slavonic Papers*, 10, no. 3 (1968) pp. 273–294.

Kakliugin, 'Organizatsiia Vlasti na Donu v Nachale Revoliutsii' in *Donskaia Letopis'*, vol. 1.

——, 'Donskoi Ataman P.N. Krasnov i ego Vremia' in *Donskaia Letopis'*, vol. 3.

Kalinin, M.I. *Rech' na Pervom Vserossiiskom S'ezde Trudovykh Kazakov* (Moscow, 1920).

Kaminskii, F.M. *Kazachestvo Iuzhnogo Urala i Zapadnoi Sibiri v Pervoi Chetverti XX Veka* (Magnitogorsk, 2001).

'Kazachii Soiuz' *Kazachestvo: Mysli Sovremennikov o Proshlom, Nastoiashchem i Budushchem Kazachestva* (Paris, 1928: facsimile edition, Rostov-na-Donu, 1992).

Kharlamov, V.A. *Kazach'ia Dolia: Zapiski Poslednego Predsedatelia Donskogo Voiskovogo Kruga* (Rostov-na-Donu, 1990).

——, *Kazachii Deputat Gosudarstvennoi Dumy (1906–1917)* (St Petersburg, 1995).

Kharuzin, M. *Svedenie o Kazatskikh Obshchinakh na Donu: Materialy dlia Obychnago Prava* (Moscow, 1885).

Khodarkovksy, M. 'The Stepan Razin Uprising:Was it a "Peasant War"?', *Jahrbucher fur Geschichte Osteuropas*, 42, no. 1 (1994) pp. 1–19.

——, *Russia's Steppe Frontier: The Making of a Colonial Empire 1500–1800* (Bloomington, 2002).

Kirienko, N.N. *Revoliutsiia i Donskoe Kazachestvo* (Rostov-na-Donu, 1988).

Kislitsyn, S.A. *Gosudarstvo i Raskazachivanie 1917–1945* (Rostov-na-Donu, 1996).

Kliuchevskii, V.O. *Sochineniia* (8 vols, Moscow, 1957).

Kononovich, L.G. (ed.) *Kuban' i Kazachestvo (konets XVIII v -1920g)* (Rostov-na-Donu, 2003).

Korchin, M. *Donskoe Kazachestvo* (Rostov-na-Donu, 1939).

Korf, S.A. *The Constitution of the Cossacks* (Paris, 1919).

Kostomarov, N. *Kazaki* (Moscow, 1995).

Kotel'nikov, E. *Istoricheskoe Svedenie Voiska Donskago o Verkhne-Kurmoiarskoi Stanitse* (Novocherkassk, 1886).

Kozlov, A.I. (ed.) *Vozrozhdenie Kazachestva (Istoriia, Sovremennost', Perspektivy)* (Rostov-na-Donu, 1995).

Kozlov, A.I. (ed.) *Problemy Istorii Kazachestva XVI–XXvv* (Rostov-na-Donu, 1995).

Kozlov, A.I. *Kavkaz v Sud'bakh Kazachestva (XVI–XVIII vv)* (St Petersburg, 1996).

Krasinski, G. *The Cossacks of the Ukraine* (London, 1848).

Krasnov, N.I. *Voennoe Obozrenie Zemli Donskago Voiska* (St Petersburg, 1870).

Kriukov, F.D. *Rasskazy Publitsistika* (Moscow, 1990).

Kutseev, V.V. *Etnicheskaia Istoriia Kazakov* (Krasnodar, 1995).

Kutsenko, I.A. *Kubanskoe Kazachestvo* (Krasnodar, 1993).

Lazarev, A.V. *Donskie Kazaki v Grazhdanskoi Voine 1917–1920gg: Istoriografiia Problemy* (Moscow, 1995).

Lenivov, A.K. *Donskoi kazachii slovar'* (Munich, 1971).

Lesur, C.L. *Histoire des Kosaques* (2 vols, Paris, 1813).

Le Vasseur, Guillaume, Sieur de Beauplan, *A Description of Ukraine*, trans. and ed. A.B. Pernal and D.F. Essar (Cambridge, Mass., 1993).

Liberman, A. (ed.) *O Nachale Voin i Smut v Moskovii* (Moscow, 1997).

—— (ed.) *Khroniki Smutnogo Vremeni* (Moscow 1998).

Listonadov, A.M. (ed.) *Donskoi Fol'klor* (Rostov-na-Donu, 2002).

Longworth, P. *The Cossacks* (London, 1969).

MacCulloch, D. *Reformation: Europe's House Divided 1490–1700* (London, 2003).

Mackenzie-Wallace, D. *Russia*, 2nd edn. (2 vols, London, 1877).

Madariaga, I. de *Russia in the Age of Catherine the Great* (London, 1981).

Makhenko, S.G. (ed.) *Donskoi Fol'klor* (Rostov-na-Donu, 2002).

McGrew, R.E. *Paul I of Russia 1754–1801* (Oxford, 1992).

McNeal, R.H. *Tsar and Cossack 1855–1914* (London, 1987).

McNeill, W. *Europe's Steppe Frontier 1500–1800* (Chicago, 1964).

Mamonov, V.F. 'Teorii i fakty' in Bondar, *Ocherki Traditsionnoi Kul'tury*, pp. 140–187.

Mankova, A.G. (ed.) *Zapiski Inostrantsev o Vostanii Stepana Razin* (Leningrad, 1968).

Manz, B.F. *The Rise and Rule of Tamerlane* (Cambridge, 1989).

March, G. *Cossacks of the Brotherhood: The Zaporog Kosh of the Dnieper River* (New York, 1990).

Margeret, J. *The Russian Empire and the Grand Duchy of Muscovy: A 17th Century French Account*, trans. and ed. C.S. Dunning (Pittsburgh, 1983).

Marx, F. *The Serf and the Cossack: A Sketch of the Condition of the Russian People* (London, 1855).

Martin, T. *The Affirmative Action Empire: Nations and Nationalism in the Soviet Union 1923–1939* (New York, 2001).

Mashin, M.D. *Orenburgskoe Kazach'e Voisko* (Cheliabinsk, 2000).

Mavrodin, V.V. *Krest'ianskaia Voina v Rossii v 1773–1775 godakh* (3 vols, Leningrad, 1966).

Medvedev, Captain *Sluzhba Donskogo Voiska v Sviazi c ego Ekonomicheskim Polozheniem* (Moscow, 1899).

Mekhovskii, M. *Traktat o Dvukh Sarmatiiakh* (Moscow, 1936).

Mel'nikov, N.M. 'A.M. Kaledin (Lichnost'i Deiatel'nost). Vospominaniia.' in *Donskaia Letopis'*, vol. 1.

Menning, B.W. 'The Emergence of a Military Administrative Elite in the Don Cossack Land, 1708–1836', in W.M. Pinter and D.K. Rowney (eds) *Russian Officialdom: The Bureaucratization of Russian Society from the Seventeenth to the Twentieth Century* (Chapel Hill, 1980), pp. 130–161.

Mikhailovich, K.M. *Protiv Stalina: Vlasovtsy i Vostochnye Dobrovol'tsy vo Vtoroi Mirovoi Voine* (St Petersburg, 2003).

Minsk, I.I. *Kazachestvo v Oktiabr'skoi Revoliutsii i Grazhdanskoi Voine* (Cherkassk, 1984).

Moravcsik, Gy. (ed.) *Constantine Porphyrogenitus De Administrando Imperio*, trans. R.J.H. Jenkings (Dumbarton Oaks, 1967).

Mote, F.W. *Imperial China 900–1800* (Cambridge, Mass., 1999).

Muratov, Kh. I. *Emel'ian Ivanovich Pugachev* (Rostov-na-Donu, 1979).

Murin, V.B. (ed.) *Kartiny Bylogo Tikhogo Dona* (2 vols, St Petersburg, 1908: facsimile edition, Moscow, 1992).

Murphy, B. 'The Don Rebellion March-June 1919', *Revolutionary Russia*, 6, 2 (1993) pp. 315–350.

Muzhev, I.F. *Kazachestvo Dona, Kubani, i Tereka v Revoliutsii 1905–1907* (Ordzhonikdze, 1963).

Nedbai, Iu.G. *Istoriia Kazachestva Zapadnoi Sibiri 1582–1808* (4 vols, Omsk, 1996).

——, *Kazachestvo Zapadnoi Sibiri v Epochu Petra Velikogo* (Omsk, 1998).

Nelepin. R.A. *Istoriia Kazachestva* (2 vols, St Petersburg, 1995).

Niessel, H.A. *Les Cosaques* (Paris, 1899).

Nikitin, N.I. *Nachalo Kazachestva Sibiri* (Moscow, 1996).

Nomikosov, S. (ed.) *Statisticheskoe Opisanie Oblasti Voiska Donskogo* (Novocherkassk, 1884).

Obolensky, D. *The Byzantine Commonwealth: Eastern Europe 500–1453* (London, 1971).

Okinshevich, L. *Ukrainian Society and Government, 1648–1781* (Munich, 1978).

Oliphant, L. *The Russian Shores of the Black Sea in the Autumn of 1852, with a voyage down the Volga, and a tour through the country of the Don Cossacks* (Edinburgh, 1853).

Omel'chenko, I.L. *Terskoe Kazachestvo* (Vladikavkaz, 1991).

O'Rourke, S. 'Women in a Warrior Society: Don Cossack Women 1861–1914' in R. Marsh (ed.) *Women in Russia and Ukraine* (Cambridge, 1996), pp. 45–54.

——, 'The Cossacks' in E. Acton, V. Iu. Chernaiev and W.G. Rosenberg (eds), *Critical Companion to the Russian Revolution* (London, 1997) pp. 499–506.

——, 'The Don Cossacks During the 1905 Revolution: The Revolt of Ust-Medveditskaia Stanitsa,' *Russian Review*, 57, 4 (1998) pp. 583–598.

——, *Warriors and Peasants: The Don Cossacks in Late Imperial Russia* (London, 2000).

Oskolkov, E.N. 'Sud'by Krest'ianstva i Kazachestva v Rossii: Raskrest'ianivanie i Razkazachivanie' in Ratushniak, *Problemy Istorii Kazachestva*.

Ostrowski, D. *Muscovy and the Mongols: Cross-Cultural Influences on the Steppe Frontier, 1304–1589* (Oxford, 1998).

Ovchinnikov, R.V. (ed.) *Dokumenty Stavki E.I. Pugacheva, Povstancheskikh Vlastei i Uchrezhdenii: 1773–1774 gg* (Moscow, 1975).

——, *Manifesty i Ukazy E.I. Pugacheva: Istochnikovedcheskoe Issledovanie* (Moscow, 1980).

——, *Sledstvie i Sud nad E.I. Pugachevym i Ego Spodvizhnikami* (Moscow, 1995).

——, *Emel'ian Pugachev na Sledstvii* (Moscow, 1997).

Ozerov, A. and A.G. Kiblitskii *Vozrozhdenie Kazachestva v Novoi Rossii* (Rostov-na-Donu, 2004).

Paul of Aleppo *Travels of Macarius: Extracts from the Diary of the Travels of Macarius Patriarch of Antioch, written by his son Paul Archdeacon of Aleppo in the years of their journeying, 1652–1660* (London, 1836).

Pavlov, A. and M. Perrie *Ivan the Terrible* (London, 2003).

Perekhov, Ia. A. *Vlast' i Kazachestvo: Poisk Soglasiia* (Rostov-na-Donu, 1997).

Perrie, M. *Pretenders and Popular Monarchism in Early Modern Russia* (Cambridge, 1995).

Philips-Price, M. *My Reminiscences of the Russian Revolution* (London, 1921).

Pissot, N.I. *Precis Historiques sur les Cosaques. Nation sous la Domination des Russes: Leur Origine, Etablissement et Accroissement; Leur Grandeur et Abaissement; Leur moeurs et Usages* (Paris, 1812).

Platonov, S.F. *The Time of Troubles: A Historical Study of Internal Crisis and Social Struggle in Sixteenth and Seventeenth Century Muscovy*, trans. J. Alexander (Kansas, 1970).

Plokhy, S. *The Cossacks and Religion in Early Modern Ukraine* (Oxford, 2001).

——, *Tsars and Cossacks: A Study in Iconography* (Cambridge, Mass., 2002).

Popov, A.G. *Istoriia Voiska Donskago* (Novocherkassk, 1812).

Popov, I.A. *Materialy k Istorii Dona* (Novocherkassk, 1900).

Potto, V.A. *Dve Veke Terskago Kazchestva 1577–1801* (Vladikavkaz, 1912).

Prianishnikov, I.P. *Materialy dlia Istorii Voiska Donskago* (Novocherkassk, 1864).

Pronshtein, A.P. *Zemlia Donskaia v XVIII Veke* (Rostov-na-Donu, 1961).

——, *Don i Nizhnee Povolzh'e v Period Krest'ianskoi Voiny, 1773–1775: Sbornik Dokumentov* (Rostov-na-Donu, 1961).

Pushkin, A.S. *Istoriia Pugachevskago Bunta* (St Petersburg, 1834).

Pudavov, V.M. *Istoriia Voiska Donskogo i starobytnost' nachal kazachestva* (Novocherkassk, 1890).

Raeff, M. 'Pugachev's Rebellion' in R. Forster and J. Green (eds) *Preconditions of Revolt in Early Modern Europe* (Baltimore, 1970).

Ratushniak, V.N. *et al. Problemy Istorrii Kazachestva: Sbornik Nauchykh Trudov* (Volgograd, 1995).

Ratushniak, O.V. *Donskoe i Kubanskoe Kazachestvo v Emigratsii (1920–1939)* (Krasnodar, 1997).

Rediker, M. *Between the Devil and the Deep Blue Sea: Merchant Seamen, Pirates and the Anglo-American Maritime World 1700–1750* (Cambridge, 1987).

Reshetova, N.A. *Intelligentsiia Dona i Revoliutsiia* (Moscow, 1998).

Riabov, S.I. *Voisko Donskoe i Rossiiskoe Samoderzhavie 1613–1725* (Volgagrad, 1993).

Rigel'man, A. *Istoriia o Donskikh Kazakakh* (Moscow, 1846).

Rolle, R. *The World of the Scythians* (Berkeley, 1989).

Romano, A.L. *Coup d'Oeil Philosophique sur le Pays Occupe par les Cosaques du Don* (Milan, 1807).

Rozner, I.G. *Iaik Pered Burei* (Moscow, 1966).

Ryzhkova, N.V. *Za Veru, Otechestvo i Drugi Svoia: Donskie Kazaki v Velikoi Voine 1914–1917gg* (Rostov-na-Donu, 1998).

Sagnaeva, S.K. 'Ural'skoe Kazachestvo' in Bondar', *Ocherki Traditsionnoi Kul'tury*, vol. 1, pp. 256–262.

Savel'ev, A.P. *Trekhsotletie Voiska Donskago 1570–1870* (St Petersburg, 1870).

Savel'ev, E.P. *Drevniaia Istoriia Kazachestva* (3 vols, Novocherkassk, 1915).

Savchenko, S.N. *Ussuriiskoe Kazach'e Voisko v Grazhdanskoi Voine na Dal'nem Vostoke (1917–1922)* (Khabarovsk, 2002).

Scherer, J. B. *Annales de la Petite-Russe: ou Histoire des Cosaques-Saporogues et des Cosaques de l'Ukraine* (2 vols, Paris, 1788).

Seniutkin, M. *Dontsi: Istoricheskie Ocherki Voennykh Deistvii. Biografii Starshin Proshlogo Veka, Zametki iz Sovremennago Byta i Vzgliad na Istoriiu Voiska Donskago* (Moscow, 1886).

Serczyk, T. 'The Commonwealth and the Cossacks in the First Quarter of the 17th Century,' *Harvard Ukrainian Studies*, II, 1 (1978), pp. 73–93.

Sergeev, V.N. *Politicheskie Partii v Iuzhnukh Kazach'ikh Oblastiakh Rossii 1917–1920* (3 vols, Rostov-na-Donu, 1993).

——, *Dvizhenie za Vozrozhdenie Kazachestva* (Rostov-na-Donu, 1993).

—— and D. Iu Shapsugov (eds) *Parlamentskaia Deiatel'nost' Rossiiskogo Kazachestva (1906–1917)* (Rostov-na-Donu, 2003).

Shcherbina, F.A. *Istoriia Kubanskago Kazach'iago Voiska* (2 vols, Ekaterinodar, 1910–1913).

Shishkin, V.I. (ed.) *Sibirskaia Vandeia 1919–1920* (2 vols, Moscow, 2000).

Shenk, V.K. (ed.) *Kazach'i Voiska* (St Petersburg, 1912).

Shibanov, N.S. *Kazach'ia Golgofa* (Cheliabinsk, 2004).

Sholokhov, M. *And Quiet Flows the Don*, trans. S. Garry (Harmondsworth, 1967).

——, *The Don Flows Home to the Sea*, trans. S. Garry (Harmondsworth, 1970).

——, *Virgin Soil Upturned*, trans. S. Garry (Harmondsworth, 1977).

——, *Harvest on the Don*, trans. H.C. Stevens (Harmondsworth, 1978).

Shuldiakov, V.A. *Gibel' Sibirskogo Kazach'ego Voiska 1917–1920* (2 vols, Moscow, 2004).

Sinor, D. (ed.) *The Cambridge History of Early Inner Asia* (Cambridge, 1990).

——, 'The Hun Period' in *The Cambridge History of Early Inner Asia*.

Skorik, A.P. *et al. Vozrozhdenie Kazachestva: Istoriia i Sovremennost': Sbornik Nauchnykh Statei k V Vserossiiskoi mezhdunarodnoi Nauchnoi Konferentsii* (Novocherkassk, 1995).

Skorik, A.P. *Kazachii Don: Ocherki Istorii* (2 vols, Rostov-na-Donu, 1995).

Skrynnikov, R.G. *Sibirskaia Ekspeditsiia Ermaka* (Novosibirsk, 1982).

Smirnov, N.N. 'Zabaikal'skoe Kazachestvo' in Bondar', *Ocherki Traditsionnoi Kul'tury*, vol. 1, pp. 287–300.

Solovev, V.M. *Anatomiia Russkogo Bunta: Stepan Razin: Mify i Real'nost* (Moscow, 1994).

Stanislavskii, A.L. *Grazhdanskaia Voina v Rossii 'XVII': Kazachestvo na Perelome Istorii* (Moscow, 1990).

Stevens, C.B. *Soldiers on the Steppe: Army Reform and Social Change in Early Modern Russia* (Dekalb, 1995).

Struys, J. *The voiages and travels of J.S. through Italy, Greece, Muscovy, Tartary, Media, Persia, East India, Japan*, trans. by I. Morrison (London, 1684).

Subtelny, O. 'Cossack Ukraine and the Turco-Islamic World,' in I.L. Rudnytsky (ed.) *Rethinking Ukrainian History* (Edmonton, 1981), pp. 120–134.

——, *Ukraine: A History* (Toronto, 1988).

Sukhanov, N.I. *The Russian Revolution 1917: A Personal Record*, trans. J. Carmichael (Princeton, 1954).

Sukhorukhov, V.D. *Statisticheskoe Opisanie Zemli Donskikh Kazakov* (Novocherkassk, 1891).

——, *Istoricheskoe Opisanie Zemli Voiska Donskago* (Novocherkassk, 1903).

Svatikov, S.G. *Rossiia i Don (1549–1917). Issledovanie po Istorii Gosudarstvennago i Administrativnago Prava i Politicheskikh Dvizhenii na Donu* (Belgrade, 1924).

Sysyn, A. *Between Poland and the Ukraine: The Dilemma of Adam Kysil, 1600–1653* (Cambridge, Mass., 1985).

Tabolina, T.V. (ed.), *Vozrozhdenie Kazachestva 1989–1994* (Moscow, 1994).

Tabolina, T.V. (ed.), *Rossiiskoe Kazachestvo* (Moscow, 2003).

Taylor, A. *American Colonies: The Settling of North America* (Harmondsworth, 2001).

Toekava, K. *Orenburg I Orenburgskoe Kazachestvo vo Vremia Vostanniia Pugacheva 1773–1774 gg* (Moscow, 1996).

Tolstoy, L.N. *The Cossacks*, trans. R. Edmonds (Harmondsworth, 1960).

Trenev, K. *In a Cossack Village*, trans. J. Atkinson (London, 1946).

Tret'iakova, V. *Tragediia Kazachestva* (Moscow, 1996).

Trotsky, L. *The History of the Russian Revolution* (3 vols, London, 1932).

Trut, V.P. *Kazachii Izlom* (Rostov-na-Donu, 1997).

——, *Kazachestvo v Rossii v Periode Pervoi Mirovoi Voiny* (Rostov-na Donu, 1999).

Tsybin, V.M and E. A. Ashanin *Istoriia Volzhskogo Kazachestva* (Saratov, 2002).

Venkov, A.V. *Antibol'shevistskoe Dvizhenie na Iuge Rossii na Nachal'nom Etape. Grazhdanskoi Voiny* (Rostov-na-Donu, 1995).

Voskoboinikov, G.L. *Bor'ba partii za Trudovoe Kazachestvo 1917–1920gg.: O Deiatel'nosti Kazach'ego Otdela VTsIK* (Grozny, 1980).

Weber, M. *Economy and Society: An Outline of Interpretive Sociology* (2 vols, Berkeley, 1978).

Worobec, C.D. *Peasant Russia: Family and Community in the Post-Emancipation Period* (Princeton, 1991).

Wortman, R.D. *Scenarios of Power:: Myth and Ceremony in Russian Monarchy* (2 vols, Princeton, 1995).

Wynar, L. (ed.) *Habsbourgs and Zaporozhian Cossacks: The Diary of Erich Lassota von Steblau, 1594* (Littleton, Colorado. 1975).

Ying-Shih Yu 'The Hsiung-nu' in Sinor, *The Cambridge History of Early Inner Asia*.

Zasedatel'eva, L.B. *Terskie Kazaki* (Moscow, 1974).

Zolotarev, I.I. *Kazach'e Samoupravlenie na Donu* (Rostov-na-Donu, 1999).

Zolotov, V.A. *Istoriia Dona, Epokha Kapitalizma* (Rostov-na-Donu, 1974).

Zvezdova, N.V. *Vremmenoe Pravitel'stvo i Kazachestvo* (Rostov-na-Donu, 2003).

Index

Lightning Source UK Ltd.
Milton Keynes UK
UKOW06f0142011215

263833UK00001B/7/P